PRINCIPLES OF PUBLIC FINANCE

J. Ronnie Davis
*Dean, College of Business
and Management Studies
University of South Alabama*

Charles W. Meyer
*Department of Economics
Iowa State University*

PRENTICE-HALL, INC., Englewood Cliffs, N.J. 07632

336.73
D 26 p

Library of Congress Cataloging in Publication Data

Davis, J. Ronnie.
  Principles of public finance.

  Includes bibliographical references and index.
  1. Finance, Public. 2. Finance, Public—United
States. I. Meyer, Charles W. II. Title.
HJ141.D384   1983   336.73   82-23138
ISBN 0-13-709881-2

Editorial/production supervision and
  interior design: *Barbara Grasso*
Cover design: *Photo plus Art*
Manufacturing buyer: *Edward O'Dougherty*

© 1983 by Prentice-Hall, Inc., Englewood Cliffs, New Jersey 07632

All rights reserved. No part of this book may be
reproduced, in any form or by any means,
without permission in writing from the publisher.

Printed in the United States of America

10 9 8 7 6 5 4 3 2 1

ISBN 0-13-709881-2

PRENTICE-HALL INTERNATIONAL, INC., *London*
PRENTICE-HALL OF AUSTRALIA PTY. LIMITED, *Sydney*
EDITORA PRENTICE-HALL DO BRASIL, LTDA., *Rio de Janeiro*
PRENTICE-HALL CANADA INC., *Toronto*
PRENTICE-HALL OF INDIA PRIVATE LIMITED, *New Delhi*
PRENTICE-HALL OF JAPAN, INC., *Tokyo*
PRENTICE-HALL OF SOUTHEAST ASIA PTE. LTD., *Singapore*
WHITEHALL BOOKS LIMITED, *Wellington, New Zealand*

To Mary Christine and Amanda Lee
Donelle and Eric

UNIVERSITY LIBRARIES
CARNEGIE-MELLON UNIVERSITY
PITTSBURGH, PENNSYLVANIA 15213

Contents

4. The Federal Budget Process   75

5. Analysis of Government Policies   99

6. Equity in Tax Treatment   119

7. Shifting and Incidence   137

8. Taxation of Personal Income   158

Chapter 8 Appendix   196

9. Taxation of Business Income   203

Preface

Principles of Public Finance is intended primarily for use in the introductory course in public finance. The emphasis is on developing an understanding of the basic principles and concepts that economists use to explain and evaluate the performance of the public sector. We have attempted to accommodate students with a limited background in economics by using only those theoretical techniques ordinarily covered in the standard principles course. Possible exceptions are the discussion of efficiency conditions in Chapter 2 and indifference curve analysis of labor supply in the appendix to Chapter 8. Both of these topics can be skipped without loss of continuity. Our classroom experience convinces us that students can gain a sophisticated understanding of public sector economics through judicious application of simple analytical tools.

A number of individuals have read and commented upon preliminary drafts of portions of the manuscript. Among those who have been most helpful are Roy Adams of Iowa State University, Gerald Auten of Bowling Green State University, Ann Horowitz of the University of Florida, Charles Knoeber of North Carolina State University, Jerry Miner of Syracuse University, David Sjoquist of Georgia State University, and Timothy Smeeding of the University of Utah. We acknowledge their assistance without implicating them in the result. For assistance in preparation of the manuscript, we wish to thank Sandy Aspengren, Beth Tesdahl, Nancy Wolff, Jane Clark, and Lorine Newcomer.

J. Ronnie Davis
Charles W. Meyer

1

The Public Sector

The subject matter of public finance is the description and analysis of the economic activity of government. Of course, there is disagreement over the range of legitimate governmental economic activity. While governmental responsibility is conceded in some cases, it is disputed in others. The proper scope of government actions is, therefore, a matter of concern to students of public finance. Central to the study of public finance is analysis of the impact of government on the behavior and well-being of households and firms. The subject of study becomes individual decision making units of the private sector, with certain governmental decisions taken as given. In this important sense, government and governmental activities are a major thread woven into the social fabric.

The actions of governments affect the lives of everyone in society. Legislative enactments, administrative decisions, and judicial interpretations govern and modify our behavior. Economic policies of government address the problems of allocation of scarce resources, stabilization of the economy, and distribution of incomes and wealth. Implementation of these policies requires taxation, public borrowing, and public expenditure. Public finance deals with the effects—intended and unintended—of government revenue and expenditure policies on the fulfillment of allocation, distribution, and stabilization objectives.

ECONOMIC EFFECTS OF GOVERNMENT POLICIES

Almost any revenue or expenditure policy has some effect on the allocation of society's scarce resources. Through market and political institutions, preferences are expressed and choices are made that concern want satisfaction. When government collects money to spend on typewriters, computers, and aircraft carriers, it is bidding labor, energy, materials, plant, and equipment away from production of apartments, automobiles, wheat, and other nongovernmental uses.

Markets are the primary means of allocating resources, mainly through the direction given by relative prices determined by market forces. Markets may fail to allocate resources efficiently, however, when they fail to serve as a means of generating socially correct relative prices. Consequently, too many of some goods and services and not enough of others may be produced. There are many potential causes of market failure. Monopoly power over prices distorts signals about relative costs of different goods and services. Consumers and producers often lack information about consumption and production opportunities. Resource mobility from one industry to another may be so limited that allocation does not respond to the direction given by changes in relative prices.

Other potential causes of market failure include the pressure of "externalities" and "public goods." In the case of externalities, acts of producing or consuming have effects external to the firms or consumers in control of the activities. Such effects can confer benefits or impose harm on others. For example, it is generally believed that, when an individual is educated, all of society benefits, but when an individual pollutes the environment, others suffer. The externally affected parties may not have any effective means of expressing their preferences for more or less of the activities. When external benefits and external costs are not reflected in the demand and supply forces that determine relative prices and give direction to resource allocation, goods and services may be overproduced or underproduced. In the case of public goods, markets fail to achieve an efficient level of output of goods characterized by nonrivalry in consumption. These goods may be consumed by many persons simultaneously without any one person diminishing any other's consumption opportunities. Examples include national defense and transmission of television programs. In many cases, it is not feasible for firms producing public goods to charge a market price that excludes persons who do not pay it. Firms seeking to realize profits from the sale of goods and services may not produce these public goods at all, even though there is a substantial demand for them. For example, a lighthouse may not be provided even though a large number of boat and ship owners would benefit from its services. There may be no feasible way in which to exclude those who benefit but do not pay.

Economic policies can be devised to deal with the problems of underproduction or overproduction of goods that create externalities. For example, when externalities are beneficial, government can encourage production and consumption through subsidies. When they are harmful, government can discourage production and consumption through taxation.

In addition to expenditure and tax policies, government regulation can be used to encourage or discourage certain activities. Often, government itself chooses to produce goods and services. Government provision is most common in the case of public goods that cannot feasibly be provided privately, such as national defense or flood control.

Where markets fail, however, governments do not necessarily succeed. When markets are preempted by government, decisions are shifted to the political process with all of its imperfections. Society is faced with a choice between two imperfect alternatives. Implications of this choice are discussed in the chapters that follow, particularly Chapters 2 and 3.

In addition to its effect on allocation and thus on the mix of goods and services produced, government also affects the distribution of income. Society may prefer distribution of incomes among its members that differs from that generated through markets. There is an obvious ethical question concerning the acceptable degree of inequality consistent with social order. There is also an economic question. Production of goods and services is dependent on incentives that motivate individuals to supply the needed inputs of capital and labor. Thus, the mode of distribution is central to the incentive system and, in this way, to production itself. Through markets, those who offer the services of factors they own are rewarded according to their contribution to production of goods and services that satisfy wants. Substantial inequality of income can be the result of unequal resource endowments. Unreasonable discrimination and other patterns of behavior unrelated to markets along with market imperfections such as monopoly power may add to inequality.

When there is a sense that certain classes of people will not receive socially acceptable rewards through markets, persons and organizations in the private sector engage in philanthropy and charity that, in effect, transfer income. However, private redistribution of income may not be sufficient to satisfy a social sense of justice. Government may then use its tax and expenditure power to transfer incomes. Progressive tax rate schedules tend to redistribute income to some extent.

On the expenditure side, there is a vast amount of activity that is intended to redistribute income. For example, aid to families with dependent children and social security payments transfer income directly. Other programs redistribute income by providing goods and services that benefit certain classes of people. Low-income housing projects benefit families that qualify, and veterans' hospitals provide medical services to ex-military personnel. Some of these programs may have perverse effects. A welfare program may diminish incentives to work, and the earnings of some recipients may be lower than they would be without assistance. Minimum wage laws may cause unemployment or reduce hours worked and lower the total earnings of those employed at the minimum wage.

Finally, the overall level of tax revenues and expenditures can have important effects on the aggregate levels of output, income, and prices. In the private sector, aggregate levels of demand and supply may not be stable enough to provide for acceptable levels of employment and prices. History is replete with evidence that, without government stabilization efforts, markets can fail in this respect. The basic instruments of stabilization policy are monetary policies that control the stock of money and fiscal policies that increase or decrease rates of taxation and levels of government expenditure. The historical record, especially since the late 1960s, also provides evidence that government stabilization policy may not succeed and, on occasion, may even make matters worse rather than better.

MEASURES OF
GOVERNMENT ACTIVITY

There is no truly adequate and feasible measure of the importance—or in a limited sense, the economic importance—of governmental activity. Some of the impact of governmental action is noneconomic or nonquantifiable. This may be the case with its effect on freedom. Some governmental activity may be economic and quantifiable in character but may involve incommensurable values. For example, when the value of government services is estimated, there are few prices to use as a means of estimating the value of such goods to society. Costs tend to be used instead. Cost, however, may overestimate the value of some public services and underestimate that of others.

Nonetheless, there are several useful cost-oriented measures of governmental activity. Total governmental expenditure is commonly used, particularly since data are easily available. Often, this measure is adjusted for price changes or stated relative to gross national product (GNP). Another measure is purchases of goods and services, which excludes transfer payments from total governmental expenditure. Finally, government employment is an appropriate measure for some purposes.

In Figure 1–1, government expenditures are shown for each calendar year since 1946.[1] Total expenditures grew from $46.7 billion in 1946 to more than $950 billion in 1980. In 1981, government expenditures exceeded $1 trillion for the first time. The federal share of total government expenditure has declined gradually since 1946 from more than 70 percent to about 60 percent.

Of the major components of spending, state-local expenditure on education and welfare has increased most rapidly since 1946. Together, these two functions accounted for half of state-local expenditure by 1980. At the federal level, expenditures on income security and health increased at the

---

[1]The data show expenditures of the federal, state, and local government sectors of the national income and product accounts (NIPA).

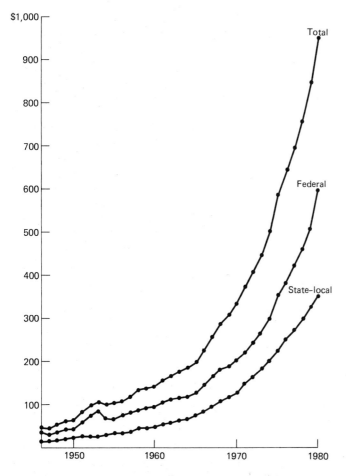

FIGURE 1-1   State-local, federal, and total government expenditures by calendar year (billions of dollars). Expenditures are shown for each calendar year since 1946. The federal share of total government expenditure has declined gradually to about 60 percent.

most rapid rate. By 1980, the health, education, and welfare functions represented almost half of federal expenditure. National defense had dropped to less than 25 percent. Reordering of priorities can have a significant impact on such relative shares. For example, in an address to a joint session of Congress on February 18, 1981, President Reagan called for greater spending to rebuild the nation's defense capabilities. He also asked for a reversal of the trend toward greater federal roles in social programs.

There are several problems in using aggregate government expenditures as a measure of the economic importance of government over time. Unadjusted data reflect changes in prices as well as real growth of government activity. Also, some growth of government expenditure would be expected along with growth of population and growth of the economy. Even when adjusted for changes in the price level, population, and the level of economic activity, trends in government expenditures do not tell the whole story. For example, law requires that new automobiles be equipped with seat belts and pollution control devices. These devices and seat belts are produced and installed, but these mandated costs of compliance are not included in government expenditures.

In Figure 1–2, government expenditures are shown in constant dollars. Expenditure in current dollars is reproduced from Figure 1–1, and

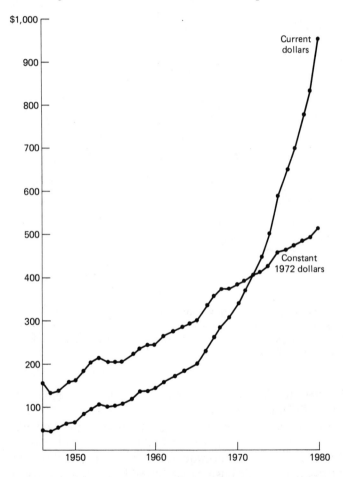

FIGURE 1–2 **Total government expenditure in current and constant 1972 dollars (billions of dollars).** Expenditure in current dollars is reproduced from Figure 1–1. Expenditure has been adjusted for inflation and is shown in current 1972 dollars. Part of the increase in expenditure since 1946 is due to inflation.

each year's total is adjusted by the implicit price deflator (1972 = 100) for government purchases of goods and services. Thus, the deflated expenditures provide a series for government expenditure in constant 1972 dollars. It is clear that part of the increase in expenditure since 1946 is due to inflation. Real per capita expenditure—measured in constant 1972 dollars—increased from $1,116 in 1946 to $2,327 by 1980. This growth must be attributed to factors other than inflation and population growth.

Various measures of government expenditure provide some indication of the economic importance of government activity. Each is helpful, but none provides a reading on the size of the public sector *relative* to the private sector or to the economy. Expressing government expenditure as a percentage of GNP can provide some sense of the relative growth of the public sector. This percentage is shown in Figure 1–3 for each year since 1946. It is clear that the public sector has grown more rapidly than the private sector; as measured by expenditures, the public sector has grown to more than one-third of aggregate economic activity.

Measures of cost do not indicate *how* the public sector meets the demand for public services. Some government programs absorb resources. In other words, they divert resources from the private sector. National defense, public safety, space exploration, and highways all absorb resources that could have been employed in the private sector. Other programs merely transfer purchasing power from one group of individuals in the pri-

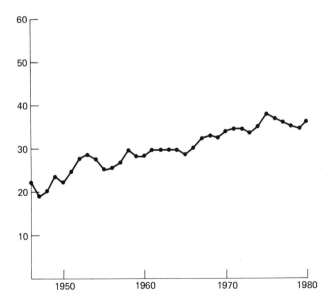

FIGURE 1–3 Total government expenditure as a percentage of GNP. Expenditure is shown as a percentage of GNP. This gives some indication of the size of the public sector relative to the economy. The public sector has grown to more than one-third of aggregate economic activity.

vate sector to another. Social security, public assistance, and unemployment compensation consist simply of transfer of income from one group to another. No inputs are reallocated from the private to the public sector. These income transfers do not affect the amount of output available in the private sector. They simply change patterns of demand (and supply) as the result of differences in demand between "donors" and recipients.

The extent to which government decisions *control* the allocation of resources is measured most appropriately by government purchases of goods and services. When purchasing power is transferred from one group to another, government does not control the allocation of resources. The recipients' decisions determine the allocation. When government hires factors of production or when government purchases final goods and services, government decisions control the allocation.

State-local purchases of goods and services have increased dramatically since 1946. The increase has been most pronounced since the mid-1960s. The increase was 170 percent from 1970 to 1980. Expenditures for education, highways, and health have accounted for most of this growth.[2] Federal purchases of goods and services have grown slowly by comparison. Purchases increased by only 108 percent from 1970 to 1980. National defense is the predominant federal government purchase. Defense spending grew slowly over that period. Expenditure on general government rose sharply, largely because of pay raises for federal employees.[3]

The most interesting difference between patterns of government purchases at the two levels is that state-local expenditure is almost entirely government purchases of goods and services, while only about one-third of federal expenditures are government purchases. Since about 1950, government purchases have accounted for more than 90 percent of state-local expenditures. At the federal level, however, government purchases have declined steadily as a share of federal expenditures. State-local and federal government purchases have been around 20 percent of GNP. The decline in the federal ratio of government purchases to GNP has been offset by an increase in the state-local ratio. Relative to the economy, government absorption of resources has not increased significantly since the early 1970s.

Not all government purchases represent government "production." Some are purchases of goods and services from firms in the private sector. One indication of the extent to which government is active in production—

---

[2]Mostly, the increase in health and hospital expenditure reflects increases in costs rather than extensions of services. Welfare services also grew rapidly. They are financed largely by federal grants, and growth has been most significant since 1970. These represent actual services to welfare recipients and should not be confused with cash transfers.

[3]A major component of general government outlays is interest paid on the national debt. These payments are treated as transfers in the national income accounts, since most of the debt was accumulated during past wars and recessions. Current productive capacity is unrelated to these federal obligations, which explains why the interest payments are not treated as a return to capital.

presumably for nonprofit motives—is government employment of factors of production. In the 1970s and early 1980s, government employed about 18 percent of all wage and salary workers.[4] The federal government employed about 3 percent of workers, and state-local governments employed about 15 percent. Since World War II, federal employment has declined steadily as a percentage of all workers. State-local employment increased steadily as a percentage of all workers until the late 1970s.

To a degree, these employment patterns reflect expenditure trends. State-local expenditure is services oriented. At a local level, for example, governments employ people to provide education, police and fire protection, refuse collection and disposal, and many other services. Any growth in these services normally requires additional employment of workers. In contrast, federal expenditure growth has been much greater for transfer payments. An increase in transfers need not require many additional employees.

It should be clear that there are various measures of the economic importance of government activity. It is also clear that the public sector has grown in importance. The growth is evident not only in absolute terms, but also relative to the private sector. What accounts for the absolute and relative growth of the public sector? Some of the growth is responsive to the demand for more public services. The "responsive elements" in the growth of public spending are the factors that affect demand: income, relative prices, and population. How much growth can be explained by these responsive elements?

The Income Elasticity of Demand for Government Goods and Services

For most goods, an increase in income, other things being equal, will lead to an increase in demand. The income elasticity of demand is a measure of how responsive demand is to an increase in income. It is defined as the percentage change in quantity demanded divided by the percentage change in income. If the income elasticity of demand is 0.5, for example, the quantity demanded increases by 5 percent when income rises by 10 percent.

In absolute terms, the growth in real income will explain part of the growth in real government spending. This simply means that the income elasticity of demand for public services is positive. Growth in real income will explain the *relative* growth of the public sector, however, only if the demand for public services is more responsive to increases in income than

---

[4]"Total wage and salary workers" excludes proprietors, self-employed persons, domestic servants, and unpaid family workers, as well as persons in the armed forces.

is the demand for goods and services supplied by the private sector. There is another way of thinking about this. If the public sector grows faster than the economy as a whole, then it is growing faster than income. This suggests that the income elasticity of demand for public services must exceed unity if it is an explanation for the *relative* growth of the public sector.

Empirical studies have estimated comparative income elasticities. A study by Thomas Borcherding indicates that income elasticity is somewhat lower for public services than it is for goods and services supplied in the private sector.[5] Borcherding placed the income elasticity of demand for public services at 0.75. This means that, if all other factors affecting the demand for public services are held constant, then public expenditures would rise by only three-fourths as much as income. Growth of income explains some absolute growth in the public sector, but this finding does not explain growth in the relative size of the public sector.

Productivity and the Price Elasticity of Demand for Public Services

Price elasticity of demand is a measure of the responsiveness of demand for a good or service to its price. It is defined as the percentage change in quantity demanded divided by the percentage change in price. If the percentage change in quantity is greater than that in price, then price elasticity exceeds 1.0, and demand is said to be price elastic. When the percentage change in quantity is less than that in price, price elasticity is less than 1.0, and demand is said to be price inelastic. Other things held constant, when the price of a good or service rises, total expenditure on the good or service falls if its demand is price elastic. Total expenditure rises if its demand is price inelastic.

Studies have shown that growth of productivity in the public sector is low compared with that in the private sector.[6] Baumol has hypothesized that public sector productivity is relatively low because government services are labor intensive.[7] The consequence of the unbalanced growth of productivity in the two sectors is that, in real terms, the relative costs of goods and services provided by government tend to rise. As productivity rises in the private sector, wages and salaries rise without necessarily caus-

[5]Thomas E. Borcherding, "The Sources of Growth of Public Expenditures in the United States, 1902–1970," in Thomas E. Borcherding, ed., *Budgets and Bureaucrats: The Sources of Government Growth* (Durham, N.C.: Duke University Press, 1977), pp. 45–70.

[6]For example, estimates indicate that there were no net gains in productivity for six state and local services studied for the five-year period, 1962 to 1967. See Robert M. Spann, "Rates of Productivity Change and the Growth of State and Local Governmental Expenditures," in Borcherding, ed., *Budgets and Bureaucrats,* pp. 100–29.

[7]William J. Baumol, "Macroeconomics of Unbalanced Growth: The Anatomy of the Urban Crisis," *American Economic Review,* 57 (June 1967), 415–26.

ing any increase in the general price level.[8] Maintaining a force of employees in the public sector requires government employers to pay wages and salaries that are roughly equivalent to those in the public sector. Thus, as wages and salaries rise with productivity gains in the private sector, government employers find it necessary to offer matching wages and salaries even though there are no productivity gains in the public sector. The unit costs of goods and services supplied by government must rise relative to the unit costs of goods and services produced in the private sector. This is equivalent to an increase in the relative price of public services.

Borcherding estimated the price elasticity of demand for public services to be 0.56, which means that demand is price inelastic.[9] If there is an increase in the relative price of public services, as Baumol suggests, then total expenditure on them would be expected to increase because demand for them is price inelastic. This effect, which stems from relatively low productivity growth and price inelasticity of demand in the public sector, contributes to the growth of total government expenditure and also to the growth of the relative size of government.

Population Size and Density

It can be assumed that population size affects the demand for goods and services supplied by government. The demand should increase with population. If there are no scale economies from providing the goods and services through government, then spending should increase by the same *percentage* as population. If there are scale economies, then the unit costs of goods and services supplied by government tend to fall, which is equivalent to a fall in the relative price of such goods. The effect on spending depends on the economies realized and the price elasticity of demand. Two studies found no statistically significant scale economies or efficiencies in consumption.[10] If this is the case for public services in general, then spending increases should be proportional to population increases.

As population increases, it tends to be more dense. A more densely settled and more urbanized population increases economic and other types of interdependencies among persons. There is greater potential for conflict in areas of health, sanitation, environment, safety, and congestion. More

[8]Empirical evidence shows that productivity gains are lower for the service sector than for the goods sector in the private economy. This means that the price of services tends to rise over time. See Victor R. Fuchs, *Productivity Trends in the Goods and Services, 1929–1961*, NBER Occasional Paper No. 81 (New York: Columbia University Press, 1962). Also, see John W. Kendrick (assisted by Maude R. Pech), *Productivity Trends in the United States*, NBER General Series No. 71 (Princeton, N.J.: Princeton University Press, 1961).

[9]Borcherding, ed., *Budgets and Bureaucrats*, p. 49.

[10]See Thomas E. Borcherding and Robert T. Deacon, "The Demand for the Services of Non-Federal Governments," *American Economic Review*, 62 (December 1972), 891–901; and Theodore C. Bergstrom and Robert Goodman, "The Price and Income Elasticities of Demand for Public Goods," *American Economic Review*, 63 (June 1973), 280–96.

governmental action in such areas may be required in response to density, but the type of action need not involve substantial increases in government spending. Zoning, building and sanitation codes, and traffic controls require some government spending, but the outlays are relatively small. Increasing density and urbanization of a given population size seem to be relatively minor in relation to the growth of public spending.

Income, Relative Prices, Population, and the Growth of Public Spending

In part, the growth of government spending has been a response to income growth, a rise in the relative prices of public services, and population growth. Borcherding estimates that income growth accounts for about one-fourth of the increase in public spending, rising costs facing price-inelastic demands for about one-tenth of the increase, and population increase for about one-fifth. Together, these responsive elements account for only about one-half of the increase in total spending. He concludes that these factors explain why one-fifth of our GNP is spent through the public sector.[11] This suggests that other unidentified elements account for as much as one-half of the growth of public spending. What are the other factors? One might be the imperfect way in which the demand for public services is expressed through political institutions.

The demand for the goods and services that government supplies is transmitted through the political process. Information, incentives, and the nature of outcomes are quite different from the market process. For example, the average citizen may underestimate the costs of public services, and the public may think that government goods and services are provided at bargain prices. Special interest legislation concentrates benefits on a particular group, yet the costs may be spread over the entire population. Bureaucracies often advocate as large a budget as they can get approved, because pay, power, and prestige tend to be related positively to the budget size of an agency or department. These are defects in the sense that informed demands for public services are not transmitted properly through the political process. There is very little empirical evidence on defects in the political process as an explanatory element in the growth of government spending.

Resistance to the Growth of the Public Sector

From the mid-1970s on, there was a growing movement to restrict the growth of state-local taxes and expenditures. The modern movement to limit government activity began in California with an attack on property

[11]Borcherding, ed., *Budgets and Bureaucrats*, p. 56.

taxation. In 1978, led by an obscure California legislator, Howard Jarvis, voters overwhelmingly approved the Jarvis–Gann Amendment, which entered Proposition 13 into the California constitution. Central to Proposition 13 was restriction of the property tax rate to no more than 1 percent of assessed value. It also rolled back property assessments to market value on the 1975–1976 rolls and factored in a 2 percent growth rate. The immediate effect of Proposition 13 was to cut property tax collections from $12 billion to $5 billion.

Proposition 13 was followed by passage of Proposition 4, which was essentially an attempt to restrict increases in government activity still further. Proposition 4 limited increases in public spending to increase in population and to the consumer price index (CPI) or state per capita personal income, whichever is lower. The message of Propositions 13 and 4 seems to be a general protest against the size of the public sector. The tax and expenditure limitation movement has spread dramatically. Seventeen states approved limits of some kind during the period 1976–1979 alone. It seems likely that, as a result of such limits, state-local governments will be forced to increase their productivity, rely more on fees and charges for services, and shift some services to the private sector.

At the federal level, there is also evidence of a protest against the size of the public sector. President Reagan was elected in a landslide in 1980. Although there were a number of issues in the campaign, the emphasis was on limiting government activity. With his inauguration, there was focus on a single priority—budget reductions. In his address to a joint session of Congress on February 18, 1981, he presented a program calling for fundamental redirection and reduction of the size and role of the federal government. With the public enthusiastically behind him and a changed Congress in disarray, President Reagan won sweeping victories to cut spending and taxes.

The major question about such protests against the size of the public sector is whether the resistance will continue. Informed opinion about the state-local limitation movement is that fiscal austerity will prevail even if the movement per se loses some of its momentum. In effect, this is a forecast that such limits will have serious effects. At the federal level, the jury is still out. There are deep rifts over spending levels and priorities. President Reagan encountered stiff congressional opposition to his 1982 and 1983 budgets. However, the expectation is movement to a new consensus on spending philosophy. It is likely that such consensus will seriously limit the role, scope, and size of the federal government.

SUMMARY

The growth of the public sector underscores the need to understand the *principles* of public finance. Description alone is not sufficient to master the study of the public sector. Analysis of democratic decision making, taxation, expenditure, and federalism is essential to a true understanding of the impact of public sector activity on the economy as well as on individual firms and households. Through description of institutions and, in particular, analysis of economic effects, the principles of public finance can serve as an introduction to political economy and the wide range of issues facing a fiscal system in a democratic society.

2

Market Failure, Public Goods, and Externalities

Economists long have been aware of the effectiveness of the market system as a mechanism for allocating scarce resources. Indeed, the enduring message of Adam Smith's *Wealth of Nations* (1776) is that only through reliance on free markets can a society realize its full economic potential. Since Adam Smith, economic theorists have demonstrated with increasing rigor the circumstances under which competitive markets can bring about efficient use of scarce resources.

Most defenders of free markets, including Smith, have conceded that, in some instances, markets will fail to allocate resources efficiently. The causes and degree of market failure vary from case to case. In some markets, productive capacity becomes concentrated in the hands of one or a few firms, which then use their market power to restrain output and raise prices. In other cases, market prices fail to reflect fully the costs or benefits associated with production or consumption of marketed goods. When this happens, markets generate false signals, and we get what are called *externalities*. Examples include environmental pollution, as when power generating stations or smelters impose costs on others by polluting the atmosphere. Some externalities are beneficial, as when education provides benefits to society in general, not just to persons being educated. Finally, some goods or services may be consumed jointly by large numbers of people. Flood protection and national defense are examples. Goods of this type are called *public goods*. We will see later that, in many (but not all) cases, if public goods are to be provided at all, they must be provided by government.

Market failures are of importance in the study of public finance because they provide a justification for limited governmental intervention in a market economy. As we saw in Chapter 1, the level of governmental participation in the U.S. economy has grown markedly in this century. Much disagreement over the proper role of government persists among economists and others. One reason is because of differing perceptions about the seriousness of market failure. Another is because of disagreement over the ability of government to deliver services in an efficient manner.

In this chapter, we examine in detail some of the causes of market failure. In particular, we emphasize failures associated with public goods and externalities. Our goal is to reach a clearer understanding of the arguments used by economists to justify governmental activity. We also learn why the conditions that justify intervention serve at the same time to limit the ability of government to correct the misallocation caused by the existence of public goods and externalities.

Before turning to an analysis of public goods and other causes of market failure, it will be helpful to explore the concept of efficiency as it is used in economic theory. In this way, we provide ourselves with a benchmark against which to compare the inefficiencies caused by various types of market failure. The discussion in the next section draws heavily on intermediate micro theory. Readers unfamiliar with this level of analysis can skip to the succeeding section without a significant loss of continuity.

EFFICIENCY AND COMPETITION

Imagine an economy consisting of two types of decision makers, households and firms. Households consume goods and services. They also own and supply the labor, capital, and natural resources used in production. Firms buy the services of the factors of production in the factor markets. They use the purchased factors to produce goods and services to be sold to households in the markets for consumer goods. To facilitate the functioning of the markets for factors and goods, a commodity such as gold may serve as money, that is, as a medium of exchange and standard of value. A pure market economy with a flow of goods and services in one direction and a flow of money in the other is depicted in the circular flow diagram of Figure 2–1.

The use of resources in a pure market economy is controlled by consumer sovereignty. Each household allocates the income it receives from the factor markets among the available consumer goods and services in accordance with its own preferences. Firms respond by producing the goods that consumers demand. Consumers use their dollars to tell the economic system how to allocate resources—one dollar, one vote as it is sometimes stated. Note that there is no role for government in the system just described.

The appeal of a market system derives from the apparently automatic

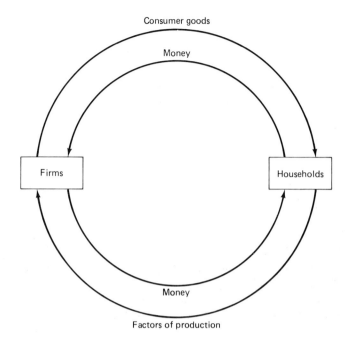

Consumer goods

Money

Firms

Households

Money

Factors of production

FIGURE 2–1   Circular flow diagram. In a pure market economy, firms produce consumer goods for sale to households. In order to produce the goods, firms must purchase the services of factors of production from households. The flow of goods and services through markets for consumer goods and factor markets is shown by the clockwise arrows. Money, the medium of exchange, flows in a counterclockwise direction, generating income for households and revenue for firms.

way in which it allocates scarce resources in accordance with consumer demands. No central direction is necessary. This is the notion exemplified by Adam Smith's famous and impersonal "invisible hand." The decisions of individual consumers and producers acting in their own self-interest serve to allocate resources to their most productive uses.

Several conditions must be satisfied, however, if a market economy is to allocate resources in an efficient manner. An economy must satisfy the conditions for efficiency in consumption, efficiency in production, and efficiency in the relationship between consumption and production. We turn now to a discussion of the requirements that must be met if these efficiency conditions are to be attained.

Efficiency in Consumption

We begin by making two assumptions about the consumer. First, we assume that all consumers try to allocate expenditures so as to maximize utility. The ability to spend, and hence to gain utility, is constrained by the consumer's money income and by the prices that must be paid for goods and services. Second, we assume that the increment in utility that a consumer receives from the consumption of a good declines as the amount consumed during a given time period increases. In more technical terms, the marginal utility, *MU,* obtained from consumption of a good diminishes with each increment in consumption.

To illustrate how a consumer proceeds to maximize utility, let us begin with an example. Suppose that the price of candy bars is twice the price of apples but that, at current levels of consumption, a consumer gets three times as much utility from eating one more candy bar as from eating one more apple. Clearly, the consumer could get more utility by giving up two apples and buying one candy bar. Recall that, as consumption of candy bars increases, marginal utility declines. On the other hand, as consumption of apples is reduced, the marginal utility from their consumption rises. In this example, substitution would continue until one candy bar yielded only twice as much utility as one apple. The reader should be able to demonstrate that, when this point is reached, a dollar spent on candy bars yields the same amount of utility as a dollar spent on apples.

Our result can be expressed succinctly in algebraic terms. We begin by defining the ratio of marginal utilities, or MU_c for candy bars and MU_a for apples. This ratio is termed the *marginal rate of substitution,* or *MRS*. In this case, the *MRS* is between candy bars and apples, or MRS_{ca}. When the consumer is allocating expenditures between candy bars and apples so as to maximize utility, the MRS_{ca} is equal to the ratio of the price of candy bars, P_c, to the price of apples, P_a. In equation form, the result may be expressed as[1]

$$MRS_{ca} = \frac{MU_c}{MU_a} = \frac{P_c}{P_a}$$

More generally, if a consumer is to maximize utility, the equality between *MRS* and the ratio of prices must hold for every pair of goods consumed. When this result is achieved, it is no longer possible for the consumer to increase utility by reallocating consumption expenditures among different goods. As a consequence, the consumer has attained a state of *equilibrium.*

The analysis may be extended from the individual consumer to all consumers. Assume that all consumers have attained a state of equilibrium in consumption and that all consumers face the same set of prices. Thus, each consumer will be equating the *MRS* between any pair of goods to the ratio of prices of the goods. If all consumers face the same set of prices, it follows that the *MRS* between any pair of goods will be the same for every consumer. Consequently, it would not be possible to bring about a mutually beneficial reallocation of consumer goods between any pair of con-

---

[1]It is demonstrated in micro theory that this equation is satisfied when an indifference curve is tangent to the consumer's budget line.

sumers. All potential gains from such a reallocation have been exhausted. The economy has attained a state of efficiency in consumption.

Efficiency in Production

The individual firm operating in a perfectly competitive environment is a *price taker*. Its output is so small relative to the size of the market that it has no perceptible effect on price, as in the case of an individual corn farmer. Likewise, the firm's demands for inputs are so small that it has no perceptible effect on the prices of factors of production. A perfectly competitive firm of this type is faced with only one marketing decision: how much to produce. It will choose the output at which market price equals marginal cost.

As long as the cost of an additional unit of output is less than the price, the firm has an incentive to expand output. The firm has no incentive to move beyond that point, because in this range, it costs more to produce an additional unit of output than the firm receives from its sale. It follows that, if the firm is to maximize profits, it must produce at the point where marginal cost equals price, and it must do so at minimum cost.[2] Because inputs such as capital, labor, raw materials, and energy can typically be substituted for each other—within limits—the firm must choose the least costly combination of inputs needed to produce a given output. To make this selection, the firm must have knowledge of the relation between inputs and output, obtained from its production function. It must then combine this information with data on the price of each input.

To illustrate the procedure for selecting the least-cost input combination, let us assume that the firm uses a combination of two inputs, capital, K, and labor, L. Each is purchased at a price per unit—P_k for capital and P_l for labor—that is determined in the factor markets. Recall that the firm takes prices as given. From its production function, the firm determines the increment in output, or marginal product, that it can obtain by hiring one more unit of capital or labor. In our two-factor example, the increments are the marginal product of capital, MP_k, and the marginal product of labor, MP_l. For each level of output, the firm must choose the combination of capital and labor that equates the ratio of marginal products to the ratio of factor prices. In algebraic terms, this equality may be expressed as follows:

$$\frac{MP_k}{MP_l} = \frac{P_k}{P_l}$$

This equation tells us that, if the price of a unit of capital, P_k, is twice the price of a unit of labor, P_l, an input combination should be chosen so that,

[2]Under perfect competition, maximum profits are driven to zero in the long run. Positive profits will disappear because of entry of new firms. Production at any level of output other than that where price equals marginal and average cost will result in negative profits.

at the margin, a unit of capital contributes twice as much to output as a unit of labor. Only if this condition is satisfied can output be produced at minimum cost. Suppose, for example, that capital and labor are combined so that the marginal unit of capital adds three times as much to output as the marginal unit of labor. If a unit of capital is three times as productive as a unit of labor but costs only twice as much, the firm can cut costs by hiring more capital and less labor. Substitution of capital for labor should continue until the ratio of marginal products is brought into line with the ratio of prices. Substitution in the opposite direction would be called for if a unit of capital were less than twice as productive as a unit of labor.

The ratio of marginal products is termed the *marginal rate of technical substitution,* or *MRTS.* In our example, the marginal rate of technical substitution between capital and labor, or $MRTS_{kl}$, must be equal to the ratio of factor prices. Otherwise, output will not be produced at minimum cost. Algebraically, this condition is expressed as follows[3]:

$$MRTS_{kl} = \frac{MP_k}{MP_l} = \frac{P_k}{P_l}$$

The equality between the marginal rate of technical substitution and the ratio of factor prices must hold for all pairs of factors used by a firm. If production in the economy is to be efficient, this condition must be satisfied for all firms in all industries. Otherwise, it would be possible to increase the value of output from a given set of inputs by reallocating factors of production among firms.

Returning to the individual firm, to maximize profits, it must choose not only the optimal *mix* of inputs but also the optimal *level* of each input. The optimal level for each input is reached when the price of the marginal unit purchased is equal to the value of its contribution to output. If a firm producing candy bars can hire a unit of labor for $50 a day, it should continue to hire additional units of labor so long as an additional worker can add at least $50 worth of candy bars per day to output. In algebraic terms, input of labor should be expanded to the point where the value of the marginal product of the last unit of labor hired, VMP_l, is equal to the price of labor. Since the VMP_l is equal to the marginal product of labor multiplied by the price of candy bars, P_c, the following equation must be satisfied:

$$VMP_l = P_c \cdot MP_l = P_l$$

The same equality must hold for capital and any other input used by the firm. This condition holds for all factors of production and for all firms when the economy is in a state of efficiency in production. It is then im-

---

[3]It is demonstrated in micro theory that this equation is satisfied when an isoquant is tangent to an isocost line.

possible to reallocate factor inputs in any way without reducing the value of total ouput.

Using the theoretical tools of microeconomic theory, it can be shown that the perfectly competitive firm satisfies the conditions of productive efficiency when it is in long-run competitive equilibrium. It can also be shown that, when all inputs are employed at the level at which *VMP* equals factor price, the output of the firm will be at the level at which marginal cost of output is equal to the price of output. This is an important result, because it indicates that, at the margin, the cost of producing a unit of output is equal to the price that consumers are willing to pay for it.[4]

The Link Between Consumption Efficiency and Production Efficiency

When all firms and industries in an economy are in long-run perfectly competitive equilibrium, all firms are producing at the point where price equals marginal cost. Picking at random any two firms in different industries, say, the candy bar and apple industries, we get the following equalities between the price of candy bars, P_c, and apples, P_a, and their respective marginal costs, MC_c and MC_a:

$$P_c = MC_c$$
$$P_a = MC_a$$

If we take the ratio of the marginal costs of candy bars and apples, we get the rate of trade-off between them in production. For example, if the value of inputs needed to produce a candy bar is at the margin twice the value of inputs needed to produce an apple, the rate of trade-off in production is 2. This rate of trade-off is called the *marginal rate of transformation*. The marginal rate of transformation between candy bars and apples, MRT_{ca}, is thus given by the equation

$$MRT_{ca} = \frac{MC_c}{MC_a}$$

Remembering that under perfect competition price equals marginal cost, we get the following relationship between MRT_{ca} and the prices of candy bars and apples:

$$MRT_{ca} = \frac{MC_c}{MC_a} = \frac{P_c}{P_a}$$

---

[4]A number of intermediate texts in microeconomics contain a detailed exposition of product and factor market equilibrium of the competitive firm. One example is Jack Hirshleifer, *Price Theory and Applications*, 2nd ed. (Englewood Cliffs, N.J.: Prentice-Hall, Inc., 1980), pp. 259–302.

In our example, if the MRT_{ca} is 2, a candy bar will cost twice as much to produce as an apple.

Recall that, when consumption is efficient, each consumer allocates expenditures among goods so that the ratio of marginal utilities, called the marginal rate of substitution, is equal to the ratio of prices. When production is efficient, the trade-off in production—the marginal rate of transformation—is equal to the ratio of prices. If efficient allocation among consumers is to be consistent with efficient allocation in production, price ratios in the consumption and production sectors must be equal. Only if this condition holds will the trade-off in consumption be equal to the trade-off in production.

For candy bars and apples, efficient allocation requires that the following equation be satisfied for all consumers and all producers:

$$\frac{MU_c}{MU_a} = MRS_{ca} = \frac{P_c}{P_a} = MRT_{ca} = \frac{MC_c}{MC_a}$$

or, more succinctly,

$$MRS_{ca} = MRT_{ca}$$

This says that the rate at which consumers are willing to substitute one good for another equals the rate at which the output of one good can be substituted for the other in production. More succinctly, it says that the trade-off in consumption equals the trade-off in production. If this condition holds for all combinations of consumers and for all pairs of goods, it is not possible to rearrange either production or consumption patterns without making someone worse off. Such an economy is said to have attained a *Pareto optimum,* a condition defined first by the Italian economist Vilfredo Pareto.

Economic theorists have provided rigorous proof of the equivalence between Pareto optimality and perfectly competitive equilibrium. The proof is quite abstract and is derived from strict assumptions about both the consumer and producer sectors that cannot possibly be satisfied in the real world.[5] The exercise is useful, however, because it provides us with a reference point for analyzing the behavior of actual economies. By examining the ways in which an actual economy fails to satisfy the conditions necessary for attaining a competitive, Pareto optimal solution, we gain an understanding of the sources of market failure.

[5]The proof of the equivalence of competitive equilibrium and Pareto optimality is outlined in Tjalling Koopmans, *Three Essays on the State of Economic Science* (New York: McGraw-Hill Book Company, 1957), pp. 3–105.

SOURCES OF MARKET FAILURE

Many things can prevent an economy from reaching a Pareto optimal equilibrium. The competitive, Pareto optimal solution is regarded as an ideal or norm for allocation of resources. Because resources are in their most productive uses, the value of total output as measured by a standard of value such as money is maximized subject to given technology, consumer tastes, and distribution of ownership of factors of production. If the economy fails to reach this ideal state in all markets for all goods, we have what is called *market failure.*[6] This does not mean that the market system fails altogether. Rather, it means that something prevents it from satisfying all the requirements for efficient allocation. We turn now to a discussion of the major sources of market failure. Some are of particular interest to students of public finance, because they provide a rationale for provision of some goods and services by the government.

Imperfect Competition

No actual market is perfectly competitive, but the departure from the competitive ideal is much greater in some industries (e.g., automobiles, electrical power) than in others (e.g., agriculture, textiles). Departure from the competitive norm is often related to economies of scale. If the output of a single firm must be large relative to the size of the market to achieve production at minimum per unit (average) cost, surviving firms will tend to grow in size and decrease in number to take advantage of scale economies. In the extreme case, the most efficient production unit (in terms of unit cost) may be a single firm—the so-called "natural" monopoly—that supplies the entire market.

Recall that a perfectly competitive firm maximizes total profit by extending output to the point where price, P, equals marginal cost, MC. The perfectly competitive firm is a price taker. Its output is such a small portion of industry output that it has no noticeable effect on market price. The demand curve it faces is horizontal, so the sale of one more unit increases revenue from sales by the unit price. In other words, price equals marginal revenue, MR. If the firm is a monopolist, the demand curve it faces coincides with the market demand curve, which generally is negatively sloped.

To increase its sales during a given time period, a monopoly must cut the price it charges for all units it sells. Suppose that the firm can sell 100 units per week at $2.00 each, but to increase its sales to 101 units, it must cut the price per unit to $1.99. Marginal revenue equals $0.99, which is the

---

[6]For a thorough treatment of market failure, see J. Ronnie Davis and Joe R. Hulett, *An Analysis of Market Failure* (Gainesville: University Presses of Florida, 1977).

price of the marginal unit, \$1.99, less \$1.00, the loss in revenue on the first 100 units resulting from the price cut of 1 cent. The monopolist who wishes to maximize profit will produce the output at which $MR = MC$, but at this point $P > MC$.

Assume for the moment that all industries but one are competitive, while one is monopolistic. In the competitive industries $P = MC$, but in the monopolistic industry $P > MC$. Consumers value output in the monopolistic industry at a price greater than cost so that the total value of output could be increased by shifting resources out of uses in which $P = MC$ into uses in which $P > MC$ until $P = MC$ everywhere.[7] In the absence of outside intervention, however, the monopolist will have no economic incentive to expand output beyond the level where $MR = MC$ so that we would not expect such a reallocation to take place. Market imperfection thus restricts the power of dollar votes—consumer sovereignty—over the allocation of resources.

Dominance of an industry by a few firms is more typical than is the single-firm monopoly. In this case, output of one firm accounts for a share of the market large enough that its pricing policy has a significant (noticeable) effect on market price. The pricing policies of the individual firms are interdependent, giving rise to oligopoly. Economic theorists have had only limited success in constructing models that will predict the outcome. There is no reason to believe, however, that market forces will tend toward a solution that will equate P to MC.

Even if a relatively large number of firms produce similar products, they will not be perfectly competitive unless buyers consider output to be homogeneous. If buyers differentiate among the products of firms and develop preferences for particular products, the sellers will retain at least some market power; that is, they will have some ability to vary the quantity sold by varying price. Consequently, in profit-maximizing equilibrium, $P > MR = MC$. This departure from the perfectly competitive norm is called *monopolistic competition*. It is somewhat descriptive of conditions in some retail markets where consumer preference may reflect location, store hours, or the shopkeeper's personality as much as the physical characteristics of the items sold.

Government policies designed to counteract imperfections arising in cases of monopoly or oligopoly include antitrust laws designed to discourage price fixing or merger among competitors, schemes for taxing monopoly profits, government regulation and government ownership, and operation in the "public interest." In general, these activities of government receive more attention from specialists in industrial organization than from public finance economists. The latter are more concerned with analysis of

[7]More is involved in meeting the conditions for efficient allocation than equating price to marginal cost in all markets. For a more thorough discussion, the reader is referred to the chapter on welfare economics found in most intermediate texts in microeconomic theory. One such source is J. P. Gould and C. E. Ferguson, *Microeconomic Theory*, 5th ed. (Homewood, Ill.: Richard D. Irwin, Inc., 1980), pp. 440–59.

the effects of taxation on the functioning of markets and with expenditure programs that absorb large amounts of scarce resources.

Public Goods and Externalities

Some goods possess characteristics that make it impossible for the market to provide them efficiently if at all. These goods, variously called *public, social,* or *collective goods,* provide benefits simultaneously for two or more people; often, they provide benefits for large numbers of people. Examples include street lights, transmission of television signals, and national defense. Because of partial or total market failure, public goods are usually financed by government through taxes.

Externalities occur when market prices fail to reflect all the costs or benefits arising from the consumption or production of goods or services, or when efficient allocation is hindered by an inability to define or enforce property rights. Examples of externalities include environmental pollution, benefits to society in general from education of individuals, and traffic congestion.

Both public goods and externalities are discussed in detail in the following section.

Redistribution

The distribution of income in a free enterprise economy is determined by the distribution of earnings of factors of production. The distribution of factor earnings, in turn, depends on the distribution of marketable labor skills and wealth.

The nature and quality of life within a society are strongly influenced by the way in which income is distributed. Because of its effect on the general atmosphere of a society, its income distribution has been likened to a public good, "consumed" in a sense by everyone.[8] If society is dissatisfied with the distribution derived from the play of market forces, it may intervene through government to alter the outcome. Virtually everything that government does is likely to have some effect on the distribution of income and wealth, but some policies and programs are designed explicitly for the purpose of redistribution. Of major importance in this regard are the social insurance and welfare programs described in Chapter 13. The choice of sources of tax revenue and of tax rate structures is also strongly influenced by distributional considerations.

Cyclical Instability

The history of market economies is marked by instability of prices, output, and employment in the aggregate and in individual industries. In-

[8]Lester Thurow, "The Income Distribution as a Pure Public Good," *Quarterly Journal of Economics,* 85 (May 1971), 327–36.

stability is attributed to a variety of causes. Changes in technology and consumer tastes can generate unemployment, investment booms, and bankruptcies that send shocks through the economy. So can wars, oil embargoes, and crop failures. The role of money is cited by some as a crucial factor. Its use is required for smoothly functioning markets in diverse goods and services. Specialization and division of labor would be greatly restricted under a barter system. Yet, if the money supply increases more rapidly or slowly than real output, the general price level is likely to rise or fall accordingly. Short-term changes in the holding of money balances can lead to economic dislocation. If a fraction of the money supply is removed from the circular flow and is hoarded, an excess supply of goods and services at going prices will result. Sudden dishoarding may lead to excess aggregate demand. If prices are flexible, a reasonably rapid adjustment is possible, but not without some change in the distribution of income and wealth. If prices are "sticky," as is likely when most markets are imperfectly competitive, more prolonged dislocations with accompanying unemployment may occur. Society tends to look to government to take stabilizing action by expanding aggregate demand during recessions and restraining it during inflationary booms. These goals may be pursued through taxation and government spending, which affect aggregate demand, as well as through control of the money supply, a function that most national governments reserve for themselves.

The performance of governments in maintaining a stable economy has not been very encouraging. Some critics contend that government, especially through unwise monetary policy, is the major cause of business cycles.[9] Yet maintenance of a stable economy is a commonly accepted justification for government intervention. One reason is because only government possesses the policy instruments needed to control and stabilize the economy. Another reason is that only government has an incentive to give major consideration to the effect of its actions on the state of the economy, even though economic considerations are often overridden by political factors.

Economic Growth

Economic growth may be defined as the rate of increase in per capita real income over time. An important determinant of growth is the rate of capital formation, which in a market economy depends on how individual decision makers allocate income between consumption and investment. The growth rate that results may not meet with society's approval. Traditionally, governments have intervened in various ways to raise the growth rate above the level determined in the market. They do this by encouraging

---

[9]The best known proponent of this view is Milton Friedman, whose views are summarized in "The Role of Monetary Policy," *American Economic Review*, 58 (March 1968), 1–17.

more saving and capital formation, by underwriting technological advancement, and by improving the quality of the work force. Among the techniques used are tax breaks for investors, allocation of government tax revenue to investment projects, and government subsidies to such growth-inducing activities as basic research and education.

During the 1970s, the apostles of zero economic growth concluded that economic growth is undesirable and should be brought to a halt.[10] Thus far, this attitude has not been reflected directly in government policy, but some of the goals of zero-growth proponents have been promoted through the unintended consequences of government intervention. Notable examples are policies to promote conservation of resources and to control pollution.

♦ PRIVATE GOODS AND PUBLIC GOODS

If the benefits from the consumption of a unit of a good are confined to the individual who consumes it, the good is a *pure private good*. When one person consumes a unit of a pure private good, all others are precluded from consuming that same unit. Hence, we say that there is *rivalry* in the consumption of a pure private good. Whether the good is produced and/or distributed by the public sector or by private business firms is irrelevant for classification purposes; it is rivalry in consumption that characterizes it as a private good.

If the benefits from the consumption of a unit of a good may be consumed jointly by more than one consumer in such a way that consumption by one person in no way reduces the amount that can be made available for consumption by others, the good is a *pure public good*. Because consumption of a unit of a pure public good by one person in no way reduces the amount of that same unit that can be consumed by others, we say that consumption of a pure public good is characterized by *nonrivalry*.[11]

The benefits of some public goods are shared by a large number of individuals. Examples are defense against foreign attack, space spectacu-

[10]For a summary of the zero-growth controversy, see E. J. Mishan, "Growth and Antigrowth: What Are the Issues?" in Andrew Weintraub, Eli Schwartz, and J. Richard Aronson, eds., *The Economic Growth Controversy* (White Plains, N.Y.: International Arts and Sciences Press, 1973), pp. 3–38.

[11]The distinction between pure private and pure public goods was clarified by Paul A. Samuelson, in "The Pure Theory of Public Expenditures." *Review of Economics and Statistics,* 36 (November 1954), 387–89, and "Diagrammatic Exposition of a Theory of Public Expenditure," *Review of Economics and Statistics,* 37 (November 1955), 350–56. A more recent treatment by Samuelson appears in "Pure Theory of Public Expenditure and Taxation," in J. Margolis and H. Guitton, eds., *Public Economics* (New York: St. Martin's Press, 1969), pp. 98–123. Samuelson emphasized that the characteristic of nonrivalry in consumption is the *only* characteristic of a public good that distinguishes it from a private good.

lars, and major flood control projects. Only a few persons may receive benefits from other public goods. For example, a fence placed along the property line between two residential lots provides the benefits of privacy to members of both households. For this small group, the fence possesses the basic characteristic of a public good, nonrivalry in consumption.

The number who benefit from a public good may influence the way in which it is financed. Thus, national defense is financed by government through taxes (and, perhaps, through borrowing and conscription), while a fence is usually erected by one or both of the affected households with one or both absorbing the cost. It is the characteristic of nonrival consumption, not the institutional arrangement through which it is provided, that determines whether a good is public or private.

The characteristic of nonrival consumption leads to a set of requirements for efficient provision of public goods that differs from those for private goods. The efficiency conditions for the two types of goods are presented in the discussion that follows. To simplify the graphics, we assume that the goods in question are consumed by only two persons, Albert and Bonnie. The basic principles to be explored are equally applicable to cases involving large numbers of consumers.

Efficient Provision
of a Private Good

The market demand curve for a private good is obtained by summing the quantities that each consumer will purchase at each price. In Figure 2–2, we show the demand curves D_a and D_b for two consumers, Albert and Bonnie. At price P_1, Albert demands the quantity OA_1, while Bonnie demands OB_1. Hence, at P_1 market demand is $OA_1 + OB_1 = OC_1$. Note that the quantities shown on the horizontal axis are added to obtain the total quantity demanded. Points on *market* demand curves for private goods are obtained by *horizontally* summing the demand curves of individual consumers. By repeating the process for different prices, we can get as many points on the market demand curve, *DD*, as we wish.

Adding a market supply curve, *S*, we get the equilibrium price, P_e, and quantity, OC_e, that clears the market. Both Albert and Bonnie pay the *same price, P_e,* but they consume *different quantities, OA_e and OB_e.* In most markets for private goods, consumers must take the market price as given, but they are free to choose the quantity they buy. Therefore, each consumer will adjust consumption to the quantity at which his or her evaluation of the marginal unit is equal to the market price. Each consumer is paying a price that equals his or her evaluation of the marginal unit, and neither has any desire to change the quantity consumed. If the good is produced by a perfectly competitive industry, each firm maximizes profit by producing at a rate that equates price to marginal cost. Hence, in the ab-

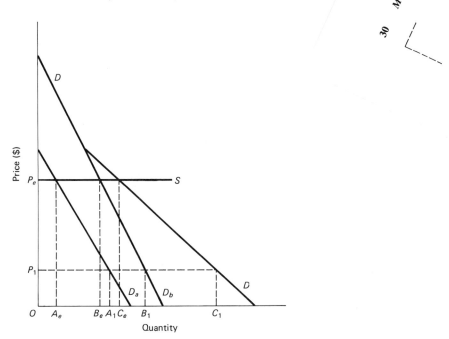

FIGURE 2–2   Derivation of demand curve for a private good. Given the demand curves D_a and D_b for two individuals, Albert and Bonnie, their combined or market demand can be obtained by summing horizontally the quantities demanded by each consumer at each price. Horizontal summation of D_a and D_b yields the market demand curve DD. Equilibrium output is at C_e, with Albert demanding A_e units and Bonnie demanding B_e units. Equilibrium price is P_e.

sence of external effects not reflected in cost, the value that consumers place on the marginal unit produced, as reflected in market price, equals the cost of producing it, as reflected in factor prices. More succinctly, price equals marginal cost.

Efficient Provision
of a Public Good

Let us continue with our two-person example and derive the conditions for efficient provision of a *public good*. Suppose that Albert and Bonnie are property owners who live along a stretch of river bank as shown in Figure 2–3. The river occasionally overflows its bank between the two hills and floods the property of both individuals. If both owners can agree to build a levee along the river bank between the two hills, they can gain some protection from flooding. The higher they build the levee, the less likely it is that flooding will occur.

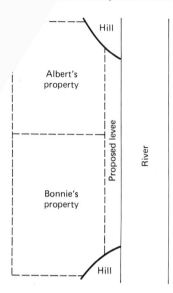

FIGURE 2–3 **Flood protection as a public good.** A levee between the two hills simultaneously protects the property of Albert and Bonnie. Consumption of flood protection is therefore nonrival, giving it the distinguishing characteristic of a public good.

Note that more protection for one property owner (a higher levee) also means more for the other. Benefits to Albert and Bonnie from the levee are characterized by nonrival consumption. Therefore, the levee is a public good for the two consumers.

We make the simplifying assumption that the demand curve of each consumer is fully and voluntarily revealed. This assumption allows us to focus our attention on the differences in the efficiency conditions for private and public goods. Later in the discussion, we explain why the assumption is not likely to be realistic.

The demand curves of Albert and Bonnie are labeled D_a and D_b in Figure 2–4. They show the price that each is willing to pay for flood protection, which we assume can be measured by the height of the levee. Because of the jointness characteristic, both must consume the same quantity of flood protection. If the levee is higher on Albert's portion of the river bank, the extra height will do him no good. He has no more protection than Bonnie. The valuation per unit that each places on a given quantity is shown on the vertical axis. Thus, for the *quantity* OE_n on the horizontal axis, Albert values the levee at OT_a dollars per foot and Bonnie at OT_b dollars. For a height of OE_n, Albert and Bonnie together value the levee at $OT_a + OT_b = OT_c$ dollars per foot. Because both are consuming the good simultaneously, the total valuation, OT_c, represents the evaluation that the entire (two-person) public places on the quantity OE_n. In other words, OT_c and OE_n are coordinates of a point on the demand curve, DD, for the levee. Note that the vertical coordinate is the sum of the vertical distances from the quantity axis to the individual demand curve of each individual (in this case, OT_a and OT_b). Other points on DD are obtained in the same

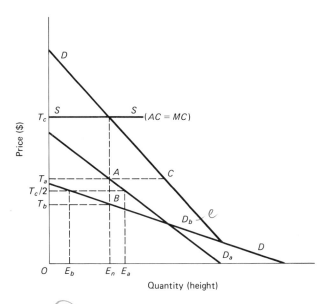

FIGURE 2–4   **Derivation of demand curve for a public good.** Given the demand curves D_a and D_b for two consumers, Albert and Bonnie, their combined demand can be obtained by summing vertically the price that each is willing to pay for each successive unit of output. Vertical summation yields the aggregate demand curve DD. Equilibrium output is at E_n. Consumers are in equilibrium at output E_n when Albert pays a price of T_a and Bonnie pays a price of T_b for the marginal unit.

manner, giving us a demand curve for a public good that is a *vertical* summation of individual demand curves.

Turn now to the supply curve, S, which intersects the demand curve, DD, at output OE_n. To the left of OE_n, the demand curve DD lies above the supply curve, indicating that Albert and Bonnie together place a higher value on additional flood protection than it costs to provide it. To the right of OE_n curve, DD lies below the supply curve, indicating that they value it at less than cost. It appears, therefore, that OE_n represents equilibrium output. Each individual will be in equilibrium when the price each pays is equal to the valuation that each places on the marginal unit of the good. This occurs when Albert pays a price (or tax) of OT_a per unit, or OT_aAE_n in total, and Bonnie pays OT_b per unit, or OT_bBE_n in total.[12]

---

[12]The condition described is a *Lindahl equilibrium,* first described by Swedish economist Erik Lindahl, a pioneer in the development of public goods theory. In the discussion in the text, it is assumed that each consumer pays a price equal to his or her evaluation of the marginal unit for *all* units each consumes jointly with the other. The equilibrium conditions for a public good require, however, that this price apply only to the marginal unit. See James M. Buchanan, *The Demand and Supply of Public Goods* (Chicago: Rand McNally & Company, 1968), pp. 37–39.

Note the contrast between a private and a public good. Each consumer pays the same market price for a unit of private good but the quantity can be varied according to differences in demand. With a public good, differences in preferences can be allowed for only if individuals pay different prices for the same quantity. In some instances, that price may be zero. In Figure 2–4, for example, if the supply curve were to intersect the *DD* curve to the right of the point where D_a intersects the quantity axis, Albert would be in equilibrium only at a price of zero. The two individuals would be in equilibrium with Bonnie paying the full cost.

But how is all of this related to our earlier discussion of efficient allocation of resources? You will recall that, when both Albert and Bonnie are in equilibrium, not only is each one paying a price per unit that equals his or her own marginal evaluation of that unit, but, in addition, the sum of these prices or marginal evaluations is equal to the supply price. If the supply price is equal to marginal cost, as would be the case if the good is provided by perfectly competitive firms, we have the public good counterpart to the $P = MC$ rule for efficient allocation of private goods; that is, $OT_a + OT_b = MC$.[13]

Turning again to the original equilibrium position as shown in Figure 2–4, what happens if Albert and Bonnie pay prices other than OT_a and OT_b? Suppose, for example, that each is charged the same price, one-half of OT_c per foot, for OE_n feet of levee. At this price Albert would prefer to see the height of the levee raised to OE_a while Bonnie would prefer a height of only OE_b. Only if by chance their demand curves should intersect or coincide at the quantity OE_n would an arrangement to split the cost equally cause each to agree on the efficient output.

Liars and Free Riders

Is it reasonable to assume that we can induce or even force consumers to reveal their true demand for a public good? When only two individuals are involved, as in our example, it is conceivable that an efficient solution will be reached through negotiation, but there is no guarantee that this will happen. Each party is in fact ignorant of the other's true preferences, and both may lie about their own preferences in the hope of getting a better "deal" in the negotiations. The example of a backyard fence may illustrate what we mean. Both neighbors may desire a fence, but each may refuse to admit it in the hope that the other party will give in and absorb

[13]A situation in which each consumer is charged a price equal to his or her marginal evaluation, as illustrated in Figure 2–6, obviously satisfies the efficiency condition. It is shown in the more advanced literature that allocation may be efficient even if individuals do not pay a price equal to their marginal evaluation, so long as the summed marginal evaluations equal marginal cost. See Jesse Burkhead and Jerry Miner, *Public Expenditure* (Chicago: Aldine-Atherton, Inc., 1971), pp. 41–49, 74–82. A more advanced treatment is given in Martin C. McGuire and Henry Aaron, "Efficiency and Equity in the Optimal Supply of a Public Good," *Review of Economics and Statistics*, 51 (February 1969), 31–39.

the entire cost of building a fence. Or each party may understate true demand, hoping for a lower share of the total cost. The misrepresentation is akin to that engaged in by two people negotiating the sale of a house or an automobile.

As the number of individuals involved becomes larger, negotiation becomes increasingly difficult, and prospects for an efficient solution become even more remote. Suppose, for example, that those who consume a good jointly try to get information by asking each other how much they are willing to pay for various quantities. The stated demands of the respondents could be summed to get aggregate demand. When this information is combined with cost data, optimal output could be determined.

Aside from the expense and inconvenience involved, the answers obtained from such a procedure are not likely to be very accurate, since it is not likely that respondents will have an incentive to tell the truth. If the cost is allocated among consumers in accordance with their stated preferences, demand will be understated. By lying, a person can cut down his or her share of the cost. The "liar's problem" is most serious when the number of beneficiaries is large and the effect of any one person's contribution is small.

Suppose that Albert is fearful that, if his country does not have a large defense establishment, it will be invaded by a hostile foreign power. He nevertheless may be acting rationally if he refuses to make a voluntary contribution to a fund for financing the armed forces. His individual contribution, even if quite generous, is not likely to have a noticeable effect on the amount of defense provided. He would be better advised, therefore, to contribute nothing to the defense fund and spend his income in other ways and hope that others will make voluntary contributions. If others do, Albert will benefit from the defense forces financed by their contributions and become a *free rider*. The problem is that everyone favoring national defense is faced with the temptation to become a free rider. If everyone else responds in the same way as Albert, we will have little or no national defense. For this reason, if given a choice between defense forces maintained by voluntary contribution or by a compulsory tax levy applied to all taxpayers, many taxpayers will choose the latter. If popular support for large defense expenditures is strong, it is likely that people will impose upon themselves a system of compulsory taxation to raise the necessary funds. It makes sense for individual taxpayers to favor such an arrangement even though their shares of the cost exceed the amount they would contribute under a voluntary scheme. The benefits that each receives from the quantity of the public good financed through taxes paid by others more than compensate for the taxes each expects to pay under a compulsory tax-expenditure scheme.

The use of compulsory taxation will tend to increase the provision of public goods above the level attainable from voluntary contributions, but it still provides no means for equating taxes to benefits at the margin. Lacking the information needed to equate an individual's tax "price" and marginal evaluation, we resort to the political mechanism for allocating the cost of public services among individuals via such means as taxation of income, market transactions, or property. In practice, expenditure decisions often are divorced from concern over who bears the tax burden. Hence, it is not surprising that most individuals feel that some government programs are not worth what they cost them in taxes and should be curtailed, whereas others are worth more than they cost and should be expanded. Failure to equate marginal cost with marginal benefits, both among individuals and in the aggregate, is inevitable. We can state the conditions that must be satisfied for efficient allocation but we have found no practical way in which to meet them.[14]

Some Misconceptions About Public Goods

Economists have a habit of dividing the economy into two parts—a private sector composed of households and privately owned business firms and a public sector that includes governments at various levels. Therefore, it is tempting to conclude that all goods sold in the private sector are private and that all goods financed by the public sector are public. Unfortunately, as we have already indicated, things are not that simple.

Public goods are characterized by nonrival consumption; that is, a given unit can be consumed simultaneously by two or more individuals. Such goods can be financed in a variety of ways. If the number involved is small, a group of individuals may form a voluntary organization to provide a good or service. A swimming pool, within capacity limits, is basically a public good, and in some parts of the country, clubs have been formed for the purpose of providing a neighborhood pool for members.

Often, the choice of private or group provision is influenced by relative costs. Each family in a neighborhood could build its own "private" swimming pool, but the cost to each would be considerably greater than it would be under a sharing arrangement. Note that, even if each family were to build its own pool, this would not eliminate the public characteristic of the pool. Our example of the levee is also relevant here. Albert could construct a levee along the border on all four sides of his property as shown by the dashed line in Figure 2–3 but at a cost that is higher than sharing or even of absorbing fully the cost of a levee between the two hills on the river bank. The swimming pool example differs somewhat, however, be-

[14]Some clever schemes have been devised for inducing consumers to reveal true preferences for a public good, but they do not appear to be practical enough for use in the real world. An important exposition of one such technique is T. Nicolaus Tideman and Gordon Tullock, "A New and Superior Process for Making Social Choices," *Journal of Political Economy*, 84 (December 1976), 1145–59.

cause the reduced cost of sharing is offset by the increased congestion and loss of control over use of the facility that accompanies sharing.[15]

Another source of confusion about public goods is the importance of the "exclusion characteristic." A private good can generally be sold in the market, because buyers cannot obtain its benefits unless they pay for it. Those who do not pay go without. It is true that the market provides a means for excluding nonpayers from getting the benefits of *most* private goods. Likewise, it is true that it is not feasible to exclude nonpayers from benefits of *many* public goods. Defense against foreign invasion is a good example. It is not feasible for an individual firm, or the members of the military-industrial complex acting in concert, to sell us the services of the defense establishment on an individual basis. It is simply not possible to protect some residents of the country—the payers—from enemy attack while leaving others—the nonpayers—unprotected.

It is not likely that anyone would be willing to provide national defense unilaterally. It is conceivable that some public goods may be so provided, however, even if exclusion of nonpayers is impossible. This may occur if the price versus demand relationship is right.

Returning to our example of the levee, assume that the supply curve in Figure 2–4 coincides with the horizontal line T_aAC. If the price and unit cost fall to OT_a, Albert would be willing to provide OE_n units unilaterally while Bonnie would become a "free rider." At a per unit price of OT_a, however, the good is underprovided. Efficiency requires that output be extended to the quantity corresponding to the point C on DD, where the summed evaluation of the two consumers equals the supply price. Perhaps if Albert provides OE_n on his own, Bonnie will agree to chip in enough to extend output to the efficient level where the summed evaluation per unit equals the supply price, but we cannot predict with certainty that the bargaining tactics of the two individuals will lead to this result.

We have already indicated that sale through the market is not feasible for *some* public goods, but there are exceptions. In other words, nonpayers can be excluded from the consumption of some public goods, and, therefore, the good can be sold in the market by profit-seeking firms. One such good is television transmission. An hour's worth of television viewing can be consumed by one viewer without in any way affecting the amount of viewing available to others. Hence, it meets our nonrivalry criterion for being a public good. Through the use of cables, it is possible to exclude nonpayers. Only viewers who pay a subscription fee are hooked up to the cable system. One problem with this arrangement is that all viewers are

---

[15]The swimming pool case is an example of what is called club theory. The seminal reference is James M. Buchanan, "An Economic Theory of Clubs," *Economica,* 32 (February 1965), 1–14. Club theory is surveyed in Todd Sandler and John T. Tschirhart, "The Economic Theory of Clubs: An Evaluative Survey," *Journal of Economic Literature,* 18 (December 1980), 1481–521.

required to pay the same fee for a given package of services. This arrangement can result in an inefficient allocation of resources when consumption is nonrival.

To aid our discussion, we make several simplifying assumptions. Output is measured in terms of hours of TV broadcasting. Fees are based on hours of transmission. Each hour of programming is assumed to be a perfect substitute for any other hour, so the only question for viewers to answer is how many hours of transmission to purchase, not when or what program. Programming is provided under conditions of constant cost so that $AC = MC$, and we shall assume that the broadcaster is required by regulation or competition to equate hourly fees collected from viewers to marginal cost.

We return to our two-person world and show in Figure 2–5 the demand curves of Albert and Bonnie, D_a and D_b, for hours of viewing. Since TV transmission is a public good characterized by nonrivalry, optimal provision occurs at OE_n hours where the combined (vertically summed) evaluations of Albert, OT_a, and Bonnie, OT_b, equal marginal cost. Again, we have the public good equilibrium solution depicted earlier in Figure 2–4; but, as in the earlier example, we have no knowledge of the demand curves of the two consumers.

Suppose that to avoid this difficulty pay TV is introduced and each individual is required to pay a price equal to one-half of marginal cost, or $OT_c/2$. Only if both Albert and Bonnie are willing to pay this price for an additional hour of viewing will the cost be covered. At the price $OT_c/2$, Bonnie is willing to pay for only OE_b hours. Because Bonnie is not willing to pay for additional programming, hours of transmission will not be extended beyond this amount. OE_b is less than OE_n, indicating suboptimal provision. By charging both individuals the same price for a given quantity of a jointly consumed good, adjustments for differences in demand are precluded, and a suboptimal amount of the good is provided. Since exclusion is possible, it is theoretically feasible for a firm selling cable TV to experiment with different pricing schemes. A price structure that would expand output toward the efficient level might eventually be found. In the more realistic large-number case, it is not feasible to experiment with each consumer individually. At best, only broad categories of consumers (say, homeowners, apartment dwellers, hotels, and bars) could be identified and charged different prices. Market segmentation of this type might move equilibrium output closer to the efficient level, but the outcome is at best likely to continue to fall short of the optimal solution.[16]

---

[16]For an analysis of the tendency toward underprovision of excludable public goods, see William H. Oakland, "Public Goods, Perfect Competition, and Underproduction," *Journal of Political Economy*, 82 (September 1974), 927–39.

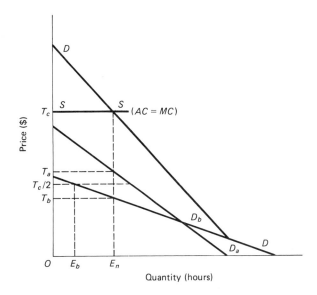

FIGURE 2–5 **Demand and supply of television transmission.** Vertical summation of individual demand curves D_a and D_b yields the aggregate demand curve for TV transmission, *DD*. Equilibrium output is E_n, but if each consumer is charged the same price, $T_c/2$, for each hour of transmission, total revenue will pay for only E_b hours. Output will be suboptimal.

We have shown that, when nonpayers can be excluded, it may be possible to provide a public good in the market and cover its cost with market receipts. Society, therefore, has the option of financing the good collectively through compulsory taxation or voluntary contribution or by charging a price and excluding nonpayers. Regardless of the method of finance, however, the presence of nonrivalry in consumption rules out optimal provision. Furthermore, both exclusion and collective provision absorb resources. In our example, resources are used to build and operate the cable system, but resources are also used if the good is to be financed through taxation. Negotiations among individuals or lawmakers and collection of revenue through taxation or voluntary contributions all require the use of scarce resources.

In some cases, public goods are provided by sellers of private goods through "tie-in" sales, as exemplified by commercial television in the United States. TV is free to the viewer, but it is financed by advertisers who presumably pass the cost on to consumers of their products. Thus, when you buy a Chevrolet, you are also, no doubt inadvertently, buying the TV programs that Chevrolet sponsors. The clumsiness of this arrangement as a way of making known your tastes in TV programming is obvious. Even so, lacking the relevant information about individual preferences, we cannot be certain which institutional arrangement will yield the most efficient result.[17]

GOVERNMENT PROVISION
OF PRIVATE GOODS

We have seen that the market system can be used in some cases as a means of providing public goods. Likewise, private goods could be provided outside the market. For example, we could vote to tax ourselves to finance the purchase of oranges and distribute them free of charge to anyone who wants them. We would expect to find little public support for such a program, however, because most taxpayers are likely to conclude that they would be made worse off. It oranges were available free of charge to individual consumers, everyone would increase consumption up to the point of satiation. The result would be a substantial increase in consumption of oranges, but at a tax cost that most taxpayers would find unattractive.

If we were to try to provide all private goods in this manner, the attempt would be a failure. We could not collect enough in taxes to finance a supply of all private goods sufficient to satiate everyone's appetite for them. Because economic goods are scarce, that would be impossible. If the market system were to be dispensed with, some other scheme of allocating or rationing would have to be used. Everything could be given out on a first-come, first-served basis, but then we would spend many hours standing in queues. The same number of units of each good might be given to each consumer, but given differentiated tastes, trade in the form of barter (i.e., markets) would spring up anyway. Of equal concern is the disincentive to work that would accompany nonmarket provision of all private goods. Love, threats, patriotism, and hero medals are at best uncertain substitutes for the economic motive.

EXTERNALITIES

An externality occurs whenever the market price of a good fails to reflect fully the cost or benefits associated with its production or consumption.[18]

---

[17]For an elaboration on these points, see Jora R. Minasian, "Television Pricing and the Theory of Public Goods," *Journal of Law and Economics,* 7 (October 1964), 71–80, and a caustic reaction by Paul A. Samuelson, "Public Goods and Subscription TV: Correction of the Record," *Journal of Law and Economics,* 7 (October 1964), 81–84.

[18]The origin of modern externality theory is found in Pigou's analysis of the divergence between private and social net product, although he did not use the term "externality." See A. C. Pigou, *The Economics of Welfare,* 4th ed. (London: Macmillan & Company Ltd., 1932), pp. 172–203.

For our purposes, it will be useful to distinguish between two types of externality, those arising because of failure to define or enforce property rights to private goods and those arising from the joint supply of private and public goods.

The first type, arising from failure to establish marketable property rights to private goods, we refer to as *ownership externalities*. The second type has been called *spillovers, positive and negative technological externalities, public good externalities,* and *mixed goods.* Most of the externalities that are cited as sources of market failure are of the latter type, including those responsible for environmental pollution.[19]

Ownership Externalities

In a few cases, difficulty in defining or enforcing property rights to private goods may make government provision or control desirable. Marine fisheries are a prime example. Fish are obviously private goods. Consumption by one person precludes consumption by anyone else. Once the fish are caught, property rights to the catch are easily enforced, but this is not true of fish swimming in the ocean. Scientists have learned a great deal about how to harvest fish from the sea so as to maximize the value of the catch over time. If catches exceed a certain rate, the stock of fish will gradually be depleted. In fact, this is happening to such varieties as haddock.[20]

If a single fishing firm had a monopoly on fishing in a large, well-defined ocean fishing area, the profit motive would encourage the firm to fish at a rate that would ensure maintenance of a plentiful supply of fish over time. In practice, many vessels from a number of countries may fish in the same waters. No single vessel has an incentive to limit its catch in the interest of conservation, because most of the benefits of conservation will go to others.

If a fishing area is under the sovereignty of a single nation, that nation can foster efficient husbandry of fishing resources by controlling the catch. This might be achieved directly by a government monopoly—public production and sale of a private good—or by regulation of private fishing firms. The catch of private firms might be regulated directly through publicly enforced limits similar to those in effect for game fish or through an excise tax that would discourage fishing by raising costs.

So long as fishing areas remain outside some sort of regulatory control, overfishing in the short run can be expected to deplete supply in the long run. For this reason many nations, including the United States, have

[19]For a careful distinction between types of externality, see F. M. Bator, "The Anatomy of Market Failure," *Quarterly Journal of Economics,* 72 (August 1958), 351–79.

[20]For a discussion of the harvesting problem and a criticism of the approach to externalities taken in this chapter, see Stephen N. S. Cheung, "The Structure of a Contract and the Theory of a Nonexclusive Resource," *Journal of Law and Economics,* 13 (April 1970), 49–70.

chosen to extend their territorial waters out to 200 miles from their shores and to exercise control over the size of the catch.

The fishery example demonstrates that, even in the case of private goods, the inability to enforce property rights, that is, the inability to exclude, can generate inefficiencies. Oil pools that underlie the holdings of many property owners are another example. Each individual owner has an incentive to pump oil rapidly. Otherwise, neighbors will get to it first. If oil is extracted too rapidly, however, the total amount that can be obtained from the pool is reduced significantly. Again, some form of regulation is needed.

Public and Private Goods
in Joint Supply

When a single production unit yields two or more different goods as outputs, we have goods in joint supply. A common textbook example is the steer (production unit), which yields two distinct consumer goods, beef and hide. Both are private goods, and joint supply does not result in any allocational difficulties. There is no externality.

An externality occurs when a production unit yields one (or more) public good(s) in joint supply with a private good.[21] Education is an example. It yields private benefits to the family unit of the recipient in the form of increased earning potential, an improved household environment, and—in the case of younger children—a babysitting service. Consequently, a private demand for education exists, and it could be sold through the market by profit-seeking firms. The private demand curve for education for an individual student, D_1, is shown in the upper panel of Figure 2–6. Assuming $P = MC$, if education is a strictly private good, efficient output would be attained at E_1 years of schooling.

Education is also thought to provide benefits of a public nature to others. By increasing earning potential, it reduces the likelihood that an individual will require welfare payments or, it is alleged, turn to crime. Education offers society a means of training an individual for citizenship, including participation in democracy and inculcation of social values and behavioral norms. It also keeps youngsters off the streets. Hence, a demand exists for the public good component of education. Parenthetically, the level of this demand is related to the effectiveness of schools in providing the public benefits just cited.

In the lower panel of Figure 2–6, the demand curve, D_2, for the public component of the education of an individual student is shown. Curve D_2 is obtained by summing vertically the demand curves of individuals receiving public benefits. Since both private and public benefits are supplied jointly

[21]A standard reference on public-good-type externalities is J. M. Buchanan and W. C. Stubblebine, "Externality," *Economics*, 29 (November 1962), 371–84.

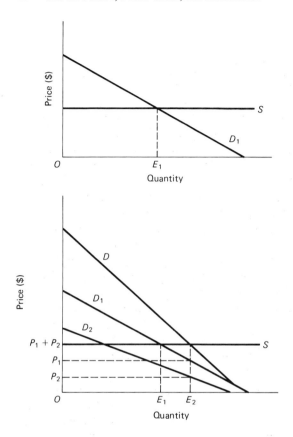

FIGURE 2–6   Education, a private and public good in joint supply. The upper panel shows the supply curve and the private demand curve D_1 for education of an individual student. Equilibrium is at E_1 years of schooling. In the lower panel, the public component of demand, D_2, is added. Combined private and public demand, shown by demand curve D, is obtained by vertical summation of D_1 and D_2. Optimal output is at E_2. Consumers are in equilibrium at E_2 when the student's family pays a price of P_1 and taxpayers (in the aggregate) pay a price of P_2.

by a year of schooling, the total demand, curve D, is obtained by summing *vertically* the private and public demand curves D_1 and D_2.[22] Optimal provision occurs at E_2 years of schooling, with the student's family paying P_1 per year and taxpayers paying P_2.

The information needed to reach point E_2 is not generally attainable. In the case of the public good component, the reasons are identical to

[22]Vertical summation of D_1 and D_2 is due to the presence of *joint supply,* not "publicness." For a clarification of this distinction, see Paul A. Samuelson, "Contrast Between Welfare Conditions for Joint Supply and for Public Goods," *Review of Economics and Statistics,* 51 (February 1969), 26–30.

those cited in the case of a pure public good. Even the private component of demand would generally be unknown in the example cited. The size of the public subsidy, P_2 in Figure 2–6, is affected by the willingness of the student's family to pay for his or her education. Therefore, the family has an incentive to understate its private demand, even if it leads to some loss of schooling, in an effort to get a larger public subsidy.[23]

In practice, when the public component is considered to be of major significance, as for example in primary and secondary education or immunization against contagious diseases, society may choose to pay for the good with tax revenue and make it freely available to all consumers. Nevertheless, in the technical sense, the good is still classified as a public and private good in joint supply. As in the case of pure private and public goods, it is the characteristics of the good, not the arrangement under which it is provided, that determines its classification.

Private Good and Public Bad in Joint Supply

In the education example, the public component in joint supply with a private good is presumed to provide positive benefits. In many cases, however, the production or consumption of a private good will impose costs (or negative benefits) on other firms and/or households that are not accounted for in private market prices. Because decision makers are likely to consider only the costs imposed on themselves, the costs their activities impose on the rest of society will not be accounted for in their decisions.

Let us take as an example noise pollution from the take-offs and landings of jet airliners. The noise creates a negative benefit for nearby residents. The benefits are negative, because the residents are willing to pay to have the noise level reduced. For those living near an airport, the noise is a jointly consumed *public bad* in joint supply with a private good, travel by air. The allocational problem involved is illustrated in Figure 2–7.

Private demand for air travel is shown by the curve D_1, and private equilibrium output is at level E_2. The demand for the public bad, obtained by summing vertically the demand curves for noise reduction across all individuals who are willing to pay for a quieter environment, is shown by D_2. It is shown as a negative demand, or negative benefit, to emphasize its similarity except for sign to the previous example where both components of demand are positive.

Because each unit of output simultaneously supplies a private good and a public bad, the demand curve for the two components, labeled D, is obtained by summing vertically the private and public demand curves, D_1

[23]For a more thorough discussion of education, see J. Ronnie Davis and John R. Morrall, *Evaluating Educational Investment* (Lexington, Mass.: D. C. Heath & Company, 1974), pp. 9–36.

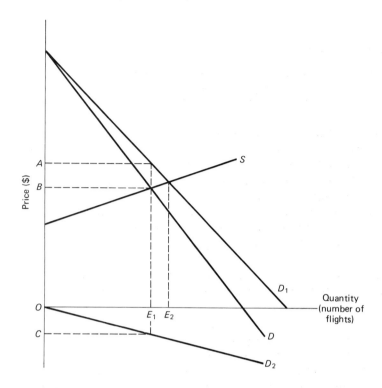

FIGURE 2-7   Pollution, a private good and public bad in joint supply. Curve D_1 shows the private demand for airline flights. The negative demand for the accompanying noise pollution is shown by curve D_2, which measures the price that affected individuals would pay for a quieter environment. The combined private and public demand, shown by demand curve D, is obtained by vertical summation of the positive private demand curve, D_1, and the negative public demand curve, D_2. Note that private equilibrium E_2 is greater than optimal output E_1.

and D_2. Optimal provision is at the level E_1 or $E_2 - E_1$ units less than private market equilibrium.

The preceding analysis is based on the assumption that noise sufferers exercise their negative demand for noise by taxing themselves and using the proceeds to pay airlines to reduce the number of flights and in that way to reduce the amount of noise. In effect, a more quiet environment becomes a public good characterized by nonrival consumption by all who live in the area. As in the previous examples, the practical difficulties of getting people to reveal their preferences arise here as well.

The aircraft noise model can be applied to a variety of cases in which a private good and public bad are in joint supply, but it is not sufficiently general to apply to all cases. For example, you may be incensed by the implication that those who suffer from pollution should be taxed so as to bribe the polluters to cut back on their output of a public bad. Society could choose to reassign rights, guaranteeing us a pollution-free environment unless the potential polluter compensates the sufferers at a rate equal to the costs (negative benefits) they incur because of the pollution. Analytically, this case is similar to the previous example. Returning to Figure 2–7, the airlines would be required to pay a tax per flight equal to the distance between D_2 and the quantity axis. In equilibrium the tax would be equal to AB ($= OC$) per flight, with the receipts allocated among the damaged parties in accordance with their demands for compensation. Note that in this case the problem of getting people to reveal their true preferences is reversed. Each individual now has an incentive to overstate his or her demand for compensation, because a receipt rather than a tax is involved.[24]

The aircraft noise example is intended to illustrate the optimal output for a private good and a public bad in joint supply. In practice, the problem is likely to be more complex. Instead of reducing noise by cutting flights, for example, it may be cheaper to build quieter airplanes or to move persons living in proximity to the airport to new and quieter surroundings.

Growing concern over environmental problems has stimulated considerable discussion of ways in which taxes can be used to regulate the level of pollution and other public bads. Some suggested remedies are discussed in Chapter 10 on sales and excise taxation.

A NEUTRAL FISCAL SYSTEM

The concept of neutrality is an old one that initially required that taxes and expenditures exert no influence, at the margin, on the choices of either consumers or producers in the private sector. In other words, taxes and expenditures should not distort such decisions as work versus leisure or consumption versus saving by households, or decisions on optimal factor inputs or output by firms. Of course, our fiscal system violates the requirements for neutrality in many ways. At times, the violation is deliberate, as in the taxation of liquor and tobacco, and at times not, as in the influence of the progressive income tax on the pattern of saving and investing in the economy.

There is a growing recognition by economists and others that government really is a means through which individuals may choose to provide themselves with certain goods and services. As a result, the concern for

[24]Aside from the liar's problem, the demand for relief from a negative externality may be greater if the sufferers receive compensation than if they pay for relief. This is because of the income effect. They are richer in the former case. Thus, D in these two cases will not coincide. See E. J. Mishan, *Cost Benefit Analysis*, new ed. (New York: Praeger Publishers, Inc., 1976), pp. 139–44.

neutrality has shifted from that of avoiding any effect at the margin on private choices to that of satisfying criteria of efficiency analogous to those by which market performance is judged.

It will be recalled that a necessary condition for the efficient provision of goods and services in the market economy is that price equal marginal cost. If there are some goods for which this equality does not hold, then a nonoptimal situation exists. It is possible, by changing some prices and outputs, to improve the welfare of one or more consumers without making anyone worse off. The requirements of fiscal neutrality extend this principle to the public good case. Each individual should pay a tax (price per unit) equal to his or her marginal evaluation of benefits received, and each good should be provided in sufficient quantity to make the sum of such taxes (per unit) equal to marginal cost. These conditions are satisfied in Figure 2–4 when output is at OE_n, Albert pays a tax price of OT_a per unit, Bonnie pays OT_b per unit, and the total tax price $= OT_a + OT_b = OT_c = MC$.

Obviously, a fiscal system that is neutral in this sense must base taxation on the benefit principle.[25] Since we cannot ordinarily measure the marginal benefit that each individual receives from public goods, the neutral fiscal system emerges, not as a blueprint for practical application, but as a standard of efficiency against which actual fiscal systems may be compared.

IS FISCAL NEUTRALITY DESIRABLE?

By now it should be apparent that, even if an economy with public goods and taxes has time to adjust to long-run equilibrium, an efficient allocation of resources—given tastes, technology, and distribution of ownership of factors of production—is unattainable. Thus, we cannot expect the value of output to be maximized subject to the constraints cited. If one agrees that resources should be allocated strictly in accordance with consumer sovereignty, failure to achieve economywide efficiency is unfortunate.

Consider, however, some other factors that may influence our willingness to accept the results of consumer sovereignty even if the market functioned perfectly. Of most importance is the dependence of any efficient outcome on the distribution of income. If that distributional pattern is, for example, so unequal as to offend society's concept of fairness, another outcome may be preferable, even if it fails to meet all the requirements for allocative efficiency. In principle, an alternative distribution might be found that would not preclude efficient allocation, but this would

---

[25]See Chapter 6 for a discussion of this principle.

require a redistribution that would not affect economic decisions at the margin, and that is difficult to implement. For example, an income tax that finances redistribution would interfere with efficient allocation by creating a difference between the value of a factor to its employer (income before taxes) and its owner (income after taxes). This is discussed in greater detail in Chapters 7 and 8.

Consumer ignorance creates further doubt about the desirability of unchecked consumer sovereignty. In some instances, it is argued that consumers do not know what is "best" for them. Hence, we exercise government control over the sale of drugs, pesticides, and other potentially harmful products. We force students to attend school for a designated number of years on the grounds that neither students nor parents are qualified to determine minimal educational needs. Goods such as education, which combine elements of publicness with a big-brother-knows-best attitude, have been termed *merit wants,* and their existence is alleged to justify interference with consumer sovereignty.[26]

Returning to public goods, fiscal neutrality requires allocation of costs in accordance with marginal benefits. If applied to all public goods, this would mean that altruistic individuals who demand public outlays for libraries and museums or for antipoverty programs would have to pay for them while misanthropes who oppose all such undertakings would pay nothing. Such would be the case if consumer sovereignty were applicable to public goods. For this reason, some are thankful that it is not.[27]

SUMMARY

A perfectly functioning market system would, by definition, allocate resources efficiently in accordance with consumer sovereignty, but no actual economy functions with perfection. Elements of monopoly, cyclical instability, consumer ignorance, and the existence of public goods are among the causes of market failure. The failure of markets to function efficiently provides a rationale for government intervention in the market system in the interest of better allocation of resources, but even if the government had as its only goal the efficient allocation of resources, the goal would not be attainable. The existence of public goods is enough to preclude efficient allocation, because the requisite information is unattainable.

Failure to attain information is not an excuse for total inaction. Some public goods could not be provided at all by profit-seeking firms, and we are probably better off if we tax ourselves to provide them, albeit ineffi-

[26]Richard A. Musgrave, *The Theory of Public Finance* (New York: McGraw-Hill Book Company, 1959), pp. 13–14.

[27]See, for example, Earl R. Rolph and George F. Break, *Public Finance* (New York: The Ronald Press Company, 1961), p. 89.

ciently. We say "probably" because we lack the information needed to prove or disprove the statement.

Society may also choose to put constraints on the functioning of consumer sovereignty, often in the alleged "interest" of the consumer. Finally, allocation in a market system is strongly influenced by the distribution of income. Society, acting through government, may take steps to alter the distribution even though the redistribution process itself creates additional market inefficiencies.

In this chapter, we have focused on market failure. In Chapter 3, the discussion shifts to consideration of various voting models. Recent developments in public choice theory, dealing with a variety of democratic decision rules, provide an interesting counterbalance to the standard analysis of market failure. Public choice theory provides economists, political scientists, and other social scientists with a number of testable hypotheses about voting behavior. It also gives us insight into the circumstances under which various voting rules will fail to provide us with a satisfactory representation of voter preferences.

3

Public Choice

Professor Milton Friedman was irritated by the late President Kennedy's 1960 inaugural address. He questioned the famous passage, "Ask not what your country can do for you—ask what you can do for your country." Even though the president undoubtedly chose this language mainly to arouse the spirit of idealism, Friedman objected to it nonetheless on intellectual grounds that neither half of the statement properly defined a relationship worthy of the ideals of democracy. "What your country can do for you" implied that government is a patron and the citizen its ward. "What you can do for your country" suggested that government is a master and the citizen its servant.[1]

Friedman's objection was that government is neither patron nor master. Instead, he argued, government is only a means through which citizens cooperate collectively to achieve certain goals and purposes. It is only an institution, in other words, through which certain services can be purchased or, presumably, special interests traded. In this sense, a system of governments is like a system of markets: each system is a means of providing particular goods or services. This vision of government is commonly called the *individualistic* or *voluntary exchange approach* to the study of public choice. As such, the voluntary exchange approach views government as a means of meeting demands that private business firms are unwilling or unable to satisfy adequately in the marketplace.[2]

[1]Milton Friedman, *Capitalism and Freedom* (Chicago: University of Chicago Press, 1962), pp. 1–6.

[2]For an articulate statement of this approach, see James M. Buchanan, "The Pure Theory of Government Finance: A Suggested Approach," *Journal of Political Economy*, 57 (December 1949), 496–505.

By focusing on the individualistic theory of the state, the voluntary exchange approach to public choice deemphasizes "society" as something existing distinct from the individuals who compose it. Also, it tends to deemphasize "public interest" as something distinct from the wants and needs of individuals. According to this approach, as a matter of fact, serving individual interests is what governments and markets are for. Moreover, the voluntary exchange approach assumes that self-interested behavior is found in the voting booth as well as in the marketplace. Many people may object to this assumption. Yet these same people may support a candidate pledged to a program that benefits themselves at the expense of others.

Perhaps those who object to the assumption of self-interested behavior in public choice justify their own self-interested actions on the grounds that they are merely choosing between candidates, which is the fundamental exercise of a democratic right. The inconsistency between justification and objection may be suspect, however. Given an opportunity, tenants—who outnumber landlords—might vote for rent controls while invoking slogans to the effect that it is just to serve the will of the majority. Farmers might vote to replace property taxation with income taxation, which, if successful, shifts some of the burden of local taxation away from farmers and onto wage earners. Their justification might be that social well-being is promoted by phasing out regressive taxes. Automobile manufacturers might lobby for higher tariffs and lower import quotas on cars, all the while appealing to an impressive variety of bromides and sophisms having to do with the public interest rather than their own.

The main shortcoming of the voluntary exchange approach, the critics argue, is that we all know that government is not merely a means of collective cooperation. We know this, they insist, just as surely as we know that not even for the most democratic governments is the state merely the collection of individuals who compose it.[3] To the contrary, the critics suggest that government consists of a distinct group of people who represent particular constituencies and who have a certain allegiance to a particular political party. Thus, it would seem that governments do have ends. The party in power wants reelection; the party out of power wants election.

This criticism need not invalidate the voluntary exchange approach, however. These ends of government itself give rise to public sector entrepreneurs who are somewhat analogous to those in the private sector. In the private sector, entrepreneurs are profit seekers who must serve the interests of consumers well if they are to be successful in realizing the profits they seek. In the public sector, entrepreneurs would be vote seekers who

---

[3]For a criticism of the voluntary exchange approach, see Leland B. Yeager and David G. Tuerck, *Trade Policy and the Price System* (Scranton, Pa.: International Textbook Company, 1966), pp. 72–73.

must serve the interests of citizens well if they are to be successful in realizing the votes they seek.[4]

Even the critics of the voluntary exchange approach would agree that slogans get us nowhere in studying democracy or public choice. Mainly, economists are interested in studying the conditions under which people choose to rely on government as a means of providing for the satisfaction of wants or needs. Also, economists are concerned with the consequences of substituting "one-person, one-vote" for "one-dollar, one-vote" decision making. In other words, economists are interested in the effect that government intervention in the economy has on, say, the allocation of resources or the distribution of income.

VOLUNTARY EXCHANGE AND THE EXCLUSION CHARACTERISTIC

The voluntary exchange approach, to reiterate, views government as a means of meeting demands that private business firms are unwilling or unable to satisfy adequately in the marketplace. This approach raises an apparent paradox. If people truly want certain goods or services, then why would firms not supply adequate quantities? The answer is that, despite the fact that people really want certain goods or services, they may be unwilling to volunteer payment to firms to supply satisfactory or tolerable supplies. Because they really want these goods or services, however, they may consent to and actually prefer forced payment! The reason that people prefer coercive to voluntary payment for the goods and services they want may be the *exclusion characteristic.*

The benefits of some goods and services can be confined to the persons who pay for them. For example, unless baseball fans are willing to pay the price stipulated by vendors, they are excluded from the enjoyment of a hot dog and a beer at a Fourth of July doubleheader. Where this exclusion condition holds, consumers must bid for and pay for the goods and services wanted. Otherwise, they do not get them: "nonpayers" are excluded from the benefits of goods for which this condition holds. On the other hand, as we saw in Chapter 2, the benefits of some goods and services cannot be confined to the persons who pay for them.[5] For example, the traditional fireworks display between the July Fourth baseball games can be seen (and heard) by persons outside as well as inside the ball park.

[4]For a study based in part on "vote seekers," see Anthony Downs, *An Economic Theory of Democracy* (New York: Harper & Row, Publishers, 1957).

[5]This does not necessarily suggest that exclusion is impossible. It merely suggests that exclusion may be economically infeasible in the sense that there are high costs incurred in excluding nonpaying customers.

Nonpayers cannot be or are not excluded from enjoying the pyrotechnics. The costs of excluding those who have not paid to enter the ball park are prohibitively high. In this case, the exclusion condition does not hold.

There are, of course, many examples of goods or services for which there is no exclusion characteristic. Some were mentioned in Chapter 2. All of us benefit more or less from a military force that serves as a deterrent to foreign attack. To one degree or other, all of us are protected from crime by an effective system of local police forces. A well-defined and stable framework of laws and justice protects everybody's civil liberties. Largely, the benefits of such services as national defense, crime protection, and law, order, and justice are, respectively, foreign attacks not waged, crimes not committed, and lawsuits not tried. As such, the benefits of a system of justice, for example, are not limited to the few who, in their lifetimes, get involved and are exonerated in a lawsuit.

If such services were provided through a system of markets, many people either deliberately or otherwise would not get around to paying for them. Each person may conclude that, if everyone else contributes, one's own contribution to the provision of the service will be a negligible part of the total amount and that the quantity provided will be almost the same even if no contribution at all is made. Each person may also conclude that, if no one else contributes, practically none of the service will be provided. Consequently, each person may decide that he or she is better off, no matter what other people do, if no contribution is made. This strategic behavior is called *the free rider problem*. It is a problem because, if enough people try to ride free, there may be no ride.

Profit-seeking firms are likely to provide too little or none at all of services from which nonpayers cannot be excluded.[6] Voluntary exchange in the market depends importantly on buying and selling property titles to the thing exchanged. This condition does not hold strictly in cases where the use or value of a thing is available even to persons who have not purchased a claim. If quantities provided through markets are intolerably small, however, a person still might express a willingness to share in paying for them, providing that he or she is assured that others will do likewise. Government provides the means whereby citizens can agree to share the cost and, if any one of them is tempted to ride free, enforce the agreement. Resolution of the free rider problem lies in this *consent to be coerced.*

---

[6]In his *Wealth of Nations,* Adam Smith recognized this problem. "According to the system of natural liberty," he said, "the sovereign has . . . the duty of erecting and maintaining certain public works and certain public institutions, which it can never be for the interest of any individual, or small number of individuals, to erect and maintain; because the profit could never repay the expense to any individual or small number of individuals, though it may frequently do much more than repay it to a great society." Adam Smith, *An Inquiry into the Nature and Causes of the Wealth of Nations* (New York: Modern Library, 1937, published originally in 1776), p. 651.

VOLUNTARY EXCHANGE
AND THE PRINCIPLE
OF UNANIMITY

Consenting to be coerced suggests that each person requires assurance that others also pay a share of the cost. Thus, each person agrees to pay, provided that payment by all others is enforced. Such agreements can neutralize the disincentives to contribute. Ironically, however, requiring unanimous agreement may not only fail to neutralize the disincentives, but may actually add to them.

If unanimous consent is required to make an agreement effective, then no one person could ever have a decision imposed on him or her by others. However, the costs of securing unanimous consent could prove to be prohibitive. In other words, as the requirements for agreement become more inclusive, the threat of costs imposed by others declines, but the expected cost of reaching an agreement increases. It is more difficult to specify a proposal that secures the consent of three-fourths of the members of a group than it is to specify one that can secure the consent of a simple majority. It is even more difficult to state explicitly a proposal that would secure the consent of nine-tenths of the same group. Even though the threat of costs being imposed on any one person by others declines as the requirement for an agreement becomes more and more inclusive, any one person's consent becomes more and more indispensable. This ever-increasing indispensability of consent creates an incentive to behave strategically in an effort to realize greater gains at lower costs than the original terms of the proposal specify. If unanimity is required, any one person can delay an effective agreement by becoming a strategic holdout.[7] At an extreme, any one person can hold out to have benefits conferred at no cost.

Replacing the strict requirement of unanimity with qualified or simple majorities could reduce the costs of reaching a decision, but it would increase the costs that could be imposed externally without securing consent. Choosing a rule that governs decision making could be made on the basis of cost minimization. Consider panels (a), (b), and (c) in Figure 3–1. In panel (a), bargaining costs are illustrated. These costs include the value of time, effort, and other outlays involved in bargaining. Such costs are shown as increasing with the group size required for an effective decision. The total voting population is represented by N. In panel (b), politically external costs are illustrated. These are costs imposed on an individual as the consequence of effective action taken by others. In other words, they are costs that occur when an individual is coerced into accepting an effective

---

[7]Delay itself can be costly. If unanimity results in protracted bargaining over cost sharing of some project, then the longer the delay, the more potential returns remain unrealized. The present value of a project can decline substantially with delay. See Chapter 5 for a discussion of this point.

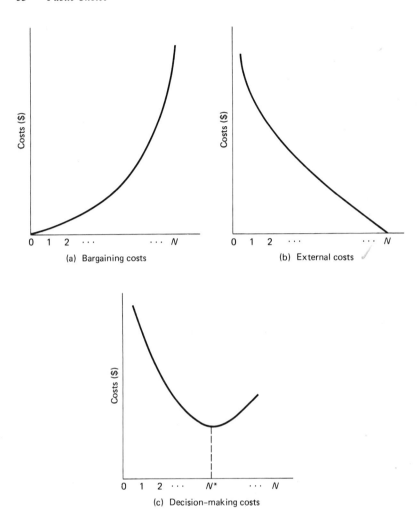

FIGURE 3–1   **The costs of decision making.** In panel (a), bargaining costs are illustrated. The costs include the value of time, effort, and other outlays involved in bargaining. Bargaining costs increase with group size. The total voting population is *N*. In panel (b), politically external costs are illustrated. These costs occur when a person does not agree with an effective action taken by others. External costs decline as group size required for an effective action increases. In panel (c), bargaining costs and external costs are summed. The summed costs decline until *N** is required for an effective action and then rise if a larger group size is required. The costs of decision making are minimized when *N** persons are required for agreement. *N**/*N* is not unanimity, nor is it necessarily a simple majority.

decision with which he or she does not agree. To the extent that those opposed pay a part of the cost of an action imposed by a controlling group, politically external costs are borne. Such costs are shown as decreasing with the group size required for an effective decision.

In panel (c), bargaining and external costs are summed for each group size required for an effective decision. These summed costs decline until a certain number of individuals, N^*, is required for an effective decision, and then they increase if a larger number is required. Thus, the summed costs reach a minimum when N^* individuals are required for agreement. On grounds of cost minimization, therefore, the most efficient voting rule is to require N^*/N of individuals to agree before a decision is politically effective. Note that unanimity is not efficient. Note also that the proportion, N^*/N, that minimizes decision-making costs need not be a simple majority or even a majority![8]

MAJORITY RULE AND CYCLICAL MAJORITIES

The discussion of minimizing decision-making costs suggests that unanimity is not efficient. It does not suggest, however, any particular voting rule less than unanimity. Nevertheless, suppose that, on cost-minimization grounds, a majority voting rule is adopted in a three-person community, or in a community in which there are three equal-sized groups, say, farmers, wage earners, and owners of businesses.[9] Also, suppose that each of the three persons or groups has a different level of demand for a certain service. In Figure 3–2, each person's or group's demand is shown as D_1, D_2, and D_3. Suppose that each pays the same price, P_0, per unit of the service.[10] If these three persons or groups vote on the level of service to be provided, all three will favor providing at least Q_1. Two of the three—a majority—will vote to expand provision to Q_2. Only one of the three—a minority—will vote to expand the quantity provided beyond Q_2. Under majority rule, therefore, provision would be extended to Q_2. If the nature of the choice is that a single quantity is chosen for the entire community, then the quantity preferred by the median voter will be chosen.[11] In effect, ma-

---

[8]This discussion is indebted to James M. Buchanan and Gordon Tullock, *The Calculus of Consent* (Ann Arbor: University of Michigan Press, 1962), pp. 63–84. The proportion N^*/N may not be the same for each individual.

[9]Choice of such a small-scale model need not be of concern because this simple model still illustrates the salient properties of majority rule.

[10]If each person faces the same price per unit, P_0, of the service, then this implies that the per unit cost of the service is $3P_0$. For the case where groups face different prices, see J. Ronnie Davis and Charles W. Meyer, "Farmer Conservatism and the Incidence of Taxes," *American Journal of Agricultural Economics*, 54 (August 1972), 485–89.

[11]This point is shown by Duncan Black, *Theory of Committees and Elections* (Cambridge: University of Cambridge Press, 1958), pp. 16–25.

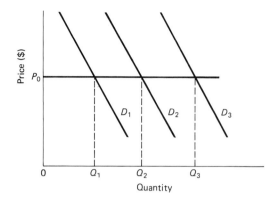

FIGURE 3–2   Three demands for level of service. Demand for a given service is shown by D_1, D_2, and D_3 for each of three persons or groups. If the three vote on the level of provision, all three will favor at least Q_1. Two of the three—a majority—will vote to expand provision to Q_2. Only one of the three will vote to expand the quantity provided beyond Q_2. Under majority rule, provision would be expanded to Q_2, which is the preference of the "median voter."

jority rule delegates choice to the person whose preferences are median for the group.[12]

Some issues of this type have a majority motion, others do not. Those that do not are called *cyclical majorities* and are discussed in a subsequent paragraph. First, however, consider an issue that does have a majority motion. Assume that there are three voters and three alternatives to choose among, as illustrated in Figure 3–3. Suppose that voters A, B, and C are deciding how much military spending they prefer: *s* dollars, which is a small amount; *m* dollars, which is a medium amount; or *l* dollars, which is

FIGURE 3–3 Preference ordering for three voters. Voters A, B, and C rank their preferences for alternative budget sizes *s, m,* and *l.* The medium budget, *m,* is a majority motion. When paired against the small budget, *s,* the medium budget is preferred by two of the three voters. When paired against the large budget, *l,* the medium budget is still preferred by two of the three voters.

		Voters		
		A	B	C
Ranking	1	s	m	l
	2	m	l	m
	3	l	s	s

[12]The median voter is the "swing voter." On city or county commissions and on school boards, there may be a succession of decisions regarding the level of provision, each one decided by a vote of 2 to 1 or 3 to 2. Often, the deciding vote is cast each time by a member whose preferences lie between those of the other members so that the one member is identified and referred to in local news media as the swing voter on the commission or the board. At times, a group within an entire constituency is clearly the swing vote.

a large amount. Voter A prefers s to m and m to l; B prefers m to l and l to s; and C prefers l to m and m to s. These preferences are shown in Figure 3–4, where the ordinal ranking is given on the vertical axis, the alternatives on the horizontal, and the lines drawn to connect the preferences as they are ranked by the three voters. The medium budget is a majority motion. It cannot be defeated by any other motion: when paired against the small budget, m wins 2 to 1, and when paired against the large budget, m also wins 2 to 1.[13]

Suppose, however, that C is one of those people or groups that likes extremes, preferring the larger budget to the smaller one, and the smaller budget to the medium one. Such preferences are not altogether unusual. They may reflect the sentiments or attitudes of those who would rather lose than compromise, who would rather do something well or not at all. Indeed, during the Vietnam debate of the 1960s, a sizable and vocal group—mainly conservatives such as Senator Barry Goldwater—wanted as their first choice to win a "military victory," but if enough financial support, labor, and material were not deployed to do the job, then it preferred "bringing the troops home" to a "no-win policy." This is an example of the order of preference (1) large budget, (2) small budget, (3) medium budget.

If A's and B's preferences are the same as before, the preferences of the three voters are as shown in Figure 3–5. Given these preferences, a majority motion does not exist! Any motion—that is proposed can be defeated by some other motion. If the large budget is proposed, a majority prefers the medium budget; if the medium budget is proposed, a majority prefers the small budget; and if the small budget is proposed, a majority prefers the large budget. When there is no majority motion, the outcome

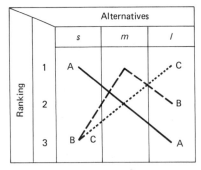

FIGURE 3–4 Preference functions: single-peaked. Ordinal rankings are given on the vertical axis, and alternative budget sizes on the horizontal. The solid, dashed, and dotted lines are drawn to connect the preferences as they are ranked by the three voters, A, B, C, respectively. Their choices can be arranged on straight lines such that they prefer an alternative closer to their first choice to any alternative farther away. The lines connecting the preferences of each of the three voters have one "peak."

[13]When more than two alternatives are considered, they must be voted upon in successive elimination among surviving pairs. This rule of majority voting is followed by the U.S. Congress, state legislatures, and other deliberative bodies.

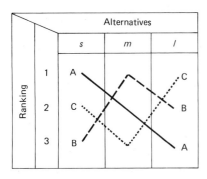

FIGURE 3–5 Preference functions: double-peaked. The preferences of voter C are not single-peaked. C prefers an alternative that is farther away to one that is closer. In the example, C prefers the large budget, *l*, to the small budget, *s*, to the medium budget, *m*. There are two "peaks" when a line is drawn to connect C's preferences. In the case illustrated, no majority motion exists. If any one budget size is proposed, a majority prefers a different budget size.

of voting can depend on the order in which alternatives are paired.

Suppose, for example, that the voting rules provide for two motions to be run off and then for the winning motion to be paired against the remaining alternative. The motion that prevails in the latter pairing is declared the *majority decision*. In this manner, therefore, if the small and medium budgets are offered for a vote, the small budget will win; and if the small budget is then paired against the large budget, the large budget will win and be declared the majority decision. However, if the first vote is between the medium and large budgets, the medium budget wins; but when it is paired against the small budget, the small budget wins and is declared the majority decision. Finally, if the first vote is between motions for the small and large budgets, the large budget wins; but it is defeated by the medium budget in the second pairing, and the medium budget is declared the majority decision. Thus, clearly, the outcome under this voting rule depends on the order in which the alternatives are considered.

The circumstances under which a majority motion does not exist is called a *cyclical majority*.[14] Duncan Black has shown that there is no problem of cyclical majorities as long as preferences are *single-peaked*.[15] To illustrate this point, reconsider Figure 3–4. Given the preferences of the three voters, their choices could be arranged on straight lines such that they preferred an alternative closer to their first choice to any alternative farther away. The lines connecting the preferences of each of the three voters had one peak.[16]

In Figure 3–5, however, the preferences of voter C are not single-peaked. Because C prefers 1 to *s* to *m*, there are two peaks. The double-

[14]Some have called this case "the paradox of voting." However, there is no paradox. In other words, there is no actual logical contradiction involved.

[15]Black, *Theory of Committees and Elections*, pp. 46–51.

[16]The level of expenditures on a given service may be ranked in the manner discussed earlier. However, choice between different services is not so straightforward. There is no self-evident ordering analogous to the case for budget size when choice is among alternative outlays of a given amount on, say, education, highways, and police protection. Yet issues may be bundled into packages that permit decisions analogous to budget size.

peaked preference function is because C's preference as second choice is an alternative—the small budget—which is farther away than a closer one—the medium budget. When a voter has double-peaked preferences, then a cyclical majority *may* occur.[17] With three motions as considered in the preceding examples, the probability that a majority motion does not exist approaches 9 percent as the number of voters becomes large.[18]

Basically, the problem of cyclical majorities is that democratic, majority voting does not lead to genuine expressions of majority will. Modern democracies accept the rule that certain conflicting preferences should be resolved by majority vote, but the possibility of cyclical majorities raises a basic question about the collective rationality of the political process. Kenneth Arrow, as a matter of fact, has proved mathematically that, when individual preferences differ, they cannot be combined so that they reflect the views of the citizens in a consistent manner unless certain restrictive conditions are met.[19] Arrow's proof, sometimes called the *general possibility theorem,* does not apply when individual orderings are single-peaked.

Although theorems such as Arrow's prove that the problem of cyclical majorities can exist, it is not clear from such work whether the problem is an important one. In a study by the political scientist, William Riker, only two tentative examples of *Arrow's paradox* (i.e., cyclical majorities) were found.[20] We seldom if ever notice legislative bodies or club meetings hopelessly bogged down because of an obvious cyclical majority problem. Perhaps this is because such bodies are continually making choices, and not all groups or their representatives have equally strong preference orderings for all alternatives. For example, rural representatives might be greatly concerned about legislation that affects agriculture but care little about legislation that affects manufacturing. Urban and rural representatives might agree to some vote trading, so that they negotiate support for their pet projects. Such vote trading to achieve a majority is sometimes called *logrolling.* Logrolling provides a means whereby persons who have strong feelings about one issue but not about other issues can trade their votes on the unimportant issues in return for the votes of those with different intensities of preference. In this way, logrolling may circumvent problems of cyclical majorities.

[17]Multipeaked preferences do not necessarily cause a cyclical majority problem. For example, suppose that voter A prefers *s* to *m* to *l;* B prefers *m* to *s* to *l;* and C, whose preferences are double-peaked, prefers *l* to *s* to *m.* Then, the small budget would be a majority motion.

[18]Frank DeMeyer and Charles R. Plott, "The Probability of a Cyclical Majority," *Econometrica,* 38 (March 1970), 345–54.

[19]Kenneth Arrow, *Social Choice and Individual Values* (New York: John Wiley & Sons, Inc., 1951).

[20]W. H. Riker, "Arrow's Theorem and Some Examples of the Paradox of Voting," John M. Claunch, ed., in *Mathematical Applications in Political Science* (Dallas: Arnold Foundation, 1965), pp. 41–60.

MAJORITY RULE AND REPRESENTATIVE DEMOCRACY

Individual voters do not always participate directly in decision making. Modern democracy, in other words, is not a direct democracy in which citizens vote directly on specific taxes or expenditures. Direct democracy in this sense would be a very costly way in which to decide a large number of complex issues. Representative democracy is intended to serve as a means of delegating most decisions to elected representatives. Presumably, those elected are representative of the preferences of a constituency on each specific issue decided. In this way, the costliness of informed participation in decision making can be reduced. The reason is that the representative can specialize in learning about and evaluating the impact of each issue. Voters have only to choose someone they believe will be truly representative of their interests.

The potential for gains from specialization is greater when the number of representatives is relatively small. Consequently, a large number of voters will be represented when the potential benefits of specialization are realized. In this way, delegation of decisions has the effect of empowering representatives to make and enforce policy and at the same time lessen the control of any one voter over decision making. Most representative democracies have a bicameral legislature in which representatives are divided into two separate houses. Each voter participates in choosing a representative in each house. Representation may be by geographic area and by population or by geographic area only. The U.S. House of Representatives is an example of the former; the U.S. Senate, the latter. State legislatures typically have two houses with the former type of representation. In any event, issues must be passed by a majority of both houses. The executive—the president or the governor of a state—typically has veto power over any issue passed by the legislative bodies.

Legislative bodies can be dominated by a minority. Consider a representative body of 15 members, each of whom has 9 constituents. There are 135 persons represented, therefore, by 15 representatives. If 5—a majority—of the 9 constituents of any one of the representatives favor some measure, take for granted that a vote-seeking representative will vote in favor of that measure. If a majority of the *representatives* favors the measure, then it passes.

In Figure 3–6, a matrix of constituents and their representatives illustrates a case in which a measure favored by a minority of constituents may be favored by a majority of representatives. Constituents who favor the measure are denoted with an X and those who oppose it, with a dash (—). Five of representative R_1's constituents favor the measure, and four oppose it. Since a majority of constituents favor the measure, R_1 will vote for

		Representatives														
		R_1	R_2	R_3	R_4	R_5	R_6	R_7	R_8	R_9	R_{10}	R_{11}	R_{12}	R_{13}	R_{14}	R_{15}
Constituents	1	X	X	X	X	X	X	X	X	—	—	—	—	—	—	—
	2	X	X	X	X	X	X	X	X	—	—	—	—	—	—	—
	3	X	X	X	X	X	X	X	X	—	—	—	—	—	—	—
	4	X	X	X	X	X	X	X	X	—	—	—	—	—	—	—
	5	X	X	X	X	X	X	X	X	—	—	—	—	—	—	—
	6	—	—	—	—	—	—	—	—	—	—	—	—	—	—	—
	7	—	—	—	—	—	—	—	—	—	—	—	—	—	—	—
	8	—	—	—	—	—	—	—	—	—	—	—	—	—	—	—
	9	—	—	—	—	—	—	—	—	—	—	—	—	—	—	—

FIGURE 3–6   The representative problem. Each of 15 representatives has 9 constituents. If 5 or more of a representative's constituents favor some measure, then the representative will vote in favor of that measure. If at least 8 of the representatives vote in favor of a measure, the measure passes. Constituents who favor a certain measure are indicated by an X, and those opposed by a dash (—). A majority of representatives will vote in favor of this measure even though it is favored by only 40 of the 135 constituents.

it. This is also true of representatives R_2, R_3, R_4, R_5, R_6, R_7, and R_8. However, since all constituents of representatives R_9 oppose the measure, R_9 will vote against it. This is also true for representatives, R_{10}, R_{11}, R_{12}, R_{13}, R_{14}, and R_{15}. In this event, 8 representatives will vote in favor of the measure and only 7 against. Consequently, this representative body may pass a measure that supports the interests of only 40 of the 135 constituents. Less than 30 percent of the total constituency could impose its will on the other more than 70 percent. As the number of constituents increases, the percentage that may rule approaches 25; that is, a one-fourth minority could impose its will on the three-fourths majority.

If voters somehow can express the intensity of their preferences, then this problem may be circumvented to some extent. For example, suppose that a number of decisions is involved so that trading votes is possible. If the majority felt strongly that the measure should not be passed, then it could compensate the ruling minority for its losses with a favorable vote on some other less objectionable measure that also is in the minority's interests. As a matter of fact, the 95 "losers" could offer some of the 40 "winners" a political plum of some sort to persuade them to express opposition to what otherwise would be their interests. In this way, the ruling minority could be rendered ineffective, unless, of course, the minority could replace the defecting coalition members.

This raises a problem facing such coalitions: *discipline*. Suppose that voter $5R_8$, one of the 9 constituents of representative R_8, decided that not enough compensation is being received from the coalition that has been formed and thereby threatens to defect unless the share is increased. The other 39 members of the coalition must either give in to the threat or strike a different bargain that would appeal to, say, voter $6R_8$, who is another constituent of representative R_8. Agreement is required among all coalition members, therefore, and getting such agreement is difficult, especially under conditions of large numbers.

The promise of vote trading and the internal problem of discipline need not prevent minority interests from dominating a majority. In some so-called "farm states," agricultural interests are actually in a decided minority. However, if all persons with agricultural interests belong to the same political party—say, the Republican Party—they may be a majority of that party's membership and thereby control its leadership and its predisposition to agriculture. If that party in turn has a majority in the state legislature, then the policies preferred by the minority may be enacted and the interests of the minority protected on a continual basis. In some so-called "labor states," organized labor may be in a distinct minority, but by belonging to the same political party—say, the Democratic Party—its members can have a powerful influence on the party and, if the party is in power, on policies that affect the interests of organized labor.

VOTERS IN DEMOCRACY

As voters, citizens determine who will lead and direct government. A person's vote depends on many factors, but it is taken for granted that a voter will support candidates expected to further a voter's self-interest. In other words, marketplaces and polling places are means of pursuing whatever goals people have. Pursuit of self-interest in a system of competitive markets tends to promote socially desirable results. It is not self-evident, however, that, as voters pursue their goals through the political system, they will prefer efficient policies. It is also not self-evident that the political system itself channels preferences into efficient choices or protects against obviously inefficient policies. Policies that are efficient are those for which benefits exceed costs. Voters, however, are concerned only about whether policies benefit them more than they cost them. If a candidate supports policies for which a bare majority expects the benefits to exceed the costs, then voters may elect the candidate to office even though the costs to everyone may exceed gains to beneficiaries.

Rational Voter Ignorance

No matter what goals people strive to achieve through the political system, voters tend to be poorly informed about choices and the consequences of decisions. Most of us have probably commented on more than one occasion that intelligent social and political decision making and action are predicated on knowledge and that ignorance is an enemy of democracy. Information is costly, however, because acquiring knowledge takes time, effort, and money that otherwise could be allocated to recreation, investments, or other activities that have a more direct and significant impact. A person informed on air pollution, for example, would require knowledge of scientific data on air quality; medical data on the relationship between a change in air quality and the frequency and severity of attacks of asthma, emphysema, bronchitis, and so forth; ecological data on the effect of changes in air quality on the environment; economic data on the alternative means of improving air quality; and perhaps much more information, not to say the ability to interpret and analyze the data.[21]

Because information is costly, ignorance may not be irrational. Some—even a great deal of—ignorance may be rational for this reason alone.[22] There is another reason, also. What benefit does a person receive from being highly informed? Consider that the probability of a person's vote being the deciding one, thereby meaning the difference between victory and defeat for a motion, issue, or candidate is infinitesimally small in typical local, state, and federal elections. Whatever the benefits to a person from passage of an issue or election of a candidate, they must be discounted by the probability of the person's vote being the deciding one. Even if the expected benefits from passage of an issue or election of a candidate are $1 million, the expected value of voting is only $1 if the probability of any one person's vote being the deciding one is one in a million. When discounted by this probability, sizable benefits from being informed and casting an intelligent ballot are exceeded overwhelmingly by even

----

[21]As the old saying goes, there is more than one way to skin a cat. Improving air quality is just one way of, say, increasing life expectancy. There are many different measures that would increase the U.S. population's average lifetime. The different measures might be compared by cost to increase average lifetime by one year. The Societal Analysis Department of General Motors studied various measures in this light, and their findings are interesting. Basically, the researchers put relative numerical values on the cost of various measures. Establishing a special ambulance service for heart-attack victims was the most cost-effective, with an estimated cost index of 192. Requiring people to use seat harnesses in automobiles had a cost index of 3,250; lighting all expressways, an index of 310,000; and requiring automobile manufacturers to meet the 1981 tailpipe emission standard for carbon monoxide, an index of 27.5 million, which was the least cost-effective measure studied. See Arlen J. Large, "The Risk-Benefit Debate," *The Wall Street Journal*, June 11, 1980, p. 22.

[22]In economics, the term "rational" means choosing effective means in helping the decision maker to achieve his or her own objectives, whatever they are. The objectives themselves are not considered either rational or irrational, unless they are self-contradictory or mutually exclusive.

small costs of voting such as driving to the polls. Consequently, for the simple reason that a person's vote is often one among millions and will have no perceptible effect on the result, people have little incentive to obtain information about government, who runs the government, issues being considered by representatives, or the effects of issues and policies.

Studies have estimated the effects on voter turnout of variables that influence the benefits and costs of voting. In one study, an inverse relationship was found between voter turnout in U.S. gubernatorial elections and size of voting population as well as between turnout and one-sidedness of the outcome.[23] These results are consistent with the theory just outlined. Another study examined voter participation in presidential elections from 1868 to 1972.[24] Campaign expenditures were used as a proxy for the information available to voters, and a statistically significant and positive effect on voter turnout was found. The level of real government expenditures was used as a proxy for expected benefits, and there was a positive relationship with respect to turnout. Also, there was an inverse relationship between size of winning majority and turnout.

Why Do People Vote?

The theory of rational voter behavior suggests that more people will vote when the expected benefits are higher and the expected costs are lower.[25] The theory also suggests that even those who do vote will want to keep their costs low. These costs include the cost of information. Two further points need to be made in connection with rational ignorance. First, rational ignorance accounts in part for the low intellectual level of political campaigns. Slogans, oversimplifications, misleading and misrepresented claims, and unsubstantiated assertions all are common in politics. Yet voters do not have the information to judge what politicians say, and politicians do not have the incentive to provide balanced and truthful views. Second, people sometimes have a great deal of practically costless information, as well as a high degree of sensitivity, about their source of income. Farmers, for example, have a lot of knowledge and information about the kind of measures that benefit and harm them. Persons employed in a particular industry will have some idea about how various programs

[23]Yoram Barzel and Eugene Silverberg, "Is the Act of Voting Rational?" *Public Choice*, 16 (Fall 1973), 51–58.

[24]Burton Abrams and Russell Settle, "The Determinants of Voter Participation: A More General Model," *Public Choice*, 27 (Fall 1976), 81–89.

[25]Of course, some vote for the psychic satisfaction of getting revenge on some politician or because they ignore the unlikelihood of casting a deciding vote. Or, perhaps because of the same reasons that they go to baseball games: going to a game has no effect on the outcome, but following and arguing about baseball are fun, and appearing well-informed about current standings and past and present players enriches the appreciation of the game. In other words, perhaps some people go to the polls because they are politics fans, just as some people go to the ball park because they are baseball fans.

affect them because they automatically know a lot about this area of economic activity. *Income-source groups,* in other words, are likely to know how policies will affect them. Persons outside an income-source group, the consumers, may not know how their interests are affected. This situation often leads voters to judge politicians wholly on the basis of information that voters have accumulated from their sources of income. Also, politicians are led to favor "producers" more than consumers in their actions.[26] In other words, vote-seeking politicians respond more to the systematic, highly vocal, intensive special interests of producer lobbies than to the often unexpressed wishes of consumers.

POLITICIANS AND DEMOCRACY

People elected as representatives of a constituency are similar to businesspersons. There are some important dissimilarities, however. In business, an entrepreneur does not require approval of a majority of the public to make decisions effective. In politics, a majority is frequently required. In politics, a minority that opposes a program may be forced to share in paying for it. In business, people who do not care for a product cannot be forced to purchase it. Yet there are similarities, one that is central. In business, entrepreneurs serve the interest of consumers when they offer a product or several products that consumers want. In politics, politicians serve the interests of voters when they offer a policy or several policies that voters want. To stay in office, a politician seeks votes. This observation suggests that the behavior of politicians can be explained by the objective of maximizing the votes they expect or of realizing a majority of votes.[27] In either event, politicians must judge their actions in terms of votes expected to be gained or lost.

There are two important factors that influence the politician's attempt to maximize votes or to realize a majority. The first is that, for rational reasons, voters are relatively ignorant of the proposals and actions of politicians as well as the effects of these proposals and actions. The second is that the proposals and actions are usually confounded so that votes are gained or lost on the basis of positions taken on several issues. Thus, voters consider rival politicians who have records of support of or opposition to many separate issues. These two factors have consequences on government policies.

[26]See Downs, *Economic Theory of Democracy,* pp. 164–204, for a formal derivation of this hypothesis.

[27]There may be other objectives that figure in a politician's self-interest, but these objectives imply that the behavior of politicians is motivated by self-interest and that staying in office is central to a politician's self-interest.

Special Interests and Lobbies

Voter ignorance tends to encourage special interest legislation that concentrates benefits on a particular group and perhaps at the same time spreads the costs over the entire population. The benefits may be highly visible to the favored minority, but the costs may be rather invisible to the majority paying the bill. The costs may be very difficult even to determine, or the costs per member of the majority may be relatively small. In this way, a politician can gain votes from members of the favored group without losing votes from the majority paying the hidden costs. Farmers who receive price supports, mothers who receive aid to families with dependent children, veterans who receive tuition subsidies, the elderly who receive social security benefits, all are relatively aware of the benefits from these programs. However, the persons whose incomes and wealth are actually reduced by corporate income taxes, the portion of social security taxes nominally paid by employers, and excise taxes are relatively unaware of the burden they are bearing. The reason is that taxes on businesses are shifted in part to consumers in the form of higher prices and even to workers and suppliers in the form of lower wages and prices paid for materials. Deficit financing also obscures the costs of programs.

If voter ignorance tends to encourage special interest legislation, then it also tends to encourage special interest groups, pressure groups, and lobbies. These are organized attempts to influence legislation that favors groups having a common interest. The Farm Bureau, the American Medical Association, the AFL-CIO, the National Rifle Association, and Common Cause are all lobbies that try to have impact on legislative bills introduced or the content of bills under consideration as well as to persuade representatives to support or oppose certain bills.

Despite the encouragement of such groups, however, there are problems that handicap the formation of lobbies. The principal reason is that benefits realized through the influence of a lobby are often available to all those persons who share a common special interest. If the benefits are available even to those who do not contribute in any way to a lobby, then many, perhaps most, persons who benefit may try to "ride free."

Most of the powerful lobbies are organizations that provide some service or services to members only, and the lobbying activities are a by-product.[28] In other words, an organization grows large because it provides its membership with services well worth the dues, and once it is large and has available a large amount of revenues from dues, it can engage in lobbying activities. Often, it has been noted that workers pay dues to labor unions in return for employment opportunities. This benefit is available to

---

[28]See Mancur Olson, Jr., *The Logic of Collective Action* (Cambridge, Mass.: Harvard University Press, 1965), pp. 132–67.

dues-paying members only. Revenue from dues can be used by union leadership to finance lobbying activities to further legislation that favors labor in general, even unorganized labor. Whenever lobbies are active, they can also influence politicians by informing constituents about how pending legislation affects persons who share a common special interest and about the politicians most likely to further those interests by voting favorably. In this way, lobbies often can mobilize voters to turn out and cast ballots for those politicians.

Some groups share common special interests but do not have these interests represented by organized lobbies. The so-called "Great Society" programs that increased the level of transfer payments to unprecedented heights during the 1960s benefited the poor and the elderly. What these groups lacked in organized lobbies, they made up with large numbers who tended to vote as a bloc for politicians who favored them.

Logrolling

The other factor that influences a politician's attempt to maximize votes or to realize a majority is that politicians gain or lose votes on the basis of many issues. This factor, along with voter ignorance, tends to encourage logrolling. Logrolling, which was discussed earlier in this chapter, is vote trading to achieve a majority. Logrolling would not be necessary if a majority of voters supported an issue, so that logrolling is understood to be the case of achieving approval of issues favored by a minority.

Logrolling can be either explicit or implicit. *Explicit logrolling* occurs when one representative agrees to vote for something that another representative wants in return for the other's vote on a second issue. For example, suppose that the congressional delegation from Florida wants approval of a national solar energy research laboratory located in southern Florida. It may go to the Mississippi delegation and offer support of a national oceanographic laboratory located in Mississippi in return for that delegation's support. It may go to the Texas delegation and offer to support irrigation projects for Texas in return for that delegation's support, and to the Idaho delegation with an offer to support flood control projects for Idaho in return for that delegation's support, and so forth. In this way, the Florida delegation might trade for a majority of votes required to locate the solar energy laboratory in Florida.

Implicit logrolling occurs when measures favored by different politicians are packaged in one piece of legislation and voted on as a single bill. By voting for the whole legislative package, a representative is voting on measures favored by other representatives, and the other representatives are voting for measures that the representative favors. At times the package of measures involves the same program, while at other times the package may involve quite different programs. A case of the former type of implicit logrolling may be a package of interstate highway construction projects in a number of states so that it benefits a majority of constituencies. A case of the latter type may be appropriations bills enabling construction of a courthouse in one district, a school in a second, a hospital in a third, an agricultural experiment station in still another, and so forth.[29]

The logrolling process at its best can promote and protect minority interest. There may be a particular measure for which there is an "intense" minority, which is to say a minority that feels very strongly about an issue. Under majority voting, however, such intensity of minority preferences may be ignored without logrolling. With logrolling, minorities can seek approval of a measure by agreeing to support other measures on which there are other intense minorities. The problem is that logrolling tends to overrepresent minority interests by making it too easy to achieve a majority vote on a measure opposed by a majority.

The Two-Party System

In the United States, politicians are usually identified with a particular political party. Of course, it is not necessary for a politician to belong to or be associated with a political party. A politician could express a platform that is strictly personal. Then why do politicians associate with a political party? The main reason is that membership in a party is a way of providing voters with information about views on important issues. If voters know that a candidate is a Democrat or a Republican, then they have some idea about the kinds of measures and issues that the candidate is likely to support or oppose. In fact, voters themselves associate with political parties for many reasons but certainly among them is the fact that voters feel their preferences on important political issues are close to those identified with a particular party.

In a sense, the name Republican or Democrat is similar to a brand name. A company like Procter & Gamble is a multiproduct firm supplying Jif, Prell, Folger's, and many other brand-name products. P & G is careful about its line of products, and any new product introduced is intended to be consistent with its high standards. Ray Kroc built the McDonald's franchise by taking strong measures to assure that each member of its chain turned out a product of standard quality and in a clean, wholesome atmosphere. Holiday Inn requires that motels in its international chain satisfy certain conditions, and in fact it advertises itself as the "no-surprise" motel chain because they are all so similar. In business, brand names convey information about products and the quality that can be expected. In the case of franchises or chains, individual cases that diminish the value of the brand name or the reputation of the franchise must be required to conform to standards or else lose rights to franchise. This tends to be true in politics

---

[29]For an excellent discussion of logrolling as a form of political exchange, see Richard B. McKenzie and Gordon Tullock, *Modern Political Economy* (New York: McGraw-Hill Book Company, 1978), pp. 404–5.

also. Leaders of a political party must protect the value of reputation of
the party name so that it continues to convey the desired information. Representatives often "vote along party lines" for this reason. Otherwise,
leaders will at least try to punish in some way a politician who diminishes
the value of the party name.

In the United States, each of the two major political parties selects a
candidate, and the two candidates run against one another for a particular
office. At times, there are candidates from other parties or independent
candidates. In any event, majority voting usually determines the candidate
who will serve. When there are more than two candidates, the one with the
most votes wins, even though the winning candidate may have only a plu-
rality rather than a majority. Basically, however, there is a two-party system with majority voting to determine winners.

Suppose that voters can be distributed along an ideological spectrum
from liberal to conservative.[30] Also, suppose that candidates are distinguishable by ideology and that voters will support the candidate they perceive to be closer to their ideology. In Figure 3–7, a distribution of voters
is illustrated. The distribution suggests that most voters are neither staunch
liberals nor staunch conservatives but are moderates or "middle-of-the-
roaders."

Under these conditions, which are not really far fetched, politicians
would not choose political positions at either tail of the distribution. If a
Democrat chose position D_L in the liberal tail, a Republican could win the
election by establishing a position slightly to the right of the Democrat's
position, say, at R_L. The Democrat would take all the votes to the left of
D_L, but the Republican would take all the votes to the right of R_L, which
would be much more than a majority. On the other hand, if a Republican
chose position R_C in the conservative tail, a Democrat could win the election by establishing a position slightly to the left of the Republican's position, say, at D_C. The Republican would win the votes to the right of R_C,
but the Democrat would take all the votes to the left of D_C, which would
be much more than a majority.

The better part of wisdom is establishing a position near the middle
of the distribution. Both the Democrat and the Republican would try to articulate a political platform that establishes a position in the middle, say,
at D_M and R_M, and close to one another. They do this to avoid being out-
maneuvered—to try to win certainly, but also to avoid losing. Of course,
many voters will be critical that politicians take such similar stands.[31] They
would prefer candidates who represent views closer to their own. How-

[30]The discussion of a two-party system is indebted to McKenzie and Tullock, *Modern
Political Economy*, pp. 389–91.

[31]George Wallace, former governor of Alabama, often said of the two major parties that
"there's not a dime's worth of difference between the two of them."

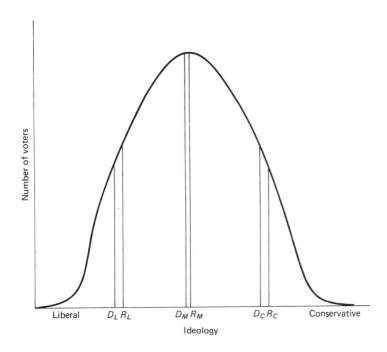

FIGURE 3–7   Importance of the middle of the voter distribution. Voters are distributed along an ideological spectrum from liberal to conservative. Candidates are distinguishable by ideology. Voters support the candidate they perceive to be closer to their ideology. In a two-party system, there is a tendency to choose an ideology close to the middle of the distribution. If party D chooses position D_L in the liberal tail of the distribution, then party R can win by choosing position R_L. If party R chooses position R_c in the conservative tail, then party D can win by choosing position D_c.

ever, rivalry between candidates of the two parties will lead them to the middle of the distribution.

The distribution of voters is not known and, for that matter, is not static. Consequently, a central problem of politics is for the Democrat and the Republican to estimate the distribution and then to establish a position in the middle of the estimated distribution. Needless to say, either one or both of the parties can err in perceiving the "mood" of the people and in establishing a middle stand on the issues. The Democrat may believe that the distribution is skewed to the left, and the Republican, to the right. These distributions are illustrated in Figure 3–8. The Democrat would then try to establish a position at D, and the Republican at R. If the middle of the distribution is in fact closer to D than to R, then the Democrat would win; if closer to R than to D, then the Republican would win. "Learning" is likely, of course. The two candidates may discover in the course of a campaign that they have been mistaken and can move right or left in order

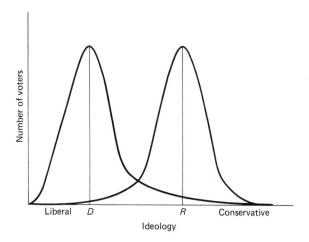

FIGURE 3-8   Uncertain distribution of voters. The true distribution of voters along an ideological spectrum is unknown. In a two-party system, each estimates the distribution and establishes a position in the middle of that distribution. If party *D*'s estimate is closer to the true but unknown middle of the distribution, then party *D* wins. If party *R*'s estimate is closer, then party *R* wins.

to be closer to the middle of the true but unknown distribution.[32] In any event, the bottom line of this simple analysis is that rational politicians will try to establish middle-of-the-road positions with respect to the distribution of voters in their constituencies or to move to the center when they learn what the actual distribution is.

BUREAUCRACY

In general usage, the term "bureaucracy" refers to any large organization. Government bureaucracy is an organization of nonelected public officials who are responsible for implementing governmental policies and programs. A government bureau differs from a business organization operated for profit. Among the differences is that a government bureau does not sell its services directly to the public. For performing its services, a bureau receives payment from the legislature. Bureaucrats do not necessarily benefit from cost savings or profit from providing a better product. The bureaucrat is not necessarily rewarded for efficiency and does not necessarily have an incentive to satisfy those who receive the bureaucrat's services. Finally, bureaucrats are generally protected from competition.

---

[32]Another complication of this simple analysis is that candidates are chosen in party primaries. Each candidate in a primary must strive for the middle of his or her own party's distribution to be nominated for election.

Bureaucrats are presumed to be rational in the same sense that voters and politicians are. Given the constraints imposed on them, bureaucrats will make decisions that benefit themselves. What are the objectives of bureaucracies? Although to say so is simplification of complex organizations, it is in the interest of bureaus to maximize the size of their budgets. This follows from the general observation that promotion possibilities, salaries, power, influence, prestige, and public respect all tend to increase with size. Bureaucrats gain with expansion of the bureau. Taking for granted that bureaucrats attempt to maximize their budgets does not mean that they will be successful. Representative bodies must approve budget requests.[33]

There is one consequence of ignorance that should be pointed out. The product or service of a bureau is usually a "package" of several "attributes." In other words, a good or service may have different characteristics that can be emphasized in different proportions. Manufacturers produce bread and cereal that differ in taste, texture, nutrition, size, and convenience. The same is true of services provided by government bureaus. Some characteristics or attributes are highly visible and easily measured. Politician ignorance may lead bureaus to emphasize the most visible and easiest measured characteristics in their services. At least one study of this hypothesis claims that VA hospitals emphasize visible, measurable attributes such as average length of stay and deemphasize invisible, less easily measurable characteristics such as the quality of services.[34]

BUDGET SIZE IN DEMOCRACY

Is government too big? The political process is highly complex. The institutions through which decisions are made contain numerous forces with conflicting tendencies. For many years, economists have analyzed the political process and institutions to examine the influences on governmental size. There is less disagreement among economists concerning the forces themselves than about their relative importance. Depending on relative importance, some economists have concluded that the size of government is too small, and others, that it is too large.

Some years ago, in a book written for popular reading, John Kenneth Galbraith argued that the public sector is too small because advertising and emulation lead people to be more aware of the gains from consuming private goods than from consuming goods provided by some level of govern-

[33]For a pioneering study of bureaucracy, see William A. Niskanen, Jr., *Bureaucracy and Representative Government* (Chicago: Aldine-Atherton, Inc., 1971).

[34]Cotton M. Lindsay, "A Theory of Government Enterprise," *Journal of Political Economy*, 84 (October 1976), 1061.

ment.[35] Galbraith emphasized that these forces distort choice. At about the same time, another economist, Anthony Downs, also argued that governments spend too little.[36] The distortion that he emphasized was rational voter ignorance. He concluded that voters tend to underestimate the benefits of government expenditures and overestimate the costs. The benefits are "remote" and "uncertain," and people are more aware of costs. Downs concedes that several other forces cause a bias toward budgets that are too large. None of these other forces is as important or powerful, Downs has argued.

In an important book that enlivened a spirited debate, James M. Buchanan and Gordon Tullock argued that government and budget size are too large.[37] The force that they thought to be dominant is the logrolling process that concentrates benefits on one group and spreads costs more evenly over the population as a whole. Elsewhere, Tullock and the late Harry Johnson have suggested that some parts of the budget are overextended and that other parts are underextended.[38] They did not agree on the components in each category. In this same tradition, the authors have emphasized the opportunities for coalitions to play "negative-sum games" as the dominant force.[39] In our study, we concluded that budget size in democracy is too large. Under majority rule, coalitions of any size greater than one-half the voters can control the composition and size of the budget. Coalitions are potentially effective if expected benefits exceed expected costs for each member of the coalition. In such cases, costs may exceed benefits when summed over population. A "game" may be "positive sum" for a majority but "negative sum" for the population.[40] Yet this type of game may be played and is commonly played in democracies. This is particularly the case, for example, when special interest groups manage

---

[35]See John Kenneth Galbraith, *The Affluent Society* (Boston: Houghton Mifflin Company, 1958).

[36]See Anthony Downs, "Why the Government Budget Is Too Small in a Democracy," in Edmund S. Phelps, ed., *Private Wants and Public Needs* (New York: W. W. Norton & Company, Inc., 1965), pp. 76–96. The article was published originally in 1960.

[37]See Buchanan and Tullock, *Calculus of Consent*, p. 169. Also, see Buchanan, *Public Finance in Democratic Process* (Chapel Hill: University of North Carolina Press, 1967), p. 91n; and Buchanan, "Simple Majority Voting, Game Theory and Resource Use," *Canadian Journal of Economics and Political Science*, 27 (August 1961), 337–48.

[38]See Gordon Tullock, "Problems of Majority Voting," *Journal of Political Economy*, 67 (December 1959), 571–79; and Harry G. Johnson, "The Economic Approach to Social Questions," *Economica*, 35 (February 1968), 1–21.

[39]For a more thorough discussion of this section, see J. Ronnie Davis and Charles W. Meyer, "Budget Size in Democracy," *Southern Economic Journal*, 36 (July 1969), 10–17.

[40]Negative-sum games are those for which the costs exceed the benefits. If logrolling is allowed and games are defined broadly to include what amounts to a series of games, a negative-sum game in a narrowly defined sense may become a cost of playing a broadly defined positive-sum game. A positive-sum game is one for which the benefits exceed the costs. A zero-sum game is one for which the benefits and costs are equal. Poker, for example, is a zero-sum game because what the winners win is equal to what the losers lose.

to use the democratic process to secure for themselves benefits financed by taxpayers in general.

In fact, each of these forces influences decisions. There are thousands of decisions that determine government and budget size. There are undoubtedly some programs too large and others too small. This merely recognizes that the forces that tend to overextend spending dominate in some cases, and those that tend to underextend spending dominate in others. Even if economists agreed that, in the aggregate, government budgets are too large or too small, this would not imply that all programs should be reduced in scale or scope or that all programs should be expanded.

WHY NONMARKET PROVISION?

For any group of substantial size, democracy means that the group must act through agents who, as the personnel of government, are held responsible to the society as a whole and who act by making and administering laws. Under ideal circumstances, these laws would reflect unanimous agreement reached through free and informed discussion, and they would not need any literal enforcement. Neither ideal can be realized, partly because, as Frank Knight puts it, man is by nature a law-breaking animal as well as a disagreeing one. Much compulsion is necessary to interpret and administer laws, and because this action is taken by agents, a relation is created between rulers and ruled that would be absent in an ideal democracy that serves as the roots of the individualistic postulate.

If we turn to government as a means of providing certain goods and services, however, we must be prepared to tolerate nonoptimal results. As we have seen, the result in some cases may be that the decision to provide a service at a certain level of provision may be purely arbitrary. In the first place, we might not know what the optimal level of provision is because the exclusion condition does not hold. Whereas the market may underprovide such services, democratic government may overprovide them. In the second place, the cyclical majority problem may lead to intransitivity in the result, so that, no matter what alternative is chosen, a majority prefers a different one. Representative government can lead to inefficient solutions where a minority rules or where actions are taken for which the benefits fall short of the costs. If we turn to government as a means of escaping the consequences of market failure, what have we gained if there also are consequences of nonmarket failure?

The answer, not a satisfying one, is perhaps that we compare the likely outcome of market provision with that of government provision and then choose the more tolerable result. For most goods and services, we are prepared to rely on markets even though we all may agree that the result is either underprovision in cases where benefits cannot be confined or overprovision in cases where costs cannot be confined. The reason for tolerating such inefficiency is a judgment that government intervention may lead to even more unsatisfactory results. Consider national defense, however. The consequence of market provision, depending as it does on voluntary payments, might prove to be disastrous, because underprovision of national security could leave us unprepared to deter foreign attacks.

4

The Federal
Budget Process

There is a relationship between public choice and a government budget. Resources available to government are limited, but public demands on them are not. A process must be found to apportion available funds among competing public demands. Behind every government budget, therefore, is the necessity of choice. In a sense, politics is conflict over who gets what government has to give. The outcomes of this struggle are embedded and recorded in the budget. Thus, a government budget is seen as an attempt to allocate financial resources through political processes to serve differing human purposes.[1]

The budget process is something of a mystery to most people. The language, structure, and procedures of the process are complex.[2] Yet major news stories of any given year turn on some aspect of the budget process. President Nixon impounded funds appropriated by Congress and was the target of Title X of the Congressional Budget and Impoundment Control Act. The Ford administration was sued by the comptroller general of the United States over a deferral request contained in a message to Congress. President Carter and Congress were so deadlocked in 1979 that a budget was not approved until almost three months after the fiscal year had started. In November 1981, there was "the day the federal government

---

[1]This is the view expressed in Aaron Wildavsky, *Budgeting: A Comparative Theory of Budgeting Processes* (Boston: Little, Brown and Company, 1975), pp. 3–5.

[2]For an overview of the budget process, see David J. Ott and Attiat F. Ott, *Federal Budget Policy* (Washington, D.C.: The Brookings Institution, 1977). For an introduction to the political aspect of the budget, see Dennis S. Ippolito, *The Budget and National Politics* (San Francisco: W. H. Freeman and Company, 1978). For an understanding of Congress and the budget, see Allen Schick, *Congress and Money: Budgeting, Spending and Taxing* (Washington, D.C.: The Urban Institute, 1981).

stood still," when President Reagan vetoed a congressional resolution and caused a funding failure that technically stopped federal activities. Many millions of interested citizens followed these stories, which were reported in depth by national media.

The budget process can be understood best in terms of a cycle of events that takes place over a time span of several years. Basically, a budget cycle consists of four phases: preparation, approval, execution, and audit. *Preparation* and *approval* take a great deal of time prior to the date when the budget becomes operational. There must be enough time to consider policy issues, conduct analysis, plan the budget, and permit the executive and legislative branches to modify the budget proposal. *Execution* is the phase that begins when the operating budget goes into effect and ends one year later. After the end of the budget year, time is required to close accounts and to *audit* and *evaluate* policies and programs. This final phase can take several years. At a given time, there is no single budget cycle in operation. Budget cycles overlap. On the same day, an agency head may work in preparation of the budget for the next fiscal year, make decisions on the current operating budget, and revise evaluations covering last year's programs.

BUDGET PREPARATION

Budget preparation is primarily an executive function.[3] The president relies on a budget office. The Budget and Accounting Act of 1921 established the Bureau of the Budget (BOB). At first, BOB was a unit of the U.S. Treasury. In 1939, BOB was moved to the Executive Office of the President, which placed BOB directly under the president. The bureau was reorganized in 1970 by President Nixon, who renamed it the Office of Management and Budget (OMB).

In effect, preparation of a budget is preparation of a plan for the upcoming year or years. Recall that the purpose of budgeting itself is to provide a system for allocating scarce funds among competing public demands. There are several steps in this phase of the budget cycle, but preparation basically begins with budget requests. Then, decisions must be made on the requests. Finally, the decisions are presented in a set of budget documents.

Budget preparation depends on information. To facilitate preparation, OMB issues instructions to executive agencies for preparing and submitting budget estimates. Most of the instructions are concerned with expenditures, but information beyond dollar requests is required. Judgments must

---

[3]For a description and an analysis of budget preparation, see Robert D. Lee, Jr., and Ronald W. Johnson, *Public Budgeting Systems*, 2nd ed. (Baltimore: University Park Press, 1977), pp. 109–51.

be made about program effectiveness. OMB's instructions to an agency indicate the program data that are expected. Instructions also provide guidance to agencies so that their responses are somewhat bounded. The simplest form of guidance is to assume no change in programs. The only increments in an agency's current budget would be any increased costs of operating existing programs.

Agencies play an advocacy role in behalf of the programs for which they are responsible. Agency bureaucrats are specialists in their fields. They are familiar with their successes and are guarded with their failures. They may genuinely believe in the importance of their activities and the contributions they make, and they may be convinced that expansion is easily justified. However, they may also make a case for expansion for the self-interested reasons that salaries, power, recognition, and prestige tend to increase with agency size. These forces are active within an agency at the time that budget requests are under review. From the bottom up, there are attempts to gain the approval of superiors for additional funding requests. Ultimately, agency heads must decide, knowing that an agency is likely to get less than it asks for.

OMB examines budget requests and later makes recommendations to the president. This role is only one of many served by OMB. The office reviews new legislation proposed by agencies. It conducts management studies of agencies. There is a budget examiner, or perhaps more than one, assigned by OMB to review an agency. Considerable tension can develop between an OMB budget examiner and an agency. After its request has been reviewed, budget hearings are held with agency officials. Representatives of the agency must defend their requests and the effectiveness of their programs. Once more, tensions tend to be considerable.

The president's chief budget officer is the director of OMB. OMB itself is directly under the president's supervision. There are obvious political considerations in formulating recommendations to the president. The recommendations of a budget examiner are made in the light of the president's priorities. Eventually, top officials of OMB bring together the recommendations, revise the requests, develop estimates of revenues expected for the fiscal year, and draft a comprehensive budget document. There are other groups that have influence on the president's budget. His Council of Economic Advisors and the Treasury Department are generally consulted on revenue forecasts. Political advisors on the White House staff, party leadership in Congress, and other persons also have an important impact.

Many different considerations are factored into the president's budget proposal. Through OMB, agencies have been given some guidelines in terms of programs and dollars. Now, the president considers recommendations by OMB that, to a degree, have been structured by the executive's own program priorities. The president will also consider economic policy.

Some desired program expansion may have to be curtailed or postponed due to the president's concern that expenditures be held down. The president will also consider the legislative environment as well as his understanding of the public's mood. At times, the president will put something in the budget because polls indicate strong public support, or take something out because congressional leadership says that a program has no support. At other times, the president goes against the polls and the advice of political leadership. In any event, many different influences have impact on the president's decisions. During the weeks when the president is deliberating, a proposed program change may be approved and then rejected, while another is first rejected and then accepted. The appearance that decisions are made and then reversed is the normal course of many considerations being taken into account at once.

At the end of the budget preparation phase, a set of recommended programs and policies is presented in a document. The document is a budget, but it is only a proposal until Congress approves it. In fact, the president releases several budget documents. The Congressional Budget and Impoundment Control Act of 1974 requires the president to release the *Current Services Budget* no later than November 10. The intent is to estimate the costs that would be required to carry existing programs forward to the following fiscal year. In other words, this budget estimates how much it would cost next year to pay for this year's programs, assuming no changes in the programs or level of commitment. The data required to prepare this budget document are collected from agencies by OMB during the budget request process.

In January, within fifteen days after Congress convenes, the president releases the *Budget of the United States* and submits it along with his budget message to Congress. This document is a very large, weighty volume that contains several hundred pages. There are narrative discussions of programs supported with financial data. The *Budget in Brief* is released at the same time. This is a digest that is intended for the general public.

The *Budget Appendix* and *Special Analyses* are also released in January. The *Appendix* is an important document that presents vast detail about departments, bureaus, and agencies. Appropriation language is proposed, and tabular data are presented for "objects of expenditure" such as personnel, supplies and materials, and equipment. Some program information is presented. For example, work load data are reported for some activities. *Special Analyses* is a document that varies in content from year to year. It is a collection of discussions and tables on selected items.

When the budget is presented to Congress in January of each year, the budget cycle is already several months old. Yet the budget is still only a proposal. Congress must act on the budget and send appropriations bills back to the president for signature into law. The approval phase of the budget cycle is therefore primarily a legislative activity.

BUDGET APPROVAL

The structure and procedures of congressional approval were reformed by the Congressional Budget and Impoundment Control (CBIC) Act of 1974.[4] The CBIC Act moved to integrate the revenue and expenditure processes by creating two new committees, the House and Senate budget committees, and a permanent office to provide independent analyses and data to congress, the Congressional Budget Office (CBO). The CBIC Act was a budget reform intended to solve some problems of long historical standing and to improve the process of congressional approval.[5] It is helpful to see the CBIC Act in the light of budget reform history.

Budget Reform

In early U.S. history, the budget process was simple. The House Ways and Means Committee, which was established in 1802, initiated both taxing and spending bills. In the Senate, budget responsibility was held by the Finance Committee. The executive branch periodically challenged congressional control, but Congress basically managed national finances until the Civil War. The spending process struggled under the House and Senate committees. An appropriations committee was appointed in both the House (1865) and Senate (1867). Jurisidiction over taxes was left with Ways and Means and Finance. The budget process in Congress was fragmented and decentralized still further when, after the Civil War, standing legislative committees gained some control over appropriations. During this period, federal agencies submitted spending requests directly to some twelve committees. This system continued until 1921.

The Budget and Accounting Act was passed in 1921. It established an executive budget system. The act gave the president responsibility for gathering requests from all executive agencies and submitting an annual budget to Congress. To help the president, the Bureau of the Budget was created and placed in the Treasury Department. In 1939, it was moved to the newly formed Executive Office of the President. The act also clarified jurisdiction and centralized procedures in the Congress. Control of spending was returned to the appropriations committees. Other standing committees were responsible for authorizing substantive legislation. Appropriations committees could not take legislative actions, and the legislative committees could not take spending actions.

After 1921, executive control over the budget expanded. This was particularly true during the presidency of Franklin D. Roosevelt. There

[4]For a careful study of this legislation, see James P. Pfiffner, *The President, the Budget, and Congress: Impoundment and the 1974 Budget Act* (Boulder, Colo.: Westview Press, 1979).

[5]For a description and an analysis of budget approval, see Lee and Johnson, *Public Budgeting Systems*, pp. 175–207.

were periodic movements to reform the budget process. After World War II, Congress moved to establish a legislative budget. The Legislative Reorganization Act of 1946 established a Joint Committee on the Budget to study the president's budget and report on a legislative budget to both houses. The resolution was intended to place a ceiling on overall spending and, based on revenue estimates, recommend a deficit or surplus. This movement faltered and by 1950 had foundered.

Congress still had no effective way of controlling spending. In the 1960s, new social legislation and Vietnam caused federal spending and budget deficits to grow dramatically. There was renewed interest in limiting expenditures. Between 1967 and 1972, Congress passed some sort of limitation every year except 1971. The Revenue and Expenditure Control Act of 1968 included a spending limitation that put a lid on both budget authorizations and outlays. Congress passed statutory limits on expenditures again in 1969 and 1970. Expenditures exceeded the limits in each year that ceilings were approved. The basic problem was the growth of the portion of the budget classified as relatively uncontrollable. Examples are interest on the national debt and entitlement programs such as social security that require payments of benefits to all who qualify.

There was no spending limitation in 1971. And President Nixon attacked congressional budget procedures. In July 1972, he demanded that expenditures for fiscal 1973 be held below $250 billion. Congress agreed that outlays should be reduced and limited, and both the Senate and House passed ceilings. They did not agree to give the president discretion to make the necessary cuts, however.

By the early 1970s, therefore, there were a number of problems with the budget process. The budget had grown in size and in complexity. Under direct presidential supervision, BOB (later OMB) had increased in importance. Even within Congress, the grip on spending was loosening. Authorizing committees were finding ways to influence spending without going through the appropriations process. Appropriations committees were not timely in completing their work. Many agencies operated on continuing resolutions because Congress had not passed appropriations bills by the start of the fiscal year.

Yet recognition of the inadequacies of congressional budget procedures was probably not sufficient to mobilize support for budget reform. Many students of budget reform believe that the momentum for reform came from the impoundments of the Nixon administration. President Nixon simply refused to spend money authorized and appropriated by Congress for particular programs. Money had been impounded by other presidents, but no president had acted on the scale of President Nixon. It has been estimated that he had impounded as much as $18 billion by 1973. Congress was outraged because it was believed that he was selectively withholding money from programs that he disliked. The president defended his actions on the grounds that Congress was not accepting the responsibility for consequences of excessive spending. Outraged and humiliated, Congress acted on reform.[6]

The CBIC Act was reform legislation that was intended to address many of the obvious shortcomings of congressional budget procedures. Three shortcomings bear note. First, the system fragmented responsibility. No one committee was responsible for the budget as a whole. Second, appropriations committees had been weakened by spending outside the appropriations process. The integrity of the process was eroded further by failure to pass appropriation bills by the beginning of a fiscal year. Third, Congress had no independent information and advice that were the equivalent of that available to the executive branch through OMB. Congress had staff, but basically it depended on the executive for information. The CBIC Act had remarkable support and became law amidst the environment of dramatic events that ended with President Nixon's resignation. It passed the House by 401 to 6 and the Senate by 75 to 0. President Nixon signed the bill into law in July 1974. He resigned his office less than one month later.

The House and Senate Budget Committees

Title I of the CBIC Act created the House and Senate budget committees. The CBIC Act states that members of the House Budget Committee shall be selected without regard to seniority and that service is limited to no more than four years out of any ten.[7] The CBIC Act also specified that membership shall include five members from the Appropriations Committee, five from the Ways and Means Committee, eleven from the standing committees, and one member each from the majority and minority leadership. The committee was later enlarged to twenty-five members by increasing to thirteen the representatives of standing committees. The Senate Budget Committee did not provide for any representation from other committees or from party leadership. No tenure limitations were imposed on service. In the Senate, the Budget Committee was created as a standing committee with an undefined and unrestricted membership.

The responsibilities of the two committees were practically identical. Each committee was given the responsibility for reporting two "concurrent resolutions" each fiscal year. These resolutions set forth (1) the appropriate level of *total* budget outlays and of *total new* budget authority, (2) an

---

[6]For a historical summary and an analysis of budget reform, see Lance LeLoup, *The Fiscal Congress* (Westport, Conn.: Greenwood Press, 1980), pp. 3–14.

[7]Ordinarily, there is a seniority system in Congress. Chairmanship of a congressional committee comes with years of continuous service on the same committee. The requirements of membership on the House Budget Committee were part of a "new blood" sentiment. The tenure limitations were changed from four to six years prior to the start of the Ninety-sixth Congress, which convened in 1979.

estimate of budget outlays and an appropriate level of new budget authority for each major functional category, (3) the amount of surplus or deficit in the budget that is appropriate in light of economic conditions, (4) the recommended level of revenues, and (5) the appropriate level of public debt. The intent was to provide a means for Congress to take an overview of the budget. In this way, Congress could play a more active role in formulating fiscal policy.

Congressional Budget Office

Title II of the CBIC Act created CBO as a permanent office. Section 202 specified that the CBO's duties and functions are to assist the two budget committees and the committees on Appropriations, Ways and Means, and Finance "in the discharge of all matters within their jurisdictions." The assistance included (1) information with respect to the budget, appropriations bills, and other bills that provide budget authority; (2) information with respect to revenues, estimated revenues, and changing revenue conditions; and (3) such related information as requested by the committees. In fact, CBO is responsible for providing budgetary information and analytical support. In politics, information is power, and the control of information is the heart of power. Congress had been dependent on the executive branch for all its budgetary information. There was great skepticism about the information given by the "Nixonized" OMB, but Congress had no equivalent of OMB to check out the accuracy or completeness of information given. CBO gave Congress that capability.[8]

Thus, CBO was created to provide Congress with a badly needed independent source of budgetary information. However, Congress was slow in appointing a director of CBO. Charles Schultze, Kermit Gordon, and others were considered, but after six months, Alice Rivlin was appointed as its first director. She argued that CBO was *not* the congressional equivalent of OMB. The job of CBO was not that of formulating a congressional budget as OMB formulates the executive budget, she said.[9] The two offices were equivalent only in the respect that both provide budgetary information and analysis.

Section 308 of Title III of the CBIC Act sets out a number of reports, summaries, and projections expected of CBO. Basically, this section says that analysis is to be provided in various ways. One is "scorekeeping." CBO is required to compare pending and enacted legislation with totals specified in budget resolutions passed by Congress. In other words, CBO sees how consistent the parts are with the whole. This is very demanding

[8]See LeLoup, *The Fiscal Congress,* pp. 15–19.

[9]Director Rivlin's appointment was controversial, especially among conservatives. Almost immediately there were charges that CBO was an advocate of liberal policies and was biased against the defense budget. See Joel Havemann, *Congress and the Budget* (Bloomington, Ind.: Indiana University Press, 1978), p. 107.

on time and resources. CBO also "costs out" bills. Here, CBO projects the five-year costs of authorization bills to estimate the long-run spending implications of current legislation. CBO also submits an annual report of current levels of taxation and spending projected for five years, a report on alternative levels of taxation and spending with analysis of fiscal and priority choices, and policy analysis reports, which are special studies of current issues that affect the budget.

The Committee Structure of Authorization and Appropriations

The U.S. Constitution divides the legislature into the House of Representatives and the Senate. Congress conducts its legislative business through committees.[10] Legislation is taken up by parallel committees in the House and Senate. The committees act on legislative bills and, when favorable action is taken, report out bills that are acted upon by the full membership of their respective chambers.[11] Often, there are differences between the bills approved in the House and Senate. In that event, a conference committee is appointed from membership of the two committees that prepared the legislation. It then reports out a revised bill to be acted on by both chambers. When both House and Senate have acted favorably on *identical* bills, the legislation is sent to the president for signature. Only upon signature does the legislation have the effect of law.

Congress makes spending decisions by creating budget authority that allows agencies to obligate, commit, and disburse federal funds. The most common form of budget authority is appropriations. Congress does not actually determine budget outlays, which are equivalent to the annual expenditures made by the federal government in a given year. Congress approves budget authority while estimating budget outlays for a given year. The congressional committees involved in these spending decisions are authorization committees and the appropriations committees of the House and Senate.

Authorization Committees

The rules of the House and Senate require that no appropriation shall be granted for any purpose not authorized by law. The authorizing committees are of a legislative rather than a budgetary nature. Their function is to take up substantive policy proposals and recommend legislation. The committees consider policy in their respective areas. For example, the

[10]Woodrow Wilson once wrote that "Congress in session is Congress on exhibition, whilst Congress in its Committee rooms is Congress at work." See Woodrow Wilson, *Congressional Government*, 15th ed. (Boston: Houghton Mifflin Company, 1900), p. 79.

[11]Congress deals with some twenty thousand bills each year. The majority are never reported out of committee for action on the floor.

House Agriculture Committee and the Senate Committee on Agriculture, Nutrition, and Forestry consider authorizations for crop support prices. The Armed Services committees in the House and Senate handle military authorizations. The Veterans' Affairs committees consider authorization for programs that benefit veterans. Most of the budget is under *permanent* authorization, which provides indefinite legislative authority for agencies and programs. Usually, such authorizations say that sums "necessary and proper" to carry out a program should be appropriated.[12] Other authorizations are annual or multiyear, usually between two and five years. When agencies do not have permanent authorization for one or more of its programs, they must go to Congress for authorizations hearings on an annual or multiyear basis. Such programs might not be reauthorized. Congress may choose to review and change a permanent authorization, but it does so periodically rather than at regular intervals.

Most of the actual committee work in Congress is done by subcommittees. There are about 150 subcommittees in the House and 100 in the Senate. The authorizing committees and their subcommittees tend to be advocacy committees. To illustrate, one of the ten subcommittees of the House Agriculture Committee is the Subcommittee on Cotton. The membership and chair of the Subcommittee on Cotton are usually representatives from cotton-growing states and districts. Membership of the House Agriculture Committee, for that matter, is usually comprised of representatives from agricultural states and districts. Congressional representatives routinely request assignments to committees that formulate and administer policies that affect vital economic and other interests of a representative's district. A U.S. representative from Iowa will ask to be assigned to the Agriculture Committee and to the Subcommittee on Livestocks and Grains. One from Florida might ask for the Science and Technology Committee and to the Subcommittee on Space Science and Applications. The reason is clear: to protect the NASA programs at Cape Canaveral.

To the extent that subcommittees are advocates of particular programs, they join forces with agencies and interest groups that also play an advocacy role in behalf of those programs. Since Congress relies on the recommendations of committees and subcommittees, a policy advocated by a subcommittee, an agency, and an interest group often becomes a policy of the federal government. This is the reason that political scientists refer to the coalition of a subcommittee, agency, and interest group as a "subgovernment." For example, the chair of the House Dairy and Poultry Subcommittee, the assistant secretaries and deputy assistant secretaries who run the Agricultural Stabilization and Conservation (ASCS) programs for milk, and leadership of the National Milk Producers Federation are a subgovernment in the formulation and administration of policies affecting

---

[12]For example, CBO was given permanent budget authority. Section 201(f) says, "there are authorized to be appropriated to the Office for each fiscal year such sums as may be necessary to enable it to carry out its duties and functions."

milk. The chair of the House Tobacco Subcommittee, the bureaucrats who run the ASCS tobacco program, and the leadership of the Tobacco Institute are the subgovernment in tobacco.[13]

The House and Senate Appropriations Committees

Only Congress can appropriate money. The power of the purse is provided in Article I, Section 9 of the U.S. Constitution: "No Money shall be drawn from the Treasury, but in Consequence of Appropriations made by Law." The House and Senate appropriations committees consider agency requests and make recommendations to their respective memberships. In fact, the committees are broken down into subcommittees such as defense, agriculture, public works, and transportation. The work of the committees is done mostly by the subcommittees.[14]

In the House, there are fifty members on Appropriations. Each member of the committee sits on one or more of the thirteen subcommittees. The subcommittees hold open hearings that take testimony from agency leadership, economic advisors, and any others who are invited because budget proposals have some impact on groups that they represent. After these open hearings, the subcommittees hold closed meetings to determine recommendations. Then they report on appropriations bills to the full membership of Appropriations. These bills are rarely amended in any substantive way by the full committee. A bill is then reported to the full membership of the House. It is also unusual for the bill to be changed on the floor. Thus, the appropriations subcommitteees basically determine the appropriations bills that are eventually passed by the full House. The thirteen chairs of appropriations subcommittees are consequently among the most powerful members of Congress.

The Senate Appropriations Committee does not exert the same kind or degree of influence.[15] It has twenty-seven members, which is *relatively* larger than the House committee. As in the House, each of its members serves on subcommittees. In the House, however, there are twice as many members. House members can specialize in particular parts of the budget. In the Senate, members may serve on as many as eight subcommittees,

[13]See Randall B. Ripley and Grance A. Franklin, *Congress, the Bureaucracy, and Public Policy* (Homewood, Ill.: Dorsey Press, 1976), p. 78.

[14]A study in the early 1970s reported that 96 percent of appropriations meetings were subcommittee meetings. The full committee met to ratify decisions taken by subcommittees. See Richard Fenno, *Congressmen in Committees* (Boston: Little, Brown and Company, 1973), p. 95.

[15]This is less true than before the CBIC Act of 1974. Before 1974, the House committee took up appropriations first and then sent them to the Senate. Thus, the House focused on the proposed budget, while the Senate focused on the actions taken by the House. The executive tried to minimize cuts in the House and then restore funds in the Senate. The Senate Appropriations Committee became an "appeals level" in the appropriations process. After 1974, the House and Senate appropriations committees worked simultaneously rather than serially.

which does not permit the same degree of specialization. The hearing process is similar to that in the House. A major difference is that debate is unlimited in the Senate, and committee recommendations are often amended significantly on the floor.

What this means is that there is not a single omnibus appropriations bill. There are separate appropriations bills from each of the subcommittees of the appropriations committees. There are eleven major parallel appropriations bills acted on in House and Senate. These are the executive agency bills. These appropriations bills provide the level of financial support for executive agencies, and they may also include other controls. For example, they may write policy directives or program restrictions into an appropriations bill. The executive agency appropriations bills are (1) Agriculture; (2) Defense; (3) Foreign Aid; (4) Housing and Urban Development, Veterans' Administration, and National Aeronautics and Space Administration; (5) Interior; (6) Labor and Health, Education, and Welfare; (7) Military Construction; (8) Public Works and ERDA; (9) State, Justice, Commerce, and Judiciary; (10) Transportation; and (11) Treasury and Postal Service.

Identical parallel appropriations bills must be passed by both the House and the Senate before the bills are ready to send to the president for signature into law. If there are differences, a conference committee of House and Senate members tries to reach a compromise that will be supported by both bodies. When an appropriations bill passes on Capitol Hill, it is sent to the White House. The president can either sign the bill or veto the *entire* bill. There is no *item* veto that enables the president to sign into law only those parts of the bill that are consistent with executive priorities and preferences. The House and Senate may override the veto by a two-thirds vote in each chamber, but if the veto is sustained, the bill is referred back to their respective committees for review. This can be a very time-consuming process of negotiation between the president and Congress.

Entitlements

The distinction between the process of authorization and appropriations is blurred by *backdoor spending*. Backdoor spending provides spending authority without action by the appropriations committees. Two types of backdoor spending, *contract authority* and *borrowing authority,* were brought under the appropriations process by the CBIC Act. A third type, *entitlements,* was not. Entitlements are payments that the federal government is obligated to make when the legal requirements for receiving the payments are fulfilled. In other words, entitlements are open-ended guarantees of benefits to all qualified applicants. The outlays on an entitlement are thus determined by the size of the pool of eligible recipients. Examples of entitlements are unemployment compensation, welfare, food stamps, veterans' benefits, Medicare, and black lung victims' benefits. The payment levels are established by programmatic rules set forth in legislation and administrative regulations. These open-ended programs require annual appropriations, but the appropriations committees have no choice but to provide the required funds.

When the CBIC Act was being considered in Congress, the House wanted to require annual appropriations for entitlements, but the Senate wanted to apply this requirement only to new entitlement programs. The conference agreement adopted the Senate version. Programs with entitlement authority prior to the effective date of the CBIC Act were excepted from the provisions of Section 401, which dealt with bills providing new spending authority.

Ways and Means and Finance Committees

The House Ways and Means and Senate Finance committees have almost complete control of the revenue side of the budget. For this reason, they are sometimes called "tax-writing committees."[16] They are responsible for tax legislation and tax rates. Tax-cut legislation in 1964 and 1968 as well as the Economic Recovery Tax Act of 1981, which included a relatively large reduction of tax rates, were all taken up first by the Ways and Means and Finance Committees. The impact of their control is not limited to tax rates and the level of revenue. Taxation is also used to provide incentives and disincentives. So-called "tax expenditures" have grown rapidly because of actions taken by the two committees. Tax expenditures are losses of revenue caused by exclusions, exemptions, deductions, preferential tax rates, tax credits, or tax deferrals.[17]

The CBIC Act of 1974 attempted to improve coordination of taxing and spending in the budget system. The coordination is only at the highest level of aggregation on the tax side, however. Budget reform in the act was expenditure reform. There were substantial changes in the authorizations and appropriations process, but except for integration of total revenues into the budget resolutions, taxation and the revenue side are spared from the budget process. The new budget process had very little impact on the tax-writing committees.[18]

---

[16]However, the committees also have direct spending jurisdiction over some of the largest expenditure items in the budget. For example, social security, unemployment insurance, Medicaid, aid to dependent children, revenue sharing, and interest on debt are under their jurisdiction.

[17]See LeLoup, *Fiscal Congress,* pp. 127–28.

[18]There was reform in 1973 and 1974 that had impact on Ways and Means. It had nothing to do with the CBIC Act, however. The chair of the House Ways and Means Committee was Wilbur Mills. He had abolished subcommittees in the 1950s and refused to reinstate them. In 1973, the House Democratic caucus moved to require all committees with more than twenty members to be broken into at least four subcommittees. In 1974, the committee itself was enlarged from twenty-five to thirty-seven members and a fifth subcommittee was added. Mills resigned in December 1974 as the result of the Tidal Basin scandal and his admission of alcoholism. The committee had six subcommittees in the Ninety-sixth Congress.

The Procedures and Timetable
of Congressional Approval

The CBIC Act reformulated congressional budget action. New procedures and a new timetable for the congressional budget process were spelled out. The timetable of the new budget process is shown in Table 4-1. The process can be broken into four stages:

1. January 15 to April 15: Gathering information, analysis, and reporting the first concurrent resolution.
2. April 15 to May 15: Adopting the first resolution.
3. May 15 to September 14: Enacting the appropriations bills.
4. September 15 to October 1: Adopting the second concurrent resolution and reconciliation.

Each of the stages moves the process ahead on a schedule that should make a budget by the start of the fiscal year.[19]

Stage 1: Report the first concurrent resolution.   On or about January 15, the president submits the annual budget message to Congress. The House and Senate budget committees hold hearings soon after the message. Testimony is taken from a large number of government officials, members of Congress, experts outside government, leadership of interest groups, and other national organizations and members of the general public. For example, the director of OMB is certain to be scheduled to appear. The chair of the Council of Economic Advisors and the Secretary of the Treasury are also scheduled. The point of the hearings is to provide a forum for information and diverse opinion. In particular, the budget committees want testimony on the record regarding economic outlook, alternative fiscal policies, and budget priorities.

No later than March 15, the standing committees in the House and Senate are required to submit their "views and estimates" to their respective budget committees. These "views and estimates" are the standing committees' legislative and spending plans for the coming fiscal year. The intent is to have each standing committee estimate the amount of new budget authority and budget outlays resulting therefrom that it is likely to approve. This is guesswork. Even the chair of a committee may not have the foggiest idea of what action a committee will take on some programs. As a result, some chairs of committees prepare a simple list of "views and estimates" on a single typed page. Other committees conduct lengthy proceedings and then prepare a detailed report. The Joint Economic Committee (JEC) is also required to submit its views and estimates to both budget

---

[19]For an excellent discussion of the new budget process, see LeLoup, *Fiscal Congress,* pp. 26–32.

TABLE 4–1 Congressional Budget Process Timetable

ON OR BEFORE	ACTION TO BE COMPLETED
November 10	President submits *Current Services Budget.*
15th day after Congress meets	President submits his budget.
March 15	Committees and joint committees submit reports to budget committees.
April 1	Congressional Budget Office submits report to budget committees.
April 15	Budget committees report first concurrent resolution on the budget to their Houses.
May 15	Committees report bills and resolutions authorizing new budget authority.
May 15	Congress completes action on first concurrent resolution on the budget.
7th day after Labor Day	Congress completes action on bills and resolutions providing new budget authority and new spending authority.
September 15	Congress completes action on second required concurrent resolution on the budget.
September 25	Congress completes action on reconciliation bill or resolution, or both, implementing second required concurrent resolutions.
October 1	Fiscal year begins.

committees. In addition, the JEC submits its recommendations as to the fiscal policy appropriate to the goals of the Employment Act of 1946. Finally, the Joint Committee on Internal Revenue and Taxation is required to submit its views and estimates.

By April 1, CBO submits its annual report to the budget committees. The statutory requirements of the CBIC Act call for a report with respect to fiscal policy, including (1) alternative levels of total revenues, total new budget authority, and total outlays (including related surpluses and deficits) and (2) the levels of tax expenditures under existing law, taking into account projected economic conditions and any changes in such levels based on proposals in the budget submitted to the president. The report is also required to include a discussion of national budget priorities, including alternative ways of allocating budget authority and budget outlays among major programs or functional categories.

Based on testimony received in hearings, the views and estimates of standing congressional committees, the CBO report, and the president's budget request, each of the budget committees must report to its respective chamber the first concurrent resolution by April 15. The first resolution sets forth targets rather than binding ceilings for the budget. The language of the CBIC Act is "appropriate" level of total budget outlays and of total new budget authority. The budget target is then broken into targets for each major functional category. The first resolution also sets forth the recommended level of revenues, the appropriate amount of surplus or deficit in the budget, and the appropriate level of the public debt.[20]

Stage 2: Adopt the first concurrent resolution.   The full membership of the House and Senate consider the recommended first resolution that their respective budget committees have reported for action. The deadline for adoption is May 15, but the first resolution must be acted on much earlier to allow time for a conference committee to resolve any differences in the resolutions passed in the House and Senate.

May 15 is also the deadline for standing committees to report out *all* legislation that recommends new budget authority. Any such bill or resolution not reported by May 15 can be reported only by waiver. For example, in the House, the Committee on Rules must determine that emergency conditions require a waiver.[21] On the other hand, neither the House nor the Senate may *consider* any spending, revenue, debt, or entitlement legislation until *after* adoption of the first resolution. The figures agreed to in conference are targets for such legislation. There is a "joint explanatory statement" that accompanies a conference report on a concurrent resolution. It allocates spending targets among the standing committees of the House and Senate. This makes the bridge from functional totals to administrative jurisdiction. Finally, each appropriations committee subdivides the targets among its thirteen subcommittees. In this way, Congress takes an overview of the budget and agrees to figures that are nonbinding ceilings for the total budget, for functional categories of spending, and even for each of the thirteen appropriations bills reported by appropriations subcommittees.

Stage 3: Enact the appropriations bills.   After passage of the first resolution, the appropriation process proceeds as it has for some years. Ways and Means and Finance consider the revenue portions of the budget. Subcommittees of the appropriations committees consider specific appropriations bills. They schedule hearings and receive testimony. Executive agency heads appear to justify their programs and defend their budget requests. There are some differences since the CBIC Act. The subcommittees are expected to stay within the functional ceilings expressed in the first resolution. The budget committees are watchdogs. The ceilings of the first resolution are not binding, and a subcommittee may be lax in staying

---

[20]A report is required to accompany the first resolution. The report includes comparisons of (1) revenues estimated by the committee with those estimated in the budget submitted by the president and (2) appropriate levels of total budget outlays and total new budget authority as set forth in the first resolution with the budget request submitted by the president.

[21]The waiver provisions have been used extensively. For the period 1976–1978, 101 waivers were requested. Only 2 were not recommended favorably. See LeLoup, *The Fiscal Congress*, pp. 139–41.

within the figure agreed to. The budget committees try to see that legislation does not significantly exceed the targets. They have no formal powers to require observance, however, and depend on persuasion and influence for effect. CBO also serves a watchdog function. CBO issues frequent reports during the process. The "scorekeeping" reports compare spending actions with the targets of the first resolution.

Not later than the seventh day after Labor Day, Congress must complete action on all spending bills. In fact, the CBIC Act says that the appropriations committees should, "to the extent practicable," complete action on *all* regular appropriations bills before any one of them is brought to the floor for consideration. If the second concurrent resolution is timely, final action on the appropriations bills must be taken early in September.

Stage 4: Adopt the second concurrent resolution and reconciliation. By September 15, Congress is expected to complete action on the second concurrent resolution. This second resolution either reaffirms or revises the first resolution. If the second resolution revises the figures agreed to in the first resolution, then the second resolution may direct certain committees to amend bills under their jurisdiction by specific amounts. The reconciliation process calls for such committees to "determine and recommend changes to accomplish a change" of a specific amount. Recommendations are submitted to the budget committees. After receiving *all* such recommendations, the budget committees report to their respective bodies a reconciliation bill or resolution. The process of reconciliation, if needed or used, must be completed by September 25. The fiscal year starts only five days later, on October 1.

Congress may not adjourn *sine die* until action has been completed on the second resolution or a reconciliation bill, if needed. After passage, Congress may not consider any legislation that would exceed the approved totals. In this sense, the figures of the second resolution are binding. However, Congress is allowed to pass additional resolutions at any time.

The Track Record of the New Budget Process

Gerald Ford was the first president to submit a budget under provisions of the CBIC Act. His 1976 budget was submitted in January 1975. Implementation was not mandated until the following year, but Congress decided to have a trial run with the new procedures. The process was tried and, procedurally, made the grade. What effect, if any, it had on policy is unclear. President Ford's 1977 budget was submitted in January 1976. It was the first full implementation of provisions of the CBIC Act. All deadlines of the timetable applied. Most deadlines were met. The first resolution was adopted in time. All regular appropriations bills were passed by

October.[22] The second resolution was passed in September. However, it was not used to revise decisions made in the first resolution. The second resolution ratified decisions taken in May. Procedurally, it was a success. Not only was the timetable respected, but the budget committees worked reasonably well and CBO gave Congress a vital new source of economic data.

President Ford's 1978 budget was a lame duck. After his successor, President Carter, took office days after the budget was submitted, the budget committees moved to draw up a third resolution, which included spending and revenue measures that would have increased the amount of deficit. President Carter had proposed a fifty-dollar individual rebate and a jobs program. Later, he withdrew the rebate proposal. Congress did not revise its third proposal, however. These difficulties contributed to the first defeat of a budget resolution. When the first resolution on the 1978 budget came to a vote on April 27, it was defeated in the House, 320 to 84. A revised resolution finally passed the House on May 5, and a conference report passed on May 17. Signs of strain were beginning to show. They would spread. Still, only three regular appropriations bills were delayed beyond October 1, 1977.

In 1978, there was a serious debate in the House over the size of the budget and the amount of deficit. The conference report on the first resolution still passed by May 17, but only by 3 votes, however. The Senate continued to be more orderly and at least gave the appearance of being less partisan in deliberating over budget resolutions. Most regular appropriations bills were passed by October 1, 1978, and all were passed by mid-October.

By late 1979, the new process came under severe stress. The fiscal 1980 budget became the target of far-reaching political battles. Inflation had risen to an annual rate of 13 percent. President Carter and Congress clashed over budget priorities as "stagflation" became a topic of ordinary conversation throughout the country. Congress was more conservative politically and more assertive in its use of the new structure and procedures provided in the CBIC Act. In particular, CBO challenged OMB projections and assumptions. Congress preferred a comparatively restrictive budget, one that would reduce the deficit below the $30 billion figure submitted by the president.

In May 1979, the conference report on the first resolution was defeated in the House. A revised report was passed on May 24. The differences deepened in September. Fights had prolonged decisions, deadlines were broken, and deadlocks developed. For the first time since implementation of the new process, the fiscal year started without a congressional

---

[22]This was the first time since 1948 that all these regular appropriations bills were passed by the start of the fiscal year. During 1972–1975, none was passed by the start of the fiscal year.

budget. Also, for the first time, the reconciliation process was applied in the Senate. The budget was not approved until late November 1979, almost two months after the start of fiscal 1980. Only three appropriations bills had been enacted by October 1. The new process was suddenly producing results not much better than the old process.

In 1980, Congress was unable to pass any budget on time and applied the reconciliation process to the first budget resolution. No second resolution passed. President Carter and Congress could not agree on a budget, and the fiscal 1981 budget was not completed. The inauguration of President Reagan brought focus to the priority of budget reduction. This led to early budget victories. Then delay and deadlock developed. At the time that President Reagan was submitting his fiscal 1983 budget, there seemed to be a possibility of going through fiscal 1982 on temporary or continuing resolutions. Appropriations bills had not even been sent to him for his signature. A second budget resolution still had to be passed.

Some critics were not surprised by the breakdown of the budget process. They suggest that the CBIC Act did not really change the congressional structure. The four taxing and spending committees (ways and means, finance, and the appropriations committees) were left intact. The budget committees just added a new layer to the existing structure. Rather than streamlining the budget process, this had the effect of making the process more unwieldy. However, the critics do not necessarily argue for still another reform. They tend to say simply that structural reform alone will not solve problems rooted in deep divisions over spending levels, spending priorities, and political philosophy.[23]

BUDGET EXECUTION

The execution phase of the budget cycle begins with the start of a fiscal year.[24] Provided that Congress has passed appropriations legislation and the president has signed it into law before October 1, then funds are available for operation of agency programs. When Congress has not completed its work on time, it can pass a continuing resolution that allows agencies to spend at the previous year's level until regular appropriations legislation is passed and signed by the president. Even continuing resolutions must be signed by the president to become law. If neither appropriations bills nor continuing resolutions are passed by Congress and signed by the president prior to the start of a fiscal year, then technically the federal government comes to a screeching halt. This happened in November 1981 when Presi-

[23]See Norman J. Ornstein, "The Breakdown of the Budget Process," *The Wall Street Journal,* November 24, 1981, p. 22.

[24]For a description and an analysis of budget execution, see Lee and Johnson, *Public Budgeting Systems,* pp. 209–17.

dent Reagan refused to sign a continuing resolution and no appropriations bills had been signed into law.

Following congressional passage of an appropriations bill (or continuing resolution) and its signing by the president, agencies must submit a plan to OMB concerning how the funds will be spent. This is a proposed plan for apportioning expenditures over time. The plan indicates the funds that are required for operations. Ordinarily, funds are apportioned on a quarterly basis. OMB may revise the proposed plan before approving it. After OMB approval, the apportionment is allotted to the various units in an agency. The allotment process authorizes expenditures by unit. Each approved plan is forwarded by OMB to the Treasury so that the spending agency can make disbursement out of appropriate federal accounts.

There is more to execution than merely apportioning available funds. At times, an appropriation bill is highly specific with respect to certain object classes of expenditure—personnel, equipment, and travel, for example. There may be a narrative that describes the services that an agency is expected to provide or those it is prohibited from providing. Such specificity does not permit much discretionary power or control by the executive branch. Generally, there is considerable flexibility in the administration of executive agencies.

The president cannot approve apportionments for programs without appropriations or exceed amounts appropriated for specific items. On the negative side, the president does not have item veto. The president can veto an entire appropriations bill if there are funds in the bill for a program of which the president does not approve. If Congress overrides the veto, then the president is stuck with the problem of spending funds appropriated for a program that is disliked for some reason. The president might attempt what amounts to an indirect item veto by simply refusing to spend the funds appropriated for the program in disfavor. Such refusals are called *impoundments*. Impoundments have been highly controversial historically. Thomas Jefferson was evidently the first president to impound funds, and most presidents since Jefferson have also impounded funds. Almost always, Congress was angered, but President Nixon's unprecedented scale of impoundments caused such outrage that the practice was brought under control by the CBIC Act.

Impoundments

Neither the U.S. Constitution nor congressional enactments dealt with impoundment prior to 1974. Prior to the Nixon administration, presidents had used impoundment sparingly. When it was used, it was mainly to defer expenditures for one reason or other. President Nixon's impoundments greatly exceeded those of any of his predecessors. By 1973, estimates of the amount of funds that he had impounded ranged from $15 billion to $18 billion. More than a hundred federal programs were affected. Funds were withheld from highway, space, defense, health, air pollution, housing, and other programs.

President Nixon argued that the president has a constitutionally implied power to impound. He based his case on the constitutional requirement that the president faithfully execute the laws. Since the Constitution says that the president should "take care that the Laws be faithfully executed," he argued that there is an implied power to impound funds under certain economic conditions because of the president's responsibilities under the Employment Act of 1946. That act authorized the president "to avoid economic fluctuations . . . and to maintain employment, production, and purchasing power." The Nixon administration argument was that Congress had no means of coordinating revenue and spending legislation. Therefore, the president had responsibility for limiting expenditures or raising revenues when congressional actions would cause an intolerable rate of inflation.

President Nixon's critics argued that his decision to withhold funds amounted to an item veto and that he was simply preventing policies of which he did not approve from being implemented. Also, there was evidence that the Nixon administration was using impoundments as a way of forcing changes in policy. For example, many grant-in-aid programs to state and local governments were regarded as ineffective, and the administration favored replacing them with block grants in specific areas such as criminal justice and community development. Impoundment halted spending on the programs judged ineffective. Evidently, the strategy was that, by cutting off money, there would be mounting pressure on Congress to take up and approve block grant legislation.

The strategy outraged Congress and many state and local government officials. In 1973, the State of Missouri filed suit against the Secretary of Transportation to release impounded highway funds. In *Missouri* v.*Volpe*, the federal district court held that this particular impoundment was unlawful. This was the first of many court challenges. In other cases challenged, impoundments were also overturned and much of the money was released. The one case that reached the Supreme Court dealt with grants for sewers and sewage treatment plants. The Ford administration continued the impoundment originated by the Nixon administration. The Supreme Court decided that the president could not overturn the congressional decision that these funds were urgently needed. The urgency of the problem prohibited any such delay in spending. In effect, the courts ordered release of the funds. The courts did not decide whether the president has any constitutional power to impound funds.[25]

[25]See Lee and Johnson, *Public Budgeting Systems*, pp. 196–200.

Deferrals and Rescissions

Court challenges were not the only measures to rein in the president on impoundments. Congress wrote impoundment control into the budget reform legislation under consideration. Under provisions of Title X of the CBIC Act, a distinction is made between temporary actions (deferrals) and permanent actions (rescissions). Under the new law, when the president believes that part or all funds of a given appropriation are not needed to carry out the full objectives of its programs, the president can send a special message to Congress requesting a rescission of budget authority. The president can also request a rescission for fiscal policy or other reasons. The message required is lengthy. It must specify the amount of budget authority to be rescinded, the specific programs involved, the reasons why budget authority should be rescinded, the effect of the rescission on the budget and economy, and the effect of the rescission on the programs for which the budget authority is provided. The president's rescission request is automatically *rejected* unless Congress passes a bill to that effect within forty-five days. The process for deferral is similar. Whenever the president, the director of OMB, or the head of any department or agency proposes to defer any budget authority provided for a specific program, the president has to submit a special message to Congress that is similar to a rescission proposal. It must specify the amount of budget authority to be deferred, the specific program involved, the period of time during which the budget authority is to be deferred, reasons for the deferral, effects of the deferral on the budget and economy, and the effect of the deferral on the programs for which the budget authority is provided. The difference is that the president's deferral request is automatically *accepted* unless *either* the House *or* the senate passes a resolution disapproving the proposal.

Other components of impoundment control were powers given to the comptroller general of the United States, who heads the Government Accounting Office (GAO), an agency of Congress. First, the comptroller general was given power to file civil suit where the executive branch has withheld budget authority contrary to the provisions of the CBIC Act. Second, the comptroller general was given power to reclassify requests. If the comptroller general believes that what the president calls a deferral is really a rescission, the deferral request can be reclassified as a rescission by a report to both House and Senate setting forth reasons for the reclassification.

Impoundment control was intended to put a stop to President Nixon's substitution of his own spending priorities for those of Congress. Ironically, the provisions took effect after he had resigned. President Ford was the first to execute a budget under the impoundment controls. Disputes arose over interpretations of Title X of the CBIC Act and the procedures it established. For example, the comptroller general reclassified several deferrals as rescissions because there would have been insufficient time to spend the money once the deferrals expired.

The first suit brought under the act was *Staats* v. *Lynn,* filed in April 1975.[26] The suit involved what the Ford administration called a deferral of approximately $264 million for a low-income housing program (Section 235 housing) of the Housing and Community Development Act. The funds had been impounded originally by the Nixon administration, and the Ford administration tried to continue the impoundment by sending Congress a deferral request. However, the legislation was due to lapse on August 22, 1975, leaving only fifty-two days in which to obligate the money. Comptroller General Staats decided that this was a de facto rescission, not a deferral, and under the law he reported the "error" in a formal message to Congress. Congress had forty-five days in which to act or the money had to be spent. It did not act, and yet the president did not release the funds. The comptroller general notified Congress of his intention to bring a lawsuit. The Senate passed a resolution in support of the comptroller general's position. The Ford administration still refused to spend the money, arguing that the funds had been impounded under President Nixon and that Title X provisions were not retroactive. The administration also challenged the legality of a suit brought by the comptroller general against the executive branch. On October 17, 1975, before *Staats* v. *Lynn* was decided, Carla Hills announced that the Section 235 program would be reactivated and the funds would be released. The court case was dropped. Congress had won.

There were still other disputes during the Ford administration. But most of the procedural problems were settled by 1977, which marked the beginning of the Carter administration. There are some wrinkles that mar the smoothness of the procedures, however. For example, when Congress overrides a veto of an appropriations bill, the president can request a rescission. If Congress rejects that rescission, the president can request a deferral. If Congress rejects the referral, then a substitute deferral can be proposed. This could be a time-consuming process that never quite brings a conflict to closure.

BUDGET AUDIT

The final phase of the budget cycle is the budget audit.[27] The principal overriding purpose of this phase is to provide assurance of executive compliance with the provisions of appropriations bills. Auditors check the

[26]James T. Lynn was director of OMB. President Ford and Carla A. Hills, Secretary of Housing and Urban Development, were also defendants.

[27]For an excellent description of government accounting and auditing, see Thomas D. Lynch, *Public Budgeting in America* (Englewood Cliffs, N.J.: Prentice-Hall, Inc., 1979), pp. 167–208.

books maintained by an agency to check on the correct operation of the accounting system, including validating inventories and existing equipment, proper legal authority to perform an activity, and adequacy of internal control. For recent years, auditing has also included studies of program effectiveness.

Congress supervises appropriations and apportionments through the General Accounting Office, headed by the comptroller general. The GAO was established in 1921 by the Budget and Accounting Act. It was made answerable to Congress rather than to the president over the objections of President Woodrow Wilson. The justification was that an auditing office should be outside the executive branch. The comptroller general is appointed by the president, however, but only upon the advice and consent of the Senate. The appointment is for one term of fifteen years.

CONCLUSION

The federal budget process is a system that engages many units and interests in decision making. Reforms have attempted to improve decision making, particularly by enlarging on the amount and type of information available to and utilized by decision makers. Information must be interpreted, however, and budgetary information is interpreted inevitably by executive and legislative officials who operate from different political bases.

The CBIC Act of 1974 disturbed the balance of power between the executive and legislative branches, but one must be cautious in assessing shifts in power. CBO and the budget committees helped Congress to consider fiscal policy, but the president still has the capability to make fiscal policy. The president's budget has been sustained as the reference for congressional deliberations. While the CBIC Act enabled Congress to alter the president's budget, it is still the president's budget to which Congress is reacting. Reform has strengthened the ability of Congress to do its job in the budget process but not at the exclusion of presidential power.

5

Analysis of Government Policies

People of good faith can disagree on the extent to which expenditures should be used to provide for the goods and services that satisfy certain desires. In recent years, however, a major effort has been made with considerable success to bring modern techniques of management and economic analysis to bear on budget decisions. This is not to say that such techniques solve once and for all the problem of spending government revenues efficiently and wisely, but it has been found that such techniques can help in analyzing public spending policies.[1]

What such analysis attempts to do is to bring into proximity both the costs and benefits of alternative proposals to aid in the rationality of policy determination. Benefit-cost analysis, as it is usually called, is intended primarily to provide information. Second, benefit-cost analysis can help citizens and officials to see problems of choice properly in terms of alternatives and to identify choices that are preferred on the basis of a comprehensive picture of the benefits and costs of alternative proposals.

Actually, benefit-cost analysis has been used by the Army Corps of Engineers for over forty years, beginning with an evaluation of its river and harbor projects. The Flood Control Act of 1936 explicitly established the fundamental criterion for evaluating water resource projects: the benefits should exceed the costs. The 1936 act did not specify the methods for estimating benefits and costs, however, and the Army Corps of Engineers, the Bureau of Reclamation, the Soil Conservation Service, and the Tennessee Valley Authority all developed different criteria. In the 1950s, var-

---

[1]For a very readable study of policy analysis, see Robert L. Lineberry, *American Public Policy: What Government Does and What Difference It Makes* (New York: Harper & Row, Publishers, 1977), pp. 108–38.

ious attempts were made to standardize criteria for planning and evaluation. The attempts failed, either because the proposals had no official standing or because they were regarded as representing views too narrow for evaluating river development projects. In 1961, President Kennedy promised a review of standards and criteria for water resource investment. After a report to the Bureau of the Budget (BOB) by a panel of consultants and recommendations by an interagency committee, President Kennedy finally approved in 1962 a set of techniques for benefit-cost analysis to be used by all federal agencies and the BOB.

Since the early 1960s, the Bureau of the Budget (now the Office of Management and Budget), the National Bureau of Standards and most U.S. government agencies, various agencies of state and local governments, and others have explored possible uses of benefit-cost analysis and have found imaginative, practical applications. One of the major applications continues to be the comparison of natural resource policies, including proposals to reduce air and water pollution. But the applications now extend far beyond natural resources. Human investment policies, for example, are evaluated frequently with such analysis. In any event, the elements of the analysis are common: basically, the benefits and costs must be identified and measured, and some means of analyzing the benefits and costs must be developed so that alternatives can be evaluated in terms of preference.

MEASURING BENEFITS

At the heart of the analytical problem of measuring the benefits of public investment projects and of public services in general is the underlying problem of identifying and estimating output. To measure benefits sensibly, the output of a project or program must be identified, and the future quantity of output must be estimated and evaluated by appealing to market prices or to some alternative means of establishing the value of output. If output cannot be identified, if future amounts cannot be estimated, or if dollar value cannot be established, then there is a breakdown in the measurement of benefits for the purpose of comparison to costs. Even if the output of a project can be identified as readily as, for example, the electrical power produced by a dam, there are likely to be other less clearly identified outputs such as flood control as well as by-products such as recreational facilities. Although less specific and less marketable, these subsidiary and perhaps unintended outputs involve benefits nonetheless and should be measured and evaluated.

Suppose that the difficulties of identifying the outputs are solved. Then the future quantities of each of these outputs must be estimated somehow. Care must be taken here even where output is marketable so that physical capacity and future sales are not mistaken. Where output is marketed, it is sales of output, not the capacity, that is of interest. Future sales themselves are subject to uncertainty and may fall far short of capacity. Nonmarketed outputs are even more difficult to value into the future. Once outputs have been identified and projected, there still remains the price or valuation problem. With marketable outputs, the amount sold and the price charged may not be independent; with indirect or intangible outputs that are not marketed, benefits cannot even be priced except possibly implicitly. Therefore, measuring and evaluating the benefits of public projects and programs can be difficult indeed, and a clear understanding of the problems and conventional solutions is essential.

There are difficulties in measuring or even in defining the output of many governmental services. In some cases, these difficulties have the effect of making direct measures of the productivity of government output infeasible. Practical, if imperfect, analogues to such measures must be developed. If distinctions can be made between goods and services, one is that the output of goods is typically easier to measure than that of services. The reason seems clear. The output of goods usually is in the form of rather clearly identifiable physical units that can be counted easily. With services, the output may take the form of some highly abstract unit hardly amenable to either definition or measurement. "Crimes prevented" is an example of such a service provided by police.[2] Many goods provided by the various levels of government are "public goods." Recall from Chapter 2 that two or more persons *can* consume a public good without diminishing the quantity available to each other. There is no market or nonmarket algorithm for the efficient provision of such goods. Efficiency requires a system of multiple discriminatory prices based on each individual's marginal evaluation of output available for consumption. The problem is that an individual's "tax price" will increase if a high value on additional units of a public good is revealed. Consequently, there is an incentive to conceal true preferences for such incremental quantities. As the discussion in Chapters 2 and 3 demonstrated, it can be difficult or even impossible to determine what citizen preferences truly are, the value citizens truly put on quantities of output, and the level of output that is truly preferred by citizens.

Therefore, there is difficulty in measuring the amount of output a government program is producing and how much it is worth. The problem is information—actually the lack of it. A private business generally can measure its volume of output in physical units or, where this is not feasible, at least get information about the marginal revenue it would receive if it changed its level or "mix" of output. In either case, the market can pro-

---

[2]If fire protection is protection against fire, then what is police protection?

vide the firm with a value for its output. Governments, on the other hand, know only their expenditures on some programs. They may not know what they produced or what the quantity or the impact of the output was. Because of the public goods nature of many programs, even if governments did know what and how much they produced, they still would not be able to find out what the output was worth to citizens, their "customers."

Particularly where output is not marketed, estimation procedures must be developed that first account for output and then "price" it. In such cases, imputed or implicit prices may have to be estimated. Even in evaluating the output of a public project that is marketed, market prices may be inappropriate measures of its worth and need "correcting." Estimated and corrected prices are called "shadow prices."

There are two important cases of correcting market prices. The first case is where output is marketed at a price below the market level. Revenue from the sale of the output would understate its value. Irrigation water is an intermediate good used in the production of some crops. If the water is available to farmers at a price below the market level, then revenue from the sales of irrigation water would understate the value of its benefits. The market price that farmers would be willing to pay should be estimated in "pricing" the irrigation water.

Two points should be noted in connection with such use of corrected market prices. One is that there should be evidence that the *uncorrected* prices are not clearing the market. In other words, if prices are alleged to be below market levels, then there should be some evidence of market shortages or of nonmarket rationing such as licenses, maximum amounts for use, or other regulations intended to allocate output on some basis other than price. The second problem involves the avoidance of double counting. In estimating the value of benefits of water to farmers, it would be inconsistent to use the higher shadow price for estimating the value of a dam's output *and* as the basis for estimating the farmers' additional net income or profits. This would be double counting because the added profits already have been included among the benefits when the higher shadow price is used to evaluate the output "more appropriately."

A second case where market prices may need "correcting" involves externalities, which were discussed in Chapter 2. There may be significant by-products associated with marketed output. These effects on others may either impose costs or confer benefits. The ecology may be damaged. New, otherwise infeasible, recreational uses may be realized. Such costs and benefits would not necessarily be reflected in market prices. Corrections to market prices themselves might be estimated, or the external costs and benefits might be estimated independently. In the latter case, the estimates would be subtracted from or added to the uncorrected market value of output.

MEASURING COSTS

In the strictest sense, the cost of a given public project is its opportunity cost, that is, the value of the resources in their best alternative uses. Generally, *market prices* for services and materials are used to estimate costs in this sense, but the limits to relying on market prices for estimation of benefits and outputs are equally applicable when measuring costs. Where there is doubt about the applicability of market prices for factors or where they are not readily available, then *corrective* or *imputed shadow prices* might have to be used.

One major issue regarding costs that need "correcting" involves the question of unemployment. Suppose that a project makes use of labor that otherwise would be unemployed. Whatever compensation is paid for the services of such resources would be above their value in idleness, which is their alternative "use." Should compensation be corrected and shadow prices substituted for market prices under this condition? Should costs be estimated below actual wages and other payments? Generally, they are not. The reasons are many, but, mainly it is because the resources are assumed to be idle temporarily rather than permanently. The alternative to working on the project is assumed to be employment in the private sector as the result of stimulative fiscal and monetary policies that expand aggregate demand for output. As long as full employment is a national goal and as long as the goal is roughly approximated by public policy, then it seems reasonable to rely on market prices rather than on shadow prices.

Shadow prices must be estimated for some inputs, particularly where market prices are not available and where, therefore, the sum of market prices might not truly reflect opportunity costs. Suppose that a project makes use of capital that some level of government claims is no longer required for public use. Such examples abound in work force and health care projects where facilities are provided free of rental charges to the sponsoring agency. Should the imputed rental cost of facilities be included among the costs of the project, even though it is claimed that the facilities would be idle otherwise? Generally, the market price of the use of the facilities is estimated. The imputed rent is included among the project's costs because, even though no rent is exacted, use of the facility is not "free." If not required for public use, the facilities might be leased or sold to private firms.

A project may involve costs not incurred internally but, from society's point of view, are costs nonetheless. The Cross-Florida Barge Canal would have imposed heavy ecological damage. Several species of wildlife would have been endangered because their natural habitats, including delicately balanced patterns of water and plant life necessary to mating and propagation, would have been jeopardized. These are intangible costs essentially external to the project itself. From the view of society, they represent a loss, perhaps irreversible and irreparable. The environment—the air, the water, the peace and quiet, the wonders of nature—is a resource. Like labor, capital, and natural resources, the environment is scarce and has alternative uses. When land along the Mississippi Gulf Coast is used for construction of Interstate 10, then it cannot be used as breeding grounds for the sandhill crane, an endangered wildlife species. Completing interstate construction in that area has an opportunity cost, therefore. One of the costs of I-10 is the possible loss of the sandhill crane. Completion of the Cross-Florida Barge Canal has opportunity costs in the same sense. The intangible nature of such costs makes them difficult to measure and, in some cases, even to identify. Yet, socially, it is important to include estimates of such costs.

BENEFIT-COST ANALYSIS

After the benefits and costs of potential, and perhaps competing, public investment projects are identified and estimated in terms of dollars, the projects may be analyzed in those terms. The analysis itself requires close attention to and application of certain models that facilitate comparison and information prior to decision making. Because of the element of time, however, the benefits and costs must be *discounted*. Also, because there is more than one way of comparing the costs and benefit of projects, there is more than one analytical model.

Discounting

Suppose that the benefits and costs of a given public undertaking accrue and are incurred over a number of years but that they can be disaggregated into discrete years. In Table 5-1, the dollar benefits and dollar costs of a public investment project are shown in columns 1 and 2, respectively. In the example, the project requires a period of five years for completion of construction, so that no benefits are expected to accrue until the sixth year. After the $35 million cost of construction incurred in the first five-year period, operating costs of $3 million annually are incurred over the life of the project, which is twenty years. The net benefits—benefits (column 1) minus costs (column 2)—are shown in column 3, so that over the life of the undertaking, the net benefits total $55 million. These net dollar benefits are *undiscounted,* however, and it is their *present value* that is critical to analysis.

Even without the specter of inflation, a future dollar is worth less than a present dollar because a present dollar can be deposited in, say, a savings and loan institution and earn interest. In the same way, future net dollar benefits are worth less than present net dollar benefits. The real re-

TABLE 5-1 Calculation of Present Value of Net Benefits
(in millions of dollars)

YEAR	(1) ANNUAL BENEFITS ($)	(2) ANNUAL COSTS ($)	(3) BENEFITS MINUS COSTS ($)	(4) DISCOUNT EXPRESSION	(5) DISCOUNT FACTOR ($i = 0.06$)	(6) PRESENT VALUE ($)
1	0	3	−3	$1/(1+i)$	0.943	−2.829
2	0	7	−7	$1/(1+i)^2$	0.890	−6.230
3	0	10	−10	$1/(1+i)^3$	0.840	−8.400
4	0	10	−10	$1/(1+i)^4$	0.792	−7.920
5	0	5	−5	$1/(1+i)^5$	0.747	−3.735
6	5	3	+2	$1/(1+i)^6$	0.705	1.410
7	7	3	+4	$1/(1+i)^7$	0.665	2.660
8	9	3	+6	$1/(1+i)^8$	0.627	3.762
9	10	3	+7	$1/(1+i)^9$	0.592	4.144
10	12	3	+9	$1/(1+i)^{10}$	0.558	5.022
11	12	3	+9	$1/(1+i)^{11}$	0.527	4.743
12	12	3	+9	$1/(1+i)^{12}$	0.497	4.473
13	12	3	+9	$1/(1+i)^{13}$	0.469	4.221
14	11	3	+8	$1/(1+i)^{14}$	0.442	3.536
15	10	3	+7	$1/(1+i)^{15}$	0.417	2.919
16	9	3	+6	$1/(1+i)^{16}$	0.394	2.364
17	8	3	+5	$1/(1+i)^{17}$	0.371	1.855
18	7	3	+4	$1/(1+i)^{18}$	0.350	1.400
19	6	3	+3	$1/(1+i)^{19}$	0.331	0.993
20	5	3	+2	$1/(1+i)^{20}$	0.312	0.624
Totals	135	80	55	—	—	15.012

sources presently available may be invested in different ways that increase the goods, services, or real resources available at various times in the future. Discounting is needed to reduce such future values to current values for the purpose of comparing and analyzing the investment of resources in alternative uses.

Suppose that a high school student were given a $1,000 gift for college four years hence. If the gift were deposited in an institution paying a 6 percent rate of interest annually, the gift would be worth $1,000 plus $60, which is $1,000 times $(1+0.06)$, by the end of the year. If the $1,060 were left deposited, it would be worth $1,123.60, which is $1,000 times $(1+0.06)^2$, by the end of the sophomore year. If the $1,123.60 were left deposited, it would be worth $1,191.02, which is $1,000 times $(1+0.06)^3$, by the end of the junior year, and if the $1,191.02 were left deposited, the student would have $1,262.48, which is $1,000 times $(1+0.06)^4$, by graduation and in time for college. The original gift has earned interest at a compound rate because both principal and interest have been left deposited.

Suppose, on the other hand, that a student given the $1,000 gift chose to deposit now only enough of the gift so as to have $1,000 at the time of entering college. How much would the student have to deposit? This is a problem of *discounting* because the question is, how much is $1,000 to be paid four years from now worth today. First, what is $1,060 to be paid in one year worth today? How much would have to be deposited today in order to be worth $1,060 in one year? These are different expressions of the same question. The answer is known from above—$1,000—but how is it arrived at? The answer is, *dividing* by the discount factor $(1+0.06)$, so that $1,060/(1+0.06)$ is $1,000. The sum of $1,060 also can be *multiplied* by $1/(1+0.06)$. Now, what about $1,123.60 to be paid in two years? Dividing by $(1+0.06)^2$ or multiplying by $1/(1+0.06)^2$, the answer again is $1,000. The supposition, however, is that the student wants to know how much must be deposited now in order to still have $1,000 by the time of graduation and college, and the answer is $1,000 *divided* by $(1+0.06)^4$, which is $792.09. The same answer can be arrived at by *multiplying* $1,000 by 0.7920937, which is $1/(1+0.06)^4$. Thus, in this case, $1,000 four years in the future is worth $792.09 today, because $792.09 can be invested now, and, at a 6 percent rate of interest, it will be worth $1,000 in four years. The $1,000 has been discounted to the present, and its present value is $792.09.

Similarly, benefits that accrue and costs that are incurred in the future are discounted to the present to determine their present value. Columns 4 and 5 are used to discount the net dollar benefits in column 3. In column 4, the discount expression is given for each year, and in column 5, the 6 percent discount factor is solved for each year. By multiplying the discount factor times the net dollar benefits, each year's benefits and costs are discounted to the present, and the present value of the net benefits of a given public project can be determined. Annual present values are shown in column 6. Thus, the undiscounted net benefits of $55 million shown in column 3 are worth only \$15.012 million in present value. The present value of net benefits is, therefore, the summation of a series of annual net benefits discounted to the present.

$$\text{Present value} = \frac{(B-C)_1}{(1+i)} + \frac{(B-C)_2}{(1+i)^2} + \cdots + \frac{(B-C)_n}{(B-C)^n} = \sum_{y=1}^{n} \frac{(B-C)_y}{(1+i)^y}$$

for a project of n years.

It is important to note that a discount rate higher than 6 percent will involve a greater discount factor in column 5 and that the present value of net benefits will be reduced. As a matter of fact, if a sufficiently high discount rate is used, the present value of *net* benefits will become negative, because an increase in the discount rate has a greater effect on more distant discount factors. This raises the question of what discount rate to use in estimating present values.

One alternative is to rely on *private rates of return* established in competitive capital markets. The objective would be to use the rate of interest that reflects consumer choice between present and future consumption and that reflects the opportunity cost of withdrawing resources from the private sector, given the actual dollar cost involved. The problem is that there is no single rate of interest established in capital markets that can be used confidently as the appropriate discount rate.

A second alternative is most commonly used. This is the use of a *social rate of discount,* a sort of shadow price approach to the question of the appropriate discount rate. Because of the difficulties of determining *the* private rate, a practical approach is used to settle on *a* rate that approximates the social rate of time preference. Generally, this rate is the yield on long-term federal government securities. Not only is this rate the government's cost of borrowing, it also is regarded as the best indicator of time preference of individuals for current versus future income. A *higher* rate would *reject* some projects the public prefers because the discounted benefits exceed discounted costs; a *lower* rate would *accept* projects the public values less than current alternative uses of required resources.

Ranking

In any given year, there may be many projects for which the present value of net benefits is positive and even sizably positive. This indicates that, given the estimate of net benefits and the discount rate, these projects use resources to generate future benefits that are greater than the current value of these resources. This does not indicate, however, that each and every project for which the present value of net benefits is positive should be or can be undertaken. In the first place, many of them may be competitive and mutually exclusive. For example, several may be proposals for hydroelectric plants of various capacities at the same site or for water pollution treatment facilities located at various locations along a given stream or for various work force retraining programs to aid in the employment of a given group of idle workers. Second, government or a government agency faces budget constraints. Even if the present value of net benefits is positive, it may not be possible to fund all projects.

For these reasons, some means of *ranking* projects must be developed. Basically, there are three means commonly used for ranking and decision making: (1) the present value of net benefits, (2) the benefit-cost ratio, and (3) the rate of return.

Present value of net benefits. This means of evaluating projects has been discussed in some detail and illustrated in Table 5–1. For the purpose of ranking projects, however, three examples of projects are illustrated in Table 5–2. To simplify the examples, in each case the only costs

TABLE 5-2   Calculation of the Present Value of Net Benefits for Three Projects

I

YEAR	(1) BENEFITS	(2) COSTS	(3) NET BENEFITS	(4) PRESENT VALUE OF NET BENEFITS ($i=0.06$)
1	$ 0	$25,009,228	−$25,009,228	−$23,593,611
2	11,000,000	0	11,000,000	9,789,960
3	9,000,000	0	9,000,000	7,556,673
4	6,000,000	0	6,000,000	4,752,562
5	2,000,000	0	2,000,000	1,494,516
Totals	$28,000,000	$25,009,228	$ 2,990,772	$ 0

II

YEAR	(1)	(2)	(3)	(4)
1	$ 0	$49,964,164	−$49,964,164	−$47,136,002
2	28,000,000	0	28,000,000	24,919,899
3	14,000,000	0	14,000,000	11,754,668
4	9,000,000	0	9,000,000	7,128,843
5	7,000,000	0	7,000,000	5,230,807
Totals	$58,000,000	$49,964,164	$ 8,035,836	$ 1,898,215

III

YEAR	(1)	(2)	(3)	(4)
1	$ 0	$91,943,348	−$99,943,348	−$94,286,174
2	31,000,000	0	31,000,000	27,589,888
3	39,000,000	0	39,000,000	32,745,148
4	40,000,000	0	40,000,000	31,683,748
5	13,000,000	0	13,000,000	9,714,356
Totals	$123,000,000	$91,943,348	$23,056,652	$ 7,446,966

are, say, construction costs incurred in the first year, during which there are no benefits. Thereafter, there are no operating costs, and the benefits are exhausted in the fifth year. Using a discount rate of 6 percent, the present value of net benefits is, respectively, (I) $0, (II) $1,898,215, and (III) $7,446,966. First, this ranking method rejects projects having a negative present value of net benefits, so that project I is at the margin of being rejected outright. Second, it ranks projects from the highest present values of net benefits to the lowest, so that, as long as funding permits, project III is preferred to project II.

Benefit-cost ratio.   The benefit-cost ratio is a much-used means of evaluating and ranking projects. It is similar to the present value of net benefits. Rather than dealing with net benefits, it expresses the present value of benefits as a ratio to the present value of costs. The same three examples of projects are shown in Table 5–3. Again using a 6 percent discount rate, the present value of benefits is given in column 2 and of costs in column 4. The ratio of benefits—the sum of column 2—to costs—the sum of column 4—is shown in column 5. The benefit-cost ratio for each of the three projects is, respectively, (I) 1:1, (II) 1.04:1, and (III) 1.08:1. This means of evaluation rejects any project having a benefit-cost ratio of less than one to one, because the present value of benefits would be less than the present value of costs. Project I is again at the margin of rejection. Also, it ranks projects from the highest benefit-cost ratio to the lowest. Accordingly, project III would be ranked higher, funds permitting, than would project II.

Rate of return.   The rate of return is also used as a means of evaluating and ranking projects. Instead of taking a discount rate as given, the rate-of-return approach in effect *solves* for the rate of discount. The internal rate of return, as it is sometimes called, is the rate of discount that is required to make the present value of net benefits equal to zero. Recall the present value of net benefits: the present value of net benefits is based on a *given* discount rate that appears in the denominator of the discount expression—as in column 4 of Table 5–1—and that *determines* the discount factor—as in column 5 of Table 5–1. Thus, the discount rate must be known or chosen *before* it can be substituted in the denominator of the discount expression for the purpose of determining the discount factor. What the rate-of-return approach does is to *solve* for the rate in the denominator by setting the present value of net benefits equal to zero. Basically, this procedure compares the internal rate of return with the social discount rate. The same three projects used in the examples above are again shown in Table 5–4. The net benefits are shown in column 3 as they were in Table 5–1. The internal rates of return that equate the sum total of column 4 to zero have been solved for, and the discount factor, r, based on the solution

TABLE 5–3   Calculation of the Benefit-Cost Ratio for Three Projects

I

YEAR	(1) BENEFITS	(2) PRESENT VALUE OF BENEFITS ($i = 0.06$)	(3) COSTS	(4) PRESENT VALUE OF COSTS ($i = 0.06$)	(5) BENEFIT- COST RATIO
1	$ 0	$ 0	$25,009,228	$23,593,611	—
2	11,000,000	9,789,960	0	0	—
3	9,000,000	7,556,573	0	0	—
4	6,000,000	4,752,562	0	0	—
5	2,000,000	1,494,516	0	0	—
Totals	$ 28,000,000	$ 23,593,611	$25,009,228	$23,593,611	1:1

II

YEAR	(1)	(2)	(3)	(4)	(5)
1	$ 0	$ 0	$49,964,164	$47,136,002	—
2	28,000,000	24,919,899	0	0	—
3	14,000,000	11,754,668	0	0	—
4	9,000,000	7,128,843	0	0	—
5	7,000,000	5,230,807	0	0	—
Totals	$ 58,000,000	$49,034,217	$49,964,164	$47,136,002	1.04:1

III

YEAR	(1)	(2)	(3)	(4)	(5)
1	$ 0	$ 0	$99,943,348	$94,286,174	—
2	31,000,000	27,589,888	0	0	—
3	39,000,000	32,745,148	0	0	—
4	40,000,000	31,683,748	0	0	—
5	13,000,000	9,714,356	0	0	—
Totals	$123,000,000	$101,733,140	$99,943,348	$94,286,174	1.08:1

is shown in column 4. The rates of return for each project are, respectively, (I) 6 percent, (II) 8.3 percent, and (III) 9.7 percent. This means of evaluation rejects any project having a rate of return less than the social rate of discount. If the social rate of discount is 6 percent, then project I is again at the margin of rejection. It ranks projects from the highest rates of return to the lowest, so that project III would be preferred to project II.

Some Questions About Benefit-Cost Analysis

The principles outlined for benefit-cost analysis leave a number of questions unanswered. Why are three means of evaluating and ranking projects needed? What about the possibility of obsolescence, technological innovation, and all the other vagaries of the future? What about inflation? What about the distributional and redistributional effects of such programs?

TABLE 5-4   Calculation of the Rate of Return of Three Projects

I

YEAR	(1) BENEFITS	(2) COSTS	(3) NET BENEFITS	(4) PRESENT VALUE OF NET BENEFITS ($r=0.06$)
1	$ 0	$25,009,228	− $25,009,228	− $23,593,611
2	11,000,000	0	11,000,000	9,789,960
3	9,000,000	0	9,000,000	7,556,573
4	6,000,000	0	6,000,000	4,752,562
5	2,000,000	0	2,000,000	1,494,516
Totals	$ 28,000,000	$25,009,228	$ 2,990,772	$ 0

II

YEAR	(1)	(2)	(3)	(4) ($r=0.083$)
1	$ 0	$49,964,164	− $49,964,164	− $46,134,960
2	28,000,000	0	28,000,000	23,872,674
3	14,000,000	0	14,000,000	11,021,550
4	9,000,000	0	9,000,000	6,542,273
5	7,000,000	0	7,000,000	4,698,463
Totals	$ 58,000,000	$49,964,164	$ 8,035,836	$ 0

III

YEAR	(1)	(2)	(3)	(4) ($r=0.097$)
1	$ 0	$99,943,348	− $99,943,348	− $91,106,060
2	31,000,000	0	31,000,000	25,760,151
3	39,000,000	0	39,000,000	29,542,328
4	40,000,000	0	40,000,000	27,620,625
5	13,000,000	0	13,000,000	8,182,956
Totals	$123,000,000	$99,943,348	$23,056,652	$ 0

First, for almost all projects, any one of these means can be used for evaluation and ranking. Contradictory results are not the general case. Peculiar patterns of benefits and costs over time can lead to ranking problems, however. In some unusual cases, the results depend on which means is used. There are some rules of thumb. If the budget constraint sets a level of expenditure and if there is no problem of mutual exclusivity or replicability, the benefit-cost ratio is the best means of ranking because it chooses projects that maximize the present value of benefits for that level of investment. If projects are mutually exclusive, the present value of net benefits is best because it chooses the project that maximizes the dollars of present value. Finally, if the project's output is marketable and if the net revenue can be reinvested, then the rate of return seems best. Given that the net revenue can be reinvested at the same rate of return, the rate-of-return method chooses projects for which the net benefits over time will have the maximum feasible present value.

Second, the vagaries of the future make private and public decision making difficult, and decision making based on benefit-cost analysis is no exception. Basically, the only answer to the questions raised by the threat of obsolescence or the promise that technological advances may lower costs is that the consequences of action or inaction must be weighted carefully. If immediate action is regarded as necessary, then threats and promises must be ignored. If immediate action is not regarded as necessary, then waiting until some of the questions regarding the future are resolved may be prudent.

Third, the answer to the question regarding inflation is simple: analysis generally assumes that there will not be any and uses current prices. There is good reason for this practice. Inflation would affect not only the estimate of costs and benefits but also the yield on long-term government securities and, thereby, the social discount rate. Inflation exaggerates future benefits in comparison with costs concentrated principally in the present, but a real discount rate that reflects the impact of inflation would tend to bring the comparison back into line. It should be noted that the yield on long-term government securities reflects expectations of inflation.

Finally, the question of equity is most difficult. Suppose that the benefits are concentrated on one group and the costs on another, or that the benefits are concentrated on one group and the costs dispersed over an entire population. Suppose that irrigation projects are being ranked and that a project is chosen that increases the income of fruit growers in California over a project that would have increased the income of sugar cane growers in Louisiana. Suppose that a small dam that provides flood control for expensive vacation homes in Colorado is chosen over a program of building basketball courts and providing coaching and supervision in the nation's inner cities. In each case, a question of equity is involved, but should distributional weights be used to account somehow for the social justice of choices made on the basis of benefit-cost analysis? If so, there is a monumental problem in specifying the system of weights. Benefit-cost studies are generally limited to allocational and efficiency considerations. The problem of choosing among projects that have differential impacts on income groups, occupation groups, and geographic areas is left to political decision makers. After all, benefit-cost studies are a means of providing information for decisions; they are not decisions themselves.

Benefit-Cost Analysis of Human Capital Investment

As mentioned earlier, benefit-cost analysis had its nascence in evaluation of physical capital projects. In recent years, however, its applications have extended to human capital investments. These extensions require some elaboration.

Investment is anything that accumulates capital, and capital is a stock of assets that yields a stream of income over time. An investment need not be a new factory, a new dam, a new bridge. It can be education or health, each of which involves an expenditure undertaken with the expectation of a higher return of net income in the future. For education, the expenditure is both direct—tuition, fees, taxes, costs of supplies—and indirect—income forgone because the student is in school rather than at work. Job training and retraining programs such as the Job Corps and the Manpower Development and Training Act were intended primarily to increase the life-time earning power of participants. They are examples of investment in human capital. As such, they can be evaluated by benefit-cost analysis.

Generally, the main benefits of investments in human capital are measured by estimates of additional future earnings discounted to the present. There may be other benefits, however. Graduates may contribute to productivity increases for others. For example, a "paraprofessional" such as a physician's aide may increase the productivity of the physician. Such benefits would need estimating in addition to the primary benefits. Cost estimation is fairly straightfoward. Agency costs are the sum of instructional and other expenses. More important, in some cases, is that trainees forgo income while they are enrolled. Costs are also discounted, and usually such programs as these are evaluated in terms of benefit-cost ratios.

Incommensurate and Nonquantifiable Factors

It must be recognized that benefit-cost analysis is not a cure-all for what ails the public sector. The analysis does not proceed briskly in lock step to objective, scientific decisions based on dispassionate measurements. In the end, benefit-cost analysis involves subjective judgments that are the grist of the decision-making mills. In making decisions, of course, the decision maker should try to consider all the gains and all the sacrifices that are involved. In this regard, the promise of benefit-cost analysis is bounded, but not so much because some gains and sacrifices are economic and others noneconomic. People value beauty, peace and quiet, music, grace, truth, purity, and countless other activities and qualities that we do not think of as being economic. However, benefit-cost analysis is limited by the existence of incommensurate effects that, while quantifiable, cannot be expressed in terms of a common denominator and by effects that simply defy quantification. An example of the former might be evidence that a programmed learning system adds to scores on achievement tests but that it also involves so much pressure on students that it tends to lead to a variety of psychosomatic disorders requiring medical treatment. An example of the latter might be the impact of a proposal on racial harmony or on protection of civil liberties.

Judgments about incommensurate and nonquantifiable factors must be made. Such efforts may be described, but they cannot be reduced to a common denominator. The difficulties here are not *caused* by benefit-cost analysis, however. The problems and difficulties that life poses for us simply mean that citizens and officials must be discriminating in deciding when and how to use certain tools of analysis. In this regard, it seems safe to conclude that benefit-cost analysis is most appropriate to and useful in decision making when narrow problems of choice are under consideration. In other words, benefit-cost analysis is most valuable when the alternatives under consideration are very close substitutes.

PLANNING-PROGRAMMING-BUDGETING SYSTEM

There has been periodic interest in applying benefit-cost analysis systematically to federal, state, and local government programs. At first, the analysis was in terms of cost-effectiveness, searching for the least costly means of accomplishing a given objective. Former Secretary of Defense Robert McNamara's "whiz kids," a group of highly skilled economists and statisticians, pioneered cost-effectiveness studies of national defense objectives. President Lyndon Johnson was so impressed with this kind of analysis that, in 1965, he ordered it applied to programs in all federal executive agencies in the form of a Planning-Programming-Budgeting System (PPBS). Basically, PPBS is analysis of public sector expenditures requiring definition of objectives, consideration of alternatives, analysis of benefits and costs of each alternative, and use of the analysis in decision making. The idea was a noble one: make decision making less partisan, less political, and more rational.

The Bureau of the Budget, which is now the Office of Management and Budget (OMB), was made responsible for implementing PPBS. As it was institutionalized, PPBS consisted of four elements. First, an agency's *program structure* was developed that would group expenditures by objective or purpose. This was required to establish the nexus between inputs and outputs and to see more clearly where money was going in terms of what was being purchased. Second, *program memoranda* were requested by BOB (1) to get an agency responsible for a program to review, reconsider, and possibly redefine the objectives of the program; (2) to state the alternative means of satisfying the objectives; and (3) to estimate roughly the benefits and costs of each alternative. Third, a *program and financial plan* was developed that showed past expenditures for each program administered by an agency, the current year's budget, and estimates of future expenditures made necessary by current and past commitments. Also, the plan showed physical and, in some cases, dollar measures of the output of each program. As such, the plan was a fairly comprehensive accounting of the programs of an agency. Finally, *analytical studies* were used to expand upon the program memoranda in terms of policy issues on which action was likely to be taken. Essentially, the analytical studies were intended to evaluate alternative policies based on program memoranda of various agencies.

The Conflict with "Muddling Through"

The problem-solving approach of PPBS emphasizes analytical criteria, particularly efficiency and effectiveness. It promotes examination of a wide range of alternatives and stresses long-run planning. In so doing, PPBS impinges directly on political processes that emphasize such criteria as consensus. Critics argue that PPBS is unrealistic because decision making in the political process is not suited to the problem-solving approach. Also, they argue, PPBS is excessive in its emphasis on efficiency while ignoring the importance of achieving consensus through adjustment and resolution of conflicting values. In requiring an explicit statement of objectives or goals, the critics point out, PPBS serves to intensify unproductive ideological debate. Basically, the proponents of "muddling through" advocate a decision-making process that minimizes debate about values, relies on advocacy as a means of reaching agreement, and focuses on incremental changes.[3]

Those who find merit in muddling through point out that a particular policy or given legislation can become hopelessly bogged down if agreement must be secured on objectives. Such disputes block agreement among diverse interests on specific measures. Successful politics cultivates agreement among individuals or groups who hold quite divergent and even conflicting ends. Effective political leadership shapes policies and legislation so that such measures are supported by groups with different goals in view. If all parties with an interest in a bill had to agree on objectives, then some support for it may be lost and the bill may be defeated.

The proponents of muddling through cherish the tradition of the advocacy process in a democratic system. They fear that advocacy will not be protected by PPBS. While the PPBS process cannot possibly ascertain the impact on all the various groups in society, the advocacy system can, they claim. There is merit in lobbying, it seems, because advocates of every interest can present what they believe to be the relationship between a policy or legislative bill and their interests. In this way, advocates of affected interests have a voice in decision making, and widely different val-

[3]These criticisms are suggested by the work of Charles E. Lindblom. See Charles E. Lindblom, "The Science of 'Muddling Through,'" *Public Administration Review*, 19 (Spring 1959), 79–88; David Braybrooke and Charles Lindblom, *A Strategy of Decision: Policy Evaluation as a Social Process* (New York: Macmillan Publishing Co., Inc., 1963); and Charles Lindblom, *The Intelligence of Democracy* (New York: Macmillan Publishing Co., Inc., 1965).

ues are reconciled by pragmatic agreement on particular means rather than by ideological agreement on specified ends.

According to this approach to policy making, therefore, a good decision is one that enjoys consensus among divergent interests and values. A good decision may not satisfy the criteria of efficiency or effectiveness. Progress toward good decisions is made by trial and error. In other words, good decisions came through successive, *incremental* approximations. Political incrementalism suggests that we should avoid radical actions because they lie beyond our foresight. Progress comes in sequential steps along a route not planned in advance but corrected and adjusted along the way.

Defenders of PPBS accept the point raised by the political approach: if PPBS survives, it must be compatible with and integrated into the political process. Basically, use of PPBS must take political process constraints into account. Otherwise, its effectiveness may be minimal. The hope among defenders is that PPBS can improve the political process. It certainly introduces a new participant—the PPBS analyst—into the decision-making process. In essence, these new participants are partisan advocates for efficiency interests, championing effectiveness criteria in policy making. If PPBS genuinely fits into the political process, it can be an effective element in the system of advocacy.[4]

Incremental versus Zero-Base Budgeting

PPBS is intended as a means of analyzing and planning budgetary allocations. As an element in the decision structure and process governing budgets, PPBS may come into conflict with the traditional budgetary practices based on incrementalism. Incremental budgeting is the tried and true system that protects an agency's budgetary base and more or less guarantees it a certain share of any increase in the budget.

An agency's base is the sum of programs it has operated over a relatively long period of time. Over time, an agency's base generally increases because the number of "customers" it serves tends to increase and the cost of serving each "customer" also tends to rise. Even if an agency undertakes no new programs, its budget will tend to increase as the result of these factors. The nature of a budgetary base of programs is that such programs are taken for granted and are not subjected to review or evaluation.

Central to incremental budgeting is the idea that last year's budget is accepted as the *starting point* for analysis with only increases (or decreases) in last year's budgets considered in determining this year's budget. In a system of incremental budgeting, budget reviews examine

[4]See Charles L. Schultze, *The Politics and Economics of Public Spending* (Washington, D.C.: The Brookings Institution, 1968), pp. 47–53, 77–102. Schultze summarizes the Lindblom criticism of PPBS and defends PPBS in a political context.

only items for which increases over last year's budget are requested. There is no examination of the objectives, performance, or even the structure of old programs, and no alternatives to old programs are considered unless new programs are proposed.

PPBS is not totally consistent with incremental budgeting. It does not accept last year's budget as the starting point for analysis. The program memorandum of PPBS is the basis for evaluating performance, and budgetary decisions are based on that evaluation. Essentially, this practice of evaluating even old programs against specific objectives and considering more effective alternatives is founded on the principle of zero-base budgeting.

In theory, *zero-base budgeting* is based on the analytical position that the agency's base contains no programs at all, no funding whatsoever. Zero-base budgeting requires in principle that an agency must justify all its programs, especially in comparison with alternative uses of the funds. At the limit, therefore, zero-base budgeting would imply an annual review and evaluation of every program of every agency. Attempting annual zero-base reviews of all programs would be extremely costly in terms of information requirements. A relatively long budget cycle would be required. A large staff of budget analysts would be necessary.[5] Also, there is risk in seeking too many fundamental changes at one time. A succession of nonincremental decisions that depart radically from past practices or nonincremental policies that require very large increases or decreases in resources committed to particular programs can lead to a lack of continuity and stability necessary to healthy program development. Proponents argue, however, that the entire structure of federal programs need not be reevaluated every year when a budget is put together. Success lies in selectivity in programs examined.[6]

Is PPBS Dead?

In 1971, the Office of Management and Budget announced that agencies were no longer required to submit program and financial plans, program memoranda, and special analytical studies along with submission of agency budget requests. Some regarded the demise of PPBS's mechanistic apparatus as a testament to analysis. In other words, the PPBS technique was getting in the way of analysis, and the flesh and bones of PPBS were allowed to die so that its spirit could live. Thus, for those who saw analysis

[5]In its instructions for 1964 agency estimates, the U.S. Department of Agriculture stated that all programs would be reviewed from the ground up. A study of how much time the USDA effort consumed conservatively estimated that at least one thousand administrators spent an average of thirty hours a week for six weeks. See Aaron Wildavsky and Arthur Hammann, "Comprehensive Versus Incremental Budgeting in the Department of Agriculture," in Fremont J. Lyden and Ernest G. Miller, eds., *Planning Programming Budgeting: A Systems Approach to Management* (Chicago: Markham Publishing Company, 1968), p. 143.

[6]For a lucid expression of this point of view, see Schultze, *The Politics and Economics of Public Spending,* p. 80.

as the heart and soul of PPBS, the OMB announcement in 1971 was evidence of the strength and durability of analysis.

Others did not regard analysis as the central concern of PPBS and believed that the OMB announcement was evidence of failure. What PPBS tried to do, they believed, was to transform budgeting from repetitive financing of permanent bureaucracies into an instrument for deciding the purposes of government programs. Analysis was not valued for its own sake. PPBS was designed with budget outcome in mind, and unless it penetrated to the form and content of the budget, it was a failure. Thus, when OMB terminated PPBS, it ended the attempt to overhaul federal budgeting.[7]

Whether analysis was the core of PPBS and was not impaired when the mechanistic apparatus was stripped away, the causes of the demise of PPBS as such are multiple. One cause, emphasized by Lindholm and Wildavsky, is that PPBS failed because of its conflict with political values.[8] Incremental decision making and budgeting provides for advocacy, analysis, and reconciliation of diverse political interests. This bargaining mode of budgeting would be threatened if budgetary choice were centralized in the hands of budget analysts. Those who pointed to this cause still championed analysis, however, but they proposed to rescue policy analysis from PPBS.

CONCLUSION

In a sense, the budgetary process is a reconciliation of conflicting claims on resources. There is no necessary or exact relationship between such claims and economic efficiency. The main and central purpose of benefit-cost analysis is to provide information about programs or policies so that relationships between impacts and resources can be estimated. As information subject to interpretation, analysis in general and benefit-cost analysis in particular are a part of rather than a substitute for politics. Budgets are still the outcome of political decision making, and the intent of analysis is to have due influence on such decisions. Because analysis is a part of politics, however, it can be compromised to support predisposed conclusions and favored policies or programs. More than one agency has manipulated costs and benefits or twisted prevailing criteria out of shape. At times, analysis is also a comfort and convenience when it can be put to political use. When an official opposes a program or policy, benefit-cost analysis can be stressed in explanations to interest groups or constituents.

    [7]See Allen Schick, "A Death in the Bureaucracy: The Demise of Federal PPB," in Robert H. Haveman and Julius Margolis, eds., *Public Expenditure and Policy Analysis,* 2nd ed. (Chicago: Rand McNally & Company, 1977), pp. 556–76.
    [8]See Aaron Wildavsky, "The Political Economy of Efficiency: Cost-Benefit Analysis, Systems Analysis, and Program Budgeting," *Public Administration Review,* 26 (December 1966), 292–310.

6

Equity in Tax Treatment

Taxation can be used to divert resources from private to public uses. Taxation is also a potential instrument of social control. Tax burdens may be allocated among income groups to promote a more equal distribution of income. The level of aggregate demand can be raised or lowered through taxation. For whatever reasons any form of taxation is imposed, however, it is normally put to the test of fairness.

For the most part, a sense of fairness or equity is the result of a social consensus of thought, with full tincture of ethical and even aesthetical values. Questions of equity necessarily involve value judgments and sentiments, the contraband of science. Consequently, no truly "scientific" approach to equity itself is practicable. The study of equity generally begins with articulation of a principle that governs tax treatment. Then it continues with establishment of standards that serve as models of fairness. Taxation passes the test of fairness by satisfying the standards.

Expenditure literature has been more concerned with efficiency. Clear principles of expenditure equity have not been developed. Constitutionally, equity is guaranteed primarily in terms of tax treatment. Equity is grounded in the legal principles of due process of law and equal protection of the law, the Fifth and Fourteenth Amendments to the U.S. Constitution. Tax treatment is legal treatment and enjoys the same protections as other rights guaranteed by law. In economics and law, therefore, the principle of equity has dealt more with taxation.

THE EQUITY PRINCIPLE

A tax system consists of the definition of what is to be taxed and the rate at which taxes are to be levied. The former is the tax base, and the latter, the tax rate schedule. Anything bought, sold, owned, received, or given away can be used as the base of a tax. The most common bases are income, receipts from sale of commodities, wealth, and value added. The federal government and some state and local governments levy a tax on various kinds of income. Taxes on wealth are levied by all levels of government, but the taxes take different forms. The federal and state governments levy taxes based on the value of a deceased person's estate. Local governments collect taxes on the assessed value of real estate and, in some cases, on personal assets as well. Excises are sales taxes imposed on purchasers or sellers of various goods and services. State and local governments rely on sales taxes, and the federal government levies taxes on liquor, tobacco, automobile tires, and a few other goods. In Europe, a common tax base is value added, which is equal to revenue from sales of goods and services minus the costs of labor and materials utilized in production. The rate at which any base is taxed can rise, fall, or remain constant as the base increases.

The foremost principle governing a tax system is that the tax burden should bear equally upon persons in substantially similar circumstances and unequally upon persons in dissimilar circumstances. The former part of this norm is called the *horizontal equity principle* because it requires that "tax equals" be treated the same. The latter part is referred to as the *vertical equity principle* because it requires that "tax unequals" be treated differently. Two questions are raised immediately. First, how may individuals be classified into categories of equals as far as taxation is concerned? Second, how differently may individuals be treated who are classified for tax purposes as unequals? The equity principle as such does not provide the answers.

If the equity principle is to be respected by specific tax systems, then definitions and measurements of equality and inequality must be developed and applied. For the most part, the requirements of horizontal equity deal with the problem of the *tax base,* which is the value or the unit that is subject to taxation. Definition and measurement of the tax base determine classes of individuals for the purpose of taxation. *Within* each of these classes, the individuals are considered to be equals because the amount of their taxable base is the same. *Among* the various classes, however, the amount of taxable base is different, so that individuals in different classes are unequals. For the most part, the requirements of vertical equity deal with the problem of the *tax rate,* which is the ratio of the tax to the tax base. If the amount of taxable base is different among individuals, these unequals may be taxed at rates that increase, decrease, or remain the same as the taxable base increases. If a class of individuals having a larger taxable base is taxed at a higher rate than a class having less, the tax rate schedule is *progressive;* if at a lower rate, then *regressive;* and if at the same rate, then *proportional.*[1]

Earlier, we said that the study of equity generally begins with articulation of a principle that governs tax treatment. Basically, that is what the equity principle is. We also said that the study of equity generally continues with consideration of standards that serve as models of fairness. Two common standards applied in testing the distribution of tax burden for fairness are (1) the ability of individuals to pay taxes and (2) the benefits that individuals receive from governmental expenditures. These standards have served as the main interpretation of equity.

ABILITY TO PAY

Adam Smith's *Wealth of Nations* discussed taxes in some detail. He began by positing four maxims of taxation: every tax should be "equal," certain, convenient to pay, and economical to collect. On the subject of equality, he said, "The subjects of every state ought to contribute towards the support of the government, as nearly as possible, in proportion to their respective abilities; that is, in proportion to the revenue they respectively enjoy under the protection of the state."[2] In an analogy, Smith said that rent, profit, and wage recipients were like the joint tenants of an estate, and the cost of government like the cost of managing it. Accordingly, the joint tenants ought to contribute to expenses in proportion to their respective interests in the estate.

Smith was proposing, therefore, that the burden of taxation should be based on the ability to pay taxes, where that ability is determined by the proportion of total income that a source of income represents. If rent was 60 percent of total income, then landlords should pay 60 percent of the tax burden. This was fair because, according to Smith, rent was revenue enjoyed under the protection of the state, and of the total revenue protected by the state, 60 percent of it was rent. Smith went on further to suggest that, within each sort of revenue, a tax should fall equally. If a landlord's rental income is 1 percent of total rent, then that landlord should pay 1 percent of the tax burden falling on rent. This would be the landlord's fair

[1]The incidence of a tax also may be referred to in the same language. When the incidence of a tax is said to be progressive, what is meant is that, as incomes increase, a larger percentage of income is paid as tax; proportional, the same percentage; and regressive, a smaller percentage. Hence, a tax with a proportional rate schedule can be a case of regressive incidence. In other words, the incidence can be distributed regressively over income groups even when the rate schedule is proportional.

[2]Adam Smith, *An Inquiry into the Nature and Causes of the Wealth of Nations* (New York: Modern Library, 1937; published originally in 1776), p. 777.

contribution to the support of government because it would be in proportion to respective ability, which, according to Smith's maxim of equality, meant that the tax was in proportion to the revenue the landlord enjoys under the protection of the state. In modern times, this implies a *proportional income tax*. He thought that this would be a tax based on the ability to pay taxes and would satisfy the maxim of "equality."[3]

Adam Smith wrote the first treatise in political economy and was the first major figure in the classical tradition of economics. This historical reference shows that, from the practical beginning of economics itself, equity has been recognized as a central problem in evaluating taxation. Also, it shows that the ability to pay taxes has long been regarded as a fair basis for distributing the burden of taxation and that income was accepted as an appropriate measure of the ability to pay taxes. It also raises a question that has a rich history of its own: What kind of rate structure is inferred from the ability to pay taxes as a standard for equity? Particularly from the mid-nineteenth century on, progressivity in rates was argued, and, as a matter of fact, in 1913 the U.S. Constitution was amended to permit progressive rates in personal income taxation.

Although political expediency should not be underestimated, it is not surprising that most governmental activities today are financed on the justification that the tax burden is distributed according to each individual's ability to pay taxes. The concept itself provides no practicable meaning or measure of ability or of the relative abilities of taxpayers. The relationship between ability to pay and base, and between ability to pay and rate, needs to be examined in some detail.

Ability to Pay and the Question of the Tax Base

Measuring the ability to pay taxes is fraught with many problems. Adam Smith made a simple case that took for granted that revenue enjoyed under the protection of the state was the measure of ability. Later, the unfolding preeminence of income as a tax base was due largely to the simple conclusion that, since taxes are paid in dollars, dollars of income are the

---

[3]Given that stocks and flows were not well distinguished at that time, Smith may have had a property tax in mind. Most economists have misinterpreted Smith on this maxim of taxation. They claim that he is supporting only benefit taxation or both benefit and ability-to-pay taxation. While it is true that he suggests that the benefit that the subjects of every state receive from government is the revenue they enjoy under the protection of the state, he makes no case for basing taxation on benefits received but, rather, in his analogy to joint tenants of a great estate, for basing taxation on respective *interests* in the state, measured by income. As a matter of fact, he later lists *uncritically* six "general rules" of taxation given by Henry Home, Lord Kames in his *Sketches of the History of Man* (1774), which include "To remedy 'inequality of riches' as much as possible, by relieving the poor and burdening the rich" (p. 779). A proportional tax on income would do this to some extent because those with higher incomes would pay more taxes than would those with lower incomes.

best indication of the dollars available to pay taxes.[4] Agreement on income, however, still requires definition of income.

Many economists would settle on a sort of visionary's definition of income as *gain*, thereby regarding income as the algebraic sum of consumption and any change in net worth during a given calendar period.[5] Income is simply consumption and accumulation, and all *accretions* to prosperity would be included algebraically, whether rent, wages, interest, or profits; whether gifts, gambling losses, or the proceeds of a wallet found lying on a street; whether expected or unexpected; whether realized (converted into cash) or unrealized; whether regular or irregular. This "accretion" concept of income is troublesome for many reasons, among them that there is a serious problem of valuation without sale. In other words, we cannot always know that the value of all assets has increased or decreased, or by how much, unless the accumulation or decumulation is realized through market sale.

Even the economists who accept the accretion concept concede a realization criterion that would not recognize gain or loss until converted. No practicable scheme can require, as the accretion concept does, that taxpayers reappraise and report all their assets annually. Income taxes inevitably rest upon business records consistent with established accounting practice, including the realization criterion. Thus, accrued gains would be taxed as income whenever property passes out of one's hands, whether by sale or by gift. If a person were to die before the property is sold or given away, the accrued gains would be taxed as income to the person's estate when the property is transferred to heirs or legatees. The realization criterion, therefore, is reasonably unobjectionable in principle as long as it results only in *postponement* of assessment. Where property passes without sale—for example, where it is transferred by gift, inheritance, or bequest—there are opportunities for *avoidance* of taxation, however.[6]

[4]Although his argument is not grounded in ability to pay, Kaldor argues against income and in favor of expenditure as a tax base. He argues the case for an expenditure tax because it is consumption that measures a person's demands on the resources of an economy. A saver does not withdraw resources from the economy to the limits of income. To the contrary, a saver is adding to resources through investment decisions. A dissaver depletes resources beyond the limits of income! The saver should be taxed less than income indicates, according to Kaldor, and the dissaver more. See N. Kaldor, *An Expenditure Tax* (London: George Allen & Unwin Ltd., 1955). This general argument is discussed later in this chapter.

[5]For a "classic" discussion of the definition of income, see Henry C. Simons, *Personal Income Taxation* (Chicago: University of Chicago Press, 1938), especially pp. 41–102. Simons himself argues that personal income "implies estimate of consumption and accumulation" (p. 49) and that personal income is "the algebraic sum of (1) the market value of rights exercised in consumption and (2) the change in the value of the store of property rights between the beginning and end of the period in question" (p. 50). For further discussion of the accretion concept, see Chapter 8.

[6]For further discussion of the realization criterion and of death taxation, see Chapters 8 and 12.

The actual personal income tax base is merely a calculation according to defined methods. Tax laws do not really define income. They merely establish rules for what must be included and what may be deducted. Such tax laws and administrative regulations are not always logically coherent, and they are not exhaustive. They are devices of accounting and of legislation that contemplate only very rough approximations of income. As Henry Simons concluded, the fact that these rules work at all is due to the cooperation of taxpayers, the paucity of ingenious lies, the availability of market prices, and information from third parties, as well as to business records and accounts that serve as standards of comparison for verifying accuracy.[7]

Some problems in defining equals. A central requirement of the ability-to-pay principle is definition of equals. There are some special problems in defining equals, among them family size, risk, depreciation, and capital gain. Each of these should be considered.

If income measures tax capacity, then ability to pay taxes presumably begins at a certain level of income. This minimum level might be the income required for subsistence or it might be greater. One method of integrating this consideration is to define equality as income less an allowance. Presently, federal income tax law provides for a $1,000 exemption from adjusted gross income for each person in a family, which is the unit on which taxes are levied. While this method addresses the definition of equals, there are two drawbacks to the solution. First, the exemption was introduced in 1949 at a level of $600. This figure was supposed to represent the cost of necessities for a typical person. If $600 was appropriate in 1949, adjusting for inflation should put the present exemption at about $2,000. Also, an exemption of fixed amount is worth more to families with high incomes than to those with low incomes. The reason is the progressive tax rate structure. Families in the marginal tax bracket of 12 percent save $120 in taxes per family member ($1,000 × 0.12 = $120), while those in the tax bracket of 50 percent save $500 in taxes per family member ($1,000 × 0.50 = $500).

Another problem in defining equals is risk. Consider that a decision now will generate income in the future. If only one result of this decision is possible, then the outcome is certain. If more than one result is possible, the outcome is risky. Suppose that persons are averse to risk (rather than neutral to risk or lovers of risk) and that they have the same utility-of-income schedule. Under these conditions, persons will not choose a risky alternative unless the income expected from that alternative is greater than the income from a riskless or certain choice. This expected differential is a premium for bearing risk. In effect, markets cause the income from a

[7]Simons, *Personal Income Taxation*, p. 105.

risky alternative to exceed the income from a certain alternative enough so that the utility is the same in the two cases. All choices of occupation and investment involve some risk, but the premium for bearing risk is unknown. It is commonly argued that, for tax purposes, persons with a given amount of risky income should be allowed to deduct the premium from the income. Think of it this way: for risk-averse persons, the utility of a certain result is greater than the utility of a risky result with the same income.

When income is used to measure ability, capacity, or equality for tax purposes, still other problems arise. Basically, the difficulties occur in measuring or even defining income from capital assets. One of these problems is depreciation and depletion. Depreciation can occur because capital is worn out by use in production. In this case, the useful life of capital can be determined by wear and tear. However, machinery is scrapped sometimes while the capital equipment is still capable of operating. The reason is that newer, more efficient, technologically better machines are introduced. Depreciation includes charges for wear and tear as well as for obsolescence. For natural resources, the quantity of the resource is reduced by production. This reduction is called depletion, and it is analogous to depreciation in the sense that it is a loss in value, a cost.

Instead of assessing in fact the value of all capital goods, rules are used to determine depreciation for tax purposes. The Internal Revenue Service specifies useful lives for a few broad classes of assets. In this way, the amount of depreciation charges that can be deducted from taxable income each year is determined. Tax laws use an entirely different method to determine an allowance for depletion. Depletion is expressed as a certain percentage of gross revenues, and the percentage allowed varies with the type of natural resource. Percentage allowances bear little relation to the true cost of depletion.

A quite different matter is the question of capital gains. Tax law considers capital gains *realized* through sale of an asset as taxable income. Even when realized, most capital gains are weighted at only 40 percent (or less) as income for tax purposes. There are many arguments in favor of special treatment of capital gains. One is that inflation causes a difference between real and nominal gains. Another is that progressive tax rates can lower the after-tax return of a risky asset more than that of a safe asset. Preferential treatment tends to equalize after-tax returns. The approach itself is questionable, however. Portfolios of assets are usually diversified with a number of safe and risky assets. Hence, total income will vary less than will the return from any particular risky asset. Risk applies to human as well as to physical and financial capital.

Consumption and wealth as measures of ability to pay taxes. While strong arguments can be made for income as the best measure of the ability to pay taxes, there are major alternative measures. Cases have been made for basing taxes on consumption or wealth, and each of these alternative measures of ability to pay should be considered.

Several different arguments have been made for consumption as a measure of ability to pay. One of the oldest is that ability should be measured by what persons take out of the economy rather than by what they put back in. In other words, consumption uses up society's scarce resources. It exhausts productive capacity. The acts of saving and investment, on the other hand, contribute to society's scarce resources by providing for enlarged productive capacity. The argument is made that taxation should be based on consumption only, whether it is consumption out of current income or out of wealth from past accumulation.

The act of saving, which is exempt from taxation if consumption is the measure of ability, may be only a means of postponing consumption until some future time. The saver merely consumes fewer goods now in order to consume more goods later. This weakens the case for not taxing saving because income is a more comprehensive base than is consumption alone. What is being measured is the ability or the capacity for paying taxes, and ability or capacity is measured by income whether the burden of taxation falls on consumption or saving.

A quite different case for excluding savings is that taxing income unfairly taxes savings twice. In other words, an income tax falls on consumption and savings in the first place, and then it falls on earnings from previously taxed savings. The counterargument is that a consumption base undertaxes saving. Income used for consumption is taxed, but income that is saved is not taxed until it is used for consumption. It escapes taxation altogether if accumulation continues indefinitely. Postponing or escaping taxation does not occur under an income base. In fact, when someone saves, any return on savings is new income. As income never before taxed, these returns are an appropriate base for an income tax.

Still another measure of ability to pay that has been proposed is wealth. Presumably, ability to pay taxes stems from the capital income from wealth. If so, a tax on the value of an asset is equivalent to a tax on the earnings or the income from the asset. Under a comprehensive income tax base, however, capital income or asset earnings should be properly subject to taxation. Certainly, some persons save and others do not, and eventually those who saved can dissave, while those who did not cannot. Those who save and accumulate wealth are in a better position, but interest income from their savings would be taxed under an income base. The central question is whether there should also be a tax on capital, on the stock of past savings. Under a comprehensive income tax base, the answer is negative because the opportunities for accumulation were available to' those who saved and those who did not. As long as it is ability that is measured, the capacity for paying taxes was measured properly when income was taxed in the first place.

Ability to Pay and the Question of the Tax Rate

As the base—say, income—increases, how much more able to pay taxes does a person become? What kind of tax rate structure is consistent with the rate at which the ability to pay taxes increases? Regressive, proportional, or progressive rates can result in those with higher incomes paying higher taxes. In Table 6–1, three rate schedules are shown. When applied to tax bases of (1) $10,000, (2) $20,000, and (3) $70,000, each rate schedule yields the same total tax revenue, $10,500. Also, each rate schedule—regressive, proportional, and progressive—results in persons with higher income paying higher taxes. Which rate structure satisfies the condition that income is taxed at rates consistent with the ability to pay taxes?

Many persons, including some economists, have asserted that the ability to pay taxes increases more rapidly than does income. This is an argument for progressive tax rates. It is common to lay the foundation for this assertion on the idea that the marginal utility of income declines. In casual conversation, you hear this idea when someone says that we ought to have progressive income taxation because an extra dollar means less to

TABLE 6–1 An Illustration of Regressive, Proportional, and Progressive Tax Rate Schedules Yielding $10,500 of Tax Revenue

REGRESSIVE RATE SCHEDULE	TAX PAID ON $10,000	TAX PAID ON $20,000	TAX PAID ON $70,000
20% on $1 to $5,000	$1,000	$1,000	$1,000
10% on $5,001 to $50,000	500	1,500	4,500
5% on $50,001 and over	—	—	1,000
Total tax	$1,500	$2,500	$6,500

PROPORTIONAL RATE SCHEDULE	TAX PAID ON $10,000	TAX PAID ON $20,000	TAX PAID ON $70,000
10.50% on $1 to $5,000	$ 525	$ 525	$ 525
10.50% on $5,001 to $50,000	525	1,575	4,725
10.50% on $50,001 and over	—	—	2,100
Total tax	$1,050	$2,100	$7,350

PROGRESSIVE RATE SCHEDULE	TAX PAID ON $10,000	TAX PAID ON $20,000	TAX PAID ON $70,000
5% on $1 to $5,000	$ 250	$ 250	$ 250
10% on $5,001 to $50,000	500	1,500	4,500
16.25% on $50,001 and over	—	—	3,250
Total tax	$ 750	$1,750	$8,000

a rich person than it does to a poor one. There is also a rich and rigorous literature on theories that deal with equalizing sacrifices of utility.[8]

These equal sacrifice theories are based on critical assumptions: (1) the base of tax is income, (2) the marginal utility of income declines, (3) utility can be compared interpersonally, and (4) marginal utility of income is the same for all persons. Based on these assumptions, a distribution of tax burden among individuals is determined that satisfies some requirement of equal sacrifice of utility. Regressive, proportional, or progressive tax rates can equalize sacrifice. It depends on the rate at which the marginal utility of income declines. If it declines at a rate less than that at which income increases, then sacrifice can be equalized with regressive rates. If it declines at a rate greater than that at which income increases, then sacrifice can be equalized only with progressive rates.

The literature dealing with equal sacrifice requires advanced knowledge of economics and mathematics. It demonstrates, however, that the "weak" assumption of declining marginal utility is not sufficient to make a case for progressive taxation. The slope of the marginal utility of income must also be known. The argument for progression requires the "strong" assumption that marginal utility declines at a greater rate than income increases. Nevertheless, arguments that link ability to pay, the weak assumption of declining marginal utility, and some inarticulate notion of equalizing sacrifice to the case for progression still enjoy some currency in casual discussion. Such arguments give only the appearance of a "scientific" case for progression, however. The legitimacy of arguments based on weak assumptions is suspect. Arguments based on strong assumptions are even more suspect. The knowledge requirements can be too great. *Assuming* that the marginal utility of income declines is one thing, but *knowing* the rate at which it declines is another. There is no "scientific" case for progressive taxation.

The sacrifice theories and assumptions of declining marginal utility are not the only sources of arguments for progression. By the late nineteenth century, for example, there were arguments that justice in taxation required more than a simple "financial" approach. This literature suggested that a broader meaning of tax justice meant taxation to correct undesirable inequality of income distribution. In the 1930s, Henry Simons (one of the founders of the so-called "Chicago School" of economic thought) argued that, whether or not we want it to, taxation has some effect on income distribution. Regardless of its base, every tax ultimately reduces someone's income. Although the discussion is frankly ethical, it seems nonetheless reasonable to ask the question as to what effects on the distribution of income are desirable. In other words, if effects on the dis-

---

[8]For a complete discussion of equal sacrifice theories, see Richard A. Musgrave, *The Theory of Public Finance* (New York: McGraw-Hill Book Company, 1959), pp. 95–115.

tribution of income are unavoidable, then what types of effects do we want?

This method of considering and analyzing taxation led Simons and others to support progression on the simple grounds that the prevailing distribution of income violated social justice.[9] As a matter of fact, Simons himself went so far as to argue that the case for "drastic" progression in taxation *must* be rested on the case *against* inequality. One consequence of *true* progressivity in tax rates is certain: it necessarily serves to lessen the inequality in the distribution of income.[10]

Consider Table 6–2, which is based on the incomes and tax rate structures in Table 6–1. First, note that the regressive tax rate structure makes the distribution of income *more* unequal. Before the tax, the lowest-, median-, and highest-income recipients have 10 percent, 20 percent, and 70 percent of total income, respectively. The median-income recipient had twice the income of the lowest; after the tax, the median-income recipient has 2.06 times the income of the lowest. The highest-income recipient had

TABLE 6–2   Effects of Regressive, Proportional, and Progressive Rate Schedules on the Distribution of Income

	PRETAX INCOME		
RATE STRUCTURE	$10,000	$20,000	$70,000
Regressive			
1. Pretax percentage of total income	10%	20%	70%
2. Posttax percentage of total income	9.5 (8,500/89,500)	19.6 (17,500/89,500)	70.9 (63,500/89,500)
Proportional			
1. Pretax percentage of total income	10%	20%	70%
2. Posttax percentage of total income	10 (8,950/89,500)	20 (17,900/89,500)	70 (62,650/89,500)
Progressive			
1. Pretax percentage of total income	10%	20%	70%
2. Posttax percentage of total income	10.3 (9,250/89,500)	20.4 (18,250/89,500)	69.3 (62,000/89,500)

[9]See Simons, *Personal Income Taxation*, pp. 17–19.

[10]If some kinds of income are exempted from taxation, then progressive taxation of *taxable* income may permit the burden of taxation to be distributed regressively over income groups that have been categorized by, say, personal income rather than by taxable income. The discussion here assumes that there are no significant differences between income and taxable income. Moreover, this discussion requires that expenditures do not undo the effect of taxes.

7.0 times the income of the lowest and 3.5 times the income of the median-income recipient; after the tax, the highest-income recipient has 7.47 times the income of the lowest and 3.63 times the income of the median-income recipient. This example illustrates the rule that regressivity makes income distribution more unequal. Second, note that the proportional tax rate structure does not affect the distribution of income. The after-tax distribution is the same as the before-tax distribution. Finally, note that the progressive rate structure makes the distribution of income *less* unequal. After the tax, the lowest-, median-, and highest-income recipients have 10.3 percent, 20.4 percent, and 69.3 percent, respectively. Also, after the tax, the median-income recipient has only 1.97 times the income of the lowest; the highest-income recipient has only 6.7 times the income of the lowest, and only 3.4 times the income of the median-income recipient. Again this example illustrates the rule that progressivity makes distribution more equal.

Historically, the importance of the redistribution argument for progressive taxation can hardly be minimized.[11] In a persuasive and influential study, two University of Chicago lawyers, Blum and Kalven, concluded that no technical argument yet advanced—the sacrifice arguments, for example—has contributed to the acceptance or the defense of progressive taxation.[12] Instead, they suggest, progressive taxation probably was and continues to be accepted because of the widespread belief that it does promote a better distribution of income.[13]

Apart from equity, there are other defenses for progressivity. Closely related to the argument that the case for progressivity is the case against inequality is the simple preference for progression as the "best" method of redistribution. Many economists and others simply prefer progressivity to direct interference with markets to redistribute income. Market intervention is regarded as an ineffective way of redistributing income because of uncertainty about its effect on the distribution of income and because intervention can interfere with efficient allocation of resources. Even farther removed from equity considerations are arguments that progressivity pro-

[11]Resting the case *for* progression on the case *against* inequality takes into account only the distributional effects of taxation. For example, it does not account for losses in production owing to effects on the incentive to work or to save. Such disincentive effects on economic growth should be weighed against any desirable effects of redistribution.

[12]Walter J. Blum and Harry Kalven, Jr., *The Uneasy Case for Progressive Taxation* (Chicago: University of Chicago Press, 1953).

[13]Empirically, it is difficult to isolate the influence of progression alone on the distribution of income. Studies indicate that the distribution of pretax and posttax income has not changed significantly since 1950. However, this conclusion is based on cash income only and excludes noncash transfer payment programs. When we take these programs into account, we find a much more equal distribution and a marked trend toward equality since 1960. See Lester C. Thurow and Robert E. B. Lucas, *The American Distribution of Income: A Structural Problem,* Joint Economic Committee (Washington, D.C.: Government Printing Office, 1972), pp. 4–5; Daniel B. Radner and John C. Hinrich, "Size Distribution of Income in 1964, 1970, and 1971," *Survey of Current Business,* 54 (October 1974), 19–31; and Edgar K. Browning, "How Much More Equality Can We Afford?" *The Public Interest* (Spring 1976), pp. 90–110.

motes the stability of society because it "buys" the cooperation of low-income groups. In other words, it might be rational for the wealthy to accept progressivity and thereby subsidize low-income groups as a sort of insurance against insurrection or less drastic threats to the privileged lives, properties, and positions of upper-income groups. Still another argument is that, if a person accepted the notion that marginal utility of income will decline as his or her income grows over time, that person may prefer progressive rates because, in effect, they allow postponement of lifetime tax obligation (assumed to be given) from the present, when income is lower, to the future, when income is higher. Finally, many persons would argue that progressivity is not so much a question of ability to pay taxes or of equity in tax treatment as it is of the ethical respect for a hierarchy of wants. They would simply argue that low incomes that would be used to buy basic food, clothing, and shelter should be taxed at a lower rate than high incomes used to purchase imported wine, hand-tailored suits, and vacation cottages.

BENEFITS RECEIVED

Recall that the study of equity generally begins with articulation of a principle that governs tax treatment and continues with consideration of standards that serve as models of fairness. The ability of individuals to pay taxes is one such standard. The benefits that individuals receive from governmental expenditures is the other major acknowledged measure of equity. The "benefit principle" states that equity in tax treatment is satisfied when the distribution of tax burden among individuals is based on the benefits each receives from governmental expenditures. This approach to equity also has a long and illustrious history. Analogies have been drawn between the benefit principle and the principle(s) governing market prices of privately produced goods.[14] In fact, it is indispensable in the performance of an "ideally neutral fiscal system," one exhibiting the same kind of economic efficiency that we ask of a market system. At the same time, however, the principle has been criticized. The benefits of most goods and services provided by the public sector are not easily measurable. The principle is not fully applicable to expenditure programs that have strictly redistributive purposes. Nonetheless, defenders of the benefit principle argue that it is applicable under certain conditions.

Total Benefits Received

One tempting interpretation of the benefit principle is that it requires each person's taxes to be equal to the *total* benefits received from publicly provided goods and services. This interpretation is hardly tenable. Rather

---

[14]See Chapter 2 for further discussion.

than go without publicly provided services altogether—that is, rather than forgo the total benefits—taxpayers may be willing to sacrifice almost all their income above a minimum subsistence level.

Normally, taxpayers or consumers are not presented with "all-or-nothing" offers but instead with offers to vote for or buy as many units as they wish at a given price. In competitive markets, for example, every unit of a good sells for what the last or marginal unit is worth to consumers. Consumers enjoy a "surplus," therefore, that is the difference between the maximum amount they would pay before going without any units of the good and the amount they actually pay. Consider Figure 6–1. If a consumer paid a price of *OE* for *OC* units of the good, the consumer's surplus would be equal to *EDA* (the shaded area), which is the difference between *OCDA* (total utility) and *OCDE,* the portion of total utility that is "priced away." In applying the benefit principle, therefore, there should be a "taxpayers' surplus" that is not taxed away just as there is a consumers' surplus that is not priced away. The principle should not be stated in terms of *total* benefits received.

Marginal (or Incremental) Benefits

A more appropriate interpretation of the benefits-received principle is that equity requires a distribution of taxes among individuals on the basis of marginal (or incremental) benefits received. Stated in this way, the benefit principle would set taxes in a way that is analogous, except for one

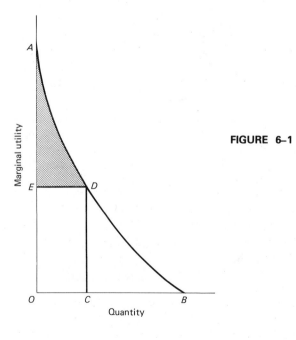

FIGURE 6–1   Consumers' (or taxpayers') surplus. Consumers' surplus is the difference between the maximum amount that consumers would pay before going without any units of a good and the amount actually paid. If consumers paid *OE* for *OC* units, consumers' surplus would be *EDA* (the shaded area), which is the difference between *OCDA* (total utility) and *OCDE* (total utility that is priced away).

very important difference, to prices in private markets. In a competitive market, there would be a *single* market price that would apply to each and every consumer, so that everyone pays the *same* price for the same good but can consume different quantities. For publicly provided goods supplied in a given quantity, there might be *many* "prices" that would apply to "consumers," so that potentially everyone pays a *different* price for the same quantity of the good.[15] Consider Figure 6–2. Assume that the marginal benefits schedule is the curve *DC* for one individual and curve *BA* for another. If an optimal quantity *OE* is provided and each individual can consume that quantity without diminishing the consumption of the other, then marginal benefit taxation would require that the one individual pay a price *OG* and the other *OF*. Under the circumstances, each of these individuals has some incentive to conceal—to understate—true evaluation of such goods of taxation.

Some Problems of Benefit Taxation

The point of benefit taxation is to tie together the decisions on taxes with those on expenditures in such a way that the benefits and costs of public services may be compared. In this respect, the advantage of the

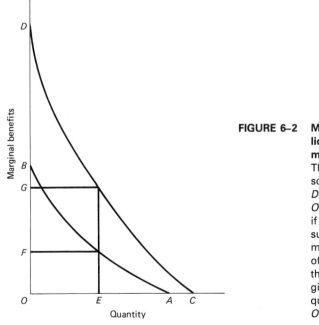

FIGURE 6–2   Multitax pricing of a public good according to marginal benefit received. The marginal benefits schedule for one person is *DC* and for another, *BA*. If *OE* units are provided, and if each person can consume *OE* units without diminishing the opportunity of the other to consume the same units, then marginal benefit taxation requires one person to pay *OG* and the other, *OF*.

[15]See Chapter 2 for a comprehensive discussion of public goods and efficiency.

principle is that it points up the problem of choice even if many of the values and quantities must be filled in or solved on the basis of judgment. There are several problems of benefit taxation, however, that limit the feasibility of its application.

Government expenditures may be separated into those for which the benefits are traceable directly to particular individuals or groups and those for which the benefits are diffused over a community or society in general. In the latter case in particular, there is no feasible way in which to measure the total or marginal benefits that accrue to specific people. Any such estimates would be arbitrary and subjective. Without markets, it is generally difficult to provide information about marginal evaluations comparable in quality to the knowledge generated by markets. This holds even for those expenditures for which the benefits might be traceable. Whether beneficiaries can or cannot be identified, there is no reliable incentive for persons to reveal fully their true preferences for public services if their tax bills rise and fall with the revealed height of their demand curves. Consequently, even when it is claimed that taxes are distributed on the basis of benefits received, beneficiaries are typically taxed or assessed on the basis of cost to government rather than benefit to the recipient.

It may be useful also to distinguish between those expenditures intended as subsidies or redistributions of income and those that are not. If benefit taxation were levied to defray the costs of programs intended to redistribute income, then it would tax away the intended subsidies. Or would it? This raises a question: Who are the beneficiaries of subsidy programs that redistribute income? The donors or donees? For example, who is the beneficiary of social security—the older nonworking generation to whom income is redistributed, or the younger, working generation that pays the subsidy to the elderly? If it is the older generation, then benefit taxation would defeat the purpose of the intended subsidy by making the donees pay for their donation. If it is the younger generation by reason that it avoids and is spared from the horror of seeing masses of old people in conditions of deprivation and the unpleasantness of a visible "illfare" among the elderly, then benefit taxation would not defeat the purpose of the intended redistribution of income. Donees would receive the donation, and donors—being the beneficiaries—would pay for the donation.

To the extent that the donees are the beneficiaries, benefit taxation would tax away the marginal benefits of redistributed income and defeat at least in part the purpose of the intended subsidy. To the extent that the donors are the beneficiaries, the measurement problem is a serious one. How could the donors be made to reveal their true preferences for or their true marginal benefits from making donations? Because of the problems of measurement and or subsidies, benefit taxation is not well suited for categories of expenditure for which the beneficiaries are difficult to identify, the benefits are difficult to measure, or the benefits are redistributed income.

Feasible Application of the Benefits-Received Principle

In cases where the benefit principle is at least roughly applicable, it may look more like a price than a tax. Highway taxes, automobile excise taxes, and motor vehicle fuel taxes are all commonly justified on the grounds that users should be the ones who pay for roads and highways. The users are regarded as the beneficiaries, and benefits are estimated by mileage and gasoline consumption. Such taxes are referred to as *user taxes,* and revenue from such sources is usually earmarked for the purpose of defraying costs of the facilities used. *User charges* are also commonly used to finance such services as toll roads, airports, waterways, and other services that involve a clear-cut *exchange.*[16] User charges are like prices, and they serve the same function as user taxes. Such charges provide revenue and distribute the costs of such facilities roughly along lines of benefits received. Such charges also perform an important rationing function.

User charges have become increasingly popular with governments. They have potential for large amounts of revenue for generally popular purposes. For example, revenue from the federal excise on gasoline is obligated by statute to be spent on new highway construction or maintenance and improvement of existing highways. In this way, users of highways pay a tax whose base is related to highway use. Other user charges at the federal level include admission charges at national parks. Revenues from the federal excise on air fares are used to defray the traffic control expenditures of the Federal Aviation Administration. State and local governments also make wide use of charges. Users of freeways, bridges, tunnels, docks, and airport terminals often are charged for use. States levy excises on gasoline usually at a higher level than the federal government. They also use the revenues for highway construction, maintenance, and improvement.

When the costs of providing a good or service are mainly fixed costs with little or no variable costs, there is a problem in deciding upon the level of the charge. A charge that is efficient would be equal to marginal cost. Since the cost of allowing an additional automobile to cross a bridge is practically zero, the efficient toll would be zero. If the bridge consequently is overused and congestion develops, then a toll greater than zero

---

[16]Charges may not be levied fully on the basis of the benefit principle. The U.S. Post Office—a quasi-public corporation—engages in direct sales to buyers. However, the per unit cost of rural deliveries is generally much higher than is that for urban deliveries. Yet all users of the postal system pay the same price, given a class of mail. Essentially, rural customers are susidized, so that prices charged by the U.S. Post Office cannot be considered in any sense as competitive market prices.

could be justified to ration access and reduce crowding. However, revenues from a toll just high enough to prevent congestion would not necessarily recover the cost of building and maintaining the bridge. In this way, there is a certain tension between cost recovery and efficiency. In fact, agencies usually compromise by averaging costs over the number of users. Average-cost pricing either subsidizes users (if marginal cost is greater than average cost) or reduces use below the efficient level (if marginal cost is less than average cost).

EQUITY REVISITED

Equity comes down to two standards that serve as models of fairness. Ability to pay taxes defines equals in a way such that persons with equal ability to pay taxes should pay equal taxes. The problems are to determine appropriate measures of the ability to pay taxes and to estimate appropriate discrimination between persons who have different abilities. Benefits received is a standard that defines equals in a way such that persons receiving equal benefits should pay equal taxes. Major problems with this standard are to identify beneficiaries and to measure the benefits received by each of them. We tend to defer to the standard of ability to pay taxes in judging the equity of financing the overwhelming majority of government services. The unfortunate consequence of reliance on the ability-to-pay principle is that efficiency considerations tend to become secondary.

7

Shifting and Incidence

Nearly all taxes are imposed on a base, such as income, retail purchases, or property, that can be varied at least to some degree by the taxpayer. By varying the amount earned, spent on taxed commodities, or held in the form of taxable property, you can exert some control over the amount of tax you pay. You can even affect the amount of tax paid on your estate by controlling its size during your lifetime and by prescribing the way in which it is to be distributed after your death. Yet you should not infer that you can reduce your tax burden at no cost to yourself. If you react to taxation by earning less income or by consuming less tobacco or liquor than you otherwise would, you are imposing on yourself another kind of burden, a reduction in your utility.

A taxpayer with market power (i.e., some control over prices) may respond to taxes by raising the prices of goods sold or by lowering the prices of goods bought. Firms are more likely than households to respond to taxes by raising prices because they typically possess more control over prices than do households over, say, wages.

The response of firms and households to taxation, both individually and in the aggregate, is the subject matter of the theory of shifting and incidence. Special emphasis is placed on the extent to which the party on whom the tax is imposed can shift or transfer some or all of the burden to others and on how taxation affects selected groups within the economy.

PARTIAL EQUILIBRIUM MODELS

Prior to the 1950s, most of the theoretical work on shifting and incidence was confined to the partial equilibrium approach. Attention was concentrated on the way in which a tax affects individual households, firms, and markets or a small number of closely related markets, for example, the markets for corn, oats, and barley. Secondary effects that the tax has on other markets and the effects on the economy of the use of tax revenue were generally regarded as being sufficiently diffused to be safely ignored. Under this approach, analysis of shifting and incidence became an exercise in comparative statics in which equilibrium solutions before and after a change in a tax were compared.

Within the partial equilibrium framework several terms are used to describe what happens when a tax is levied. The firm or individual actually paying the tax to the government experiences its *impact*. If the party experiencing the impact succeeds in transferring some or all of the money burden of the tax to another party in subsequent market transactions, *shifting* has occurred. Shifting may be *forward* from seller to buyer or *backward* from buyer to seller and is reflected in tax-induced price changes. The *incidence,* or final resting place of the money burden of the tax, is on the party or parties paying the tax directly or indirectly after the shifting process is complete. In the absence of shifting, the party paying the tax absorbs the full money burden, so that impact and incidence coincide.

Taxation of Businesses

The typical business firm pays a variety of federal, state, and local taxes. The likelihood that it will shift some or all of its tax burden to buyers or suppliers depends on such things as the elasticity of demand for its products, the tax base, and the elasticity of supply of labor and other inputs. These things are essentially external to the firm and make up the economic environment in which it operates. The internal behavior of the firm—the way in which it responds to changes in its environment—also influences shifting. The amount of shifting that occurs may change over time as competitors and suppliers react and as the firm responds by altering its output, investment, or even its location. We turn now to an examination of shifting and incidence in the short run and long run.

Short run. According to orthodox price theory, only changes that affect a firm's short-run marginal cost (cost that is a function of changes in output with a given plant) will affect a firm's price and output in the short run.[1] Sales and excise taxes on inputs purchased by a firm, payroll taxes on labor, and property taxes on inventories are among those affecting marginal cost in the short run.

Long run. In the long run, a firm can alter its investment in plant and equipment. A tax on purchases of capital goods, such as a sales tax,

---

[1]An exception is a tax unrelated to output that is high enough to force a firm out of business.

or a tax on plant and equipment, such as a property tax, affects long-run marginal cost and will therefore affect price and output in the long run.

Shifting. The ability of a firm to respond to a tax-induced increase in marginal cost by raising prices depends on competitive conditions in the market for its output. If the firm is a perfect competitor, it lacks any control over the price it may charge. In this case, the only response it can make is adjustment of output to the level at which price equals marginal cost. If the tax affects a number of other firms producing the same good, the aggregate effect of changes in output may be great enough to cause a price change, but this will come about through the functioning of the market, not through a conscious exercise of market power by any one firm.

The response of a competitive industry to imposition of a tax is illustrated in Figure 7–1. Suppose that a tax raises the unit cost of production by the amount P_2C, leading to a parallel upward shift of the supply curve from S_1 to S_2. Assuming no change in demand, equilibrium price and quantity will move from P_1 and Q_1 to P_2 and Q_2. If the supply curve slopes upward, the price increase, P_2P_1, is less than the tax, P_2C. An upward-sloping

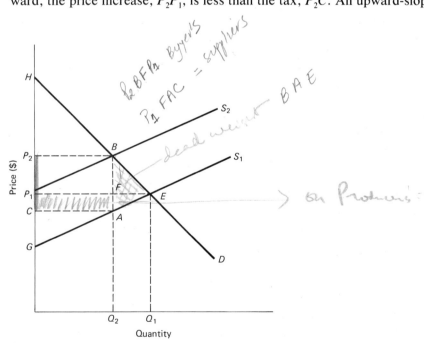

FIGURE 7–1   **Per unit excise tax in a competitive industry.** A per unit tax shifts the supply curve upward by the amount of the tax, *AB*. The total money burden, P_2BAC, consists of the buyers' share, P_2BFP_1, and the producers' share, P_1FAC. The area *BAE* measures the excess burden or welfare loss resulting from the tax.

supply curve is typical of all industries in the short run and holds in the long run for industries characterized by increasing cost.

Figure 7–1 can be used to illustrate some of the concepts introduced earlier. The government receives tax revenue equal to the tax per unit times output, as represented by the area P_2BAC, which is the total money burden or incidence of the tax as defined in partial equilibrium terms. The consumers' share of the money burden equals the price increase times output, or P_2BFP_1, which is the portion shifted forward. The remainder of the incidence, depicted by the rectangle P_1FAC, falls on owners of factors of production used by the industry.

Note that the partial equilibrium concept of incidence focuses on the distribution of the money burden of the tax but that the tax has other effects as well. One such effect is the loss of consumers' surplus on the units of commodity no longer consumed (approximated by the area BFE in Figure 7–1) and the accompanying loss of producers' surplus (area FAE).[2] These losses are called *excess burden* because they represent a welfare loss in excess of the money burden. Welfare losses attributable to excess burden are indicative of market inefficiency that generally accompanies the introduction of a tax. This can be seen in the example in Figure 7–1, where the tax causes the price paid by consumers, P_2, to exceed the marginal cost to producers, represented by point C.

In partial equilibrium analysis, we ignore any changes in relative prices of other goods and factors of production resulting from tax-induced shifts in consumer outlays, transfer of inputs to the production of other goods and services, and use of tax revenue by the government. The legitimacy of ignoring these effects is considered in the section on general equilibrium.

At the other extreme in terms of market structure is the case of a monopolist who sells a product with no close substitutes. An unregulated, profit-maximizing monopolist may be difficult to find, but the monopoly model is of some use in enabling us to predict how a firm with substantial market power will respond to taxation.

The demand, *D,* and marginal revenue, *MR,* curves for a monopolist are shown in Figure 7–2. The demand curve has a negative slope, indicating that the monopolist must cut the price on all units to increase by one the number sold. Therefore, the increment in total revenue attributable to sale of one more unit—the marginal revenue—is less than the price of that

---

[2]Consumers' surplus is the difference between the maximum amount that a consumer would pay for a given number of units of a commodity and the amount actually paid. For any point on a demand curve, it is approximated by the area below the demand curve to the price axis. Producers' surplus for any point on a supply curve is represented by the area above the curve and below the perpendicular connecting the supply curve to the price axis. It represents the rent accruing to inframarginal inputs. In Figure 7–1, at the pretax equilibrium price, P_1, consumers' surplus is represented by the area HP_1E, and producers' surplus is represented by the area GP_1E.

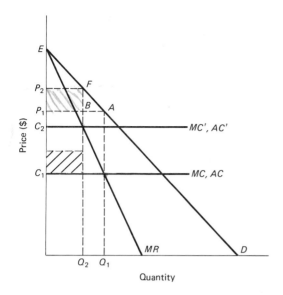

FIGURE 7-2   Per unit excise tax on a monopoly. A per unit excise tax shifts the cost
curve upward by the amount of the tax, the distance C_1C_2 on the vertical
axis. The money burden is split between consumers (area P_2FBP_1) and
producers (shaded area). The area FBA measures the excess burden or
welfare loss resulting from the tax.

unit,[3] which accounts for the fact that the MR curve lies below the D
curve. To simplify the exposition, we assume that the firm produces under
conditions of constant long-run cost, so that marginal cost (MC) = average
cost (AC). To maximize profit, the monopolist must produce the quantity
at which $MC = MR$. In the absence of a tax, this is the quantity Q_1, which
can be sold at price P_1.

Assume that a per unit tax is imposed on the monopolist, shifting the
cost curve upward from AC and MC to AC' and MC', or from C_1 to C_2
on the vertical axis. The firm now will equate MC' to MR by raising the
price to P_2 and cutting output to Q_2. Since the tax is C_2C_1 per unit, government revenue equals $(C_2C_1)Q_2$. Defining incidence as the money burden of
the tax, we see that it is shared by the buyers, who pay $(P_2P_1)Q_2$ more for
Q_2 units, and by the monopolist, who absorbs the remainder out of monopoly profits. The monopolist's share equals $[(C_2C_1) - (P_2P_1)]Q_2$, as represented by the shaded area in Figure 7-2. In addition to the money burden
or incidence of the tax, the monopolist loses profits equal to $(P_1C_1)(Q_1Q_2)$,
and consumers lose consumer surplus approximated by the triangle FBA.

---

[3]Our example applies to the case where all buyers pay the same price, that is, where
the conditions necessary for price discrimination are not met. Algebraically, if price must be
cut by ΔP to sell the nth unit, $MR_n = P_n + \Delta PQ_{n-1}$. Since $\Delta P < 0$, $P_n > MR_n$ for all $n > 1$.

From Figure 7–2, we can see that it is possible to raise the tax high enough to cause the firm to cease to produce altogether. A per unit tax greater than EC_1 would make production unprofitable at any level and drive the firm out of business. In this case, the government would receive no revenue, and there would be no tax incidence as defined in the partial equilibrium approach, but the tax would still impose an excess burden in the form of loss of profits to owners of the firm and loss of consumers' surplus to erstwhile consumers. If the purpose of the tax is to raise revenue, so high a levy would be self-defeating. Such a tax would be justified only if elimination of the firm and its product serves some social purpose.

Economic analysis is less clear cut for firms that sell in markets not characterized by either perfect competition or monopoly, that is, in markets that are imperfectly competitive. These firms can be expected to try to shift a part of their tax burden forward to buyers, but their ability to do so is limited by the response of competitors. If competitors raise prices too, forward shifting may be easy; if they do not, attempts at forward shifting may lead to a substantial decline in quantity sold.

Whether or not imperfect competitors will raise prices depends on what happens to their economic environment. In this sense, the response of a firm to a tax change is not unlike its response to any other change in the cost of doing business. For firms competing in a national market, some items are likely to move more or less in unison. The cost of capital goods, raw materials, and federal taxes are examples. Labor costs are less likely to move in unison, except under industrywide collective bargaining. Long-term trends in state and local taxes are likely to follow similar patterns across the nation, but the timing and magnitude of changes are not likely to coincide. In addition, the structure of business taxes differs among states.

If firms in an imperfectly competitive industry are more likely to raise prices when production costs and/or taxes are rising than when they are not, it follows that a firm will find it easier to shift forward a cost or tax increase shared by all of its competitors than an increase that is experienced alone or by only a minority of its competitors. Therefore, firms selling in regional and national markets may find their ability to shift state and local taxes quite limited, especially in contrast to federal taxes that apply to all domestic producers and, in some cases, to foreign competitors as well.

Obviously, these conclusions are generalizations that must be applied with care to specific cases. The analysis is perhaps most applicable to an oligopolistic market structure in which changes in major components of cost or taxes serve to trigger a price change. If all firms are affected similarly, one of them may decide to take the lead in announcing a price change with reasonable confidence that others will follow. In an industry with a single recognized price leader, the impact of tax changes on that one firm becomes more important, and the distinction between federal and state-local taxes may be somewhat less significant.

As the geographical range of a market narrows, the tax climate of competing firms is likely to become more homogeneous. In a market limited to intrastate firms, all competitors are subject to the same state taxes, and if the market is confined to a single community, local differences are eliminated as well. As the tax climate becomes more homogeneous, forward shifting of state and local taxes should become easier. One should not conclude, however, that all local retailers are so isolated from outside competition that they can recoup tax increases promptly and fully by raising prices. Even in remote communities, sellers face some competition from mail-order firms and merchants in other cities.

Finally, for some commodities, the shifting of taxes may be constrained by competition from foreign imports. The constraints are weakened by transportation costs, tariffs, and other trade restrictions, but in recent years many domestic producers have felt the sting of overseas competition.

As indicated earlier, shifting of taxes also may be backward from buyer to seller. In competitive factor markets, a tax-induced reduction in factor demand may lead to lower factor prices, causing some of the money burden to fall on factor owners. In unionized industries, the wage bargain between the employer and employees may be affected by the employer's net profits, which in turn are influenced by taxes. Forward shifting also may occur in factor markets. For example, unions may try to maintain a given level of take-home pay in the face of higher income or payroll taxes. If they succeed, the tax is shifted forward to the firm, which may or may not succeed in shifting the burden forward to its customers.

Taxation of Households

The household typically is a price taker with little or no control over the prices it pays or receives for goods and services. The partial equilibrium approach focuses on the way in which the household responds to tax-induced differences between the price including tax (paid by the buyer) and the price net of tax (received by the seller). The difference, which is equal to the tax paid on the marginal unit, is referred to as the "wedge" that is driven between the gross and net prices by the tax. In Figure 7–1 it is represented by the distance *BA*.

Partial equilibrium analysis of household response can be extended to markets for goods or services in which households trade. As in the case of firms, analysis is ordinarily limited to a single market, ignoring both the effects of the tax on other markets and the consequences of the government's use of tax receipts.

Income tax. Much of the discussion of household response to the income tax centers on the choice between work and leisure. From the point of view of the individual household, the imposition of an income tax reduces the price of leisure by driving net income at the margin below the pretax level. The lower price for leisure encourages the household to substitute leisure for work, thus reducing the supply of effort. This is an example of the *substitution effect,* a fundamental concept in consumer demand theory. At the same time, however, the imposition of the tax reduces the real income of the household below the pretax level. The fall in real income causes the household to reduce its consumption of leisure. The latter phenomenon is called the *income effect.* An indifference curve, budget constraint diagram is used to illustrate the substitution and income effects of a tax in the appendix to Chapter 8. If the substitution effect, which encourages leisure, is stronger, the household will decrease its supply of work effort; if the income effect, which encourages work, is stronger, the household will increase its supply of work effort. The role of income and substitution effects is reversed in the case of a tax cut.

The effect of an income tax on a household's allocation of income between consumption and saving can be shown best by contrasting an income tax with an equal-yield tax on consumption spending. The income tax includes in its base both current consumption and savings, whereas savings are excluded from a tax on current consumption. Thus, the consumption tax enables a taxpayer to postpone tax payment on the portion of income saved until some future date when current savings are eventually spent. If savings are never spent on consumption, the tax on income saved is avoided altogether. By postponing payment of a tax, the household retains additional funds on which it can earn interest. Consequently, a consumption tax will encourage more saving and less current consumption than will an equal-yield income tax.

Sales and excise taxes. Household consumption patterns can be affected by excise and sales taxes that apply to the sale of some goods while excluding others. If there is a relative increase in the price of taxed items, the consumer will tend to substitute untaxed for taxed items. The overall effect on the demand for untaxed items remains in doubt, however, because the income effect of partial sales and excise taxes encourages reduced purchases of all normal goods (goods for which quantity consumed is related positively to changes in real income).

From the point of view of the individual household, a property tax on residential dwellings is like an excise tax on housing and may be analyzed in the same way as partial sales and excise taxes. Hence, since housing is a normal good, both the substitution and income effects of the property tax operate to lower the amount or quality of housing consumed by a family.

Conclusion. These are just a few examples of how individual households might react to taxation. In limiting the discussion to how a single decision unit reacts, we have failed to account for the aggregate effects of major taxes on the economy. For example, one can consider the effect of an income tax on wages net of tax, but the income tax is likely to alter the before-tax wage rate as well, as we shall see in the next section. The effects of taxation on firms and households are discussed further in each of the chapters on major kinds of taxes.

GENERAL EQUILIBRIUM MODELS

The partial equilibrium approach to shifting and incidence, as we have seen, is limited to analysis of how a tax affects an individual firm, household, market, or a few closely related markets. We turn now to consideration of the limitations of this approach and then to some proposals for restating incidence theory in ways that emphasize the effects of taxation and public expenditures on the overall economy.

Recall that in the partial equilibrium approach the incidence of a tax is equal to its money yield and that shifting deals with how the incidence is distributed between buyers and sellers. There are many other effects, however, including tax-induced changes in prices of untaxed goods and services, losses of consumer and producer surplus, and, perhaps of most importance, effects of the uses of tax revenue on the economy as a whole.

The distinction between direct and indirect effects is regarded by some writers, notably Richard A. Musgrave,[4] as being arbitrary and irrelevant. He reasons that there is no justification for restricting incidence theory to consideration only of what happens in the direct line of market transactions in the taxed commodity.

A more fundamental criticism, methodological in nature, involves misuse of the *ceteris paribus* assumption. This assumption, which means literally "other things being equal," is a useful simplification in much of economic theory. In incidence theory, the assumption suggests that only a tax variable is changed while all the other determinants of economic behavior are unchanged. The consequences of the change in the tax variable are then analyzed. The difficulty is that it is not possible to change only the tax variable. At least one other budgetary variable must be changed as well. Thus, if a tax rate is increased, the additional revenue must be used somehow—to increase government expenditure, reduce some other tax or

---

[4]Richard A. Musgrave, *The Theory of Public Finance* (New York: McGraw-Hill Book Company, 1959), p. 228.

narrow the base of the tax in question, reduce borrowing, retire debt, or replace money creation as a means of financing public expenditures.

The way in which tax revenue is used can have a significant effect on the economy. If one is convinced that the offsetting budgetary efforts cancel each other, as might be the case if the government bought exactly the same goods and services that taxpayers would have bought if they had kept their tax money, or if the offsetting effects are so diffused or insignificant that they can be ignored safely, one may then be justified in using the partial equilibrium approach. These conditions may be met if the yield from the tax is relatively insignificant, but they clearly fail to apply to major revenue sources such as taxes on personal or corporate income or retail sales.

Economics of Budget Policy

As we have seen, a change in one tax variable must be accompanied by at least one other budgetary change so as to accommodate the change in tax revenue. The change in budget policy can affect the economy in many ways, and much of the recent literature on incidence consists of attempts to identify those consequences of budget policy most worth emphasizing.

The magnitude of the problem is so great that some selectivity is required. To illustrate, suppose that it is decided to compare two equilibrium solutions for the economy under two alternative budget policies. Each budget policy calls for a different tax-expenditure package with differences in equilibrium values attributed to differences in budgetary alternatives. Obviously, it is not possible to make an actual comparison of general equilibrium solutions, since it is impossible to run two successive experiments while changing only budget variables. Practical considerations aside, even if we could observe two equilibria that differ only because of budget policy, it would be necessary to find some way of aggregating and summarizing the results. A comparison of millions of equilibrium prices and quantities would not provide us with useful information; no human mind could interpret such a plethora of data.

Professor Musgrave suggests a way out of this difficulty by proposing that we focus on three consequences of budget policy: resource transfer, income distribution, and output effects.[5] In presenting his proposals, Musgrave also develops alternative definitions of incidence that are suited to a general equilibrium setting. First, we outline the three aspects of budget policy that Musgrave considers most important; then, we summarize some of the most useful concepts of incidence.

1. *Resource transfer*. When the government spends money for goods and services, it bids scarce resources away from private use. In a full-employment

[5]Ibid., pp. 207–9.

economy, this transfer reduces the amount of resources available for private use. The reduction in private consumption is the primary burden on public expenditure.

2. *Effect on income distribution.* Budget policy can alter the distribution of real income among households through the effect of taxes and public expenditure on relative prices. An individual household can experience a change in real income on the *sources* side through changes in the prices of factors of production it supplies in the factor market. Likewise, changes in real income on the *uses* side can come about through changes in the prices of goods and services it buys. Musgrave emphasizes that measurement of changes in real income must encompass the effects of price changes on both the sources and uses side, because a change in budget policy can change the real income of a household through its effect on the prices of factors of production and consumer goods. The change in real income attributable to a change in budget policy is called *incidence*. Note that, by focusing on the change in real income that is due to changes in market prices, Musgrave's version of incidence theory ignores increments in real income that the household might receive in the form of benefits from publicly provided goods. Only income available for private use is considered.

3. *Effect on output.* Budget policy operating through its effect on relative prices can influence factor supply, choice of production techniques, saving and investment, and the size and consumption of the output of an economy. Included here are output effects resulting both from voluntary changes in factor supply and from involuntary unemployment of the type envisioned by Keynes. Involuntary unemployment can be brought about by inadequate aggregate demand, which, in turn, is influenced by budgetary policy.

Incidence of Budget Policy

Musgrave's version of incidence theory owes much to the turn-of-the-century writings of the Swedish economist Knut Wicksell. Wicksell was among the first to appreciate the inadequacies of the partial equilibrium approach that dominated English language literature on taxation. We are indebted to Musgrave and Professor James M. Buchanan, who called our attention to voluminous Italian literature,[6] for overcoming our linguistic insularity and pointing out the methodological shortcomings of the English tradition.

Musgrave specifies a variety of ways in which incidence can be measured. All revolve around the effect of alternative budget policies on the distribution of income. The following discussion is limited to two of the most useful of Musgrave's concepts: differential tax incidence and balanced-budget incidence.[7]

Differential tax incidence. Differential tax incidence is defined as the effect on the distribution of income that occurs when one tax is substi-

[6]James M. Buchanan, *Fiscal Theory and Political Economy* (Chapel Hill: University of North Carolina Press, 1960), pp. 24–74.

[7]Musgrave's discussion of incidence concepts appears in Musgrave, *Theory of Public Finance,* pp. 211–17.

tuted for another, subject to the constraint that each tax yields enough revenue to finance a given set of government expenditures. The substitution may be between two different taxes, such as sales and income, or it may involve components of a single tax, such as a broadening of the income tax base accompanied by lower rates. Most incidence studies compare the tax under consideration with a distributionally neutral proportional income tax.

The concept of differential incidence is relevant for policy purposes, since much of the debate over fiscal matters centers on the best way in which to finance a given level of public expenditures. It may be worth noting that it does not make sense to speak of the overall burden of taxation in this context, because differential incidence describes the *redistribution* of burden among individuals. In the aggregate, gains and losses offset each other.

Balanced-budget incidence. Under the balanced-budget approach, the change in the real income of individuals is related to a change in public expenditures combined with a change in tax revenue, governmental borrowing, or money creation needed to offset it. In this case, one can speak of aggregate burden, because an increase in public expenditure does require a reallocation of resources from private to public use. The resulting effect on the distribution of income among individuals is called balanced-budget incidence. No attempt is made to separate the effects of raising revenue from those of spending it.

MEASUREMENT OF INCIDENCE

The difficulty of measuring the shifting or incidence of taxes should be obvious. Yet many incidence studies have been made, and their findings have no doubt had some influence on policy makers. We turn now to a discussion of some of the problems that must be dealt with by anyone who makes quantitative estimates of the way in which tax burdens are distributed.

In the partial equilibrium context, you will recall that measurement of incidence requires identification of those who bear the money burden of a tax. If the relevant supply and demand functions have been estimated, an allocation of money burden between buyers and producers can be attempted. For example, if estimates of S_1 and D in Figure 7–1 are available, an estimate of the tax-induced shift of S_1 could be made. The new equilibrium could then be determined, and the amount of shifting to buyers could be measured.

This procedure is legitimate only if the adjustment in the economy attributable to collection and expenditure of revenue from the tax has no significant effect on the factor supply or product demand functions of the taxed industry. It also presupposes the ability to make statistical estimates of the supply and demand functions. Economists have had reasonable success in making such estimates for some competitively supplied goods, notably, agricultural products. Once an industry departs significantly from the competitive norm, responses to changes in factor supply and product demand generally become more difficult to estimate. Given the stringent conditions that must be met if the estimating procedure described is to be legitimate, coupled with the comparative insignificance of most taxes that meet these conditions, quantitative estimates of incidence as defined in the partial equilibrium context are rare.

Turning to the general equilibrium approach, the various incidence concepts involve measurement of changes in the real income of individuals. Since we are dealing with changes, it is necessary to determine what the distribution of income would be under two different budget policies. The way in which budget policies are varied depends on which of the varieties of incidence as described is used.

For an individual household, the comparison requires measurement of R_1 and R_2, where R stands for real income net of taxes and the subscripts 1 and 2 refer to alternative budget policies. The incidence of a change from policy 1 to 2 (e.g., from a sales to an income tax) is

$$\Delta R = R_1 - R_2$$

Again, measurement problems arise. First, real income ordinarily cannot be measured unequivocally. If on the sources-of-income side the budget change raises the price of factors that a household sells, real income rises; if factor prices fall, real income declines. On the uses-of income side, a fall in the prices of goods purchased increases real income; a rise in prices reduces it. The ambiguity in measuring a change in real income arises if the household responds to changes in relative factor and product prices by changing quantities supplied and demanded. Should R_1 and R_2 be evaluated using quantities associated with budget policy 1 or 2 or some sort of average of 1 and 2? There is no generally satisfactory answer to this question. Some readers will recognize this as an example of *index number bias*, which is explained in most good textbooks in price theory.

Another measurement problem is due to the impossibility of observing the consequences of both policies at a single point in time. Because only one policy can be in effect at a time, the consequences of an alternative policy must be estimated rather than observed. The consequences of policies 1 and 2 could be observed over time, but a comparison of the results would not isolate the effects of the budget change, because changes in other determinants of real income would undoubtedly influence the result. Because we cannot run controlled experiments in economics, we cannot rely fully on observational results in making estimates of incidence.

Even if ΔR could be measured for each household, the results would have to be summarized in some useful way. Looking down a long list of ΔR's, some positive and some negative, would not be very informative. Some means of meaningful aggregation must be devised to make the results more understandable.

The results of most incidence studies are presented in "incidence" tables that show the percentage of income paid in tax by the "typical" or "average" taxpayer in each of several income groups. When results are presented in this way, the reader can easily determine the ways in which the percentages vary as income rises; one can see at a glance whether a tax is progressive, proportional, or regressive. This method of presenting results can be deceptive, however, because of the difficulty of estimating the effects of budget policy on the distribution of real income.

To illustrate, suppose that the percentages shown in an incidence table are obtained by dividing the amount of tax paid by the observed income, including taxes paid, of the "typical" taxpayer in each income group. The results tell us the percentage of income that is absorbed by the tax in question, but they do not give us "incidence" as was just defined. Recall that, when a tax is levied, at least one other budget variable must be changed—expenditures, another revenue source, budgetary surplus or deficit, or some combination thereof. If the set of budgetary changes has any effect on the real income of households on either the sources or uses side, *observed* income will differ from income that would have prevailed in the absence of the tax and accompanying budgetary changes.

Because observed income can be expected to differ from what income would be if the tax and accompanying budget changes were eliminated, an incidence table showing tax as a percentage of observed income does not necessarily tell us how much income has been reduced by the tax. Those who construct incidence tables usually recognize this and make adjustments to observed income that reflect their estimates of changes induced by taxation. Given the complexity of the response to budget changes within a general equilibrium context, the use of statistical estimates is limited. Adjustments are therefore usually justified by appeals to economic theory rather than to empirical evidence, and the tentative nature of the results must be kept in mind.

THE BROOKINGS INCIDENCE STUDY

The tax incidence study by Joseph A. Pechman and Benjamin A. Okner, published by The Brookings Institution in 1974, is perhaps the most thorough of such undertakings. Eight sets of incidence estimates, based on eight sets of shifting assumptions that "span the range of opinions currently held by economists" are presented for the major federal, state, and local taxes for the year 1966.[8]

Two of the eight incidence estimates are shown in Table 7–1. Taxes paid are shown as a percentage of adjusted family income for twelve income groups. Each percentage measures the average tax burden of families within the group. By looking down the columns for each of the taxes and for total taxes, one can quickly discern the pattern of progressivity or regressivity. Each percentage is obtained by dividing the adjusted family income (AFI) of each income group into the tax paid by that group. AFI is a very broad measure of income. It includes money factor income, wage supplements, imputed rent, realized and unrealized capital gains, and transfer payments.

The income data were obtained from the Brookings MERGE file, a data base that was constructed by combining data from a sample of 87,000 individual income tax returns and from a sample of 30,000 households included in the Survey of Economic Opportunity (SEO), a U.S. Census survey that collected much of the socioeconomic data used in studies of poverty.[9]

Shifting Assumptions

The two variants shown in Table 7–1 represent the most progressive (variant I) and least progressive (variant II) of the eight sets of incidence estimates. They are shown here because they are the only variants for which Pechman and Okner give percentages by income group for each of the major taxes.

In both variants it is assumed that there is no shifting of the personal income tax and that the burden of sales and excise taxes is borne in proportion to consumption of taxed items. The difference is in treatment of business and property taxes. Variant I is an application of the competitive model. Property taxes are allocated to households according to their property income, including imputed rent on owner-occupied dwellings. The corporation income tax is split equally between stockholders (allocated according to dividend income) and property owners in general. The reasoning is that competition prevents businesses from shifting taxes forward to consumers. The corporation income tax reduces the income of stockholders, but it also causes a shift of investment to noncorporate assets, thereby driving down the income of owners of these properties as well. The entire

---

[8]Joseph A. Pechman and Benjamin A. Okner, *Who Bears the Tax Burden?* (Washington, D.C.: The Brookings Institution, 1974), p. 2. For a similar effort that also includes estimated benefits of public expenditures, see Richard A. Musgrave, Karl E. Case, and Herman Leonard, "The Distribution of Fiscal Burdens and Benefits," *Public Finance Quarterly,* 2 (July 1974), 259–311.

[9]Pechman and Okner, *Who Bears the Tax Burden?* pp. 21–25.

TABLE 7–1 Effective Rates of Federal, State, and Local Taxes by Type of Tax for 1966 by Family Income Group

ADJUSTED FAMILY INCOME GROUP ($ 000)	INDIVIDUAL INCOME TAX	CORPORATION INCOME TAX	PROPERTY TAX	SALES AND EXCISE TAXES	PAYROLL TAXES	PERSONAL PROPERTY AND MOTOR VEHICLE TAXES	ALL TAXES
			Variant I				
0–3	1.4%	2.1%	2.5%	9.4%	2.9%	0.4%	18.7%
3–5	3.1	2.2	2.7	7.4	4.6	0.4	20.4
5–10	5.8	1.8	2.0	6.5	6.1	0.4	22.6
10–15	7.6	1.6	1.7	5.8	5.8	0.3	22.8
15–20	8.7	2.0	2.0	5.2	5.0	0.3	23.2
20–25	9.2	3.0	2.6	4.6	4.3	0.2	24.0
25–30	9.3	4.6	3.7	4.0	3.3	0.2	25.1
30–50	10.4	5.8	4.5	3.4	2.2	0.1	26.4
50–100	13.4	8.8	6.2	2.4	0.7	0.1	31.5
100–500	15.3	16.5	8.2	1.5	0.3	0.1	41.8
500–1,000	14.1	23.0	9.6	1.1	0.1	0.2	48.0
1,000 and over	12.4	25.7	10.1	1.0	*	0.1	49.3
All groups	8.5	3.9	3.0	5.1	4.4	0.3	25.2
			Variant II				
0–3	1.2	6.1	6.5	9.2	4.6	0.4	28.1
3–5	2.8	5.3	4.8	7.1	4.9	0.4	25.3
5–10	5.5	4.3	3.6	6.4	5.7	0.3	25.9
10–15	7.2	3.8	3.2	5.6	5.3	0.3	25.5
15–20	8.2	3.8	3.2	5.1	4.7	0.3	25.3
20–25	9.1	4.0	3.1	4.6	4.1	0.2	25.1
25–30	9.1	4.3	3.1	4.0	3.6	0.2	24.3
30–50	10.5	4.7	3.0	3.5	2.6	0.2	24.4
50–100	14.1	5.6	2.8	2.4	1.3	0.1	26.4
100–500	18.0	7.4	2.4	1.7	0.7	0.1	30.3
500–1,000	17.7	9.0	1.7	1.4	0.4	0.2	30.3
1,000 and over	16.6	9.8	0.8	1.3	0.3	0.2	29.0
All groups	8.4	4.4	3.4	5.0	4.4	0.3	25.9

*Less than 0.05%.

Source: Joseph A. Pechman and Benjamin A. Okner, Who Bears the Tax Burden? (Washington, D.C.: The Brookings Institution, 1974), p. 59. Reprinted by permission.

payroll (social security) tax, including the employers' share, is assumed to fall on labor and is allocated to workers.

Because ownership of property is heavily concentrated among high-income families, the allocation of all corporate income and property taxes on the basis of property income contributes to an overall pattern of tax incidence that is progressive throughout. Even in this version, however, the property tax and corporation income tax are mildly regressive at the bottom of the income distribution. This is due to the importance of dividends and property income among low-income elderly persons.

Variant II is based on a market power model under which it is assumed that businesses possess enough market power to shift a sizable share of taxes on business property and corporate income forward to consumers. In effect, these taxes are regarded as a form of hidden consumption tax. Specifically, the corporation income tax is split equally between consumers and recipients of property income. The property tax on land is allocated to landowners, the tax on dwellings to occupants, and the property tax on businesses (except land) to consumers. The result is a much less progressive incidence pattern.

Controversies over which set of shifting assumptions is most reasonable are examined in the following chapters, but the reader should be warned that these issues are not settled. That is why the authors of the Brookings study presented eight variants instead of one.

Differential Incidence

Pechman and Okner applied Musgrave's concept of differential incidence, estimating how the distribution of actual taxes differs from what it would have been had the same total tax revenue come from a proportional income tax. In this way they avoided the difficult job of estimating the distributional effects of government expenditures.

The careful reader will note that the data in Table 7–1 appear to differ from the concepts used by Musgrave in defining differential incidence. Recall that Musgrave defined "incidence" as the "redistribution of income for private use" brought about by a change in budget variables. But the Musgrave version is easily derived from the data in Table 7–1. Tax as a percentage of adjusted family income for all taxpayers is obtained by summing AFI over all income groups and dividing the sum into total yield for each tax. The percentages for each tax and for all taxes are shown in the row labeled "All Groups" in Table 7–1. The minor differences noted between variant I and variant II, for example, 8.5 percent for the individual income tax under variant I and 8.4 percent under variant II, are due to the effect of different shifting assumptions on estimated AFI.

Taking the percentages shown under variant I in Table 7–1, if the existing individual income tax were replaced by a porportional tax applied to adjusted family income, the rate would have to be set at 8.5 percent to generate equal yield. Under the existing income tax, the average rate for families in the $0 to $3,000 income group in 1966 was 1.4 percent. Under the proportional tax, it would have been 8.5 percent. The differential incidence is 8.5 percent minus 1.4 percent, or 7.1 percent. In other words, in comparison with a proportional income tax on AFI, the existing income tax gave families in the lowest-income group an average of 7.1 percent more income for private use. For families in the $30,000 to $50,000 income group, the existing tax took an average of 10.4 percent of income. To get differential incidence measured as a percentage of family income, subtract 10.4 percent from 8.5 percent, getting a negative 1.9 percent. Families in this income group had an average of 1.9 percent less to spend on private goods under the existing tax than under a proportional tax on AFI.

Since a proportional tax without exemptions, deductions, or exclusions reduces everyone's income by the same percentage, the relative share of each family in the distribution of income is unaffected by the tax. Any departure of actual taxes from strict proportionality *does* change the relative share of families in the distribution of income for private use, and when derived in the manner shown, the differential incidence concept provides a measure of this redistribution. In terms of progressivity, if the percentages rise as one goes down a column in Table 7–1 from low-income to high-income groups, the tax is progressive. The opposite pattern indicates regressivity.

The percentages in Table 7–1 show that the competitive model (variant I) generates progressive patterns for taxes on individual and corporate incomes and property and regressive patterns for the remaining tax categories. The overall tax structure, shown in the last column, is clearly progressive. The market power model (variant II) shows progressivity for the individual income tax, regressivity for property tax, sales and excise taxes, payroll taxes, and personal property and motor vehicle taxes. The corporation income tax and the overall tax structure show a regressive pattern among low-income groups and a tendency toward progressivity at higher levels.[10]

Variance Within Income Groups

The various percentages shown in Table 7–1 represent averages for households in each income group. While the results tell us a lot about how our tax structure affects the income distribution, they tell us nothing about the differences in tax incidence within each income group. Yet we know that families with the same income may be taxed much differently. Differ-

---

[10]Strictly speaking, the individual income tax is progressive only up to incomes of $500,000. Above this level, percentages decline, although they remain well above the all-group average.

ences in sources of income, consumption habits, property ownership, and place of residence are among the causes.

Pechman and Okner, using data from the MERGE file, present a variety of estimates of variations in the tax incidence among economic and demographic groups.[11] Among their more interesting results is evidence that within-group variance in taxes is greatest among the lowest- and highest-income groups. This result no doubt reflects a greater heterogeneity among households within these groups, but it is also attributable in part to the preferential treatment accorded certain sources and uses of income under the federal income tax.

Evaluation. The sensitivity of the results of an incidence study to shifting assumptions is well illustrated by the differences between variant I, based on the competitive model, and variant II, based on the market power model. Most uncertainty over incidence can be traced to a lack of consensus on the shifting of business taxes, and the following chapters reveal the extent of disagreement among the experts.[12]

A second question concerns the timeliness of the results. The Brookings study is based on data for 1966, but it was not published until 1974. The lag was due in part to the prodigious task of assembling the data needed to assign tax burdens to income groups. Data from several sources, including budget surveys, censuses, and tax collectors' files, had to be matched up and processed. Since much of the data is collected at irregular points in time, an annual update is not feasible.

How much does a study based on 1966 tell us about the incidence of taxes today? Owing to inflation, numerous changes in tax laws, and changes in the underlying income distribution, these results should not be taken too literally. However, the basic patterns shown in the Brookings study—given the same shifting assumptions—can still be expected to hold. Thus, the study should serve as a useful guide to tax policy.

Finally, the reader may wonder why the study includes only estimates of differential incidence. The usefulness of estimating differential incidence by comparing existing taxes with a broadly based tax proportional

---

[11]Pechman and Okner, *Who Bears the Tax Burden?* pp. 66–83.

[12]Recent advances in computational techniques make it possible to simulate the incidence of changes in taxes with computerized general equilibrium models. One such model, constructed with data from national income accounts, the consumer expenditure survey, and federal tax returns, is disaggregated into nineteen industries, sixteen consumer goods categories, and twelve income groups. A comparison of its results with those based on Pechman-Okner procedures shows nearly identical results for the personal income tax and results similar to variant II for taxes on housing and an excise tax on clothing and jewelry. The simulation model allows for adjustments on both the sources and uses side, but it does not allow for change in aggregate factor supply. See Shantayanan Devarajan, Don Fullerton, and Richard A. Musgrave, "Estimating the Distribution of Tax Burdens: A Comparison of Different Approaches," *Journal of Public Economics*, 13 (April 1980), 155–82.

to income have already been mentioned. To make the comparison, Pechman and Okner had to estimate what the distribution of income would be if the tax structure were proportional. Obviously, we have no way of knowing how accurate their estimate of this unobserved distribution, sometimes called a "counterfactual," might be.[13] The farther the counterfactual departs from the observed state of the world, the more questionable the incidence estimates become.

We may be willing to grant that economists know enough to estimate the proportional tax counterfactual with an acceptable degree of accuracy. Contrast this exercise to an attempt to estimate the balanced-budget incidence of the entire public sector. To do so, it would be necessary to compare the observed distribution of income with the distribution that would exist if government were totally absent, that is, in a state of anarchy. The techniques of social science are not adequate to such a task. We must leave the specification of this counterfactual to the musings of utopian dreamers.

SUMMARY

Government decisions to tax, borrow, and spend can have a profound effect on the allocation of resources. By raising revenue to spend on the purchase of goods and services, the public sector takes a direct hand in the allocative process. Collection of taxes and payment of transfers influence allocation indirectly via effects on economic decisions of housholds and businesses.

Partial equilibrium models of the firm and household have been used extensively to analyze the shifting and incidence of taxes. A firm or household may attempt to shift the money burden of a tax by reducing the amount of taxed items that it buys or sells. A buyer or seller with enough market power to set prices may try to shift some or all of the money burden to other transactors by raising the price of items for sale or by lowering the price of offers to suppliers. By tracing the market transactions in a taxed good or service, the economist attempts to determine the extent to which the money burden, or incidence, is shifted from the point of impact, where the tax is collected, to its final resting place.

The partial equilibrium approach considers only the direct money burden of the tax. Indirect effects on other prices and the effects of the uses of tax revenue are ignored. For minor taxes such as regulatory excises, it may be safe to ignore indirect effects. For major tax sources, however, the indirect effects are too important to ignore. Budgetary variables

[13]For a discussion of counterfactuals, see J. Behrens and E. Smolensky, "Alternative Definitions of Income Redistribution," *Public Finance,* 28 (1973), 315–32.

cannot be changed one at a time. An increase in yield of a particular tax must be accompanied by a corresponding change of at least one other budget variable—spending, reduction of another tax, or size of government surplus or deficit.

Recognition of this fact has encouraged public finance economists to adopt a general equilibrium approach to analysis of budgetary impact with particular emphasis on the effect of fiscal activities on the distribution of income. Incidence has taken on a new meaning. It is now defined as the redistribution of household income attributable to a change in two or more fiscal variables. Of particular note are the concepts of differential tax incidence and balanced-budget incidence. Differential tax incidence is a measure of redistribution of income that occurs when one tax (or set of taxes) is substituted for another of equal yield. Balanced-budget incidence measures the redistribution of household income that results from equal changes in tax revenue and government spending.

Attempts to measure incidence as defined in the general equilibrium context are complicated by uncertainty over the extent to which taxpayers shift broadly based taxes and by difficulties in estimating the employment effect of fiscal policy. In addition, a lack of adequate data on income sources, expenditures patterns, and property ownership complicates attempts to assign tax burdens to income and demographic groups. Because of the time it takes to amass the necessary data, estimates may appear to be dated before they can be published. In spite of these difficulties, attempts to estimate incidence in a general equilibrium framework are generally regarded as worthwhile because of the importance of the public sector in our economy.

8

Taxation of Personal Income

A tax on personal income is commonly regarded as the most equitable of all major taxes. Tax liability is a function of income, which is widely accepted as the best index of ability to pay. Because it is levied directly on individuals rather than on transactions or property, a personal income tax can be adjusted for factors aside from income that affect ability to pay. Adjustments for differences in family size and deductions for extraordinary expenses, such as large medical bills, are examples. If a more equal distribution of income is a social goal, a progressive rate structure can be used to help achieve it.

In the United States, the individual income tax has been the most important single source of federal tax revenue since World War II. In fiscal 1981, it yielded $284 billion, or about 49 percent of federal tax collections. Taxes on personal income have been a major revenue source for many state governments since the 1930s. Currently, forty-four states and the District of Columbia levy taxes on personal income. These taxes accounted for $37 billion in revenue in 1980, about 28 percent of state tax revenue. Local governments levy income taxes in those states where state law permits them to do so, but income taxes are generally unimportant at this level. State and especially local rates are far below federal rates.

MEASUREMENT OF INCOME

If the income tax is to meet standards of horizontal and vertical equity among taxpayers, it must be based on a comprehensive definition of income. If income earned from certain sources, say, oil wells or interest on municipal bonds, is taxed at a lower rate than is other income—or not taxed at all—tax burdens under the income tax are no longer based exclusively on ability to pay. Favored treatment to taxpayers who spend their income in certain ways leads to the same result. For this reason, the concept of a *comprehensive tax base* enjoys widespread acceptance among persons concerned with equitable income taxation. Its proponents argue that each dollar of income should be treated the same way, regardless of how it is earned or how it is spent.

Aside from considerations of fairness, a comprehensive tax base tends to minimize the effect of an income tax on the allocation of resources. Individuals seeking to avoid taxes will be encouraged to engage in economic activities accorded preferential tax treatment. The effect of preferential treatment on allocation can become quite significant, especially if rates are high. The temptation to use tax concessions as devices for encouraging certain activities is strong and often provides public officials with a justification for narrowing the income tax base. Much of the debate over income taxation grows out of concern over the trade-off between tax equity and the use of taxation as a device for social control.

For tax purposes, income must be measured over some time period. Common sense dictates that we follow the accounting convention of using a time period of one year, but sometimes this practice can be discriminatory, particularly under a graduated rate structure with rising marginal rates. Hence, the timing of receipts and outlays becomes important, and methods for dealing with variability in income flow are a major facet of tax policy.

The Accretion Concept

The accretion concept of income serves as the starting point for construction of a comprehensive tax base. Income under the accretion concept is defined as the algebraic sum of a taxpayer's consumption expenditures plus the change in net worth over a given time period. Thus, it measures the amount that an individual can spend on consumption without changing net worth. In another sense, it is a measure of the increment in an individual's capacity to exercise control over scarce resources.

The late Henry Simons, a professor of economics at the University of Chicago, used the accretion concept as the basis for his extensive work of tax reform.[1] Recall from Chapter 6 that he developed the concept as an

[1]Henry C. Simons, *Personal Income Taxation* (Chicago: University of Chicago Press, 1938). The accretion concept of income as a measure of income for tax purposes was proposed earlier by Robert M. Haig and is sometimes referred to as the "Haig–Simons" definition. The Simons definition measures income over a one-year period. Quite different rankings of taxpayers would be likely if a lifetime measure of income were used, but such measures have had little effect on tax policy. See A. Mitchell Polinsky, "A Note on the Measurement of Incidence," *Public Finance Quarterly*, 1 (April 1973), 219–30.

ethical norm. It reflected his concern for interpersonal justice in the form of horizontal equity (equal treatment of equals), as well as social justice promoted by redistribution through progressive taxation. Simons's writings demonstrate how an ethical norm can serve as a basis for critical evaluation, in this case as a basis for evaluation of alternative definitions of income for tax purposes. Subsequent defenders of a comprehensive tax base have used the accretion concept for the same purpose.

Implementing the Accretion Concept

The accretion definition serves as a starting point for deriving a base for the income tax, but, like most general precepts, it proves somewhat ambiguous in implementation. Those who agree on general principles may disagree on specific issues of tax policy and discover that the accepted definition is of little use in resolving their dispute. Even when there is no disagreement on principle, problems of administration, enforcement, and taxpayer compliance sometimes require departures from a strict application of the accretion concept.

Despite the concessions that must be made in the interest of practicability and social policy, most of the "experts" seem to agree that the accretion concept provides a useful benchmark for the construction of a tax base. It reminds policy makers of the need to justify each retreat from a comprehensive base, particularly since a narrower base means either higher rates on taxable income or lower total yield. It also provides tax administrators and the courts with a useful norm for administrative rulings and court decisions.

BASIC STRUCTURE OF THE U.S. INDIVIDUAL INCOME TAX

The U.S. individual income tax is a social artifact of great complexity. The tax code, as enacted and amended by Congress, is a lengthy and technical legal document. The code is supplemented by a number of regulations issued by the Internal Revenue Service, which administers the tax, and by decisions in many court cases.

In spite of its complexity, the basic structure of the tax can be summarized quite simply. The relation between the broad definition of income prescribed by the accretion concept and the tax base, or taxable income, may be outlined in the following way:

Accretion (consumption plus change in net worth)

Less: Exclusions (sources of income not taxed)
　　　　Adjustments to income

Equals: Adjusted gross income
Less: Income in zero-rate bracket ($2,300 for single returns, $3,400 for married
          couples filing a joint return)
          Itemized deductions in excess of zero-rate bracket (uses of income not taxed)
          Personal exemptions ($1,000 for taxpayer and each dependent)
          Equals: Taxable income

The proportion of income removed from the tax base by exclusions, deductions, and exemptions can be estimated only roughly, because we have no measure of income as defined under the accretion concept. Taking as a starting point personal income, a narrower measure of income than accretion, Joseph A. Pechman estimated that in 1974 slightly more than half of the income of individuals was removed from the tax base.[2] The reasons for removing so much income from the tax base are discussed in the paragraphs that follow.

Once the taxable income of a taxpayer is determined, the next step is to calculate the tax liability by applying one of four rate schedules to the tax base. For most taxpayers, this is accomplished by the use of a tax table. The rates in each of the schedules are graduated, meaning that income in each successive bracket is taxed at a higher rate.

Two major rate reductions have dropped rates in all brackets well below the high levels set during the Korean conflict. The first was the Kennedy–Johnson tax cut of 1964. Among its major features was a cut in the marginal top-bracket rate from 91 percent to 70 percent. The second was included in President Reagan's Economic Recovery Tax Act, passed in 1981 as the cornerstone of his plan for stimulating production in the private sector. Prior to the Reagan rate reduction, rates ranged from 14 percent in the lowest taxable bracket to 70 percent in the highest. The 1981 legislation phased in a rate reduction averaging 23 percent across all brackets. Rate reductions were scheduled in stages, to begin in October 1981 and to be completed in 1983. For years after 1983, rates will range from 11 percent in the lowest taxable bracket to 50 percent in the top bracket.

For some taxpayers, the regular rate schedules are supplemented or replaced by special procedures for averaging income over several years or for calculating a minimum tax on income otherwise not included in the tax base. Finally, some taxpayers are allowed to reduce their tax liability by subtracting tax credits. Credits are allowed for certain sources or uses of income and for income taxes paid to foreign governments by residents of the United States.

Another important feature of the U.S. individual income tax is withholding. Employers withhold from employee paychecks an amount approximately equal to the anticipated tax liability of the employee and submit the withheld amount to the U. S. Treasury. Most self-employed persons

[2]Joseph A. Pechman, *Federal Tax Policy*, 3rd ed. (Washington, D.C.: The Brookings Institution, 1977), p. 59.

are required to pay to the Treasury quarterly payments of estimated taxes. When the taxpayer files a return after the close of the tax year, any difference between tax liability and withholdings or payments of estimated tax is handled by a refund or additional payment. The withholding feature on wages was introduced during World War II when the bulk of the working population first became subject to the income tax. Withholding was extended to most dividend and interest income in 1983. Its importance should not be underestimated. First, it keeps the relationship between earnings and tax payments current. Second, the taxpayer is spared the psychological impact of having to pay a large amount of tax in one or two installments, as is the usual practice with the property tax. Withholding undoubtedly makes it easier to raise large amounts of revenue from the income tax.

Exclusions

Henry Simons placed particular emphasis on the necessity of treating income from all sources alike if an income tax is to meet the criterion of horizontal equity. Failure to do so leads to differences in the impact of the tax on persons in like circumstances. Because income by source often varies systematically among income groups, exclusions can affect vertical equity as well. Exclusion of an income source that is of greatest importance among high-income families can lead to significant disparities between the apparent progressivity built into a graduated rate structure and actual progressivity as measured by effective rates (tax liability divided by total income).

Several important sources of nonmoney income are not generally taxed. The most significant exclusions of this type are imputed rent on owner-occupied dwellings, unrealized capital gains, and employee fringe benefits. Admittedly, it would be difficult to measure some forms of nonmoney income. It is not likely that the sources mentioned will be included in the tax base, for political as well as practical reasons. Even so, it is important to understand how these exclusions affect tax equity and allocation of resources.

The inequities attributable to exclusion of imputed (or estimated) rent on owner-occupied dwellings can be illustrated by an example. Suppose that Mr. A invests $60,000 in a home, whereas Ms. B invests an equal amount in interest-bearing securities and uses the proceeds to rent housing. A is really in the business of providing housing services for himself, but he pays no tax on the rental income. B pays tax on the interest income and must pay her rent out of after-tax receipts. By not taxing imputed rent on owner-occupied dwellings, the tax law discriminates against renters and encourages persons who otherwise would rent to buy a dwelling unit. The tax code further discriminates in favor of homeowners by allowing deduction of mortgage interest and property taxes. These tax preferences encourage taxpayers to buy housing, rather than to rent and, no doubt, are partly responsible for the recent boom in condominiums. They also interfere with efficient allocation of capital by diverting investment from the industrial sector into housing.

Another major source of income that is not taxed is unrealized capital gains. A capital gain or loss occurs when there is a change in the money value of an asset. This change is reflected in a change in net worth and is therefore income under the accretion definition. If an asset is not sold, the capital gain is unrealized. One reason for not taxing unrealized gains or losses is the difficulty of measurement. Changes in the value of stocks and bonds traded on organized exchanges can be determined with little difficulty, but measurement is more difficult for less liquid assets such as real estate, equity in family-owned businesses, or art collections. Aside from measurement problems, taxation of unrealized gains would create liquidity problems for taxpayers without the cash reserves needed to meet their tax liabilities.

Because unrealized capital gains are not taxed, taxpayers are able to postpone taxes on such income indefinitely, and taxpayers have an incentive to hold on to assets that they would otherwise sell. This feature of the tax, called the "lock-in" effect, interferes with efficient allocation in the capital market. It also complicates tax treatment of realized capital gains and losses. This topic is discussed later in the chapter.

Another source of tax-base erosion is exclusion of employee fringe benefits. Some fringes are difficult to separate from legitimate costs of doing business. Employer provision of meals and lodging and other forms of "expense account living" for salespersons are examples. They must be dealt with under admittedly arbitrary regulations or "rules of thumb" designed to make compliance and enforcement manageable. Exclusion of employer contributions to group life and health insurance plans and group legal services is more questionable. The proliferation of fringe benefits is a result of a desire on the part of employees to receive tax-free income, although the employer may benefit somewhat if health insurance improves the quality of the work force. If fringes of this type were taxed as ordinary income, they would tend to disappear, since employees would prefer cash to income earmarked for certain purposes. The only offsetting factor would be lower premiums that might result from economies of scale in providing insurance coverage for large groups.

Fringe benefits in the form of employer contributions to pension plans are excluded from the tax base, but pension benefits are generally taxable. Some critics contend that employer contributions should be taxed as employee income at the time they are made rather than when they are received as benefits. They point out that this would increase tax revenue, because employees are generally in higher tax brackets while working than when retired.

In one sense, employer contributions to pension plans are accrued income, and the accretion definition presumes use of accrual accounting. It is not clear, however, that taxation of pension rights as they accrue would be equitable. The taxpayers would have to pay tax on income that may not be received for many years. Indeed, it may never be received. Employees lose pension rights if they quit a firm before they work there for a minimum number of years. They or their survivors may lose benefits if they die before retirement. Pension plans, like social security, redistribute income from the short-lived to the long-lived. Taxation of contributions, rather than benefits, accentuates this redistribution.

Aside from equity, exclusion of pension contributions encourages growth of the private pension system. Private pensions are an important supplement to social security, particularly among more affluent households. In addition, private pension funds are an important source of funds for capital markets.

Exclusion of fringe benefits is sometimes criticized on equity grounds, since employees with fringe benefits pay less tax than do comparably situated employees with money income. If the labor market is reasonably efficient, however, there will be a tendency for offsetting wage differentials to appear. Untaxed fringe benefits serve to make certain jobs more attractive, like other job perquisites such as pleasant, clean surroundings or a favorable geographical location. As workers respond to the more attractive offerings, relative wages in these jobs will tend to fall. Even if the functioning of the labor market serves to eliminate horizontal inequities among workers, however, the proliferation of fringe benefits can contribute to market inefficiencies as firms overallocate resources to the provision of in-kind benefits for employees.[3]

Transfer payments are another major form of income not usually taxed. Among the transfer payments excluded from the income tax base are public transfers, such as social security benefits, veterans' benefits, and welfare payments and private transfers, such as scholarships, benefits from private charities, and gifts and bequests.

Over the past four decades, public transfers have become increasingly important. The Social Security Act of 1935 introduced a national pension system financed by a payroll tax. Survivors benefits and disability insurance were added later. The 1935 act also introduced various programs of assistance for the needy that are financed jointly by federal, state, and local governments. Unemployment compensation, which provides temporary income for those out of work, originated in the 1930s as well.

At the time of their inception, exclusion of payments under these programs was of little importance. Owing to high exemption levels, only a

---

[3]Equity and allocational aspects of exclusion of fringe benefits are discussed in Charles T. Clotfelter, "Equity, Efficiency, and the Tax Treatment of In-kind Compensation," *National Tax Journal,* 32 (March 1979), 51–60.

small minority of income recipients paid federal income tax, and virtually none of those who did were recipients of public transfers. Even today, many who receive public assistance would not receive enough income to have to pay taxes even if their transfers were not excluded. They must pass a relatively strict "means test" that denies payments to families with income and/or assets in excess of certain limits. Other programs, notably social security benefits, unemployment compensation, and service-connected veterans' disability payments, are based on eligibility requirements that have nothing to do with needs. Consequently, most of the concerns of tax reformers are directed at these programs.

Omission of social security benefits from the tax base (coupled with no deduction of the employee's share of the social security payroll tax) dates from the program's inception in the 1930s. This practice has benefited past and current recipients of social security, who in most cases have received much more in benefits than they paid in taxes. Returns to future beneficiaries, relative to taxes paid in while working, are likely to be much lower for reasons described in Chapter 13. This will have the effect of reducing the significance of the present arrangement, although it might have considerable impact on the lifetime tax burden of specific individuals.

The total exclusion of unemployment compensation benefits for workers who are temporarily out of work aroused much criticism from those who felt that it discouraged recipients from seeking new employment. Because of the exclusion from the income tax base, the differential between unemployment benefits and after-tax wages was narrowed to the point where the economic incentive to return to work was thought to be weak. Congress responded in a modest way in the Revenue Act of 1978 by reducing the amount of unemployment benefits excluded from the tax base. The amount excluded is reduced by one-half of the amount by which gross income (including unemployment compensation) exceeds $20,000 for single workers and $25,000 for married workers filing joint returns. Consequently, only the more affluent workers are affected.

Some supporters of a more comprehensive tax base contend that gifts and inheritances should be taxed like other income. Under the accretion concept, transfer of property is clearly income unless the transfer takes place within the taxpaying unit. Taxation of gifts and inheritances as income could subject taxpayers to a much higher marginal rate than normal if the transfer is large. If the property is transferred in the form of nonliquid assets, it may be necessary to sell or borrow to meet tax obligations. Gifts and inheritances are subject to taxation under separate federal and state taxes, but there is no reason in principle why they could not be taxed as income as well, particularly if the primary social goal is to break up large concentrations of wealth.

A number of other transfers take place within the private sector, and most enjoy partial or total exclusion from the income tax base. Life insurance benefits, lawsuit settlements, workmen's compensation, and receipts in cash or kind from private charities are generally granted total exclusion. Presumably, recipients of private charity would pay little or no income tax anyway, so this exclusion is not very important, but exclusion of other receipts does appear to violate the principles of horizontal and vertical equity as outlined by Simons.

Exclusions are often used to promote specific social goals. The most significant example is the exclusion from the tax base of interest on the debt of state and local government. Interest on state and local debt has been exempt from taxation since the present income tax was introduced in 1913. Originally, the exemption probably reflected doubt about the constitutionality of such a tax, but it is now generally believed that the courts would accept it.[4] The effect of the exclusion is to make tax-free state and local securities particularly attractive to high-bracket taxpayers and corporations. As a result, interest rates are substantially below those on other debt instruments of comparable quality. State and local governments benefit by being able to borrow at low interest rates but at the cost of greater tax inequity. Because the interest exemption is most profitable to taxpayers with high taxable income, this provision is objectionable in terms of vertical, as well as horizontal, equity. Elimination of the exclusion would redress the inequity among taxpayers, but so abrupt a transition would severely upset the market for the affected securities. State and local government securities would no longer be such attractive investments, and their market price would fall precipitously. Their owners would suffer capital losses, and state and local governments would find it more expensive to borrow.

Some politicians have suggested total elimination of the tax on interest income, but it is unlikely that Congress will accept so sweeping a change. One reason is concern over revenue losses and equity. Another is that elimination of the tax on all interest income would undermine the favored status of state and local securities with consequences similar to those just described. This case illustrates how difficult it sometimes is to deal with a well-established tax loophole.

In the 1981 Economic Recovery Tax Act, Congress took a more modest step toward favored treatment of interest income. The act introduces a net interest exclusion of 15 percent of qualified interest income. This provision, which applies to interest earned after January 1, 1985, allows an exclusion of up to $450 on individual returns and $900 on joint returns. Most interest income from domestic sources qualifies for the exclusion. Net qualified interest is obtained by subtracting qualified interest expense from qualified interest income. Qualified interest expense includes all deductible interest on personal debt other than interest on mortgages and on trade or business loans.

[4]Pechman, *Federal Tax Policy*, p. 115.

Adjustments to Income

The tax code allows taxpayers to subtract certain uses of income from the tax base before arriving at adjusted gross income. These outlays are referred to as adjustments to income. They may be subtracted from the tax base even if the taxpayer does not itemize deductions, making them available to all taxpayers. Among the adjustments allowed are selected employee business expenses, payments into individual retirement accounts, and alimony.

Moving expenses incurred because of a change in location of job are allowed as adjustments to income for employees (to the extent that they are not reimbursed by employers) and the self-employed. Employees may remove from the tax base unreimbursed travel expenses associated with their jobs. These include transportation, meals, and lodging, but not costs of commuting to work. Other job-related expenses are deductible only for employees who itemize.

As we have seen, employer contributions to pension plans are not counted as taxable income of employees. To redress discrimination against the many employees who are not covered by employer-financed pension plans, Congress in 1975 introduced individual retirement accounts, or IRAs. In its original form, this feature allowed employees not covered by an employer plan to contribute a fraction of their incomes to an IRA account. IRA contributions are not to be taxed until they are returned as retirement benefits. The 1981 Economic Recovery Tax Act liberalized restrictions on tax-free contributions and extended eligibility to all employees, including those covered by employer pension plans. Employees may deduct IRA contributions of up to $2,000 per year from taxable income. If an unemployed spouse is included, contributions of up to $2,250 may be deducted. The amount deducted cannot exceed an employee's earnings. The law imposes a tax penalty on employees who withdraw contributions from an IRA account before age 59½.

The extension of IRAs to employees covered by employer pension plans compromises the original intent of the provision. Once again, the tax code favors employees who are also covered by employer plans. The purpose of the extension of eligibility is to encourage a larger flow of savings into the capital markets. This is one of many examples where the goal of tax equity is overridden by other social goals.

A similar program is in effect for self-employed persons. They may deduct up to 15 percent of self-employment income (to a maximum of $15,000) if they invest it in an approved Keogh (HR 10) retirement plan. As in the case of other private pension plans, income earned on these contributions is taxed only when it is paid back after retirement.

Alimony payments are treated as tax-free adjustments to income for the person making the payment, but they must be reported as income by the person receiving them.

Deductions

Taxpayers are allowed to deduct several categories of expenditure in arriving at taxable income. The reasons for some deductions are obscure, but in most cases the intent is either to come up with a more equitable measure of taxable income or to use the income tax as an instrument for subsidizing selected expenditures.

The current tax law contains two forms of deduction. One is a minimum deduction that is granted to all taxpayers. The minimum, formerly called the standard deduction, is now referred to as the zero-bracket amount. Beginning in 1979, the minimum was set at $2,300 for single taxpayers and $3,400 for married couples filing jointly. Taxpayers are allowed additional deductions, called itemized deductions, for selected expenditures. Itemized deductions are permited only to the extent that they exceed in total the zero-bracket amount. Thus, a married couple with deductible expenses of $2,000 would take the zero-bracket deduction of $3,400 but would not itemize. A couple with deductible expenses of $5,000 would take the $3,400 minimum and an additional $1,600 in itemized deductions. Itemizing is most common among taxpayers in the higher income brackets.

Some itemized deductions are designed to improve the measurement of income. One example is the deduction for uninsured casualty losses. A loss of property via storm, fire, or accident reduces net worth and therefore reduces income as measured by accretion. The law allows deductions for uninsured losses insofar as they exceed 10 percent of adjusted gross income. Because the law does not permit deduction of insured losses or of insurance premiums, it tends to discriminate against those who buy casualty insurance. Measurement of income is also improved by deduction of selected expenses of earning income (in addition to those classified as adjustments to income). Examples include outlays for professional books and periodicals, membership dues in unions and professional organizations, broker's fees, and special clothing or tools used on the job.

Personal exemptions, adjustments to income, and the zero-bracket amount generally remove from the tax base enough income to maintain a minimal standard of living, but an additional adjustment may be needed for taxpayers with abnormally high medical expenses. Taxpayers are allowed to deduct uninsured medical and dental expenses and medical insurance premiums in excess of 5 percent of adjusted gross income.

The deductions for contributions, state and local income, sales, and property taxes, and interest on personal debt represent an indirect federal subsidy of these uses of income. Although it is generally agreed that at least some of these uses of income are socially desirable, many advocates of tax reform argue that, if government wants to provide subsidies, it should do so directly through appropriations rather than indirectly through deductions.

Deductibility of contributions to charitable, scientific, and educational institutions helps to support activities that presumably contribute to social welfare and reduce the need for tax-financed services. Deductions for contributions to religious organizations no doubt reflect a perception among members of Congress of strong public support for nurturing organized religion.

Under the graduated rate structure of the U.S. individual income tax, the government subsidy to itemized contributions ranges from 11 cents on the dollar in the lowest taxable bracket to 50 cents on the dollar in the highest. The tax incentive to philanthropy is therefore stronger at higher income levels. Economic evidence indicates that deductibility of contributions is a powerful device for directing the income of the well-to-do toward socially beneficial uses.

A recent study by Martin Feldstein, using data from a sample of federal tax returns, indicates that elimination of this deduction would cut contributions by from 25 to 50 percent and that the loss to nonprofit organizations would exceed the tax gain to the Treasury. The loss in contributions would be greatest for educational institutions and hospitals and least for religious organizations.[5] At the time of Feldstein's study, the top marginal rates were as high as 70 percent. Observers will be watching closely to see whether the reduction of the top rate to 50 percent, which became effective in 1982, discourages high-income taxpayers from giving.

Should we use the tax law as a device to encourage contributions from the rich? William Vickrey argues that, by making philanthropy a rich person's game, we risk building a plutocratic bias into our nonprofit institutions.[6] The implications of Vickrey's warning are difficult to assess, and by its very nature, philanthropy is likely to be dominated by the rich, even without a tax break. A more fundamental issue is whether a dollar contributed by a wealthy taxpayer to a nonprofit organization is likely to be used to better advantage than is the 50 cents of tax revenue that, in the absence of deductibility, would be allocated by the government. In light of the imperfections inherent in any public choice mechanism, the answer is not at all obvious.

A provision of the 1981 Economic Recovery Tax Act is designed to encourage contributions from taxpayers who do not itemize. Most such taxpayers are in low- or middle-income groups. Even if their total deductions fall short of the zero-bracket amount, taxpayers are now allowed to deduct a fraction of their contributions. The fraction increases from 25 per-

---

[5]Martin Feldstein, "The Income Tax and Charitable Contributions: Part I—Aggregate and Distributional Effects," *National Tax Journal*, 28 (March 1975), 81–100, and "The Income Tax and Charitable Contributions: Part II—The Impact on Religious, Educational, and Other Organizations," *National Tax Journal*, 28 (June 1975), 209–26.

[6]William S. Vickrey, *Agenda for Progressive Taxation* (New York: The Ronald Press Company, 1947), p. 131.

cent of contributions (up to a $25 maximum) in 1982–1983 to 50 percent (up to a $75 maximum) beginning in 1984. This provision will expire in 1987 unless reenacted by Congress.

Deductibility of state and local taxes has the effect of reducing the net burden of these taxes for taxpayers who itemize. In this way, resistance to state and local taxes may be reduced, particularly among taxpayers in high brackets. At one time, deductibility of state and local income taxes served the additional function of preventing the combined federal-state-local rates from approaching or even surpassing the confiscatory 100 percent rate. From 1950 to 1963, for example, the top-bracket federal rate was 91 percent. If neither the federal nor state tax allowed deduction of income tax paid to the other, a state tax rate of only 9 percent could have subjected some taxpayers to a marginal rate of 100 percent, completely eliminating any incentive to earn more income. Federal deductibility reduced the effective federal rate to 82.8 percent and the effective combined rate to 91.8 percent.[7] With the top federal rate now down to 50 percent, confiscatory rates are no longer a problem. Nevertheless, deductibility of state income tax on federal returns does give states a greater opportunity to adopt progressive rate structures without putting a squeeze on high-bracket taxpayers.

The same argument cannot be used to defend deduction of sales and property taxes, but failure to allow taxpayers to deduct them would discriminate against residents of states that rely heavily on these sources of revenue. On the one hand, limitation of deductibility to the income tax would induce states and local governments to rely more heavily on this revenue source, and persons who desire greater reliance on the income tax may favor such a restriction. On the other hand, those who favor separation of revenue sources or greater state autonomy would oppose limiting deductibility to the income tax. Deductibility of the property tax draws yet another criticism, because it favors homeowners over renters, who are presumed to pay property taxes indirectly through higher rents.

The practice of allowing deductions for income, sales, and property taxes discriminates against other means of paying for public services. A number of local governments are experimenting with user charges for selected capital improvements that benefit particular property owners or for services such as refuse collection or sewage treatment. In some communities, refuse collection and even fire protection are provided by private firms. Alternatives to general tax finance may be worth encouraging, but unless deductibility is extended to these outlays, the tax law will tend to limit their use.

The deductibility of interest on personal debt is the most questionable of the subsidy-type deductions. Only if interest is a legitimate cost of earn-

---

[7]Assuming a federal rate of 91 percent and a state rate of 9 percent, the effective federal tax on a dollar of additional income would be .91 ($1.00-$0.09), or 82.8 cents. The total tax on a marginal dollar includes 82.8 cents federal plus 9 cents state tax for a total of 91.8 cents.

ing taxable income, as when one borrows to acquire an income-earning asset, is a deduction justified. It is difficult to see the propriety of subsidizing consumer installment debt. Deduction of mortgage interest on owner-occupied dwellings would be justified only if imputed rental income were taxed. This provision is yet another source of discrimination against renters, but its popularity among homeowners is likely to guarantee its continuation. The best that tax reformers can hope for is an upper limit on the mortgage deduction. It is estimated that an annual limit of $5,000 would leave about 95 percent of homeowners unaffected while removing the tax subsidy only for owners of very expensive dwellings or of the more lavish vacation homes.[8]

Exemptions

The personal exemption is intended to remove from the income tax base an amount required to cover the minimum subsistence needs of each family. The exemption is currently set at $1,000 per person. The fixed per capita exemption fails to allow for economies of scale in household living costs. Two cannot live as cheaply as one, but two adults living together can live more cheaply than can two living separately. In addition, the fixed exemption fails to reflect the lower subsistence costs of young children.

These shortcomings are offset somewhat by the zero-rate-bracket deduction. The $2,300 minimum deduction plus the exemption removes at least $3,300 from the tax base for all single taxpayers. The $3,400 minimum deduction plus exemptions guarantees married couples at least $5,400 of tax-free income. Beginning in 1985, the minimum will be protected against inflationary erosion by annual indexing.

Present law grants a double exemption of $2,000 for persons aged 65 and over and for persons who are blind. A blind person over age 65 receives a triple exemption. The double exemption for persons over age 65 cannot be justified on equity grounds. Subsistence needs do not suddenly double on one's sixty-fifth birthday. It is true that, on average, persons over age 65 have lower incomes than do younger persons, but the relevant comparison is between persons of different ages who have the same income. To provide a tax break based strictly on age violates the principle of horizontal equity or equal treatment of equals. The double exemption adds to the horizontal inequity created by excluding social security benefits from the tax base. The double exemption for the blind is a crude way of adjusting for additional expenses incurred because of blindness. If this method is to be used to allow for the added costs of being blind, a case might be made for extending the provision to persons with other severe

---

[8]The proposal to put a limit on the mortgage interest deduction apparently has the support of budget director David Stockman, architect of President Reagan's economic recovery plan. Stockman is quoted as calling such a limit a "mansion cap." See William Greider, "The Education of David Stockman," *The Atlantic Monthly,* December 1981, p. 36.

disabilities. Such an extension could become costly to administer, however, and under present law, some disability-related costs are allowed as medical deductions.

Rate Schedules

The U.S. individual income tax has four separate rate schedules. A taxpayer's filing status determines which schedule will be used. The four schedules are for married couples filing joint returns, unmarried heads of households, other unmarried individuals, and married individuals filing separate returns. The number and width of tax brackets differ among schedules, but all four have bracket rates ranging from 11 percent in the lowest taxable bracket to 50 percent in the highest. For married taxpayers filing joint returns, the zero-rate bracket applies to the first $3,400 of income. Above that level are fourteen brackets with rates ranging from 11 percent on income between $3,400 and $5,500 to 50 percent on income in excess of $162,400. Bracket rates increase in increments from one to five percentage points. For unmarried taxpayers the zero-rate bracket applies to the first $2,300 of taxable income. Above that level are fifteen brackets with rates ranging from 11 percent on income between $2,300 and $3,400 to 50 percent on income in excess of $81,800.[9]

The tax treatment of single individuals versus married couples has been a subject of controversy for years. Shortly after World War II, the United States adopted the practice of income splitting for married couples filing joint returns. The effect at that time was to double the size of rate brackets on joint returns. As a result, if two single persons earning equal incomes were married, their combined income placed them in the same bracket that they were in as single taxpayers, and the two of them paid the same total tax as before marriage. In this case, the law did not discriminate for or against marriage. If a person with taxable income married a person with no income, the taxpayer dropped to a lower bracket and paid less tax. In nearly all cases, marriage resulted in tax savings for two persons with unequal incomes.

In response to complaints about discrimination against single taxpayers, Congress in 1969 passed legislation introducing a new rate schedule for single persons, ensuring that their taxes would not exceed 120 percent of the tax paid by married couples with the same taxable income. Since 1969 there have been many cases in which married couples filing jointly pay more tax than they would pay as single persons earning the same incomes. The tax differential is most pronounced among middle-income

---

[9]Bracket and exemption limits cited are for 1984. For 1983, the 50 percent bracket begins at $109,400 of taxable income for married couples filing jointly and at $44,300 for single taxpayers. Beginning in 1985 bracket limits and the personal exemption will be indexed, as described in the next discussion.

spouses with roughly equal earnings. A few affected couples gained nation-wide publicity by getting tax divorces while continuing to live together. In 1981 Congress acted to reduce the so-called "marriage tax" by introducing a special provision for two-earner married couples. It allows a deduction of 10 percent of the first $30,000 of income earned by the spouse with lower earnings. Even with this provision, many working couples will continue to experience a marriage penalty under existing rate schedules.

A third rate schedule, with rates approximately halfway between those for single and married taxpayers, is in effect for unmarried taxpayers with dependents. A fourth schedule, for married couples filing separate returns, has the same rate structure as the schedule for joint returns, but the brackets are only half as wide. Effective rates under this schedule are higher than under the other schedules.

Income Averaging

One characteristic of a graduated rate structure is a tendency to penalize incomes that fluctuate substantially from year to year. For example, an individual with an income of $10,000 one year and $50,000 the next will generally pay more in taxes over a two-year period than will an individual who earns $30,000 in both years. To reduce discrimination against fluctuating incomes, taxpayers with sizable increases in income are permitted to use a special formula that averages income over a five-year period. To be eligible, taxpayers must have been U.S. residents over the entire period and have provided at least 50 percent of their support during each of the five years. The latter provision is intended to prevent college students who are supported by parents from averaging after they become full-time workers. Taxpayers with declining incomes are not permitted to take advantage of averaging.

Credits

Exclusions, personal exemptions, and deductions remove income from the tax base, leaving taxable income as a residual. The applicable rate schedule is then applied to taxable income to determine tax liability before subtraction of credits. Recall that tax savings from exclusions, exemptions, and deductions range from 11 cents to 50 cents per dollar, depending on the taxpayer's marginal bracket. Thus, tax saving is a function of filing status and taxable income. Because credits are subtracted from the tax liability *after* the rate schedule is applied to taxable income, they are independent of the tax bracket. Credits, therefore, add flexibility to the income tax.

Until recently, credits were used sparingly, but in 1975 Congress began experimenting with tax credits designed to benefit low-income working families. One such device is the earned income credit. It is available only to persons with dependent children who receive earned (wage or self-employment) income. The credit is equal to 10 percent of earned income up to $5,000 for a maximum of $500. For earnings above $6,000, the credit is reduced at a rate of 12.5 cents per additional dollar earned, phasing out at $10,000. In the likely case in which the credit exceeds income tax liability, the family receives a cash payment. Thus, the earned income credit is really a form of welfare payment for low-income working families with children.[10]

The credit for child care expenses is also directed at working families. Working couples and single working parents are allowed a tax credit to offset a part of the cost of work-related child care expenses for children under age 15. A similar provision is available for care of a disabled spouse or other dependent.

A retirement income credit for persons over age 65, revised several times since its introduction in 1954, is designed to reduce discrimination between income from private pensions and tax-exempt income from social security. This credit is reduced by subtracting from it any social security or other tax-free retirement income. In addition, it is phased out for those with higher incomes. As a result of the almost universal coverage of social security, the importance of the retirement credit is declining over time.

Other credits include the 10 percent credit for investment in capital equipment, described in Chapter 9, a residential energy credit for homeowners who install energy-saving items, and a credit equal to 50 percent of contributions to political campaigns. The current maximum for this credit is set at $50 for single taxpayers and $100 for married couples filing jointly. Its stated purpose is to clean up American politics by encouraging small contributions. Taxpayers with income earned in foreign countries are allowed a credit for income taxes paid to foreign governments. The credit cannot exceed the amount of U.S. tax that would have been paid on the income had it not been taxed by a foreign country. The foreign tax credit is designed to eliminate double taxation of income from foreign sources.

Opportunities exist for more extensive use of income tax credits. For example, they could be used in place of the personal exemption. Because credits are independent of the rate bracket, a substitution of credits for exemptions would reallocate some of the tax burden from low-income to high-income taxpayers. During the 1970s, Congress experimented with a mix of personal credits and exemptions, but the credits were dropped when the exemption was raised from $750 to $1,000 in 1979. A similar redistribution of tax burdens (assuming an equal loss to the federal treasury) could be accomplished by replacing some itemized deductions with credits.

Congress has considered and rejected proposals to grant tax credits

[10]The earned income credit is often described as a form of negative income tax. More precisely, the earnings credit works like a wage subsidy on the first $5,000 of earnings and like a tax on wages in the $6,000 to $10,000 range.

to parents that would reimburse them for a part of the cost of college tuition for their children. Tuition credits would shift part of the burden of rising tuition to the federal Treasury and provide an indirect subsidy to higher education. Tuition credits could be extended to parents of children in private elementary and secondary schools. This arrangement would provide some relief for state and local taxpayers by reducing public school enrollments. Proponents see it as a way of getting around the constitutional prohibition against direct aid to parochial schools. As you might expect, for elementary and secondary students, tuition credits are strongly opposed by teachers' unions and public school administrators.

Special Provisions

The tax provisions described thus far apply to so-called "ordinary income." They are augmented by special provisions dealing with capital gains and by a minimum tax on some types of income that would otherwise escape taxation.

Capital gains.   Capital gains or losses occur when there is a change in the money value of assets. When an asset is sold, the difference between the selling price and the "basis" (usually the purchase price less depreciation, if any) is the realized gain or loss. As we have seen, any change in asset value is included in income under the accretion concept, but for practical reasons, only realized gains or losses are relevant for tax purposes.

Taxation of realized capital gains is one of the most controversial aspects of tax policy. The controversy revolves around two issues. One issue concerns the treatment of long-term capital gains under a progressive rate structure. The basic question is, should a gain that has accumulated over a number of years be taxed like ordinary income in the year in which it is realized? If rates are graduated, a taxpayer might be subjected to marginal rates well above those that would have applied had the gains been taxed as they accrued. Not only is this inequitable, but it also affects the timing of decisions to sell assets, and therefore, interferes with efficient allocation of resources. A second issue relates to the effect of preferential treatment of capital gains on the willingness of individuals to invest and take risk. For many investors, the capital gains potential is a more important consideration than is the annual flow of dividends or interest. This is particularly true of the more speculative investments, such as those in new companies or in some forms of oil or mineral exploration. In these cases, it is claimed that preferential tax treatment of capital gains and liberal allowances for capital losses increase the supply of venture capital.

The case for preferential treatment of capital gains is complicated by considerations of vertical equity. As you might expect, income from realized capital gains is heavily concentrated among taxpayers in the higher brackets. Data from federal tax returns show that long-term gains account for about 2 percent of reported income for taxpayers with adjusted gross incomes of less than $50,000, compared with about two-thirds of reported income for those with incomes over $1 million.[11] Because of the heavy concentration of realized gains at the top, preferential treatment can seriously undermine the progressivity of the income tax.

The tax literature abounds with proposals for lessening the effects of "bunching" of capital gains into the year in which they are realized. Most of them involve either an averaging scheme, which taxes gains as if they had been spread equally over the years the asset was held, or prorating, where assets held over a specified length of time are taxed as if they were held for some arbitrary period of, say, three or five years. Under an averaging procedure, an individual taxpayer stands a good chance of benefiting by postponing the realization of capital gains, at least for a limited number of years. By postponing payment of taxes, the taxpayer is in effect enjoying an interest-free loan from the government. For this reason, it is sometimes suggested that the taxpayer be required to pay interest on postponed taxes.

Proposals of the type just described are quite reasonable, but if implemented, they would treat capital gains income less favorably than do the provisions generally in effect in industrialized countries. In the United States, for example, a distinction is made between short-term gains on assets held for one year or less and long-term gains on assets held for more than one year. Short-term gains are treated like ordinary income, but 60 percent of net long-term gains are excluded from taxable income. The 60 percent exclusion means in effect that the actual tax rate on long-term capital gains is 40 percent of the rate on ordinary income. Even for taxpayers in the highest (50 percent) bracket, the effective rate on long-term gains is only 20 percent.

The exclusion provision is difficult to justify. If does serve to offset the inequities of bunching, but in a very crude way. The same tax break is allowed whether an asset is held for one year and one day or sixty years. The preferential rate encourages schemes to convert ordinary income into capital gains and attempts to control these activities have generated some of the most complex provisions in the tax code.

Another feature of the tax law is the asymmetrical treatment of capital losses and capital gains. Short-term capital losses may be deducted in full from short- or long-term gains, and any remaining short-term loss may be deducted in full from ordinary income. A taxpayer with a net long-term loss is allowed to deduct only 50 percent from ordinary income up to a maximum of $3,000. Losses in excess of $3,000 may be carried forward to

[11]U.S. Department of the Treasury, *Statistics of Income, 1977: Individual Income Tax Returns* (Washington, D.C.: Government Printing Office, 1980), pp. 16, 20.

future years. Losses carried forward can be written off in full against capital gains received in future years, but no more than 50 percent of long-term losses can ever be subtracted from ordinary income.

One of the biggest tax loopholes is the failure to tax capital gains unrealized at death. Property received as a bequest is revalued for tax purposes, and the value at death becomes the basis for the recipient. No income tax is paid on gains accrued during the lifetime of the deceased. As a consequence, many elderly taxpayers have an incentive to hold on to assets that have appreciated in value. The Tax Reform Act of 1976 included a provision that would have gradually narrowed this loophole by requiring recipients of bequests to assume the basis of the decedent. Congress rescinded this "recapture" provision before it went into effect. Capital gains unrealized at death may be taxed under the federal estate tax, but the 1981 revision of this tax has greatly reduced its impact.

The tax code contains two provisions designed to ease the impact of capital gains taxation on homeowners. The "rollover" provision allows a taxpayer to postpone payment of capital gains tax on the sale of a principal residence if a new residence is purchased within two years at a price that exceeds the capital gain on the old residence. In addition, a taxpayer age 55 or over is allowed a once-in-a-lifetime exclusion of up to $125,000 in capital gain from the sale of a principal residence. The latter provision makes it possible for many older persons to move into rented quarters without having to pay a capital gains tax on sale of a home.

The inflationary environment of the past decade has created pressure on Congress to provide some means of adjusting realized capital gains for inflation. Gains are measured in current or nominal terms, but in a period in which prices have more than doubled in a decade, changes in nominal value run far ahead of changes in real value. Indeed, a study by Martin Feldstein and Joel Slemrod indicates that in 1973 sellers of capital stock paid taxes on nominal gains of $4.5 billion, which, when adjusted for inflation, became real capital losses of almost $1 billion.[12] A tax bill including indexing for capital gains passed the House of Representatives in 1978, but the indexing provision was dropped from the final version.

From 1969 to 1976, Congress adopted a series of amendments that chipped away at the preferences accorded to capital gains. This trend was reversed in 1978 when the exclusion of long-term gains was raised from 50 to 60 percent and the recapture provision for gains unrealized at death was dropped. The relaxation in taxing of capital gains is most beneficial to high-bracket taxpayers, but Congress apparently concluded that the need to induce taxpayers to save and invest justified tax concessions to the rich. Tax preferences may generate more funds for capital investment. In light of the concern about a capital shortage and the lack of growth in productivity, it

---

[12]Martin Feldstein and Joel Slemrod, "Inflation and the Excess Taxation of Capital Gains on Corporate Stock," *National Tax Journal*, 31 (June 1978), 107–18.

is not surprising that Congress has acted accordingly.[13] In a typical year, however, only about one-fourth of the taxable capital gains are on marketable securities. The remainder are on sales of such assets as urban real estate, farmland, and livestock. Tax concessions on these items do little to solve problems of slow growth in labor productivity.

Minimum tax. The minimum tax is designed to reach taxpayers with large tax preferences who otherwise would escape the income tax completely. Taxpayers are required to add to their ordinary taxable income the 60 percent capital gains exclusion and any itemized deductions (excepting medical deductions and state-local taxes) in excess of 60 percent of adjusted gross income, plus the tax savings that result from accelerated depreciation on certain real estate and business property or from tax breaks on oil and mineral exploration and production. The minimum is applied to these preferences (less an exemption of $10,000 or one-half of ordinary tax due) at a rate of 20 percent. The minimum tax provision represents a modest attempt to reduce the benefits from tax preferences. Noticeably missing is interest income from state and local securities, which remains untouched by the federal income tax.

Effects of Inflation

Inflation can affect the impact of the income tax in many ways. Some of the most important effects are on calculation of business income. These are discussed in Chapter 9. The inflationary impact on capital gains has already been considered. Recently, the effect of inflation on the real rate structure of the income tax has received much attention. A taxpayer's before-tax money income may rise at the same rate as the price level, apparently leaving real income unchanged. If the rate brackets are defined in nominal (or current) dollars, however, the rising dollar income will project the taxpayer into higher marginal brackets. After-tax real income is reduced, and the government collects an inflationary windfall.

During the past decade, Congress has provided relief from this form of "bracket creep" by increasing the size of the personal exemption and zero-rate bracket. The 1978 amendments provided additional relief by revising the rate structure. The most far-reaching change is contained in the 1981 amendments. Both the bracket limits and the personal exemption are to be adjusted upward, or indexed, by the consumer price index. Indexing is to occur each year beginning in 1985.

---

[13]Productivity is usually measured in terms of output per unit of labor input. Productivity in the private sector grew at annual rates of over 3 percent in the 1950s and early 1960s. Growth rates declined markedly in the 1970s, falling to about 0.4 percent per year in 1977 to 1979. The rate of saving and investment is only one of several important determinants of productivity growth.

The indexing procedure may be illustrated by the following example, taken from the tax schedule for married couples for the year 1984:

	BRACKET LIMITS	
RATE	BEFORE INDEXING	AFTER INDEXING
11%	$3,400 to $5,500	$3,740 to $6,050
50%	Over $162,400	Over $178,640

The example assumes a 10 percent increase in consumer prices. Note that all the bracket limits are increased by 10 percent. Thus, a couple with taxable income of $5,500 in the year before indexing would be at the upper limit of the 11 percent bracket. If their taxable income increased by 10 percent, the same rate as inflation, they would have an additional $550 of taxable income, or $6,050 in total. Without indexing, the additional $550 would be taxed at the next bracket rate of 12 percent. Their total tax payment would rise from $231 to $297, even though their real income did not change. Tax as a percentage of income would increase from 4.2 to 4.9 percent. A couple at the top bracket limit of $162,400 would experience an increase in income of $16,240 if their income rose at a 10 percent rate. Without indexing, the increment would be taxed at the top-bracket rate of 50 percent, and their total tax would go up from $62,600 to $70,720. Taxes as a percentage of income would increase from 38.5 to 39.6 percent.

If bracket limits are indexed, both couples remain in their original rate brackets. Their total tax bill rises at the same rate as inflation and money income. After-tax real income is unaffected, and they pay the same percentage of their income in tax.

Indexing has been introduced in Canada and several European countries. In the United States, the practice is spreading among the states. From an equity point of view, the practice seems desirable, because it prevents unintended changes in the rate structure and real burden of the income tax. Fiscal conservatives favor indexing as a means of restraining the growth of government in an inflationary environment. Politicians will be denied an "inflation dividend" and will be forced to raise tax rates if they wish to spend more. A major objection to indexing is that it undermines the usefulness of the income tax as a stabilization device. By constraining the growth of tax revenues when inflation rates are high, it weakens the restraining effect of fiscal policy.

TAX PREFERENCES
AND TAX REFORM

It should be clear by now that the U.S. income tax code contains many provisions that favor certain sources and uses of income. By discriminating in favor of selected economic activities, the income tax influences the allocation of resources in ways that may or may not improve economic efficiency. By narrowing the tax base, tax preferences tend to undermine the horizontal and vertical equity of the tax. Indeed, as we saw in Chapter 6, it is not generally possible to satisfy the traditional principles of horizontal and vertical equity and at the same time use the tax system to achieve allocational objectives. Finally, narrowing of the base makes it necessary to impose higher rates in order to collect a given amount of revenue.

Tax Expenditures

Some years ago a clever tax reformer coined the term "tax expenditure" to describe the revenue losses caused by the various tax loopholes. A tax expenditure is the additional revenue that the Treasury would receive under the existing rate structure if a particular tax preference were eliminated. The idea is based on the claim that there is no essential difference between a tax preference and a direct government subsidy. With a tax preference, the government loses revenue it would otherwise collect. With a subsidy, the government collects more tax revenue but spends it to encourage a favored activity or to benefit favored individuals.

The 1974 Congressional Budget Act directs the Office of Management and Budget to include an estimate of tax expenditures in the annual budget document. Since that time, tax expenditures have grown rapidly, reaching $139 billion in fiscal 1981. A summary of the estimates by major category is shown in Table 8–1.

The table shows that exclusion of employer fringe benefits, exclusion of government transfers (mainly social security benefits), the capital gains exclusion, and deduction of state and local nonbusiness taxes are the largest items. The estimated total tax expenditures of $139 billion are about one-half the yield of the individual income tax. Note that personal exemptions and the zero-bracket (standard) deductions are not included. Using tax data in Table 8–1, one can make a crude estimate that, if all tax preferences were eliminated, rates could be cut by about one-third. Because the tax expenditures are estimates, and because the components of the tax base would change in response to such a massive change in tax policy, this estimate must be treated with caution. Nevertheless, it gives us some insights into the potential trade-off between broadening of the base and reduction of rates.

Base Broadening

If elimination of a number of tax preferences would make the tax more equitable and allow sizable rate reductions, why does it have so little political appeal? One reason may be that, even with rate reductions, some taxpayers would be net losers. Those who have made major investment commitments to take advantage of tax preferences are likely losers. Investors in state and local government securities and in various real estate or

TABLE 8–1   Estimated Tax Expenditures, U.S. Individual Income Tax, Fiscal 1981

TAX PREFERENCES	TAX EXPENDITURE ($ MILLIONS)
Capital gains	$ 22,310
Exclusion of interest on state-local debt	3,865
Deductibility of state-local nonbusiness taxes	24,795
Deductibility of charitable contributions	8,860
Itemized deductions	44,505
Deductibility of mortgage interest and property tax on owner-occupied dwellings	22,340
Benefits for the elderly	12,410
Total	$139,085

Source: Office of Management and Budget, *Budget of the United States Government, Fiscal Year 1981,* Special Analysis G (Washington, D.C.: Government Printing Office, 1981).

farm tax shelters are examples. Congress has been extremely reluctant to inflict losses in such cases, and if change ever comes, it is likely to be phased in very slowly to cushion the impact.

Another reason for rejecting the base-broadening, rate-reducing option is disagreement over whose rates to cut the most. The options are infinite. The simplest would be a proportional cut in all brackets. A more radical proposal calls for greatly simplifying the tax by broadening the base and eliminating the graduated (or progressive) rate structure. The graduated rates would be replaced by a two-bracket structure with a zero rate on income up to the exemption level and a proportional or flat rate thereafter. The structure can be illustrated in simple algebraic form.

Let T = tax liabiliity
Y = income
E = exemption
t = proportional rate

The tax liability is

$$T = (Y - E)t$$

The average rate is

$$\frac{T}{Y} = \left(1 - \frac{E}{Y}\right)t$$

The average rate is less than the marginal rate, t, but it approaches the marginal rate as income rises.

This rate structure was suggested by two University of Chicago law professors, Walter J. Blum and Harry Kalven, Jr., in their 1953 book, *The Uneasy Case for Progressive Taxation.*[14] They call it a *degressive rate structure.* The idea has since been endorsed by other fiscal conservatives, including Milton Friedman and former Secretary of the Treasury William E. Simon.

It is generally suggested that adoption of a degressive rate or flat rate structure should be accompanied by simplifying the tax and broadening the base. This would be achieved by eliminating a number of deductions and the preferential treatment of capital gains. Problems associated with irregular incomes, bunching, and bracket creep would generally disappear. By expanding the base, the proportional rate on taxable income could be set at a relatively modest level. A rate of 17 or 18 percent is not unreasonable.[15]

A flat rate structure is not appealing to someone who wants to use the income tax as an instrument for redistributing income. But a comparison of a flat rate tax with the current rate structure does serve to illustrate the limited amount of progression built into the present tax in spite of its highly progressive rate structure.

Joseph A. Pechman of The Brookings Institution calculated the average effective rate on reported income for 1976.[16] Overall, the tax collected was only 12.4 percent of reported income. Average rates exceeded 30 percent only for taxpayers with incomes between $100,000 and $1,000,000. The average rate peaked at 32.7 percent in the $200,000 to $500,000 segment and dropped off to 27.9 percent for incomes above $1,000,000. The drop-off in rates at the top of the distribution is due to preferential rates on capital gains and high deductions. Since 1976, the maximum effective rate on long-term capital gains has been reduced from 35 to 20 percent, and rates in all brackets have been reduced. It is unlikely, however, that these changes have altered the general pattern of differences between statutory and effective rates.

ECONOMIC EFFECTS OF A PERSONAL INCOME TAX

An income tax with a comprehensive base offers the taxpayer only limited opportunity to avoid payment by altering economic behavior. If all sources of income are taxed, the only option open to the taxpayer is to reduce total

[14]Walter J. Blum and Harry Kalven, Jr., *The Uneasy Case for Progressive Taxation* (Chicago: University of Chicago Press, 1953), pp. 90–100.

[15]Total collections from the individual income tax have exceeded 20 percent of taxable income only slightly in recent years. With a modest broadening of the base, collections could easily be brought below the 20 percent figure.

[16]Pechman, *Federal Tax Policy,* pp. 72, 349–50.

income. That can be done by reducing hours worked, choosing a lower-paid occupation, and divesting oneself of income-producing assets. An income earner with market power may try to shift part of the burden to buyers of factor services, but the ability of most persons to do this is very limited. As a result, economists generally agree that there is little shifting of the burden of a comprehensive personal income tax.

We have seen that the U.S. individual income tax is far from comprehensive. In addition, its graduated rate structure can have allocational effects not present with a proportional rate. The general conditions that determine the degree of shifting of taxes on households were summarized in Chapter 7. We now consider in greater detail the economic effects associated specifically with the personal income tax.

Effect on Factor Supply

The income tax, like any effective tax, reduces the income available to taxpayers for private use. Tax-financed expenditures presumably provide benefits for taxpayers, so they are not necessarily made worse off. The extent to which economic well-being is altered by the tax-expenditure mechanism depends on each taxpayer's tax share and benefits from government services.

Labor-leisure choice. In Chapter 7, the effect of an income tax on the work-leisure and saving-consumption choices of households was described. We saw that by reducing the net wage an income tax reduces the price of leisure and encourages a worker to substitute leisure for work. This response, called the substitution effect, reduces the number of hours worked. The tax also reduces the amount of income a worker can earn by working a given number of hours. To offset the reduction in income, a worker will tend to work more. This response is called the income effect. Because the substitution and income effects influence hours worked in opposite directions, the net effect of an income tax on labor supply is indeterminate. The substitution and income effects of a tax are illustrated graphically in the first discussion of the appendix to this chapter.

For many workers, institutional arrangements, such as union contracts or the forty-hour workweek, limit their ability to vary hours worked even if they wish to do so. Workers who wish to change their supply of work effort may be able to do so only by changing jobs, taking a second job, or leaving the labor force completely. In these cases, continuous variation in hours worked, as assumed in the standard labor-leisure model, is not possible.

The effect of the income tax on aggregate labor supply is generally thought to be small. Most of the empirical evidence appears to support this conclusion.[17] In particular, it is tempting to conclude that modest changes in tax rates—at least within the limited range usually considered by Congress—have little effect on aggregate supply.

There is some evidence, however, that changes in marginal tax rates might influence the composition of the labor force. A recent study of working couples by Jane H. Leuthold shows that they tend to respond to higher marginal rates by increasing the husband's share and reducing the wife's share of time spent working outside the home. Leuthold also finds that a decrease in a spouse's tax rate (implying an increase in net wage rate) reduces the hours worked by the other spouse.[18]

Additional effects on labor allocation can be expected if a graduated rate structure replaces a proportional structure. Assuming equal yields, a switch to a graduated structure will redistribute tax burdens and alter marginal rates in the manner illustrated as follows:

INCOME GROUP	AFTER-TAX INCOME	MARGINAL TAX RATE
Low	Up	Down
Middle	Up	Up
High	Down	Up

For low-income workers, the income effect (higher income) reduces labor supply, but the substitution effect (lower marginal rates, higher price for leisure) increases labor supply. The net effect is indeterminate. For middle-income workers, both the income effect (higher income) and substitution effect (higher marginal rate, cheaper leisure) reduce labor supply. Among high-income workers, the income effect (lower income) increases labor supply, but the substitution effect (higher marginal rate, cheaper leisure) reduces it. The net effect is indeterminate for low-income and high-income workers and for the labor force as a whole.

A graduated rate structure can affect labor supply in another way. By narrowing after-tax income differentials, it can alter occupational choices in the direction of lower-paying alternatives. The limited evidence available indicates that tax considerations have only a minor effect on occupational choice.[19] Given the educational requirements for many of the more lucrative occupations, any tax effect is likely to be fully operative only over rather lengthy time periods.

Saving and investment.   An income tax can affect the saving of an individual in two ways. First, any tax that reduces income can be expected

---

[17]For a summary of empirical studies, see George F. Break, "The Incidence and Economic Effects of Taxation," in Alan S. Blinder et al., *The Economics of Public Finance* (Washington, D.C.: The Brookings Institution, 1974), pp. 180–91. In particular, efforts to estimate the magnitude, and in some cases even the sign of income and substitution effects, have not been very successful. This is attributed to the difficulty of controlling for other factors that affect labor supply in econometric analysis of data from sample surveys.

[18]Jane H. Leuthold, "Taxes and the Two-Earner Family: Impact on the Work Decision," *Public Finance Quarterly,* 7 (April 1979), 147–61.

[19]Break, "Incidence and Economic Effects of Taxation," pp. 190–91.

to reduce both the saving and consumption of a taxpayer. Second, an income tax that taxes interest income will affect the rate of trade-off between present and future income. Other things being equal, the tax-induced fall in interest income reduces the rate at which forgone current consumption can be converted into future consumption. The first effect is thought to be stronger and more predictable than the second.

If income is the only determinant of household saving, the effect of an income tax on savings operates through its effects on disposable income. The ratio of a change in savings to a change in disposable income is referred to as the marginal propensity to save, or *MPS*. In algebraic terms, the *MPS* and its complement, the marginal propensity to consume, or *MPC*, can be stated as follows:

$$MPS = \frac{\Delta S}{\Delta Y}$$

$$MPC = \frac{\Delta C}{\Delta Y}$$

where ΔS = change in savings
ΔC = change in consumption
ΔY = change in disposable income

Because all income must either be saved or spent on consumption, the *MPS* and *MPC* must sum to 1. If an income tax reduces the disposable income of a household, the reduction in saving and consumption will depend on its *MPS* and *MPC*. For example, if its *MPS* = 0.05 and its *MPC* = 0.95, a tax-induced reduction in disposable income of $1,000 will cut household savings by $50 and consumption by $950.

Household saving may also be affected by the rate of return on investments. This effect may be analyzed most simply by assuming a two-period decision horizon in which the household is faced with the decision of how to allocate a given current income between the present and the future period. Income in the future period is assumed to be zero. Think of it as a case in which the household saves during its working life in order to finance retirement. The interest rate is assumed not to be affected by the levying of a tax on interest income.

The amount of future consumption made possible by current savings can be shown by the following equations.

Interest not taxed: $C_f = S_c (1 + i)$ (1)
Interest taxed: $C_f = S_c [1 + i(1 - t)]$ (2)

where C_f = consumption in future period
S_c = savings in current period
i = interest rate
t = tax rate

If interest is not taxed, the household retains all the interest on its savings, an amount equal to iS_c, to spend on consumption in the future period. If interest is taxed, the household keeps after-tax interest income, or $i(1-t)S_c$, and pays a tax of tiS_c. Obviously, if S_c is the same in each case, consumption in the future period is lower with than without the tax.

The household can respond by changing the amount that it saves, but we cannot predict on the basis of theory alone what its response will be. The tax on interest income has the effect of raising the price of future consumption in terms of forgone current consumption. If the demand for future consumption is price elastic, savings will fall; if it is price inelastic, savings will rise. Either outcome is possible.

To summarize, an income tax reduces household saving by reducing income and has an indeterminate effect on savings by taxing interest income.

The effect of an income tax on aggregate saving can be analyzed only within a macroeconomic or general equilibrium framework. As we saw in Chapter 7, a tax can be introduced or changed only in conjunction with other fiscal and/or monetary variables. One tax may be substituted for another of equal yield, as in differential incidence, or a change in tax yield may be matched by a change in expenditures, as in balanced-budget incidence. A change in one tax without a change in another tax or government expenditure will alter the budget surplus or deficit. A change in the budgetary deficit or surplus must be analyzed with the aid of a macroeconomic model. Aggregate demand and equilibrium output are affected, but in a way that is dependent on the reaction of monetary authorities. Macroeconomic modeling is beyond the scope of this text, but the reader is reminded that planned saving will be realized only when equal to planned investment, that is, when the economy is in macroeconomic equilibrium.

Within the framework of differential incidence, the income tax is often compared with an equal-yield tax on consumption expenditure. An income tax includes both saving and consumption in its tax base. A consumption tax, by definition, does not tax savings. Therefore, the tax can be avoided by saving. If at some future date the individual dissaves out of past accumulations, a consumption tax must be paid. By postponing payment of the tax, however, a taxpayer has use of the money in the interim. Accumulations that are never dissaved are never subject to the tax. Consequently, a consumption tax is more favorable to saving than is an equal-yield income tax. For this reason, it is sometimes recommended that countries wishing to stimulate saving and investment should substitute a consumption tax for an income tax.

The impact of an income tax on aggregate saving is likely to be sensitive to the rate structure. To determine the effect of substitution of a proportional for a progressive income tax of equal yield, it is necessary to compare the incremental impact across income groups. If the marginal propensity to save, *MPS*, is the same for all income groups, aggregate savings will not be affected. The allocation among investment outlets may be affected, however, because households at different income levels are likely to follow different investment strategies. Evidence indicates that the *MPS* does rise somewhat as income rises, so a move toward a less progressive rate structure would increase savings.

George F. Break used estimates of the *MPS* by income group coupled with data from an incidence study to estimate the effect of a change from a progressive to a proportional rate structure. Using data for the 1960s, he found that aggregate saving would increase by an amount equal to about 5 percent of total tax yield.[20] If the same relationship held for 1980, the increment would be about $12 billion, or about 11 percent of net private saving and 15 percent of saving by households. In recent years, politicians and economists have expressed concern about an inadequate rate of saving and capital formation in the United States. The 1978 and 1981 revisions of the tax code indicate that a move toward a less progressive rate structure is a possibility, and an updating of Break's work would give us additional information on the likely effect on saving.

In the past, the general consensus among economists has been that the aggregate supply of saving is not very responsive to changes in the rate of return. If they are right, changes in the tax law that increase the rate of return would not stimulate a large increase in the flow of investible funds. The consensus view may be attributed to the failure of most empirical studies to show a significant relationship between saving and rate of return. The consensus position has been attacked recently, notably by Michael J. Boskin of Stanford University. Boskin criticizes the earlier studies and presents his own results, which show that aggregate saving is responsive to higher rates of return.[21] Boskin's results are not directly comparable with other studies, however, because he includes outlays on consumer durables, such as appliances and autos, as a form of saving and investment.

Risk taking.   The income tax may affect the willingness of a taxpayer to undertake risky investments or to choose occupations characterized by sizable variability in income. When the government shares in your income via taxation, it is in effect becoming a partner in your income-producing activities. The nature of the government's partnership depends on the rate structure and the way in which losses are treated.

If the income tax is imposed at a proportional rate and with full-loss offset, the government's share of your gains and losses is always the same. Your gains are taxed at the same rate regardless of their size, and if you

[20]Ibid., pp. 191–93.

[21]Michael J. Boskin, "Taxation, Saving, and the Rate of Interest," *Journal of Political Economy*, 86 (April 1978, Part 2), S3–S27.

suffer a loss, the government will reimburse you for a portion of it at the proportional rate.

Under the U.S. individual income tax, the government generally shares in your undertakings on somewhat less favorable terms. The graduated rate structure takes a larger share of higher payoffs, although the effect is attenuated if the payoff is a long-term capital gain. Loss offsets are sometimes imperfect. Losses on some activities may be subtracted from gains on others, but there are limits on subtracting capital losses from ordinary income.

Various theoretical models have been constructed for the purpose of exploring the relationship between the income tax and risk taking. The most generally accepted result is that a proportional income tax with full loss offset will encourage a taxpayer to increase the riskiness of a portfolio of assets.[22] In this case, introduction of the tax reduces yield and risk by the same proportion, and the investor responds by increasing before-tax yield and risk in an effort to return to the risk-yield combination that was selected prior to the introduction of the tax. If full-loss offset is eliminated or if the rate structure is graduated, risk and yield are no longer altered proportionally by the tax, and the effect of the tax on risk taking is harder to predict.

The theoretical models yield definitive predictions only in those cases in which specific assumptions are made about the preferences of asset holders concerning the trade-off between risk and yield. By their nature, such models are difficult to test empirically, and no important empirical results are available.

Should tax policy be influenced by concerns over the amount of risk taking in the economy? Any investment involves some risk. The future cannot be predicted with certainty. It is difficult to determine just when an economy is characterized by the "right amount" of risk taking. Too little could stifle innovation and result in a sluggish economy. Too much could lead to instability and bankruptcies. In a strictly formal sense, the amount of risk taking may be less than optimal because of market imperfections. Imperfections may occur if indivisibilities prevent investors from acquiring the degree of portfolio diversification they desire. Small investors are particularly vulnerable. Mutual funds are an example of an institutional arrangement that has been developed to deal with this problem. If it could be demonstrated that the level of risk taking is suboptimal, a case could be made for using tax policy as a corrective.

Some provisions in the U.S. tax code are intended to encourage risk

---

[22]Risk is usually defined in terms of some property of a probability distribution of possible outcomes. In the case of investments, it is based on the probability distribution of possible outcomes, some of which may be negative. Most theoretical models use the standard deviation as the measure of risk. For a summary of the issues and references to major contributions, see Martin S. Feldstein, "The Effects of Taxation on Risk Taking," *Journal of Political Economy,* 77 (September–October 1969), 755–64.

taking. Examples include the preferential treatment of capital gains and various concessions in taxation of business income, including accelerated depreciation, depletion allowances, immediate deductibility of research and development expenses, and the investment tax credit. These features of business taxation are described in Chapter 9.

If investors respond to tax incentives by taking on more risk, some of it will be shifted to the Treasury because of its partnership role inherent in the income tax. This does not necessarily mean that the Treasury will experience more instability in revenue flows, however, because the risk is spread over millions of taxpayers. Indeed, even if every investor were to take on a riskier portfolio of assets, it does not necessarily follow that total risk taking in the economy would increase. Risk can be reduced by diversification—by not putting all your eggs in one basket. Conversely, it can be increased by concentrating investments in fewer outlets. Simply by reshuffling investment portfolios so as to reduce diversifications, investors can take on more risk individually without increasing aggregate risk in the economy.

Supply-Side Economics: The Laffer Controversy

The conventional view of economists, as we have seen, is that the aggregate supply of factors of production is quite inelastic. Consequently, a large reduction in the effective income tax rate would have little impact on factor supplies and national product. The conventional view has been challenged by a small minority of economists led by Arthur Laffer of the University of Southern California. Laffer argues that tax rates on factor incomes are so high in the United States that they are counterproductive. The high tax rates discourage people from working and investing. If tax rates were reduced, the incentive to increase production would be so great that the tax *yield* on the additional income would actually rise.

The relationship between tax rate and tax yield is shown by the Laffer curve, illustrated in Figure 8–1.[23] The basic idea of the Laffer curve is uncontroversial. Obviously, at the origin where the tax rate is zero, no revenue will be collected. At the other extreme, point B corresponding to rate t_2 in Figure 8–1, disincentive effects would discourage all income-earning activity. This result would presumably be observed with effective rates at 100 percent (and perhaps less), where the economic incentive to produce would disappear. The controversial question is, at what effective rate would revenues be a maximum? This occurs at rate t_1, corresponding to point A on the graph. The issue is whether we are currently to the left or right of point A.

---

[23]The second part of the appendix to this chapter shows how the Laffer curve may be derived from a simple model of aggregate factor demand and supply.

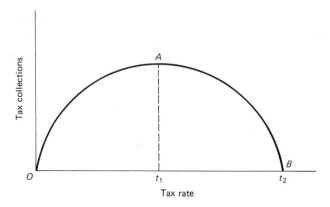

Figure 8–1   The Laffer curve. The Laffer curve shows the relationship between income tax collections and the tax rate. Revenue is maximized at point *A,* corresponding to rate t_1. At point *B,* where the rate is t_2, the disincentive effect of the tax is great enough to cause the tax base (taxable income) to drop to zero, and the tax yields no revenue.

The reasoning underlying the Laffer curve is most clear when applied to a single good. Let us take alcoholic beverages as an example. If the tax were set at $1 per fifth, the quantity sold would drop very little below the zero-tax level. Even if the tax were doubled, consumption would not change markedly, so government revenue would nearly double. A jump to $10 a fifth would be a different matter. Revenue per unit would rise, but if enough people are discouraged from drinking—or if bootlegging becomes more profitable and expands—total revenue will fall. Put the tax at $1,000 a fifth, and the tax would be useless as a revenue source.

Laffer and his followers carry the same argument over to aggregate supply in the economy. Almost all economists, including many who are quite conservative, believe that the United States is to the left of the maximum shown at point *A.* Indeed, one of Laffer's most persistent critics is Herbert Stein, a fiscal conservative, who chaired President Nixon's Council of Economic Advisors.[24] Stein and others argue that, if tax rates are cut without a corresponding cut in expenditures, the result will be a fall in tax revenue and a larger deficit. The deficit must be financed by government borrowing. Either the government must bid loanable funds away from private borrowers, crowding them out and reducing private spending, or borrow from the Federal Reserve, adding to the money supply and fueling inflation. Laffer and his followers counter by pointing to the successful Kennedy–Johnson tax cut of 1964, which was followed by a noninflation-

[24]"Two Views of the Kemp–Roth Bill," *The AEI Economist,* July 1978, pp. 1–8. Econometric models of the U.S. economy generally provide little support for the Laffer position. Supply-siders counter by pointing out that the econometric models used to refute Laffer are aggregate demand models that fail to include supply-side equations.

ary expansion of output and a drop in unemployment. Laffer's critics attribute the success of the 1964 tax cut to its effect on aggregate *demand* in an economy with excess capacity.

In spite of the skepticism with which Laffer's ideas are greeted by most economists, he has attracted an enthusiastic following among politicians. The first serious attempt to put Laffer's proposal into practice occurred in 1978 when the Kemp–Roth bill was introduced in both the House and Senate. The bill, sponsored by representative Jack Kemp (R., N.Y.) and Senator William Roth (R., Del.), would have cut income tax rates by 30 percent over a three-year period. The bill was defeated in both houses, but Kemp–Roth provided the inspiration for the massive rate cuts and investment incentives contained in the Economic Recovery Tax Act of 1981.

One feature of the debate that has not received enough attention from economists is the relationship between the tax side and expenditure side of the government budget. Government expenditures that do little to improve the well-being of the bulk of taxpayers do not have work-disincentive effects. Defense expenditures are a good example. They may be necessary, but they do not improve living standards. On the other hand, welfare expenditures may have stronger disincentive effects if they reduce the need for earnings. They may do this by reducing the need for money income. Examples include housing subsidies, food stamps, or nationalized health services. Disincentives from welfare outlays are probably stronger in some European countries than in the United States. Welfare expenditures may also cut labor supply by reducing the net gain from working. For example, if welfare payments, unemployment insurance, or disability benefits are high relative to wages, the additional income received from work may be too small to make it worthwhile. In the United States, disincentives of this type are most likely to occur under social insurance programs, discussed in Chapter 14, but they may be present among some persons with low earning potential who have an option of choosing between work and welfare.

These considerations are important if policy makers are considering a combination of tax and expenditure cuts. A tax cut coupled with a cut in welfare expenditures will have a stronger work-incentive effect than will a tax cut coupled with a cut in defense spending. Whether such a cut is desirable is, of course, a separate issue. Indeed, this issue was at the heart of the national debate over the efforts of President Reagan to reorder national priorities.

STATE AND LOCAL
INCOME TAXES

Broadly based personal income taxes are currently in effect in forty-one states. In three states, the tax is limited to income from interest, dividends, or capital gains. As of the early 1980s, total yield was about $40 billion, less than a fifth of the yield of the federal income tax and about four-fifths of the yield from the retail sales taxes. In a number of states, however, the personal income tax is the largest single source of general tax revenue. Local income taxes are less common, but they are important revenue sources in the District of Columbia and in several of the ten states that allow them.

State Income Taxes

Wisconsin enacted the first state income tax in 1911. By 1937, largely in response to financial needs of the depression, some type of income tax was in effect in more than thirty states. After a lull of two decades, the income tax began to spread again as states responded to the revenue needs of the 1950s and 1960s. In addition to equity considerations, the personal income tax appeals to state officials because of its responsiveness to growth. Revenue elasticities generally range from about 1.5 to 1.8,[25] which means that revenue grows 1.5 to 1.8 percent for each 1 percent increase in personal income. Since the revenues from most other state and local taxes rise less rapidly than income, reliance on other sources entails greater fiscal austerity or more frequent rate increases.

In most states, the income tax base is similar to the federal base. Deductions are much alike. Most states have exemptions for taxpayer and dependents, but a few rely on credits instead. Rate structures are graduated in all but five states. Marginal rates usually start at 1 or 2 percent. Top rates are often less than 10 percent and are reached at low levels, usually $25,000 or less. In three states, the state tax is a fraction of the federal liability. This procedure simplifies taxpayer compliance, but federal tax cuts can cause budgetary dislocation unless states are prepared to make immediate offsetting changes in the fractional rate. Federal deductibility of state income taxes cushions the impact on the taxpayer, particularly in higher federal brackets, as explained earlier. Some states reciprocate and allow deduction of federal income tax from the state tax base. Reciprocal deduction substantially reduces the effective state rate on high-bracket taxpayers. The results are a tendency for effective rates to become regressive at high income levels and a sizable loss of revenue to the state treasury. Complications sometimes arise when residents of one state earn income in another. These are usually handled by interstate agreements or by allowance of tax credits for income tax paid to other states.

Local Income Taxes

Local income taxes are found in a variety of forms. In most cases, they are levied at a low, proportional rate of about 1 or 2 percent. The most common base is gross earnings of individuals with no deductions or

[25]L. L. Ecker-Racz, *The Politics and Economics of State-Local Finance* (Englewood Cliffs, N.J.: Prentice-Hall, Inc., 1970), p. 47.

exemptions. The tax on gross earnings gives cities an opportunity to collect revenue from persons who work in the city and benefit from many of its services but who live in suburbs. Progressive rate structures are less common, but a progressive local tax is an important revenue source in New York City and Washington, D.C. An interesting variation is found in Maryland, where local governments levy a surtax of 20 to 50 percent of the graduated state income tax.

PERSONAL INCOME TAXATION: AN EVALUATION

The flexibility of a personal income tax makes it possible to adjust tax liability to each taxpayer's ability to pay. Exemptions and deductions can be used to adjust for differences in family circumstances. Allowances can be made for such extraordinary expenses as large medical bills or alimony payments. A graduated rate structure can be used to make the tax progressive. The personal income tax would thus appear to be the ideal instrument for implementing the principles of horizontal and vertical equity.

In practice, however, the income tax falls far short of satisfying the equity criteria of writers such as Henry Simons and his followers. The very flexibility that makes it possible for the income tax to conform to widely accepted standards of equity makes it a tempting device for promoting other social goals and for catering to favored constituencies. Consequently, many tax preferences or "loopholes" have crept into the U.S. tax code.

Some of the preferences are justified by practical considerations. Exclusion of most sources of nonmoney income is an example. Others, such as tax incentives to save and invest or to contribute to charity, promote other goals at the expense of equity. A few of the loopholes are difficult to defend on administrative, allocational, or equity grounds. Among the latter are exclusion of interest on state and local securities, interest payments on homeowner's mortgages and personal debt, and failure to tax capital gains unrealized at death.

A few years ago The Brookings Institution published a book called *Federal Tax Reform: The Impossible Dream?*[26] Its authors were optimistic enough to end the title with a question mark. From the mid-1960s to the mid-1970s, Congress did take a few modest steps toward genuine reform, but by the end of the 1970s, the reform movement waned. The move to broaden the tax base, even when it permits further rate reductions, seems to have little political appeal as the emphasis shifts to schemes to encourage saving and capital formation.

[26]George F. Break and Joseph A. Pechman, *Federal Tax Reform: The Impossible Dream?* (Washington, D.C.: The Brookings Institution, 1975).

Most of the attention of advocates of tax reform is directed at statutory inequities, but the inability of tax authorities to monitor all sources of income with equal efficiency is also a major source of unequal treatment among taxpayers. In the 1960s, a study by C. Harry Kahn revealed substantial disparities in the percentage of income from various sources that was reported on federal returns.[27] Improvements in tax administration and data processing have corrected many of the shortcomings uncovered by Kahn, but much income still escapes the authorities. The most serious cases of underreporting are found among the self-employed, small landlords, casual laborers, and persons engaged in illegal activities. There is evidence that a "subterranean economy" of substantial size operates outside the purview of the Internal Revenue Service. This economy uses currency—no checks, no credit cards—as a medium of exchange. Peter M. Gutmann of Baruch College used statistics on the growth of currency in circulation relative to checking deposits to make inferences about the size of the off-the-record economy.[28] He estimated that in 1976 it accounted for $176 billion in output, or about 10 percent of reported GNP. Aside from the revenue losses, failure to tax so large an income flow adds to the inequity of the income tax.

A feature of the income tax that is appealing to many is its progressivity. The federal income tax is the most important source of progression in our overall tax system. A cursory examination of its rate brackets, which range from 11 percent to 50 percent, conveys the impression of a highly progressive tax, but a number of provisions attenuate its progressivity. These include preferential treatment of capital gains, exclusion of interest on state and local securities, and various other provisions that are most beneficial to persons with high incomes.

As we saw in Chapter 6, there is little that economists can say about how progressive the income tax should be. Arguments based on marginal utility of income have been largely discredited. Recently, some economic theorists have developed a new approach to progression, called the theory of optimal income taxation. An identical utility function for all taxpayers specifies preferences for income and leisure. Different earning capacities are assumed, along with a ranking of alternative income distributions (or, in the terminology of welfare economics, a social welfare function). Because the income tax falls on income but not on leisure, it interferes with efficient allocation of time between work and leisure. The resulting inefficiency creates an excess burden or welfare loss. At the same time, a progressive income tax can be used to achieve a more equal distribution of income. Assuming that the postulated social ranking favors equality over

[27]C. Harry Kahn, *Business and Professional Income Under the Personal Income Tax* (Princeton, N.J.: National Bureau of Economic Research, 1964), pp. 15–50.

[28]Peter M. Gutmann, "The Subterranean Economy," *Financial Analysts Journal,* 33 (November–December 1977), 26–27, 34.

inequality, the gain in social welfare from progressive taxation can be compared with the loss from the inefficiency or excess burden. The tax structure that just balances the two is defined as optimal.

The literature on optimal income taxation is highly abstract and is based on postulated utility functions and welfare rankings. Perhaps it is worth noting that, when theorists make "reasonable" assumptions about the form the utility function and the distribution of earning capacity, the resulting tax structure is very nearly proportional.[29] All this is interesting to theorists, but the new approach has not yet had any noticeable impact on tax policy.

The inflationary pressures of the past two decades have caused the general price level to more than triple. Changes of this magnitude have an effect on the base and rate structure of the income tax that cannot be ignored. The effect on the tax base is most apparent in the case of capital gains, where increases in nominal values of assets outstrip increases in real value. The impact of a graduated rate structure is felt through "bracket creep," in which increases in nominal income may boost taxpayers into higher rate brackets even though real income remains static. In the past, Congress has responded to bracket creep with periodic and somewhat haphazard adjustments in the rate structure. The Economic Recovery Tax Act of 1981 introduced indexing of federal tax brackets beginning in 1985. Each year the personal exemption and the limits of each tax bracket will be adjusted to coincide with annual changes in the consumer price index. As a result, taxpayers whose income rises at the same rate as the general price level will no longer move into a higher tax bracket.

In spite of its shortcomings, the U.S. individual income tax is destined to retain its role as the most important single source of tax revenue in the U.S. tax system. Likewise, in most states the role of state income taxes as a major revenue source is assured. Income is still generally accepted as the best measure of ability to pay. Income tax revenue, particularly with a graduated rate structure, is highly responsive to income growth. The latter feature makes the tax attractive to public officials, because it generates needed revenue without continual rate increases. Automatic revenue growth is attenuated, however, in those jurisdictions that have adopted automatic indexing. Tax reforms that would make the tax more equitable are likely to be slow in coming. They seem to rank low on the priority list of the coalitions that dominate American politics.

[29]J. A. Mirrlees, "An Exploration in the Theory of Optimum Taxation," *Review of Economic Studies*, 38 (April 1971), 200–08.

Appendix

THE INCOME TAX AND
LABOR SUPPLY

As mentioned in Chapter 7, an income tax affects the supply of labor by an individual worker in two ways. If we assume that the gross wage is not affected by the tax, the introduction of an income tax reduces the net wage for the marginal hour of work. Letting $w =$ the hourly wage rate before tax and $t =$ the marginal tax rate, the net wage is reduced from w to $(1-t)w$. As a consequence, the price of an additional unit of leisure drops from w to $(1-t)w$, the amount of hourly wage forgone. The fall in the price of leisure causes the worker to substitute leisure for work. This is the substitution effect, and it always reduces labor supply.

Payment of the tax reduces the amount of income earned by working the pretax number of hours. The worker is made poorer by the tax. Assuming that leisure is a normal good, the fall in income will reduce the number of hours of leisure. This is the income effect, and it increases labor supply.

The income and substitution effects of an income tax may be illustrated by an indifference map showing the labor-leisure trade-off, as illustrated in Figure 8–2. The vertical axis measures income (assumed to be only from wages) and the horizontal axis measures leisure. The total time endowment in hours is measured by the distance OD. Assuming that the wage rate is constant regardless of the number of hours worked, the maximum income the individual could earn by taking no leisure is OC. The wage rate is given by the formula

$$w = \frac{OC}{OD}$$

which measures the slope of the budget line CD.

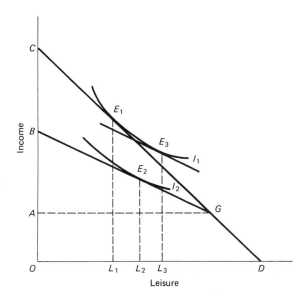

Figure 8–2   Income and substitution effect of an income tax. An income tax imposed at a fixed rate on all income above the level *OA* shifts the budget line from *CD* to *BGD*. The substitution effect is illustrated by the shift from E_1 to E_3 along indifference curve I_1. It increases the demand for leisure from OL_1 to OL_3 hours. The income effect is represented by the jump from E_3 on I_1 to E_2 on the lower indifference curve I_2. It reduces demand for leisure by L_3L_2 hours. The total effect, represented by the jump from E_1 to E_2, is the algebraic sum of the income and substitution effects. In this example, it is positive (leisure increases by L_1L_2 hours), but its sign cannot be predicted on theoretical grounds.

In the absence of a tax, and assuming that the worker is completely free to choose the number of hours worked, the individual maximizes utility at the tangency point between indifference curve I_1 and the budget line. This occurs at point E_1. The equilibrium level of leisure is OL_1. Thus, the total time endowment is divided between OL_1 hours of leisure and L_1D hours of work.

Now, suppose that the government introduces a linear progressive income tax. This is a tax with an exemption equal to *OA* dollars, as shown on the vertical axis. Above the exemption level the worker begins paying an income tax at a constant rate, *t*. Graphically, the after-tax income is illustrated by the budget line *BGD* in Figure 8–2. Notice the kink at point *G*, which corresponds to the exemption level *OA*. The marginal tax rate is measured geometrically by the formula

$$t = \frac{CB}{CA}$$

The reader may recognize this as a graphical representation of the degressive rate structure discussed in Chapter 8 (pp. 181–82).

The after-tax equilibrium is at point E_2, where indifference curve I_2 is tangent to the after-tax budget line *BGD*. The worker takes OL_2 hours of leisure. In this example, hours worked have decreased from L_1D to L_2D, with leisure increasing by L_1L_2 hours. Thus, the tax has a net work disincentive effect.

The distance L_1L_2 measures the total effect, which is the algebraic sum of the income and substitution effects. The substitution effect may be determined by drawing a line tangent to indifference curve I_1 and parallel to the segment *BG* of the after-tax budget line. (Note that the ratio *BA/AG* measures the slope of segment *BG*. This is the net or after-tax wage rate.) The substitution effect is represented by the segment E_1E_3 on I_1. It shows the amount of additional leisure that the worker would take at the new net wage rate (the "price" of leisure) if utility is held constant. In terms of hours, it is measured by the distance L_1L_3 on the horizontal axis. Because indifference curves between income and leisure are convex from below, the substitution effect must be positive.

The income effect is shown by the jump from point E_3 on indifference curve I_1 to point E_2, the after-tax equilibrium, on indifference curve I_2. The fall in income resulting from the tax puts the worker on a lower indifference curve. This fall in real income will reduce the demand for leisure, assuming that it is a normal good, by the amount L_3L_2.

The total effect L_1L_2 is the algebraic sum of the positive substitution effect L_1L_3 and the negative income effect L_3L_2. In the example, L_1L_2 is positive, indicating that the tax reduces the supply of work effort. The theory of consumer behavior on which indifference curve analysis is based can tell us the direction of the income and substitution effects, but it cannot tell us which effect is of the greater magnitude. Therefore, we cannot say on the basis of theory alone whether the total effect will be positive (as shown) or negative.

SUPPLY-SIDE ECONOMICS: DERIVATION OF THE LAFFER CURVE

Since the Great Depression of the 1930s, fiscal policy has been looked upon as an instrument for stabilizing the economy through the control of aggregate demand. The emphasis on aggregate demand grew out of the depression economics of John Maynard Keynes, which called for deficit spending by the federal government as a means of combating unemployment. Additional government spending, financed by money created by the banking system, would generate the aggregate demand needed to bring the economy's idle capacity back into production. During and after World War II, the emphasis switched to the use of fiscal policy as a means of restraining inflationary booms. During World War II, the Korean conflict, and the war in Vietnam, attempts were made to soak up excess purchasing power by raising taxes. The efforts were regarded by many economists as being too little and too late.

The prolonged stagflation of the post-Vietnam era has been accompanied by growing skepticism over the effectiveness of fiscal policy. The Keynesians, who thought in the early 1960s that they had learned how to "fine-tune" the economy, became the targets of derisive comments from the monetarist economists and conservative politicians. Attempts by Keynesians to blame the failures of economic policy on the unwillingness of politicians to follow good advice left many unconvinced, and a new view of economic reality—supply-side economics—began to emerge. Those who espouse supply-side economics blame high taxation and stifling government regulation for inhibiting the growth of the economy. They call for a large cut in tax rates, accompanied by cuts in expenditure and deregulation of industry. They contend that such a policy will unleash the productive capacity and innovative spirit of the American economy.

Among economists, the leading spokesperson for supply-side economics is Arthur Laffer of the University of Southern California. Professor Laffer unabashedly contends that a cut in income tax rates would actually *increase* tax collections. The incentive effects of the rate cut would increase the size of the tax base (income) by more than enough to overcome the effect of lower rates. Referring back to Figure 8–1, Laffer contends that the U.S. economy is on the downward segment of the Laffer curve.

Analytically, it is easy to demonstrate the conditions under which the economy can be on the upward (left of A) or downward (right of A) segment of the curve. Roy D. Adams has devised a macroeconomic model from which the Laffer curve can be derived.[30] A graphical version of his model is shown in Figure 8–3. The model is based on *Say's law*, the assumption of classical economics that the economy always generates enough aggregate demand to absorb aggregate supply. Adams's model illustrates the basic relationships among tax rates, tax collections, and aggregate supply.

In the example in Figure 8–3, labor is assumed to be the only variable input (making it a short-run model). Labor is also assumed to be homogeneous. The labor supply curve S_L, shown in panel (a), is positively sloped up to wage W_2. At this wage the quantity of labor supplied is at a maximum, L_2 on the labor supply axis. At wages above W_2, the supply of effort declines, indicating that in the aggregate income effects outweigh substi-

---

[30]Roy D. Adams, "Tax Rates and Tax Collections: The Basic Analytics of Khaldun–Laffer Curves," *Public Finance Quarterly*, 9 (October 1981), 415–30.

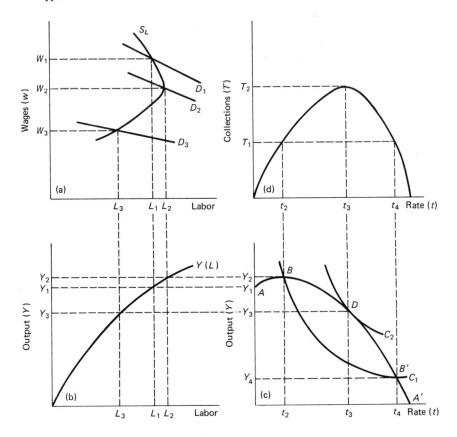

Figure 8–3   Derivation of the Laffer curve. Panel (a) shows the effect of successively higher income tax rates on equilibrium labor supply. The tax shifts the after-tax labor demand curves from D_1 (no tax) to D_2 (low tax) and D_3 (high tax). Panel (b) shows the effect of tax-induced changes in aggregate labor supply on total output. Curve AA' in panel (c) shows the relationship between tax rates and aggregate output. Isocollections loci C_1 and C_2 show combinations of tax rate, t, and output, Y, that yield equal collections. Shown in panel (d) is the corresponding Laffer curve, which gives the relationship between tax rates and tax collections. Collections are maximized at T_2 with tax rate t_3, which corresponds to labor demand curve D_3 and output Y_3.

tution effects. The reverse holds for wages below W_2. The supply curve is drawn in this way to make the model more general.

The no-tax demand for labor is represented by demand curve D_1 in panel (a). Imposition of successively higher proportional (ad valorem) income taxes introduces a wedge between no-tax demand, D_1, and net or after-tax demand (depicted by D_2 and D_3). Since labor supply depends on the net wage, successively higher tax rates will cause the equilibrium to shift from L_1 to L_2 or L_3. Note that, along the backward-bending segment of the supply curve, an increase in the tax rate increases the quantity of labor supplied.

Output is determined by labor supply and the aggregate production function, shown in panel (b). Labor input is measured on the horizontal axis, which is identical to the horizontal axis in panel (a). The vertical axis measures aggregate output, Y. Output levels Y_1, Y_2, and Y_3 are obtained from labor input levels L_1, L_2, and L_3, respectively, as derived from the production function $Y(L)$.

Curve AA' in panel (c) shows the relationship between output, Y, and the tax rate, t. Output, Y, is measured on the vertical axis, which is identical to the Y axis in panel (b). Curve AA' is constructed from a schedule of tax rates and levels of output. Recall that the tax rate affects output through its effect on labor supply (panel (a)), which in turn determines output, as shown in panel (b). Note that the backward-bending segment of the labor supply curve in panel (a) maps into the positively sloped segment AB of curve AA' in panel (c). In this range, higher tax rates bring about increased output. Along the remainder of curve AA', higher values of t bring about lower levels of Y. This negatively sloped segment of the AA' curve corresponds to the positively sloped portion of the labor supply curve.

Tax collections for the various tax rate-output combinations are determined by the formula

$T = tY$
where T = tax yield in dollars
   t = tax rate
   Y = aggregate output or income (the tax base)

Holding tax collections constant at the level $\overline{T}$ and solving for Y, we get the following relationship between income and tax rate:

$$Y = \frac{\overline{T}}{t}$$

This is an equation for a rectangular hyperbola. Two such curves, labeled C_1 and C_2, are graphed in panel (c). They are representative of a family of curves showing the locus of combinations of t and Y that yield the same level of tax collections. Adams refers to them as isocollections loci. Proceeding out from the origin, each successive curve corresponds to a higher level of tax collection.

Isocollections locus C_1 intersects the income rate curve AA' at two points, labeled B and B'. At each point, the tax collection would be the same. The lower rate t_2 applies to a larger base Y_2 at B; at B' the tax disincentive effect has reduced output to Y_4, where the rate t_4 generates the same level of tax collection. Maximum tax collection is attained at point D, the point of tangency between curve AA' and the higher attainable iso-collections locus C_2. This occurs at tax rate t_3.

The Laffer curve is shown in panel (d). It is a graphical representation of a schedule of tax rates, t, and tax collections, T. The rates collections schedule is derived from the data set used to construct the curves in panel (c). The Laffer curve peaks at rate t_3, which corresponds to tangency point D in panel (c). Collections are at the maximum attainable level, T_2. At rate t_3 the increment in revenue resulting from the tax rate increase is exactly offset by the shrinking of the tax base, Y, resulting from the work-disincentive effect of the tax. Note also that tax rates t_2 and t_4 generate an equal yield, T_1, shown in panel (d). This is to be expected, since t_2 and t_4 are the rates are which isocollections locus C_1 intersects curve AA' in panel (c).

The discussion thus far is based on the assumption that only the labor supply is responsive to change in the income tax rate. If the supply of both labor and capital respond positively to lower tax rates, the expansion of output will be greater than is illustrated. In this case, it is more likely that the expansion of the tax base will be large enough to offset the revenue effect of the rate reduction, particularly over longer time periods.

9

Taxation of
Business Income

In principle, the taxation of business income presents no special problems. The income of each business should be allocated among each owner in proportion to the owner's share in the firm's equity. In practice, that is how it is done for proprietorships and partnerships but not for corporations. Governments usually impose separate taxes with different rate structures on individuals and corporations. This procedure is followed by the U.S. government and by nearly all the states.

There are many similarities between the U.S. individual and corporate income taxes. Income is defined in a similar way. Deductible business expenses, including depreciation and depletion allowances, are treated identically. The major difference is in the rate structure. Because the two taxes are so much alike, and because most business income is generated in the corporate sector, the discussion that follows is limited to the corporation income tax.

THE U.S. CORPORATION
INCOME TAX

The U.S. corporation income tax was introduced in 1909, four years earlier than the individual income tax. It quickly became the largest single source of federal revenue and remained so until World War II, when it was surpassed by the individual income tax. It now ranks third in importance behind the individual income tax and the social security payroll tax. In fiscal 1981, which preceded passage of the Economic Recovery Tax Act, the U.S. corporation income tax yielded $61.1 billion, or about 10 percent of federal tax revenue. Its importance as a revenue source is expected to recede in the wake of the major changes contained in the Economic Recovery Tax Act of 1981. These changes include a new set of capital cost recovery provisions that will cut tax revenues markedly in future years.[1]

The U.S. corporation income tax, like the individual income tax, contains many complexities. Its basic structure is simple, however, and may be outlined in the following way.

Gross receipts
Less: Current expenses
    Depreciation allowance
    Interest expense
    State and local taxes
    Contributions (up to 10 percent of corporate income)
Equals: Taxable income

Tax liability is determined by applying a five-bracket rate structure to taxable income. The rates range from 15 percent on the first $25,000 to 46 percent on income over $100,000, as shown in Table 9–1. The four lower brackets are important for small corporations but are inconsequential for large firms with income in the millions or billions. For these firms, the tax is essentially proportional. The corporation tax includes a special maximum rate of 28 percent on long-term capital gains and a minimum tax of 15 percent on selected forms of tax-preference income that otherwise escape taxation.

If a corporation experiences an operating loss for a given year, the loss may be subtracted from taxable income of the preceding three years. This provision, called a "carry-back," makes the firm eligible for a refund. Should the loss exceed taxable income earned over the preceding three years, the remainder may be carried over and subtracted from income for the next fifteen years. The carry-back and carry-over procedure permits the firm to spread losses over nineteen years, thereby lightening the tax burden of firms in riskier lines of endeavor. If a firm with accumulated losses is absorbed by a profitable corporation, the profitable firm can subtract the losses from its own taxable earnings. This feature, which is now somewhat restricted, has been criticized for encouraging concentration of corporate ownership.

The corporate rate is applied to all corporate income whether it is retained by the corporation or is distributed to shareholders as dividends. Dividend income is also included in the income of the recipients and is

---

[1]The 1981 act prescribed new rules for depreciation allowances and investment tax credits that would have cost the federal Treasury an estimated $53 billion by fiscal year 1986. Anticipated revenue losses have been reduced significantly, however, by the Tax Equity and Fiscal Responsibility Act of 1982, which rescinds some of the major concessions in the 1981 act. Passage of the 1982 revision was prompted by the desire to reduce huge projected federal deficits.

TABLE 9-1   Rate Structure of U.S. Corporation Income Tax

TAXABLE INCOME	RATE
First $25,000	15%
$25,000 to $50,000	18
$50,000 to $75,000	30
$75,000 to $100,000	40
Over $100,000	46

taxed again as personal income. To mitigate this so-called "double taxation," Congress has granted a $100 dividend exclusion ($200 for a married couple with joint stock ownership). By setting the exclusion so low, relief is concentrated on taxpayers with small stock holdings.

Retained earnings would appear to escape double taxation, but only in a direct sense. Retained earnings add to corporate net worth, and if they are reinvested intelligently, future earnings will increase.

As a result, the value of common stock is likely to rise, and stockholders will experience capital gains. If these gains are realized subsequently, they will be taxed, albeit at preferential capital gains rates. Hence, even retained earnings can be subjected to double taxation of a sort. Because capital gains are taxed at lower rates and are not taxed at all unless realized, many shareholders prefer corporations to retain earnings rather than to pay dividends. This feature of the income tax has no doubt affected corporate dividend policy at the expense of less wealthy stockholders who have less to gain from preferential capital gains rates.

Depreciation

The productive life of capital assets usually extends well beyond the annual accounting period over which business income is measured. Some means must therefore be found to allocate the cost of capital among accounting periods. In principle, this presents no difficulty if the accretion concept of income is used. Any reduction in the value of assets, including that from wear and tear, is a reduction in net worth and reduces income accordingly. In practice, it is not feasible to make estimates of the decline in value for each item of capital equipment. Consequently, arbitrary formulas for depreciation write-offs have been accepted by accountants and tax collectors alike.

Two factors influence the rate at which the cost of capital investment can be written off. One is the number of years over which the write-off takes place. This is referred to as the *recovery period*. The other is the proportion of the cost of the asset that may be written off in each year. Various formulas have been devised for determining the annual write-off. The simplest is the straight-line formula, which allows the write-off of an equal proportion of the cost of an asset each year. For example, if the cost of an asset is to be written off over five years, the straight-line method allows one-fifth, or 20 percent, of original cost to be deducted each year. The tax code permits the use of other formulas that concentrate more of the write-off in early years of the cost recovery period. They are described subsequently.

A faster write-off concentrates more of the cost of capital in the early years. By deducting more of the cost of a capital investment in earlier years, a firm is able to postpone taxes. A firm generally prefers to postpone taxes, because it gains the use of the money in the interim. In effect, tax postponement is the equivalent of an interest-free loan. Early write-offs, commonly called *accelerated depreciation,* therefore make investment more attractive. Major relaxations of depreciation rules to allow faster write-offs occurred in 1954, 1962, 1971, and 1981. In each of these years, the administration in power was trying to revive a sluggish economy by encouraging businesses to step up investment. The desire to promote investment took precedence over the goal of obtaining a more accurate measure of taxable income. It is generally agreed that relaxation of depreciation rules stimulates investment in the short run by encouraging firms to speed up investment schedules. There is less agreement on whether it is an effective way of increasing the nation's capital stock in the long run.[2]

Accelerated cost recovery system. The time periods over which firms are permitted to write off the cost of capital assets have been successively shortened through the introduction of new depreciation guidelines in 1962, 1971, and 1981. The 1971 guidelines introduced the asset depreciation range (ADR) system. The ADR system permitted taxpayers to use service lives within 20 percent above or below the already shortened 1962 guidelines. ADR guidelines were set for over one hundred broadly defined asset categories. As expected, most firms opted for the fastest write-off allowed. The Economic Recovery Tax Act of 1981 represents a more radical departure from previous practice by introducing the *accelerated cost recovery system* (ACRS). The ACRS scheme totally abandons the accounting convention of matching the cost of a capital investment against the income it creates. Previous depreciation guidelines with over a hundred asset categories are superseded by a new classification scheme that recognizes only four categories. Capital recovery periods are set at three, five, ten, or fifteen years.

[2]Robert E. Hall and Dale W. Jorgensen found that accelerated depreciation and other tax inducements are effective ways of increasing investment. Their results appear in "Application of the Theory of Optimum Capital Accumulation," in Gary Fromm, ed., *Tax Incentives and Capital Spending* (Washington, D.C.: The Brookings Institution, 1971), pp. 9–60. Robert M. Coen, testing a different type of investment model, concludes that tax incentives have not been very effective inducements to invest. See "The Effect of Cash Flow on the Speed of Adjustment," in Fromm, ed., *Tax Incentives and Capital Spending,* pp. 131–79.

The ACRS guidelines contain the following four categories:

Three-year capital recovery	Autos, light trucks, equipment used in research and development activities, and assets with midpoint lives of four years or less under previous (ADR) guidelines.
Five-year capital recovery	Most other machinery and equipment.
Ten-year capital recovery	Public utility property with eighteen-and-a-half- to twenty-five-year lives under previous (ADR) guidelines.
Fifteen-year capital recovery	Most depreciable real estate and public utility property with depreciable life in excess of twenty-five years under previous (ADR) guidelines.

Replacement of more than a hundred asset categories by only four simplifies depreciation accounting for taxpayers. The new guidelines also shorten the write-off period for most assets. Since all assets are assigned to one of only four capital recovery periods, the extent to which depreciation is accelerated differs markedly among different asset categories. As a consequence, the potential tax savings from accelerated depreciation are distributed unevenly across assets with different actual service lives.

Depreciation formulas. The proportion of cost that can be written off each year is determined by the depreciation formula. Straight-line (SL) depreciation is the most conservative method in general use. As mentioned, SL spreads the capital cost deduction equally across all years of the recovery period. The formulas prescribed under ACRS generally permit a more rapid write-off in early years than does the SL method. A comparison of the SL method with the 150 percent declining-balance (DB) formula prescribed for most forms of machinery and equipment illustrates the difference. Assuming a five-year capital recovery period, the first-year deduction under the 150 percent DB formula is 30 percent of the cost of an asset; the first-year deduction under SL is 20 percent of cost. By the end of the third year, 78 percent of asset cost is written off under the 150 percent DB formula, compared with 60 percent under SL. Write-off is completed in five years under both formulas.[3]

---

[3]Under the 150 percent declining-balance formula, the write-off in the first year is 1.5 times (150 percent of) the straight-line write-off. Continuing with the five-year example, 30 percent versus 20 percent is written off in year 1. In year 2, 30 percent of the remaining balance is written off. In practice, the declining-balance formula is applied up to the midpoint of the capital recovery period. The straight-line method is used to write off the remaining capital cost. The ACRS write-off differs from the example in the text in one respect. It uses the "half-year convention" for all assets other than realty. Under this procedure, assets are treated as if they were in place for one-half year in calculating depreciation for the year of acquisition. Thus, for an asset in the five-year class under 150 percent DB, the write-off in the first tax year of ownership is 15 percent rather than 30 percent.

The 150 percent DB formula applies to most investments (other than real estate) placed in service in 1981 and thereafter. Formulas in effect for depreciable real estate and for other capital goods in service before January 1, 1981 allow a somewhat faster write-off in early years than either the 150 percent DB or SL methods.

Separating Current Expense from Investment

Investment in plant and equipment must be written off over a specified number of years, but outlays for labor, raw materials, fuel, and lubricants are examples of current expenses that can be deducted as costs in the year of purchase. These procedures seem to be reasonable, because they serve to assign production costs to the year in which they are actually incurred. In some cases, however, outlays that are in the nature of long-term investments can be deducted as current expenses. Major maintenance expenses are an obvious example. Exploration and development costs in the oil and mineral industries are another. Perhaps the most important are costs of research and development (R & D).

Several issues are involved. When a firm is deciding how to allocate funds between R & D activities and investment in depreciable capital equipment, the immediate tax write-off will tend to make investment in R & D more attractive, at least at the margin. Since both types of expenditures are a form of investment, the tax law undoubtedly induces reallocation, although the two forms of investment are to some degree complementary. This is because new products and processes may require new capital equipment.[4]

Some of the R & D output contains elements of publicness; other firms can borrow the new knowledge unless patent laws prevent it. The tax break can, therefore, be thought of as a public subsidy for the public component of a firm's R & D activities. The concessions also help to offset the high risks of product innovation, but the adjustments for publicness and risks are crude at best.

Depletion

The depletion of deposits of oil and minerals is similar in one respect to depreciation of capital goods. As deposits are extracted, the value of the oil or mineral right declines and in accordance with the accretion concept of income should be treated as a reduction in net worth. Tax treatment of depletion has long been a controversial feature of U.S. tax policy. For years, the oil depletion allowance has been a target of liberal critics. Con-

---

[4]The 1981 act provides additional incentives for R & D. Equipment used in R & D activities may be depreciated in three years, regardless of actual service life. The act also introduces a tax credit for incremental expenditures on R & D, as described subsequently.

gress eliminated it for large oil and gas producers in 1975 at the peak of anti-industry sentiment that accompanied the onset of the energy crisis, but it remains in effect for numerous smaller companies and owners of oil rights.

The argument for a depletion allowance is predicated on the American legal doctrine that treats rights to natural resources as private property. Thus, if oil is discovered on your property, you will become the owner of the right to extract it. Once the oil is discovered, extraction rights will take on a value equal to discounted expected returns. The discovery will provide you with a windfall in the form of increased net worth.

Recall from Chapter 8 that the accretion concept of income includes changes in net worth as a part of income. Under a strict application of accretion, the increment in net worth would appear in the tax base at the time of discovery. As oil is removed, the value of the oil rights will decline and will be reflected in declining net worth and a reduced income tax base. Conceptually, therefore, the problem of depletion presents no special difficulties once one accepts the accretion definition.

In practice, increments to net worth are not ordinarily subject to the income tax unless they are realized through sale of assets. Thus, if the right to remove oil remains in the hands of the original owner, no income tax is paid on the windfall. If the original owner sells the rights, the windfall will be classified as a capital gain and taxed accordingly. Some means must then be devised to allow the purchaser to write off the decline in property value as the oil or mineral is removed.

One alternative is to use a formula based on cost depletion. The following formula is used to determine cost depletion for any given year:

$$\text{Adjusted basis} \times \frac{\text{units sold during year}}{\text{units remaining in deposit}} = \text{depletion allowance}$$

where the adjusted basis is the original cost of the deposit to the owner plus additional capital investment in developing the site minus depletion allowances and depreciation deducted in previous years. If the deposit is developed by the original owner, the only cost would be development cost. Under cost depletion, the owner would not be allowed any depletion deduction for the declining value of the original rights. This is as it should be for tax purposes if the original windfall was *not* included in taxable income at the time of discovery. The sale value of the oil or minerals removed should be included in taxable income at the time of realization. Otherwise, the windfall gain in net worth will never be taxed.

If the rights to the deposit are sold, the cost should be included in the new owner's basis and written off in accordance with the formula given. Recall that in this case the windfall income to the original owner is taxed as a capital gain at the time the rights are sold. Under existing provisions of the U.S. personal and corporate income tax, the preferential treatment of capital gains income might encourage original owners to sell the rights in preference to exercising them themselves, but that is a weakness in the way in which we tax capital gains, not in the principle of cost depletion.

A practical problem occurs in determining the ratio of units sold during a given year to units remaining in the deposit, because it is often difficult to determine the size of a deposit before it has been exhausted. Lack of uniformity in quality of mineral deposits may distort the economic significance as well, but the problem is not so great as to make the use of a cost depletion formula impractical. We use formulas for estimating depreciation even though it is recognized that they approximate "true" depreciation only roughly.

Current U.S. tax law gives firms in the extractive industries, except for a few large oil and gas producers, an option of using percentage depletion rather than cost depletion. Percentage depletion is almost always more favorable to the taxpayer. Under percentage depletion, the firm is allowed to subtract from taxable income a percentage of the *gross* receipts from the sale of minerals, coal, and, for eligible firms, oil and gas.[5] The percentage ranges from 5 percent of gross sales for sand and gravel up to 22 percent for a number of minerals, including uranium. The allowance is subject to the constraint that it cannot reduce net income excluding depletion by more than 50 percent. The effect of the depletion allowance is to reduce the effective rate of taxation in extractive industries below the rate in most other industries.[6] The tax break is especially great for discoveries that are developed by the original owner. Because unrealized capital gains are not taxed at all, the original windfall in the value of the rights is not taxed. As the output is sold, a sizable part of the realized gain escapes taxation through percentage depletion. The favorable treatment of extractive industries could be eliminated by taxing profits from the sale of oil, gas, coal, and mineral rights as ordinary income, while allowing purchasers of the rights to write off the cost as the deposit is reduced. If rights are not sold, no depletion allowance is justified, because the allowance removes windfall income from the tax base.

Those who defend the percentage depletion allowance have long argued that it is necessary to compensate for the high risks in discovery and development, especially in the oil industry. This argument evokes visions

---

[5]The 1975 Tax Reduction Act eliminated the percentage depletion allowance entirely for major oil and gas companies and reduces it gradually for small producers. The percentage is reduced gradually from 22 to 15 percent and will be limited to sales of the first 1,000 barrels of oil or 6 million cubic feet of gas when the restrictions are implemented fully in 1984.

[6]John J. Siegfried has estimated the effective average rates on U.S. corporations in 1963. At that time, the statutory rate was 52 percent on income above $25,000. Because of tax preferences, the average effective rate was 39.4 percent. All extractive industries had below-average effective rates. Three of them, including petroleum refining and extraction, had effective rates below 20 percent. See "Effective Average U.S. Corporation Income Tax Rates," *National Tax Journal,* 27 (June 1974), 257.

of a daring wildcatter risking everything on one last crack at fortune. In reality, much of the prospecting is done by large operators, who spread the risk of exploratory drilling over a large number of attempts in much the same way as an insurance company spreads the cost of claims over a large number of policyholders. Opponents of percentage depletion regard it as another tax loophole that creates inequities among taxpayers and contributes to misallocation of resources. Misallocation occurs because the tax advantage encourages overinvestment in the extractive industries at the expense of investment elsewhere. One consequence is a more rapid depletion of natural resources than would otherwise occur.

Deduction of Taxes and Contributions

Most of the deductions included in the individual income tax are intended to meet the needs of households and are inapplicable to corporations. Some, such as state and local taxes and interest payments, are deductible as normal business expenses. Corporations are also allowed to deduct contributions to eligible nonprofit organizations up to a maximum limit of 10 percent of corporate income.

Credits

The corporate rate structure is applied to taxable income to determine tax liability gross of credits. Credits are subtracted from this amount to determine the net tax liability. The most important are the investment credit and a credit for income tax paid to foreign governments.

The investment tax credit is another device designed to encourage investment. Businesses are allowed to take 10 percent of their outlay on machinery and equipment as a credit against their income tax liability. The full credit is allowed only on items with a depreciation write-off of five years or more. A 6 percent credit is allowed for equipment in the three-year depreciation category. Unused credits may be carried back three years or forward fifteen. Because only half of the credit is deducted from depreciable value of the asset, it is really a direct tax subsidy to businesses that invest in machinery and equipment.

The investment credit first appeared as a part of the 1962 tax stimulus package. The percentage was raised from 7 to 10 percent in 1975. The entire credit was suspended for two short periods during the Vietnam era in an effort to cool down an overheated economy, but in light of more recent concern over a capital shortage, it is likely to remain as a permanent feature of the tax law.

To stimulate additional spending on research and development, the 1981 tax revision introduced an R & D credit. Firms are granted a tax credit of 25 percent of incremental expenses on R & D activities. The increment is defined as the amount by which R & D expenditures in a given year exceed like expenses averaged over the three preceding years. Depreciation charges on R & D equipment, which are granted preferential treatment under the depreciation rules, are not counted. The credit is limited to R & D activities in the physical or biological sciences and engineering. Firms may take a credit for both in-house and contract research. The latter provision makes it possible for universities and other nonprofit agencies to benefit indirectly.

Income earned in foreign countries by U.S. corporations is subject to the U.S. tax. A credit is allowed for payment of a foreign corporation income tax. The credit cannot exceed the U.S. corporation income tax liability of foreign income. Its purpose is to prevent double taxation of foreign source income.

INFLATION AND THE TAXATION OF BUSINESS INCOME

The accounting procedures used to measure income are at best somewhat arbitrary, particularly when depreciation and depletion are a factor. A further source of measurement error is introduced by inflation. One way in which to deal with inflation is to ignore it and base taxation on nominal (or current dollar) income. This is the current practice. Alternatively, nominal income can be adjusted for changes in purchasing power, making tax liability a function of real income.

Nominal measures of business income are sensitive to inflation, particularly when there is a lag between the time when a cost is incurred and the resulting revenue is generated. In particular, depreciation allowances based on the historical cost of capital equipment understate the capital consumption cost of production and cause an upward bias in measurement of income. To the extent that the bias is induced by inflation, an index of the general price level could be used to adjust capital costs for inflation. In this way, book value is increased in accordance with the inflation rate. A more precise adjustment to current capital costs could be made by valuing depreciable assets at replacement cost. The latter procedure adjusts for any change in the price of capital goods, not just changes attributable to inflation. Where changes in design and technology are important, however, it may not be possible to estimate replacement cost accurately.

Although present tax law does not permit businesses to adjust depreciation costs for inflation, capital equipment can generally be written off in a time period shorter than the actual average service life. In a firm with a growing stock of real capital, acceleration of depreciation will serve to overstate the investment write-off in nominal terms so as to offset in a rough way the downward bias from use of historical costs.

Inflation can generate inventory profits. Raw materials and goods in process may increase in value before they are converted into finished products and sold. The government allows firms to use either the first-in, first-out (FIFO) or last-in, first-out (LIFO) method of inventory evaluation. Under FIFO, inventory used up is priced at the earliest price paid for items in stock during the accounting period; under LIFO, the latest price paid for items on hand is used first. When prices are rising, LIFO will result in higher materials costs and lower income, so inventory profits and tax liability will be lower for firms using the LIFO method.

THE INCOME TAX
AND INVESTMENT

The effect of the income tax on aggregate saving and investment was discussed in Chapter 8, where it was pointed out that income taxation, insofar as it reduces the purchasing power of the private sector, can be expected to reduce both consumption and investment. Income taxes may also affect the allocation of private sector spending between consumption and investment. This occurs through its effect on the net rate of return to capital. The extent to which the net rate of return to capital affects the allocation of private sector spending between consumption and investment is a matter of dispute. Econometric evidence is inconclusive. There is no doubt, however, that the Economic Recovery Tax Act of 1981 is designed to raise the net (after-tax) return to capital investment. It is hoped that this feature of the act will serve to tilt the allocation of private sector expenditures in the direction of more investment.

Tax treatment of capital expenditures is of significance not only because of its effect on aggregate investment, but because of its effect on the allocation of capital outlays. Depreciation allowances and tax credits prescribed by the 1981 and 1982 tax acts impact in markedly different ways on different kinds of investments. Inflation adds a further complication. A thorough analysis of how all these factors affect the net return on different types of investment is complicated and will not be attempted here. Instead, a general overview will be presented. This will enable us to gain an appreciation of the ways in which the current law can be expected to affect investment decisions.

We begin by assuming a stable price level. The 1981 act allows businesses to write off the cost of a depreciable asset over a prescribed time period. This is the accelerated cost recovery system, or ACRS. In addition, firms are granted a tax credit for purchase of most types of machinery, equipment, and vehicles. The credit reduces a firm's tax liability in the year of purchase by from 6 to 10 percent of the purchase price. The attractiveness of the credit was reduced somewhat by two changes included in the Tax Equity and Fiscal Responsibility Act of 1982. That act requires firms to subtract one-half of the amount claimed as a credit (3 to 5 percent of the purchase price) from the depreciable cost of an asset. It also eliminates a leasing option that permitted firms without taxable income to lease equipment from firms that could take full advantage of the tax savings. Even with these restrictions, however, the credit remains as an important form of investment subsidy.

Investment in buildings and other structures is generally not eligible for the investment tax credit. This feature helps to tip the tax code in favor of purchases of machinery, equipment, and motor vehicles. Indeed, it has been demonstrated that, when reasonable assumptions about discount rates and returns to capital goods are used in estimating effective tax rates, the rates on some investments are *negative.* Negative rates occur whenever the present value of the tax savings from the investment credit and the accelerated depreciation schedules exceed the cost of the asset.[7] Present value is calculated for the year of purchase. The government is in effect paying firms to invest in certain kinds of equipment. The tax savings on these items can then be used to reduce the tax liability on income that a firm generates from other sources.

Investments in structures are not eligible for the credit. Therefore, income from these investments is taxed at positive effective rates. (The effective rates are below the statutory rate, however, because the capital recovery period allowed by the tax code is much shorter than the actual service life of most structures.) As a result, the tax structure tends to favor investments in shorter-lived machinery, equipment, and vehicles over longer-lived buildings and other structures.[8]

Inflation adds an additional complication, as was indicated in the preceding section. In the absence of annual indexing, depreciation allowances

[7]The present value of tax savings is calculated by discounting future tax savings. Calculation of present value is described in Chapter 5. Estimates of effective tax rates on a variety of investments under a tax scheme much like that incorporated into the ACRS and investment credits in the 1981 act appear in Charles R. Hulten and Frank C. Wykoff, "Economic Depreciation and Accelerated Depreciation: An Evaluation of the Conable–Jones 10-5-3 Proposal," *National Tax Journal,* 34 (March 1981), 52. The Conable–Jones bill contained depreciation provisions very similar to those contained in the Economic Recovery Tax Act of 1981.

[8]Ibid. Hulten and Wykoff estimate an effective tax rate on investments in nonresidential structures at 12 percent, compared with minus 68 percent on machinery and a corporate statutory rate of 46 percent. Following Conable–Jones, their estimate assumed a ten-year capital cost recovery period for real estate. The fifteen-year recovery period in ACRS serves to widen the disparity between the two categories of investment. In contrast to current law, Conable–Jones did not require firms to subtract half the value of the investment credit from depreciable cost. This feature of the current law serves to reduce the disparity. The Hulten–Wykoff estimates are based on the assumption of stable prices.

are based on original cost (or book value). Given a rate of inflation, tax savings from deductions of depreciation are less in real terms than they would be with stable prices. Inflation and the degree to which tax write-offs are accelerated combine to influence effective tax rates on investments, but in ways that are not easily summarized. With or without inflation, however, the differential impact on different kinds of investment is likely to be present.[9]

To the extent that the ACRS and tax credit provisions treat some types of investment more favorably than others, the corporation income tax interferes with the efficient allocation of capital. This has a negative effect on productivity. One way of eliminating discriminatory taxation of different categories of assets would be to bring capital recovery formulas into line with actual service lives and to adjust for inflation with annual indexing. As noted earlier, however, such a procedure would not provide the incentive to invest that is sought by policy makers. A system of first-year expensing could restore tax neutrality among different types of investment without removing the incentive created by the current tax advantages.

Under first-year expensing, businesses are permitted to write off the entire cost of a capital investment during the first year. The switch to expensing would be accompanied by the elimination of the investment tax credit. These changes would accomplish three things. First, the negative effective rates on some assets would be eliminated. Costs would be deducted in full, but the investment subsidy from the credit would be dropped. Second, the disparity in effective tax rates would be eliminated. Third, the inflationary distortions in capital cost recovery would virtually disappear. First-year expensing, like ACRS, discards any pretense of matching depreciation deductions against the income generated by capital goods. This is in keeping with the policy goal of stimulating saving and investment. Like ACRS, it would result in substantial revenue loss to the Treasury. Unlike ACRS, however, first-year expensing is neutral in its impact on different kinds of investment. For this reason, a switch from ACRS to expensing would contribute to a more efficient allocation of capital.

THE SHIFTING CONTROVERSY

Because many corporations are thought to possess significant market power, at least some short-run shifting of the tax burden is considered likely. As we saw in Chapter 7, the ability of a firm to shift a tax to con-

---

[9]Interestingly, in the Hulten–Wykoff simulation, high inflation rates virtually eliminate the large differential in effective rates that exists with stable prices. The estimated effective rates on machinery and equipment versus nonresidential structures range from minus 68 percent to 12 percent, respectively, with stable prices to 40 percent and 39 percent, respectively, with 14 percent annual inflation. These estimates are for broad asset categories and hide substantial variation across asset groups and industries. Ibid., pp. 52–53.

sumers or suppliers is determined by the structure of the markets in which it operates. In a purely competitive environment, shifting comes about through tax-induced changes in the supply of inputs or output. The amount of shifting, if any, depends on underlying supply and demand elasticities. In the oligopolistic markets in which many large corporations operate, the short-run reaction of firms is more difficult to predict. Interdependence of demand among a few competitors complicates the response of each firm.

A number of attempts have been made to estimate the degree of short-run shifting of the corporation income tax. In the United States, these efforts began in 1963 with publication of the startling econometric results of Marian Krzyzaniak and Richard Musgrave,[10] who, with others, had observed an increase in the gross (before-tax) return to capital in manufacturing that coincided with a substantial increase in the rate of the corporation income tax. Realizing that other factors in addition to shifting of the tax might account for the observed increase, they constructed an econometric model designed to separate the effect of the tax variable from other determinants of corporate profits. Using data for the years 1935 to 1942 and 1948 to 1959, they estimated that shifting exceeded 100 percent, that is, that the *after-tax* return to capital in manufacturing *increased* as a result of an increase in the tax rate.[11] If these results are correct, it would appear that the government is doing investors in manufacturing corporations a favor by raising tax rates!

These results have been viewed with suspicion, especially by some of the more orthodox price theorists. One reason is that the standard model of the firm predicts that a tax on pure economic profit will not be shifted in the short run. Pure profit is a residual (the difference between total revenue and total cost) containing no cost elements. The price and quantity that maximize profits without a profits tax will also maximize after-tax profits with a tax so long as the marginal rate does not exceed 100 percent. Of course, the base of the corporation income tax is not limited to pure profits. No deduction is allowed for the opportunity cost of equity capital, and the various provisions for deducting depreciation and other expenses are at best only rough approximations of actual costs. This is not a serious problem in applying the model to the short run, however, because the capital stock of a firm is assumed to be fixed. Hence, any return to capital is in the form of a residual or quasi-rent. A tax on such returns does not affect marginal cost and, therefore, should not affect output. A potentially more serious limitation of the standard model stems from its partial equilibrium nature. Only the effects of tax payments, not the effects of uses of

[10]Marian Krzyzaniak and Richard A. Musgrave, *The Shifting of the Corporation Income Tax* (Baltimore: Johns Hopkins University Press, 1963).

[11]Krzyzaniak and Musgrave tested a number of variations of their basic model, but they consistently came up with results indicating at least 100 percent shifting.

revenue, are taken into account. As we saw in Chapter 7, it is not ordinarily legitimate to apply such a model to a major revenue source.

As has been mentioned, the standard profit-maximization model does not necessarily apply to oligopolies. Indeed, the lack of a general model of oligopolistic behavior is an important factor hindering efforts to construct and test a model of tax shifting. Nevertheless, many economists find the implications of the Krzyzaniak–Musgrave results difficult to accept. In particular, they question the hypothesis that corporate managements administer prices so as to reach a target rate of return instead of trying to maximize profits.

Soon after publication of the Krzyzaniak–Musgrave findings, several other studies appeared showing quite different results. Of particular interest is a study by Cragg, Harberger, and Mieszkowski,[12] who attribute the rising rate of profit that accompanied tax increases to increases in aggregate demand and to a gradual tax-induced shift of capital from the corporate to the noncorporate sector. In reestimating the Krzyzaniak–Musgrave model, they added variables reflecting the unemployment rate and wartime mobilization. The addition of these two variables caused the tax variable to become insignificant, indicating that it really was demand conditions, not higher taxes, that caused the gross rate of return on capital to rise. Other studies incorporating aggregate demand variables appear to confirm the results of Cragg et al., thereby casting considerable doubt on the Krzyzaniak–Musgrave findings.[13]

The issue, however, is not yet resolved. The studies described are based on statistical estimates of a variety of profit equations that include a tax variable. Frederick D. Sebold uses another approach in which he tests a multiequation model that explicitly relates prices of inputs and output in the manufacturing sector to changes in the tax rate. By treating input and output prices separately, Sebold is able to test for forward shifting (to consumers) and backward shifting (to suppliers of factors). His results indicate that there is no backward shifting but that about 70 percent of the tax burden is shifted forward to consumers in the short run.[14]

Sebold's findings support the hypothesis that higher corporate tax

[12]J. G. Cragg, A. C. Harberger, and P. Mieszkowski, "Empirical Evidence on the Incidence of the Corporation Income Tax," *Journal of Political Economy*, 75 (December 1967), 811–21.

[13]For a summary and critique of several important studies, see William H. Oakland, "A Survey of the Recent Debate on the Short-Run Shifting of the Corporation Tax," *National Tax Association Proceedings*, 1969, pp. 525–47. A more recent survey appears in J. Gregory Ballentine, *Equity, Efficiency, and the U.S. Corporation Income Tax* (Washington, D.C.: American Enterprise Institute, 1980), pp. 12–19.

[14]Frederick D. Sebold, "The Short-Run Shifting of the Corporation Income Tax: A Simultaneous Equation Approach," *Review of Economics and Statistics*, 61 (August 1979), 401–09.

rates serve as a signal to raise prices in oligopolistic markets. His work represents a new departure that is likely to be subjected to additional tests. One feature of the current economic environment that may not be reflected adequately in Sebold's results is the increased competition from imports. Sebold tests his model with data for the years 1931 to 1941 and 1946 to 1970. During most of that period, U.S. domestic manufacturers enjoyed a more dominant role in the world economy, and that may have enhanced their ability to shift tax burdens forward to consumers.

Uncertainty over short-run shifting complicates analysis of long-run shifting. If the corporation income tax is not shifted in the short run, an increase in the tax will lower the net (after-tax) rate of return to capital in the corporate sector relative to the noncorporate sector. Over time, capital will be reallocated from the corporate to the noncorporate sector. Both the uses and sources of income will be affected. The shift in resources will increase output of the noncorporate sector, mainly agriculture, real estate, and some service industries. Corporate output, including manufacturing and transportation, will decline. Prices of noncorporate output will fall relative to prices of corporate output, benefiting consumers with relative preferences for noncorporate output. The effect of the shift in resources from the corporate sector to the noncorporate sector can be expected to change the relative prices of factors of production. The direction of change depends on a rather complicated set of relationships involving the ratio of capital to labor input, factor substitutability, and demand elasticities between the two sectors. Arnold Harberger constructed a model that accounts for these interrelationships. This model, which treats the corporation income tax as a form of excise tax on the use of capital in the corporate sector, indicates that capital bears the full burden of the tax.[15]

The Harberger model represents a major advance in the use of a general equilibrium model to estimate tax incidence. For this reason alone, it represents an important advance in incidence analysis. To make the model tractable, Harberger had to make a number of simplifying assumptions, two of which are of particular concern. One is the assumption that the supply of capital and labor in the economy is perfectly inelastic and therefore unresponsive to any change in factor prices. This proposition has not been disproven, but if it is incorrect, the conclusions drawn from the model must be modified. In particular, if the aggregate supply of capital in the U.S. economy falls in response to a fall in the after-tax rate of return, the conclusion that capital bears the full burden of the tax no longer holds. If the corporation income tax reduces the capital stock, a part of the burden is shifted to labor. A second assumption implicit in Harberger's model is that the tax does not induce short-run forward shifting in oligopolistic markets. To the extent that it does, the return to capital in the corporate sector

---

[15]Arnold C. Harberger, "The Incidence of the Corporation Income Tax," *Journal of Political Economy*, 70 (June 1962), 215–40.

is not reduced, and the long-run shifting via transfer of capital is short-circuited. A third assumption, also implicit, is that firms in the corporate sector do not attempt to avoid the tax by switching to a noncorporate form of business enterprise. Presumably, the advantages of the corporate form, including limited liability and perpetual life, make it necessary for firms that must accumulate large amounts of capital to use the corporate form.[16]

The lack of consensus on the shifting and incidence of the corporation income tax makes it difficult to prescribe sound tax policy. If the distribution of tax burden is unknown, the tax cannot be evaluated in terms of the principles of tax equity. If the burden falls on owners of capital, as suggested by Harberger, the tax is progressive. This is because of the heavy concentration of asset ownership at the top of the income distribution. If the burden is shifted to consumers, as suggested by Krzyzaniak–Musgrave and Sebold, it becomes a form of hidden sales tax that is regressive or, at best, proportional in its incidence.

INTEGRATION OF
CORPORATION AND
INDIVIDUAL INCOME TAXES

Should we have separate taxes on corporate and individual income? The answer depends on how one views the role of the corporation in our economy. Some people see the big corporation as an independent entity that receives a large income and controls a huge accumulation of wealth while being subject to little if any control by its stockholders. Viewed in this way, the corporation is seen as an independent source of taxpaying capacity. The corporation income tax becomes a politically attractive source of revenue, particularly in light of the uncertainty over its incidence.

Alternatively, the corporation may be viewed as a special form of partnership in which its owners, the stockholders, pool their resources to earn income. Seen in this light, it follows that corporate income should be treated like any other income. For tax purposes, it should be allocated among shareholders in proportion to equity holdings and taxed as part of personal income. Individual rates would apply to all corporate income, whether retained or paid out in dividends. The tax liability would fall on individuals rather than on corporations.

Full integration of corporate earnings into the individual income tax is appealing when viewed in terms of the traditional principles of horizontal

[16]This issue is discussed in Roy D. Adams, "The Demise of Corporations in Harberger's Incidence Model," *National Tax Journal*, 30 (March 1977), 91–92. The incentive to switch to a noncorporate form is generally not present in small firms with ten or fewer stockholders. These firms have the option of being taxed like partnerships, where income is allocated among owners and is taxed as personal income under the individual income tax.

and vertical equity. The present arrangement violates horizontal equity because it taxes income from corporate and noncorporate sources differentially. It violates the principle of vertical equity because it applies the same corporate rate to the income of all shareholders regardless of their income bracket. Furthermore, it subjects dividend income to double taxation, taxing it first at corporate rates and then (except for the $100-per-person dividend exclusion) at personal rates.

Unfortunately, because of serious practical problems, full integration would be difficult to achieve. Allocation of earnings to individual taxpayers can become very complicated. On a typical day, 50 million shares may be traded on the New York Stock Exchange alone. Annual earnings would have to be prorated for millions of shareholders who own stock for only one part of a year. It is not unusual for a corporation to own some or all of the stock of another corporation, so stockholder equity would have to be traced through tiers of corporate ownership. Taxation of retained earnings might create liquidity problems for some shareholders, and it would require a change in the taxation of capital gains. If retained earnings are taxed as personal income when earned, they would have to be added to the basis (purchase price) of stock. Otherwise, to the extent that retained earnings cause the price of stock to rise, they would be taxed a second time when gains are realized.

Aside from equity considerations, integration could cause the government to lose revenue. Many shares of stock are owned by nonprofit institutions or private pension funds that pay no tax or by foreigners who pay taxes only on U.S. earnings. If U.S. earnings are small, foreigners might pay little or no tax as individuals.[17]

The corporation income tax is not likely to disappear, owing to its political appeal and the problems of integrating it into the individual income tax. A less radical proposal calls for continuation of the corporation tax on retained earnings only. Corporations would be allowed to deduct dividends as business expenses. Dividend income would continue to be subject to the individual income tax, as under current law. To the extent that dividends represent the opportunity cost of equity capital, they are a legitimate business expense and should be deductible. Deduction would reduce the incentive that now exists for corporations to choose debt over equity financing for tax purposes. The serious administrative and compliance problems accompanying full integration would be avoided, and the alleged double taxation of dividend income would be eliminated.[18]

In spite of the appeal of dividend deductibility on equity grounds,

---

[17]For a more detailed discussion of the administrative and compliance problems of integration, see Charles E. McLure, Jr., "A Status Report on Tax Integration in the United States," *National Tax Journal,* 31 (December 1978), 313–28.

[18]To the extent that dividends are paid to tax-exempt organizations, some income would escape taxation completely. For a description of schemes for preventing this, see ibid., pp. 317–18.

Congress has shown little interest in the proposal. Taken alone, it would reduce tax revenue. Its potential effect on capital formation makes some people wary. Corporations would have an incentive to distribute more income as dividends, thereby reducing the supply of funds available for investment. On the other hand, to the extent that deductibility reduces the tax burden on income from equities, it would make common stock a more attractive investment option. This would be expected to increase the aggregate supply of equity capital and help to offset the negative effect of the tax on investment and capital formation. A political obstacle to deductibility of dividends is uncertainty over incidence of the corporation income tax. Potential beneficiaries are not readily identifiable, and they may not be fully aware of the tax reduction even if it is adopted. This is likely to make the measure less attractive to Congress.

STATE CORPORATION INCOME TAXES

State corporation income taxes are currently in effect in forty-four states and in the District of Columbia. They are levied typically at a flat rate, usually between 4 and 10 percent. A few states have mildly progressive rate structures. In most cases, the definition of income is essentially the same as under the federal tax. Only a few states allow deductibility of the federal corporation income tax. Since many corporations operate interstate, the proportion of income to be taxed in each state in which they operate must be determined. In most states, the "three-factor" formula is used for this purpose. Total taxable income of a corporation is multiplied by a weighted average of the portion of the firm's payroll, property, and sales within the state. To illustrate, suppose that corporation X has taxable income of $1 million and that 50 percent of its payroll, 60 percent of its property, and 10 percent of its sales are in state Y. The three percentages average out to 40, so $400,000 of the firm's income is taxable in state Y.

The three-factor formula is admittedly arbitrary. If the goal were to measure income generated within a state, a two-factor formula limited to payroll and property would be better. These are the inputs that produce the output. Inclusion of the sales factor serves to reduce the tax burden of corporations with large out-of-state sales. This feature may be attractive to states trying to attract industry, but it is obviously inequitable. Bills that would adopt federal standards for apportionment of income among states have been introduced in Congress, but they have been blocked by opposition from the states. State officials seem to prefer autonomy in this matter, even though it sometimes leads to confusion and inequity.

Although a corporation income tax is in effect in most states, it accounts for only about 9 or 10 percent of state tax revenue nationwide. It is not likely to increase in importance because of concern within states that high business taxes will arrest industrial development. Some states have adopted the ACRS depreciation schedules contained in the federal tax code. In these states, the relative importance of the corporation income tax is likely to decline as the decade of the 1980s progresses.

BUSINESS INCOME
TAXATION: AN EVALUATION

The taxation of business income presents us with some of the most intractable issues of tax policy. Examples include depreciation and inventory accounting and depletion allowances for extractable resources. Treatment of all these is complicated by inflation.

Another major question is, how should we tax corporate source income? In principle, the ideal solution is to integrate the corporation and individual taxes and subject all income to the same rate structure regardless of source. To do so requires assignment of all corporate income to individual stockholders, whether the income is paid out as dividends or is retained by the corporation. As we have seen, such a procedure would be beset by administrative complexities. Income assigned to shares owned by pension funds, nonprofit institutions, and some foreigners would escape taxation altogether. Integration without changing the tax rates on individuals would result in reduced tax revenue for the government.

Other options include partial integration or complete elimination of the tax on corporate income. Under partial integration, only the retained earnings of corporations would be subject to the corporate tax. Dividends would be exempt from the corporate tax but would continue to be taxed as personal income. Again, tax revenues would fall unless rates are increased. There is concern that corporations would reduce their retained earnings and that part of the additional divided income would be diverted from investment to consumption. On the other hand, deducting dividends from the corporate tax base would remove the discrimination that now exists between debt and equity finance. (Recall that interest payments are deductible.)

Total elimination of the tax on corporate source income is not likely to receive serious consideration. The revenue loss and the political implications of so large a tax break for business would preclude it unless another major tax on business were introduced in its place. The most likely candidate would be the value added tax, a form of sales tax described in Chapter 10. If the corporation income tax were eliminated completely, retained earnings would escape taxation unless they are realized as capital gains by stockholders. Retained earnings would thus become an even more attractive means of tax postponement and avoidance than they are under current law. In its present form, the corporation income tax gets low marks in terms of its effects on both allocation and equity. The tax raises the cost of equity capital to the corporate sector. This creates allocative inefficiencies and a loss in economic welfare by inducing a reallocation of capital from the corporate to the noncorporate sector.[19] The tax also encourages firms to exceed optimal debt-equity ratios, because it allows a deduction for interest expense but not for the opportunity cost of equity capital. Consequently, the cost of equity is greater than the cost of borrowed funds. A massive shift from equity to debt financing would be a matter of concern, because it would weaken the financial soundness of U.S. corporations and increase the likelihood of bankruptcy. The evidence indicates that the corporation income tax has caused a modest increase in debt-equity ratios, but other factors have prevented the shift from becoming excessive. One constraining factor is the rising marginal cost of debt imposed on corporations by lenders. As the debt-equity ratio rises, the probability of default increases, and lenders demand a higher risk premium. Another factor is the preference of high-bracket taxpayers for retained earnings over either interest or dividends. Recall that retained earnings are taxed only when realized as capital gains when stock is sold.[20]

In terms of equity, the U.S. corporation income tax is difficult to defend. It introduces differential rates on income from corporate and noncorporate sources, an obvious violation of the principle of horizontal equity. It is more difficult to evaluate in terms of vertical equity because of uncertainty over shifting. If the tax is shifted to consumers in the short run, it is a form of sales tax on the output of the corporate sector with an incidence pattern that is either regressive or proportional. If shifting occurs only in the long run through reallocation of capital, the tax burden is more likely to fall on capitalists. In this case, the incidence is likely to be progressive. If the tax reduces the size of the capital stock (relative to some budgetary alternative), a part of the burden is shifted to labor and progressivity is reduced.

The uncertainty over who bears the burden of the tax is an undesirable feature for those concerned with tax equity, but it makes the tax attractive to politicians. If they can impose a tax burden on us without our realizing it, they can acquire revenue without paying the political price. For this reason, and because the corporation income tax is a significant source of federal revenue, it is not likely to disappear.

[19]Harberger, using the model described, estimated the welfare loss at 0.5 percent of national income. See Arnold C. Harberger, "Efficiency Effects of Taxes on Income from Capital," in Marian Krzyzaniak, ed., *Effects of Corporation Income Tax* (Detroit: Wayne State University Press, 1966), pp. 110–17. More recent estimates showing welfare losses of comparable magnitude are summarized in Ballentine, *Equity, Efficiency, and the U.S. Corporation Income Tax,* pp. 77–82.

[20]For a discussion of the effects of the corporate tax on costs of debt versus equity finance policy, see Luigi Tambini, "Financial Policy and the Corporation Income Tax," in Arnold C. Harberger and Martin J. Bailey, eds., *The Taxation of Income from Capital* (Washington, D.C.: The Brookings Institution, 1969), pp. 185–222.

10

Sales and Excise Taxes

Many different types of taxes are levied on market transactions in virtually all countries and by all levels of government. Some are comparatively general, covering a broad range of commodities. These include retail sales, turnover, and value added taxes. *Sales taxes* of a general nature can yield large amounts of revenue at modest rates. In terms of equity, they are acceptable to those who regard expenditures as a suitable base for taxation. Because they apply to transactions, it is difficult to adjust them for individual differences in ability to pay or to impose a progressive rate structure on individuals. As a result, general sales taxes are looked upon with disfavor by those who think that the tax structure should contribute to a more equal distribution of after-tax income.

Taxes on the sale of a particular commodity or commodity group are called *excise taxes*. Aside from yielding revenue, excise taxes are often intended to serve other purposes of society. They may be used to discourage use of certain commodities or activities, as in the case of excise taxes on cigarettes, alcoholic beverages, and legalized gambling. Revenues from federal and state excise taxes on gasoline are earmarked for financing highways and roads. In this way, the tax-financed facilities are paid for by those who use them. As noted in Chapter 6, user taxes of this type represent one of the few applications of the benefit principle. Excise taxes may be levied as a percentage of selling price (called an *ad valorem* tax) or at a fixed amount on each unit sold (called a *per unit* or *unit tax*). The latter is more common in the United States. The major forms of sales and excise taxes are described in the following discussions and are evaluated in terms of equity and allocational effects.

Europe:

Turnover Vs VAT

THE FORM OF SALES TAXATION

Most commodities pass through a series of transactions on their way to the consumer. Their ingredients are sold as raw materials and perhaps as intermediate products. Finished goods may be sold to a wholesaler and retailer before the final sale to the consumer. A sales or excise tax may be levied at any stage in which a transaction occurs.

In the United States, the sales tax is usually levied at the retail level. The tax is collected by the seller, who adds it to the purchase price. Because the retail sales tax is collected at only one stage in the production-distribution channel, it is an example of a single-stage tax. Other examples of single-stage taxes are those on the sales of manufacturers or wholesalers. Since general sales taxes are ad valorem, the tax base at an earlier stage is smaller than at retail. Because of differences in markups, a sales tax levied at the manufacturing or wholesale stage can have an impact that is quite uneven among goods.

A manufacturer's sales tax is used by the federal government in Canada and by governments in a number of developing countries. Developing countries find it easier to collect sales taxes from manufacturers than from many small retailers with inadequate or nonexistent records. A single-stage tax at the wholesale level is found in only a few countries, but it is an important revenue source in Australia and New Zealand.

A sales tax levied at more than one point in the production and distribution channel is a multistage tax. The turnover tax is the most inclusive multistage tax. It applies to all intermediate transactions between firms and to retail sales to consumers. Sales of services of the basic factors of production are exempt. Governments sometimes find the turnover tax attractive, because its broad base yields substantial revenue at low rates. Because the tax falls on transactions at the manufacturer-wholesaler and wholesaler-retailer levels as well as on retail sales to consumers, it has some undesirable consequences. The tax can be avoided at one or more stages through vertical integration, causing competition to give way to increased market concentration. The multistage application of the tax causes it to impact more heavily on those commodities where vertical integration is absent, resulting in distortions in relative prices at the retail stage.

These shortcomings help to explain why the turnover tax has never been popular in the United States and why it is disappearing elsewhere. In the United States, only Hawaii extends coverage to the manufacturing and wholesale level, and only Mississippi taxes sales by wholesalers. All other states with a sales tax limit coverage to retail sales.

Turnover taxes once were a major revenue source in Western Europe, but they have been replaced by the value added tax, a multistage tax that applies only to the value added at each stage. Turnover taxes remain

a significant revenue source in the Soviet Union and other socialist countries of Eastern Europe, where the shortcomings just described are less
relevant.

RETAIL SALES TAX

The retail sales tax is the only general transactions tax in widespread use
in the United States. The federal government has left this revenue source
open to the states. The first sales taxes appeared in this country during the
1930s, when financial hardship forced state legislatures to seek a replacement for state property taxes. Twenty-four states adopted the sales tax between 1932 and 1938. An additional twenty-one states followed between
1947 and 1969 in response to growing need for state-financed public
services.

A sales tax is now in effect in forty-five states and in the District of
Columbia. In the aggregate, the sales tax is the largest single source of
state tax revenue, accounting for nearly one-third of the total. Local sales
taxes are increasing in importance in those states where they are permitted
by state law. They now account for about 7 percent of local tax revenue.

Base and Rate Structure

The sales tax is typically a single-stage, flat-rate (ad valorem) tax applied to retail sales within a state.[1] Rates range from 2 to 7 percent, with 3
or 4 percent the most common. Differences in coverage are substantial.
During the 1930s, the base was confined almost entirely to sales of tangibles, but in recent years coverage has been extended to many services.
Most states tax the receipts of hotels and motels, public utilities, and recreational activities. In some states, coverage is extended to such services
as repairs, laundry and dry cleaning, personal care, and equipment rental.

Extension of the base to services has the obvious effect of increasing
revenue with a given tax rate and may, therefore, help to forestall a rate
increase. In many cases, coverage of services facilitates administration and
compliance. If repair services are taxed, for example, it is no longer necessary to separate the cost of parts and labor to calculate the sales tax.
Finally, coverage of services removes discrimination against tangibles and
thereby makes the tax more neutral.

Because the sales tax applies only to retail sales, it is less objectionable than the turnover tax. Since many retail transactions are between
businesses, however, the sales tax is not confined strictly to consumption.
Exemption of products that are to be resold is nearly universal, as is ex-

---

[1]In terms of the relationship between its base and rate, the sales tax is a proportional
tax. As we saw in Chapter 7, however, its incidence is not distributed proportionally over
income groups.

emption of ingredients and component parts of products that are manufactured for sale (the *component-part* rule). Some states extend the exemption to sales of machinery, equipment, fuels and lubricants, and so on used directly in industrial or agricultural productions (the *direct-use* rule). The direct-use rule is clearly more liberal, but even in this case, some interbusiness transactions are taxed, such as purchases of desks and supplies for the front office.

Attempts to exempt all interbusiness transactions from the sales tax would hopelessly complicate administration and increase opportunities for evasion. For example, if furniture sold for business use is exempt, there will be a strong incentive among the self-employed to claim a business exemption on furniture acquired for personal use. Arbitrary rules on what is and what is not taxable are in effect in all states but with considerable variation. As a result, estimates indicate that retail sales to businesses account for as little as 10 percent of sales tax receipts in some states and as much as 30 percent in others.[2]

Exemption of Necessities

The sales tax is almost universally thought to be regressive and to discriminate against large families. This view is supported by results of budget studies showing that, as money income rises, the percentage of income spent on sales-taxed items declines. Since the sales tax is applied at a proportional ad valorem rate, it follows that its incidence pattern is regressive. Budget studies also support the rather obvious expectation that, within a given income category, consumption of taxed items rises with family size.[3]

While no one questions the facts gathered from budget data, some critics do question the usual interpretation. One group, exemplified by Rolph and Break,[4] point out that the standard view rests on the presumption that the sales tax is shifted forward fully to consumers. They contend that, when considered in a general equilibrium setting, the burden of the sales tax may actually fall on factors of production rather than on consumers. In effect, they contend that the burden is distributed in accordance with sources of income rather than with uses. We consider their argument later in this chapter.

[2]Daniel C. Morgan, Jr., *Retail Sales Tax* (Madison: University of Wisconsin Press, 1964), p. 27.

[3]The regressive nature of sales tax incidence patterns in each of the forty-five states with a general sales tax is documented in a monumental study by Donald Phares, *Who Pays State and Local Taxes* (Cambridge, Mass.: Oelschlager, Gunn and Hain, Publishers, Inc., 1980), pp. 119–21, 180. For an analysis of sales tax burden and family size, see Reed R. Hansen, "An Empirical Analysis of the Retail Sales Tax with Policy Recommendations," *National Tax Journal*, 15 (March 1962), 1–13.

[4]Earl R. Rolph and George F. Break, *Public Finance* (New York: The Ronald Press Company, 1961), pp. 287–95.

Another criticism is directed at the income concept used in estimating incidence. The budget studies use a definition of income that approximates the current money income received by participating families. One critic, David G. Davies,[5] points out that, in the lowest-income class, consumption expenditures exceed income. This is possible only through dissaving, presumably out of accumulations of previous income, or through borrowing in anticipation of higher future income. To put it another way, during any given year, some families will have incomes well below or well above the income they regard as average or normal. Families with incomes temporarily below normal will predominate in the lower-income groups, but they are likely to try to maintain their standard of living by spending more on sales-taxed items than they would if their income were permanently at the same low level. In higher-income groups, families with incomes temporarily above normal will predominate, but they will spend less on sales-taxed items than if their incomes were permanently at observed above-average levels. As a result, the budget studies, which usually cover a one-year period, yield results that contain a regressive bias.

Davies has reestimated the incidence pattern of the sales tax by calculating tax burden as a percentage of permanent income (approximated by averaging income over previous years with declining weights for earlier years). He finds that, when income is redefined in this way, the sales tax is approximately proportional.[6] Davies's conclusions rest on the assumption of full forward shifting to consumers.

Economists may quibble about shifting or about what income concept to use in estimating regressivity, but most of those who object to the sales tax remain convinced that its incidence pattern is regressive. Because it falls on some of the basic necessities, it is particularly burdensome to low-income households. In response, a number of states have exempted various purchases from sales taxation. Over half the states exempt prescription drugs, and a number exempt food (except for restaurant and carry-out meals). A few states grant exemptions to some types of clothing. Major exemptions entail a considerable loss in revenue. A food exemption alone usually reduces yield by about 20 percent. Substantial relief accrues to more affluent taxpayers who allegedly do not need it.

Sales Tax Credit

As an alternative to exemption, several states provide a rebate of at least some of the tax paid on purchases of necessities. To be eligible, a taxpayer must file a state income tax return. The rebate is in the form of a sales tax credit against the state income tax. If the sales tax rebate exceeds

---

[5]David G. Davies, "The Significance of Taxation of Services for the Pattern of Distribution of Tax Burden by Income Class," *National Tax Association Proceedings,* 1969, pp. 141–46.

[6]Ibid., p. 144.

a taxpayer's income tax liability, he or she receives a check from the state for the difference. Persons with no tax liability can file and get the full credit.

In its simplest form, each resident qualifies for a rebate of a fixed amount. For example, a per capita credit of $20 in a state with a 4 percent sales tax would be the equivalent of a rebate of the tax paid on the first $500 of taxable items consumed by each resident. Tax relief can be concentrated on low-income families by use of a variable credit that declines and eventually reaches zero as family income rises. This feature holds down revenue loss while providing relief where it is needed most. At present, only the District of Columbia uses a declining credit. If the credit is to be a function of income, it must be administered with care to prevent abuse. For example, parents may be tempted to file separate returns for each child in the family to collect the credit intended only for members of the lowest-income group.

Both types of credit create some inconvenience for taxpayers who would not otherwise file state income tax returns, and there is concern that, because of ignorance or oversight, some of the most needy families will fail to get their rebates. James A. Papke and Timothy G. Shahen used consumer budget data to simulate the effects of a food exemption and credits on the incidence pattern of a typical retail sales tax.[7] Their results indicate that exemption of over-the-counter food sales converts a regressive tax into one that is nearly proportional across most income groups. Assuming equal cost to the state, a per capita credit provides somewhat more tax relief for low-income families and somewhat less for high-income families than does a food exemption. For the bulk of households, the two forms of relief are nearly the same. As expected, an income-related declining credit makes the tax progressive up to the income level at which it disappears. Papke and Shahen also examined the way in which a food exemption and a credit affect horizontal equity—the dispersion in sales tax burdens among households in the same income groups. Because of differences in consumption patterns within income groups, dispersion is substantial. Neither the food exemption nor the per capita credit brings about a significant reduction in dispersion.

USE TAX

States with a sales tax have always been concerned over loss of sales to states with lower rates or no tax at all. They have responded by enacting a use tax. A use tax has the same base and rate as the sales tax, but it applies to purchases of goods outside the state for use within the state. Any sales tax paid in other states can be credited against use tax due.

[7]James A. Papke and Timothy G. Shahen, "Optimal Consumption-Base Taxes: The Equity Effects of Tax Credits," *National Tax Journal*, 25 (September 1972), 479–87.

The use tax is difficult to enforce, and evasion is widespread. For obvious reasons, out-of-state merchants and mail-order firms generally are unwilling to cooperate in collecting the use tax. State efforts to coerce them to do so have been blocked in the courts. States have had more success in collecting use tax on purchases by business firms, since they are subject to audit by revenue officials. Automobiles can be taxed at the time of application for title and registration. Otherwise, the record of compliance and enforcement is not good.

LOCAL SALES TAXES

Local governments levy sales taxes in twenty-six states and the District of Columbia. In most states, the local tax applies to the same base as the state tax. Revenues are collected by the states and are returned to the local jurisdiction in which they accrued. The local tax is thus a supplement to the state tax. This procedure minimizes administrative costs, and it avoids the confusion that results when state and local taxes apply to different commodities.

Local governments can levy retail sales taxes only if permitted by state law. Local autonomy is restricted in a number of ways. Local governments usually have the option of levying the tax, either through statute or referendum. Rates may be fixed or set within a range prescribed by the state. Local rates are usually lower than state rates, typically ranging from 0.5 to 2 percent.

Local option can lead to a "border tax" problem. If a city levies a sales tax but the surrounding county does not, for example, retailers may locate outside the city limits to avoid the tax. Undesirable urban sprawl and loss of revenue is likely to occur. For this reason, a good case can be made for levying local sales taxes at least on a countywide basis. Local sales taxes are slowly becoming a more important source of revenue, but nationally they account for only about 7 percent of local government tax receipts.

VALUE ADDED TAX

The value added tax (VAT) is the most recent form of sales tax to come into widespread use. It is now in effect in all countries of the European Economic Community (the EEC or Common Market). It is also attracting the interest of both scholars and public officials elsewhere.

The VAT is a flat-rate (ad valorem) tax applied to the value added by each firm. The base thus equals total sales revenue minus the cost of inputs purchased from other firms. By netting out purchases from other firms, the multiple taxation and pyramiding of the turnover tax is avoided. As generally practiced, the tax is applied to the total sales of a firm with a credit allowed for the VAT already paid on purchases from other firms. This procedure requires separate listing of VAT on all invoices. To qualify for the credit, each firm must be able to demonstrate that the tax on its purchases was paid by the seller. This simple requirement encourages buyers to enforce payment of the tax by sellers.

The VAT can be of three different types. The *gross product* VAT allows no credit for tax paid on purchases of capital goods. A completely general VAT of this type is therefore equivalent to a tax on gross national product. This version discriminates against investment in plant and equipment and has received little serious consideration. The *income-type* VAT applies to sales less depreciation charges and purchases other than plant and equipment from other firms. Its base is the firm's contribution to national income. A completely general VAT of this form is equivalent to a proportional tax on factor incomes. The *consumption-type* VAT applies to sales less all purchases from other firms, including capital equipment. Therefore, it is equivalent to a sales tax on final consumption. In this respect, it is superior to the retail sales tax, which, as we have seen, cannot be limited to sales to final consumers. The VAT in effect in the EEC is of the consumption type. In a growing economy (where investment exceeds depreciation), the base is narrower with the consumption type than with the income type, necessitating higher rates for equal yields. Governments apparently prefer the consumption type because it is more conducive to economic growth.

The impact of the three types of VAT is illustrated in the example in Table 10–1. The firm in the example has sales of $1,000,000, purchases of noncapital inputs from other firms of $400,000, purchases of capital goods

TABLE 10–1 Determination of the Base for Gross Product, Income-Type, and Consumption-Type Value Added Taxes

	TYPE OF VAT		
	GROSS PRODUCT	INCOME-TYPE	CONSUMPTION-TYPE
Sales	$1,000,000	$1,000,000	$1,000,000
Purchase of noncapital inputs from other firms	−400,000	−400,000	−400,000
Purchases of capital goods			−200,000
Depreciation		−100,000	
Tax base	$ 600,000	$ 500,000	$ 400,000

of $200,000, and depreciation of $100,000. Because of the different treatment of capital costs (depreciation and investment in new capital goods), the base ranges from a high of $600,000 for the gross product VAT to a low of $400,000 for the consumption-type VAT.

A VAT becomes more complicated in an open economy because of the flow of commodities in and out of the country. These flows are taxed in accordance with either the destination principle or the origin principle. Under the destination principle, the accumulated VAT on all exported commodities is refunded when they leave the country. All imports are subject to a compensatory import duty applied at the VAT rate to the value of the goods at point of entry. The EEC uses the destination principle for exports and imports. Thus, if a computer manufactured in the United States is imported into Germany, it will be subject to a German import duty levied on the delivery value of the computer. The purpose of the import duty is to remove discrimination against computers produced in Germany or other EEC countries, where domestically produced goods are subject to the VAT.

When a Mercedes-Benz manufactured in Germany is exported to the United States, the manufacturer receives a refund of the VAT paid on the export value of the car. From the German point of view, the refund is looked upon as a means of making the German car competitive with U.S. cars that are not subject to a VAT. Some Americans complain that the tax refund on European exports puts U.S. producers at a competitive disadvantage, because international agreements prohibit refunds of corporation income taxes paid by U.S. exporters. This complaint is suspect on two counts. First, it is valid only if it can be demonstrated that the corporation income tax is shifted forward in the form of higher prices of U.S. exports. As we saw in Chapter 9, the evidence in support of forward shifting is inconclusive. Second, it ignores the fact that EEC countries generally levy corporation income taxes at rates roughly comparable to U.S. rates.

Under the origin principle, exports are subject to the VAT with no refund, while imports are exempt. Since this procedure discriminates against domestic producers, it is not likely to be adopted unilaterally by any country. It could be adopted by trading partners on a reciprocal basis without discriminating against domestic producers, but only if all tax at the same rate.

Future of VAT

The comprehensive VAT was introduced in France in 1954. It spread rapidly to other countries of Western Europe after its adoption by Germany in 1968.[8] In the United States, the VAT is looked upon as a potential

---

[8]For an evaluation of experience with the value added tax in six European countries, see Henry J. Aaron, ed., *The Value-Added Tax: Lessons from Europe* (Washington, D.C.: The Brookings Institution, 1981).

source of federal revenue. It has been mentioned as a replacement for the corporation income tax, particularly since the weakening of the latter by the 1981 Economic Recovery Tax Act. A consumption-type VAT is appealing because it encourages investment by allowing deduction of capital expenditures. The refund provision on exports makes it attractive to those concerned about our competitive position in world markets. The VAT has also been mentioned as a supplementary revenue source for the ailing social security system.

Those who oppose it usually contend that it would be a form of national sales tax and, therefore, its incidence pattern would be regressive. This view is based on the assumption of full forward shifting to consumers. Many, including some of its supporters, fear that a VAT would be inflationary. This was not a problem in Europe, because the VAT replaced a turnover and other related taxes that had a similar effect on the general price level. These reservations are examined later in this chapter.

In principle, the VAT could be applied to all sectors of the economy, but in practice it is applied on a selected basis. Exemption of the public sector and nonprofit institutions is a virtual certainty. Exemption of value added in other sectors, such as agriculture, housing, the medical profession, and other politically or socially favored categories is likely. Exemptions complicate administration of the tax and may have undesirable allocational effects as well.

Even if political resistance blocks adoption of a VAT by the federal government, it might catch on at the state level. A tax similar to the income-type VAT was in effect in Michigan from 1953 to 1963. It was repealed when Michigan introduced personal and corporation income taxes. In 1976 Michigan adopted a new consumption-type VAT as a replacement for state taxes on corporate income and net worth and the property tax on business inventories.[9] In the late 1960s an income-type VAT almost passed in West Virginia. Determination of the tax base for multistate firms can be a problem, just as under a state corporation income tax, but it can be solved in a reasonable manner through separate accounts for in-state operations or by use of an allocation formula.

EXPENDITURE TAX

All the sales taxes discussed thus far are taxes on transactions. As such, they cannot be adjusted to meet the different conditions of particular taxpayers (except indirectly, as with sales tax credits). The expenditure tax is

---

[9]The original Michigan tax, called the Business Activities Tax, is described and evaluated in Robert D. Ebel, *The Michigan Business Activities Tax*, MSU Business Studies (East Lansing: Michigan State University, 1972). Its successor, called the Single Business Tax, is described in Harvey E. Brazer, "Michigan's Single Business Tax—Theory and Background," *National Tax Association Proceedings*, 1976, pp. 62–69.

offered as a form of tax on consumption that can be levied on individuals, as an income tax. Because the tax base applies to the individual taxpayer, it is possible to allow an exemption for expenditures on basic necessities and for such things as uninsured medical costs or contributions.

In principle, the accretion concept of income, described in Chapter 8, serves as a starting point for determining the expenditure tax base. Under accretion, income, Y, equals consumption, C, plus the change in net worth, ΔNW. The tax base for the expenditure tax is total expenditures during the time period in question, or

$$C = Y - \Delta NW$$

The expenditure tax differs from the income tax by excluding savings from taxation and by taxing dissavings. It is amenable to a graduated rate structure. Indeed, in contrast to the income tax, the top rate could exceed 100 percent without running into the problem of confiscatory taxation. There is no reason, for example, why people who spend more than $1 million a year on personal consumption could not be taxed $2 for every additional $1 they spend on themselves.

Because an expenditure tax exempts savings and taxes dissavings, it appeals to those who favor a reallocation of resources from consumption into saving and investment. It also appeals to those who accept the argument discussed in Chapter 6 that taxes should be based on what one consumes out of society's common pool of resources, not on what one produces.

In practice, it is generally agreed that an expenditure tax would be more difficult to administer than would an income tax. In addition to many of the problems encountered with an income tax, it would be necessary to determine net saving or borrowing of each taxpayer. This would require more extensive record keeping by taxpayers and more monitoring by tax collectors.[10]

EXCISE TAXES

Excise taxes are levied on selected commodities or commodity groups, usually at the manufacturer or wholesale level. Some excises are corrective in nature, designed to alter consumer behavior or correct imperfections. Other excises, such as the gasoline tax earmarked for roads and highways, are a form of user charge. Corrective taxes and user charges are

[10]The standard reference on the expenditure tax is Nicholas Kaldor, *An Expenditure Tax* (London: George Allen & Unwin Ltd., 1955). The contention that an expenditure tax is more difficult to administer than an income tax is challenged in P. L. Kelley, "Is an Expenditure Tax Feasible?" *National Tax Journal,* 23 (September 1970), 237–54.

defended on equity or efficiency grounds. Governments may attempt to gain revenue by placing excises on a limited number of items, especially if the demand for them is price inelastic. Such narrowly based taxes discriminate against consumers who have a preference for taxed items. For this reason, public finance economists are generally critical of excises that do not serve some other legitimate social or economic purpose.[11]

In the United States excise taxes are most important at the state level, where they account for more than 20 percent of total tax revenue. They account for about 5 percent of federal tax revenue and about 3 percent of tax revenue of local governments. The most significant in terms of revenue are taxes on alcoholic beverages, tobacco products, and motor fuel and the windfall profit tax on domestic oil production.

Sumptuary Taxes

The most pervasive of corrective excise taxes are those designed to discourage consumption of goods thought to be in some way detrimental to users or to society. These excises are called *sumptuary taxes*. The federal government and all states tax cigarettes and alcoholic beverages. Gambling is taxed where it is legal. Traditionally, sumptuary taxes have been applied to goods or activities thought to be morally questionable, thus earning the label "sin taxes." Often, they represent an alternative to outright prohibition. Given the price-inelastic demand for these goods or activities, sumptuary taxes are a stable source of federal and state revenue.

Taxes on beer, liquor, and tobacco products are generally levied on a per unit basis. As a result, the tax is a larger percentage of the selling price of cheap brands. The price differential narrows between cheap and expensive brands. Gambling taxes are generally a percentage of the "take," but they also include per unit levies on certain gaming devices such as slot machines. A number of states supplement sumptuary tax revenues by operating state monopoly liquor stores, and a growing number have sought profits from gambling through state lotteries.

If the burden of sumptuary taxes is borne largely by consumers, which is a reasonable assumption, the incidence pattern is likely to be highly regressive. This is especially true of taxes on tobacco products and beer, which account for a declining percentage of consumer expenditures

---

[11]In the literature on optimal taxation, a case is made for applying different tax rates to different commodities so as to minimize welfare loss. To take the extreme case, if the supply of a good is perfectly inelastic, there will be no change in the supply of the good if it is taxed. Thus, there will be no tax-induced misallocation, although there will be a transfer of welfare from producers to government. Where supply is not perfectly inelastic, the basic rule is that the tax-induced percentage deviation of price from marginal cost must be inversely proportional to the price elasticity of demand for each commodity. For a relatively accessible exposition, see William J. Baumol and David F. Bradford, "Optimal Departures from Marginal Cost Pricing," *American Economic Review*, 60 (June 1970), 265–83.

as incomes rise. Hence, a conflict exists between the distributional and other social goals of society.[12]

Pollution Taxes

We saw in Chapter 2 that the production or consumption of some goods may supply a private good jointly with one or more public "bads." Environmental pollutants are a prime example of a public "bad." Recall from that discussion that consumption of a public bad, like a public good, is nonrival. The negative benefits of air pollution are an example; more smog for you means more smog for your neighbor. Conceptually, a public good differs from a public bad only in that the benefits for the former are positive, whereas the benefits of the latter are negative.

The example of aircraft noise pollution analyzed in Chapter 2 and illustrated in Figure 2–7 is based on the assumption that the amount of pollution (negative benefit) is proportional to the quantity of output (number of flights). If the cost of pollution is a fixed proportion of output, negative benefits can be reduced to the optimal level by taxing output of the good, as in the aircraft example.[13] In most cases of pollution, however, the amount of pollution is not related so rigidly to output. By using different production techniques or installing abatement devices, the amount of pollution that occurs with each level of output can be varied, often substantially. Because we want to control the output of pollution, not the output of the good, it would be better to tax the output of the pollutant directly, if possible. This will give producers an incentive to deal directly with the problem.

In practice, the cost (or negative demand) from pollution is as difficult to estimate as the positive demand for a public good. In addition, if the output of pollution is to be taxed, its source must be identified and measured. Although the task may be difficult and sometimes impossible, pollution taxes are not unprecedented. For years, a tax or effluent charge has been imposed on firms discharging industrial wastes into the Ruhr

[12]Sumptuary taxes are sometimes defended on the grounds that people can avoid paying them by not consuming the taxed commodity. Henry C. Simons unleashed a colorful blast at this line of thinking. He wrote, "it seems a little absurd to go around arguing that poor people ought to do without tobacco, especially if it is taxed, in the face of the fact that they do not do anything of the kind." Simons goes on to claim that "tobacco taxes are the most effective means available for draining government revenue out from the very bottom of the income scale." See Henry C. Simons, *Personal Income Taxation* (Chicago: University of Chicago Press, 1938), p. 40n.

[13]Use of taxation to control activities that create pollution is not a new idea. The famous English economist, A. C. Pigou, suggested such taxes more than fifty years ago, but only in the last couple of decades have economists taken the suggestion seriously. For a succinct summary and criticism of Pigou and others, see Ralph Turvey, "On Divergences Between Social Cost and Private Cost," *Economica* 30 (August 1963), 309–13.

River in West Germany with proceeds being used to improve water quality.[14] In the United States, however, government has generally chosen to deal with the pollution problem by regulation rather than taxation, often with little regard for comparative costs and benefits.

If taxation of effluents is feasible, a tax is likely to be a more efficient way of achieving a given level of environmental quality than is regulation. Suppose, for example, that the government wishes to reduce the emission of an industrial pollutant by 50 percent. Regulators could achieve this result by ordering each firm to cut pollution by half. It is highly unlikely that it would be equally costly at the margin for each firm to achieve a 50 percent reduction in emissions. It would be more efficient to achieve the same result by cutting pollution where it is least costly to do so. When a per unit tax is levied on emission, firms have an incentive to control pollution as long as the cost of control is less than the tax. In this way, the cheapest control methods will be applied first. In equilibrium, each firm will spend an amount on pollution control equal at the margin to the tax. In this way, the cost of attaining a given level of environmental quality is minimized.

User Charges

In some cases, it is possible to allocate the cost of public services to those who benefit through excise taxes or direct user fees. This technique is used extensively to finance roads and highways. The federal highway system is heavily subsidized by transfers to state and local governments out of the federal highway trust fund. Revenues for the fund come from federal excise taxes on motor fuel and lubricants, vehicle accessories, and tires. All revenues from these taxes are earmarked for the trust fund. A portion of the fund is allocated to urban mass transit. Such a reallocation appears to depart from the benefit principle of taxation, but if mass transit reduces traffic congestion and parking problems, it could benefit those who continue to use roads and highways.

All fifty states levy taxes on motor fuel. Most of the revenue is earmarked for uses that are beneficial to motorists. Some states have allocated small amounts to other uses. License fees also go into road-user funds, and they are well suited to discriminating among vehicles on the basis of weight. In this way, large trucks and buses can be charged fees more in line with the higher construction and repair costs resulting from their use of highways. Some states build an element of progressivity into license fee structures by basing fees in part on the estimated market value of the vehicle.

[14]For a description of water management in the Ruhr, see Allen V. Kneese, *The Economics of Regional Water Quality Management* (Baltimore: Johns Hopkins University Press, 1964), pp. 162–87.

Federal and state road-user funds have suffered from the practice of levying the motor fuel tax on a per gallon rather than on an ad valorem basis. The tax is based on quantity sold rather than on value of sale. As a result, yields have failed to keep up with price inflation and the rapid rise in highway construction costs. The revenues have also been suppressed by periodic gasoline shortages and reduced gasoline sales induced by price increases. This experience illustrates the disadvantage of a per unit excise tax in an inflationary environment.

Other types of user taxes include the federal excise on air travel, which is earmarked for airport and airway development, and a wide variety of fees such as tolls on limited-access highways, entrance fees to public parks, and hunting and fishing licenses. Again, the receipts are used to finance services for those who pay. Note that fees charged for licenses are *not* taxes on sales of specific commodities. The rationale supporting their use is derived from the benefit principle. There are many opportunities for greater reliance on user fees and taxes. Examples include use of inland water facilities, public recreational activities, and selected municipal services such as trash removal. There are several factors preventing more extended adoption of user charges. One is the political opposition of those who would have to pay. Another is the deduction provisions of the federal individual income tax, which allow deduction of general state and local taxes but not user fees.

Finally, keep in mind that the case for user taxes or fees is strengthened if most or all of the burden is shifted onto those who consume the service. Only in this case will those who benefit be absorbing the full cost.

Severance Taxes

Severance taxes are a form of excise tax applied to the output of mineral resources, forest products, oil and natural gas, and coal. They are sometimes used as an alternative to property taxes on forest and mineral properties. Severance taxes have been in effect for years in states where oil, mineral, and timber production are important. The geographical immobility and inelastic supply of these resources make them an attractive revenue source for state governments. They are defended on the grounds that they compensate the states for the loss in wealth and other social costs that result from the exploitation of natural resource. In recent years, the explosion in energy prices has generated sizable increases in revenue for a few states with large petroleum and coal deposits. Nationally, severance taxes account for less than 3 percent of state tax collections, but in five states— Alaska, Louisiana, Oklahoma, Texas, and Wyoming—they account for from 18 to 25 percent. Consuming states have complained, and in some cases their congressional representatives have introduced legislation that would limit the ability of producing states to tax gas, oil, and coal production.[15]

The federal windfall profit tax on crude oil is also a form of severance tax. Misnamed a profit tax, it is really an excise tax on domestic oil production. It was based on the presumption that domestic oil prices were set at the level determined by the international oil cartel (OPEC). The windfall profit tax applies to the difference between the market price of crude oil and the base price that existed before price deregulation in 1979. (To keep pace with inflation, the base price is adjusted upward quarterly by a price index.) Rates range from 70 percent of the price differential on "old oil"— oil discovered before imposition of controls—down to 30 percent on newly discovered oil. Receipts are earmarked for use in generating new energy sources and for encouraging energy conservation. The windfall profit tax is supposed to be temporary, with a phase-out scheduled for sometime during the period 1988 to 1993.

Other Excises

Most excise taxes in effect in the United States fall into the sumptuary or user category, but there are a few exceptions. Regulatory excises may be used to inhibit sales of certain items and to promote other economic goals. The Wisconsin tax on oleomargarine is a good example. It was designed to narrow the spread, as it were, between the prices of butter and margarine to encourage the sale of butter in America's Dairyland. States face severe restrictions in imposing taxes that interfere with interstate commerce, but the federal government levies a variety of tariffs or customs duties on imports. The purpose of the latter is to protect favored domestic industries from foreign competition; revenue considerations are only incidental.

Proposals for taxes on luxuries are advanced as a way of taxing the rich, but they are effective only if they are levied on the sale of items bought almost exclusively by the rich. Such items are difficult to find. Progression will not be attained by taxing items "one can do without," because many such items are bought by poor people. Moreover, part of the burden of a tax on luxuries may be shifted back on suppliers who may not have high incomes.

Finally, excise taxes are sometimes levied without any social goal in mind. As mentioned, they cannot be justified in terms of equity or allocational efficiency. Several taxes of this nature once levied by the federal government were eliminated. The excise on telephone and telegraph serv-

---

[15]For a summary of the issues, see James A. Papke, "Economic Perspectives on the State Taxation of Nonrenewable Energy Sources," *National Tax Association–Tax Institute of America Proceedings,* 1980, pp. 38–41.

ice survives. It was repealed for a brief period, then reenacted as a politically feasible way of narrowing the deficit created by the Vietnam buildup.

THE SHIFTING
CONTROVERSY

We have seen that most of the discussion of policy issues is predicated on the assumption that the burden of excise and sales taxes falls on consumers. In the case of selective excise taxes, economic analysis lends support to this view. In a competitive market, the imposition of the tax will bring about a gradual withdrawal of firms and resources from the industry, reducing supply and increasing price. If long-run industry supply is perfectly elastic, the price rise will equal the tax per unit of commodity. Full foward shifting of the money burden will occur. If the market is imperfectly competitive, sellers will respond to the tax by raising prices, thus reducing quantity sold and leading to a reduction in resources used by the industry. The amount of forward shifting will be affected by the structure of the market and the response of the firms. Both the competitive and noncompetitive cases were discussed in greater detail in Chapter 7.

An excise tax, therefore, will bring about a shift of resources from the production of taxed to the production of untaxed items, raising the price of the former relative to the latter. In theory, only specialized factors will experience a significant loss in income. Other factors will shift easily into new industries. If the taxed industry is small relative to the whole economy, effects on the rest of the system can be neglected. This line of reasoning is sometimes applied to more general taxes. As a number of items taxed is increased, however, there are fewer untaxed industries where released factors can go. Furthermore, if the tax accounts for a large share of government revenue, it is no longer legitimate to ignore the consequences of corresponding budgetary changes. A general equilibrium approach must replace that of partial equilibrium.

A General Model of Sales Tax
Incidence

Critics of the conventional view of sales tax incidence usually derive their arguments from a model of a completely general sales tax. For this reason, it is useful to outline and examine such a model. Our model incorporates the following assumptions:

1. The tax is completely general; that is, it applies to the sale of all final output, including sales to the government, at a proportional rate. In practice, such a tax would be approximated most closely by a completely general tax on value added.

2. The government spends the revenue in such a way as to keep aggregate demand for real output unchanged. Recall that this corresponds to Musgrave's model of balanced-budget incidence.
3. All factor and product markets are competitive.

The first question is, what happens to the general price level? Will it rise by the amount of the tax, remain at the pretax level, or settle somewhere in between? The answer depends on the response of monetary authorities. If they allow the money supply to expand enough, the price of final output will rise by the amount of the tax, with factor prices remaining at the initial level. If this happens, the real income of factor owners will fall, because they will be able to buy less with a given money income.[16] Suppose that the money supply is held at the pretax level so that prices are constrained from rising. Then businesses will experience temporary losses, reduce their demand for factor inputs, and drive down the prices in factor markets. A new equilibrium will be established once the price of factors falls by the same percentage as the tax. Again, factor owners experience a loss in real income.

In both examples, the real income of factor owners fell, indicating that the burden of the tax is shifted backward onto suppliers of factors of production. The important thing is what happens to *relative* prices of factors and output. What happens to the absolute price level is irrelevant. Note also that the incidence of a completely general sales tax in a competitive economy is equivalent to a proportional tax on factor incomes.

Before concluding that the retail sales tax as levied in the United States is really a tax on factor incomes, one should consider some qualifications to the argument outlined earlier. First, the analysis involves comparison of two states of equilibrium (which is called *comparative statics*). It thus fails to consider transitional matters, including changes in the purchasing power of cash balances. Incomes such as pensions may not respond to changes in relative factor incomes, which would change the relationship between income sources. If there are downward rigidities in money wage rates, attempts to maintain stable prices for final output will generate unemployment rather than lower factor prices. In either case, the real income of labor falls, but the incidence pattern among workers may be quite different.

We discuss only changes in the general level of output and factor prices, but in a more realistic setting, changes in relative prices within the two market categories also will occur. Even if government expenditures leave aggregate demand unchanged, the *pattern* of demand will be altered.

---

[16]The change in money supply need not be proportional to the change in price level, because the budgetary change may alter the velocity of circulation of money. For a more detailed discussion, see Amotz Morag, *On Taxes and Inflation* (New York: Random House, Inc., 1965), pp. 24–43.

The fall in real factor income will alter consumption patterns. Both developments will induce price changes and a reallocation of output. In spite of these qualifications, however, the analysis of the incidence of a general sales tax leads us to conclude that those who contend that any sales tax is fully and immediately shifted to consumers are guilty of oversimplification.

Shifting of Partial Sales Taxes

The base of all actual sales taxes is partial. Some consumption activities, such as consumption of leisure, cannot reasonably be included in the tax base. All taxes are limited to the jurisdication of the government that levies them and, therefore, can be avoided by migration if by no other means.

In the United States, the retail sales and use taxes are now fairly close to being universal, although there are substantial interstate differences in rates and coverage. The tax is no doubt pervasive enough to have affected factor earnings as well as retail prices. In other words, distribution of the sales tax burden among households is partly a function of factor earnings and partly a function of consumption outlays.

From the point of view of a particular state, however, the conventional view of sales tax incidence may still have much validity. Officials in one state are obviously unable to influence the effect of sales taxes levied by other states on relative product and factor prices in their own state. This is unavoidable in view of the flow of economic goods and services across state borders. For most commodities sold at retail, each individual state is only a small part of a national market. For these items, any change in sales in a given state will have only a small effect on total sales and, therefore, is likely to change prices net of sales tax very little. In other words, the supply of most commodities to an individual state is highly, and perhaps perfectly, elastic.

Recall that in partial equilibrium analysis, perfectly elastic supply resulted in full forward shifting of the money burden of the tax. Because the individual state is a small part of a larger market, there is an argument for using partial equilibrium analysis to determine the incidence of the sales tax of a *single* state on its *own* residents.[17] The highly elastic supply of sales-taxed items contributes to full forward shifting of the sales tax burden to retail customers. It follows that the results of surveys of consumer spending habits may give us reasonably satisfactory estimates of the incidence of sales taxes on a state-by-state basis, even though they are less reliable in considering incidence in a national setting.

If this line of reasoning is valid, then legislators and the governor of a particular state are justified in viewing the incidence of a sales tax on

[17]Carl S. Shoup, *Public Finance* (Chicago: Aldine Publishing Company, 1969), p. 213.

residents as regressive. In this limited way, the conventional attitude toward the sales tax is vindicated.

SALES AND EXCISE TAXES:
AN EVALUATION

The retail sales tax is likely to continue as a major revenue source for state governments. It is the one major source of tax revenue that has not been tapped by the federal government. Most states now tax both sales and income, making it possible for them to avoid high rates on either. Sales tax revenue is responsive to inflation, but it is less responsive to economic growth than is revenue from the income tax. States that rely mainly on the sales tax have been forced to raise rates periodically.

The sales tax normally is paid in small amounts at a time. Consequently, taxpayers are not likely to have a very precise idea of how much per year they pay. This feature makes the tax *relatively* painless for most taxpayers and may explain its appeal to legislators, but such expediency does not contribute to informed collective decision making.

In contrast to an income tax, a broadly based sales tax applied to all consumption goods does not distort the trade-off between present and future consumption, because it does not tax interest. The retail sales tax is not a pure consumption tax, however. Some consumption expenditures, mostly services, are not taxed. Therefore, the sales tax does encourage consumers to reallocate expenditures in favor of untaxed goods and services. To the extent that capital equipment is subject to the tax, it also influences investment decisions.

The most common criticism of the sales tax focuses on its regressivity. Defenders counter with the argument that the sales tax is not as regressive as budget studies indicate. They cite the regressive bias inherent in annual budget surveys and question the assumption of full forward shifting. In addition, evidence indicates that food exemptions and sales tax credits are effective means of reducing sales tax regressivity.

Most excise taxes levied in the United States are intended to affect the allocation of resources as well as to raise revenue. Sumptuary taxes raise the price of alcoholic beverages, tobacco products, and legalized gambling and supposedly discourage their consumption. Because of inelastic demand, however, sumptuary taxes are probably more effective at raising revenue than at improving the moral climate. They are often criticized on equity grounds because they tend to be highly regressive.

Economists generally prefer taxation to regulation as a means of controlling negative externalities. Taxes on emission of pollutants encourage the efficient use of abatement techniques, but governments in this country have been reluctant to adopt them. Perhaps this reluctance can be attributed to the difficulty of identifying and measuring sources of pollution. It might also reflect a preference of the affected firms for regulation over taxes.[18] To some extent, sumptuary taxes serve to correct for negative externalities. This effect can be reinforced by, for example, earmarking some of the liquor tax revenue for treatment programs for alcoholics. In practice, however, sumptuary taxes are probably explained more by considerations of morality than by concern over externalities.

User charges are best thought of in the context of benefit taxation. Where feasible, they represent an opportunity to extend market principles to the public sector. Opportunities exist for greater reliance on user taxes or fees, and local governments hard pressed by newly imposed expenditure limitations are finding them attractive.

---

[18]James M. Buchanan and Gordon Tullock discuss the circumstances in which firms will find regulation a more profitable alternative than taxation. When this occurs, firms will be expected to use their political influence to promote regulation. See "Polluters' Profits and Political Response: Direct Controls Versus Taxes," *American Economic Review*, 65 (March 1975), 139–47.

11

The Property Tax

The property tax in America dates back to the colonial period. As recently as 1941, it was the largest single source of government revenue. It remains the major source of tax revenue for local governments. Prior to the depression of the 1930s, state governments relied heavily on property taxes, but the depression left many property owners unable to meet their payments. Legislatures responded by shifting to other forms of taxation. The property tax has never been a significant source of federal revenue. It remains as the one major tax that is administered locally and is the chief source of what financial independence local governments have left.

Financial pressures on local governments, especially for financing schools, contributed to the increase in both the absolute and relative importance of the property tax after World War II. This trend may have been checked by a series of court cases restricting the use of the local property tax for financing schools[1] and, more recently, by constitutional and statutory limits on local taxation or spending.

By the early 1980s annual property tax revenues had passed the $65 billion mark. The property tax accounts for about three-fourths of all local tax collections and about 12 percent of all U.S. tax collections.

[1]The landmark case was *Serrano* v. *Priest* (1971). The California Supreme Court held that the local property tax is unconstitutional as a source of school finance, because it results in unequal educational opportunities for pupils in poor and rich districts. Similar decisions have been rendered in cases in other states, but the U.S. Supreme Court ruled in *San Antonio Independent School District* v. *Rodriguez* (1973) that use of the property tax to finance schools is not in violation of the U.S. Constitution.

IMPACT OF THE PROPERTY TAX

For tax purposes, property is usually classified into the following categories:

1. Real estate (land, buildings, immobile improvements)
2. Tangible personal property
   a. Income-producing assets (business equipment, machinery and inventories, farm machinery, crops, and livestock)
   b. Household personal property (household goods and automobiles)
3. Intangibles (stocks, debt instruments, money)
4. Public utility and railroad property

Since the property tax is administered locally under laws of the individual states, it is not surprising that great variation is found in both coverage and rates. In the aggregate, about four-fifths of the revenue is obtained from taxes on real estate, and most of the remainder is from the tax on personal property. The importance of the realty component is a result of a gradual but persistent narrowing of the property tax base during this century. During the eighteenth and nineteenth centuries, the trend was in the opposite direction. The base was extended from land to buildings and a wide variety of tangibles and intangibles. In some states, the tax is still applied to a variety of assets in all categories. The current tendency, however, is to limit the base to real estate, utilities, and business equipment and inventories.

Another way in which to view the impact of the property tax is to examine the distribution of collections among major sectors of the economy. Although data on sources of revenue are sketchy, it appears that about half the total is paid by nonfarm households, 40 percent by nonfarm business, and 8 percent by the agricultural sector.[2]

ADMINISTRATION OF THE PROPERTY TAX

The assessment process is the initial stage in administering the property tax. Assessment involves three separate steps: (1) preparation of the tax roll, (2) valuation, and (3) review.

[2]Dick Netzer, *Economics of the Property Tax* (Washington, D.C.: The Brookings Institution, 1966), pp. 21–22. Although dated, this is the most recent treatise on the property tax in the United States. According to the Census of Governments, nonfarm residential property accounts for about 60 percent of the assessed value of real estate. Commercial and industrial property accounts for about 25 percent and farms and acreages for 12 percent. See U.S. Bureau of the Census, *1977 Census of Governments*, "Taxable Property Values and Assessment/Sales Ratios," Vol. 2 (November 1978), p. 6.

Preparing the Tax Roll

Each parcel of taxable property must be discovered and placed on the tax roll by the assessor. This step is relatively easy for real estate. Assessors have access to records of property ownership and plattings. In some cases they may also use maps and aerial photographs to discover land and buildings. Failure to include taxable real property on the tax rolls is rare but not unknown.

Personal property is more difficult to discover. Some owners deliberately hide it, and often assessors do not try very hard to find it, especially in the case of household goods. Much household personal property is of low value, making the potential revenue too small to justify the cost of assessment in terms of both the assessor's time and the householder's inconvenience. As a consequence, personal property of households is usually excluded from the tax base either by legislation or informally by deliberate policy of assessors. Automobiles are an exception. They are easily traced through registration records.

Business personal property, which includes machinery, furniture, equipment, and inventories, is less likely to escape the tax rolls. Inventories present a special assessment problem. In many states they are valued as of a particular date, such as January 1. This gives businesses an incentive to cut inventories to a minimum on the assessment date, a procedure that conflicts with optimal inventory management. Assessment on a particular date also leads to inequitable treatment of firms with a seasonal inventory pattern. These difficulties can be avoided by averaging inventories over the year, but this complicates record keeping and enforcement.

Intangibles are the most difficult class of property to discover. Assessors often rely on self-reporting, but evasion is widespread, resulting in discrimination against the honest few who report fully. As one would expect, a tax that penalizes honesty breeds additional evasion. Some states have attempted to encourage reporting of intangibles by taxing them at a lower rate. This too has failed. Administration is complicated further by numerous and sometimes confusing exclusions from the base. Many states have simply ceased to tax intangibles either by legally exempting all intangibles or by informal adoption of lax enforcement procedures.

If assessors were to be given access to data on income from financial assets collected by the Internal Revenue Service, they could uncover many intangibles. There is little evidence that this opportunity is being exploited. As a consequence, local reliance on revenues from taxation of intangibles appears to be on the way out.

Valuation

The second step in the assessment process is valuation. An assessed value must be assigned to each piece of taxable property. Assessors use different methods to value various types of property. For real estate, the standard procedures of appraisers are followed. Outside experts are sometimes employed for this purpose. Data on the ratio of assessed value to sale value may be used to check on accuracy. For homogeneous classes of property, such as most one-family dwellings and farmland, a large sample of assessment-sales ratios can usually be collected each year. The absence of dispersion in these values is indicative of uniformity of assessment procedures.

Sales data are less likely to be useful in checking the accuracy of valuations of commercial and industrial realty. Transfers of such property are infrequent in most communities. Furthermore, the specialized nature of business property makes accurate assessment more difficult. A few states have replaced local assessment with state assessment of industrial property. The limited evidence available indicates that valuations by state assessors are higher in these states than in states with local assessment.[3]

Valuation of tangible personal property presents an even greater problem to the assessor because of the heterogeneity of this class. Market values provide a guideline for evaluating inventories. For other producer and consumer durables, the assessor must have a list of estimated original or replacement costs and accompanying depreciation schedules. At best, these lists are incomplete, and their use requires the exercise of expert judgment. The magnitude of the task is such that valuation, especially by local assessors, is certain to be imperfect and somewhat arbitrary.

Valuation of intangibles, if they can be uncovered, is usually straightforward. Most stocks and debt instruments are either marketable or redeemable in fixed dollar amounts. Time and demand deposits and currency are, of course, defined in terms of dollars.

Most public utility and railroad property is valued by state assessors, although the division between state and locally assessed utility assets varies among states. State assessment of railroad and utility property is undoubtedly more efficient than is local assessment, since states can afford to employ specialists for this purpose. In the end, however, it is still necessary to devise a formula for allocating the property of a utility among the taxing jurisdictions in which it operates. To cite an example of the difficulties faced, suppose that an electrical generating plant located in one taxing district supplies power to the surrounding ten districts. Should the value of the plant be assigned entirely to the district in which it is located, or should it be allocated among the ten districts to which it supplies power? If you agree that the value should be allocated among all ten districts, should it be on the basis of power consumed, line mileage, population, or some other basis? Even this example is simplified. In practice, we encounter

[3]Netzer, *Economics of the Property Tax*, p. 95.

overlapping taxing districts (cities, counties, school districts, etc.), and modern power grids often extend over several states. Hence, it is not surprising that laws dealing with these matters lack uniformity and consistency.

Assessment Review

The third step in the assessment process is the opportunity for review. Property owners have the right to request a review of the assessor's valuation, either by a board appointed for the purpose or by a local governing body such as a county board of supervisors, and ultimately by the courts. Overvaluation is difficult to prove, however, because of the almost universal practice of assessing below market value. In about two-thirds of the states, the law calls for assessment at full market value; yet the evidence shows that, on average, real estate in all such states is assessed at well below this figure.[4] In the remaining states, where fractional valuations are specified, valuation below the statutory ratio is just as common. The practice of systematic undervaluation makes it difficult for the property owners to demonstrate that their property is overvalued even though—and this is the important point—it is overvalued *relative* to the property of other taxpayers in the same community.

In many states the valuations of individual local assessors are subject to review and equalization by a state agency. State equalization proceedings seldom deal with individual holdings. Their purpose is to equalize the ratios of assessed-to-market value of property in different assessors' jurisdictions or to equate the ratios for different classes of property, such as urban and rural real estate, within each county.

The Tax Levy

Once the listing, valuation, review, and equalization proceedings are complete, the valuations of the individual items on the tax rolls can be summed to determine the tax base within the jurisdiction of each local taxing body. After the budgeting authority within each taxing body decides on the amount of revenue to be raised by the property tax (an amount equal to total outlays less revenue from other sources), the property tax levy can be determined. The levy is usually stated in terms of mills and is computed as follows:

$$\frac{\text{Required revenue}}{\text{Total assessed value}} \times 1,000 = \text{millage rate}$$

[4]Census of Government figures show statewide averages of assessed value of real estate ranging from 3.3 percent of market value in South Carolina to 72 percent in Kentucky. See U.S. Bureau of the Census, "Taxable Property Values and Assessment/Sales Ratios," pp. 60–65.

Thus, if $10 million in revenue is to be raised from a tax base of $100 million of assessed value, the millage rate is 100.[5]

A typical parcel of taxable property will be subject to taxation by several different taxing bodies, for example, city, county, school, district, and often special units such as park boards and sanitation districts. In most cases, a single official, often the county treasurer, serves as the collection agent for all units. Interest and sometimes a penalty charge are imposed for delinquent payment. Prolonged delinquency may result in recovery of taxes due via a tax sale.

GEOGRAPHIC DIFFERENCES

A property tax in some form is in effect throughout the United States. With nearly 80,000 local governmental units operating under the laws of fifty states and the District of Columbia, great variation exists in coverage, administration, and effective rates. The role of the property tax in the overall state-local tax structure varies greatly among states. It accounts for over 60 percent of state-local tax revenue in some states and less than 25 percent in others. Property taxes are most important in the Northeast and Midwest, least important in the South. They are of variable importance in the West. Prior to passage of Proposition 13, a tax-limitation amendment, property taxes in California were among the highest in the nation. Alaska, Oregon, Montana, and Wyoming rely heavily on property taxes; Hawaii and New Mexico are at the other extreme. As the share of the property tax declines, more revenue from state sources must be transferred to local governments.

The types of property included legally in the tax base are usually prescribed by state law. A few states allow limited local option. Real estate is the major component of the tax base in all states, but even in this category significant holdings are granted exemption. Total exemption is typically allowed for real estate owned by federal, state, and local governments. The same is true for realty owned by nonprofit educational, charitable, and religious institutions, provided that it is used in their nonprofit activities. In some cases, income-earning property owned by nonprofit institutions, such as commercial property owned by churches and rented to commercial enterprises, is also exempt. Finally, the type of nonprofit organizations eligible for exemption varies among states. Groups such as veterans and fraternal organizations, labor unions, farm organizations, and chambers of commerce are often, but not always, eligible for exemption. A number of

---

[5]Since there are 10 mills in 1 cent, a millage rate of 100 means a tax of 100 mills or 10 cents per dollar of assessed value. Alternatively, the tax rate may be given as a percentage of assessed value (10 percent in this example) or in terms of dollars of tax per $1,000 of assessed value ($100 per thousand in this example).

states grant partial exemptions, most frequently for veterans and homesteads. Exemptions narrow the tax base and raise the rates on eligible property. In effect, owners of taxable property are forced to make involuntary contributions through the tax system to a variety of nonprofit institutions and other favored groups.

Partial exemption of tangible personal property is common. Major categories are legally exempt in forty states. The most common exemptions apply to household goods, automobiles, and various types of agricultural inventories and equipment. Nonfarm businesses do not fare as well. Consequently, their share of the property tax burden is increased. Four states grant total exemption to personal property. Difficulties of administration appear to be a major reason for legal exemptions and "informal" exemption of legally taxable personal property through incomplete assessment and deliberate undervaluation.

Administrative obstacles have led to the virtual disappearance of a property tax on intangibles. They are completely exempt in thirty-six states and are largely exempt or are taxed at a special low rate in most of the others.[6] As a consequence, less than 1 percent of intangibles appears on the tax rolls, and the tax on them accounts for less than 1 percent of property tax revenue.

Even if the administrative problems could be solved, it can be argued that intangibles should not be taxed because they represent claims against tangible assets that are also taxed. Compare the case of two $50,000 residences, one with a $25,000 mortgage, the other owned outright. If an intangible tax is applied to the mortgage instrument, the total levy on the owner of the mortgaged home plus the holder of the mortgage would be one and one-half times the levy on the other dwelling (assuming the same rate applies). Hence, the mortgaged dwelling is subject to "double" taxation on the amount of the mortgage.

In other cases, however, the argument needs some qualification. In the case of a corporation, for example, the value of its taxable physical assets may be less than the market value of its stock. Stock value reflects the discounted expected earnings of the firm. To tax the stock certificates leads to some double taxation. Not to tax them leads to exemption from the property tax of the amount by which the value of the stock outstanding exceeds the value of the corporation's taxable property. As one might expect, the difficulty of administration, not the theoretical argument about double taxation, is the chief reason for the demise of the tax on intangibles.

In the discussion of the assessment process, it was pointed out that assessors may value property at different percentages of full market value. When this happens to different properties within a single taxing district, it

---

[6]U.S. Bureau of the Census, "Taxable Property Values and Assessment/Sales Ratios," p. 8.

leads to horizontal inequities among property owners because the millage is applied to assessed value. Sometimes the differences are due to the inherent difficulties of evaluation, but often they are the result of a deliberate effort on the part of the assessor to influence the distribution of the tax burden. In some states close supervision by responsible state officials limits the assessor's opportunity to engage in such activities. In many cases assessors still have considerable opportunity to evade the intent of the law and usurp legislative authority for their own purposes.

Substantial differences may also exist in average ratios of assessed value to market value for property in different assessment jurisdictions within a state. If each assessment jurisdiction is completely independent, it makes little difference. Often, this is not the case. Local taxing bodies, such as school districts or counties, may overlap the jurisdictions of two or more assessors. If the state levies a property tax, all districts are involved. When taxing and assessing jurisdictions overlap, an assessor in one district is under pressure to value property at a lower percentage of full value than property assessed by others so as to shift more of the burden to taxpayers outside the area. The result is competitive undervaluation.

Undervaluation raises equity questions and limits the taxpayer's right of appeal. The practice also interferes with other fiscal objectives. State financial aid to local governments is sometimes based on assessed value per capita (or per pupil) or on property tax rates. Since low assessed values and high tax rates usually mean more state aid, local assessors have an additional incentive to undervalue. Not all districts are able to compete equally in the "race," however. Local governments often face state-imposed debt limits that are tied to assessed values. Communities with high indebtedness cannot allow assessments to drop below specified levels. States may also impose upper limits on tax rates for specific expenditures. Once the limit is reached, the only way in which to increase expenditures is to increase the base by raising assessed values.

If states refrained from basing financial assistance on assessed values or tax rates, pressure for competitive undervaluation would be diminished. Otherwise, geographical equity requires continual efforts by states to equalize ratios of assessment-to-market values. The use of assessment-sales ratio studies for all real estate that is sold can help states to attain equalization. The record in this respect is not very good. A comparison of dispersion in assessment-sales ratios for realty as reported in the quinquennial Census of Governments revealed a definite improvement during the 1960s but little change since.

The geographical differences in property taxes that we have considered up to this point are due to interstate differences in tax structure and to differences in administrative practices. We should not overlook the effects of differences in taxable wealth and the need for public services that exist among localities. Differences in taxable wealth are a result of natural, demographic, and economic factors. Wealth is not likely to be distributed evenly, even over a small area. This is especially true of metropolitan areas where the tax capacity of governmental units can be significantly affected by the way in which governmental boundaries are drawn. The fiscal problems of central cities and suburbs, which are discussed in Chapter 15, arise in part from the political fragmentation of metropolitan areas.

Likewise, differences exist in the demand for local public services. These may reflect both needs and preferences. In general, the need for services rises with increased population density. In large central cities, low-income populations require greater outlays for welfare and public safety in addition to the usual services needed in any urban community.

The effect of the forces that contribute to geographic differences in property taxes can be seen by comparing the median effective rates (tax as a percentage of estimated market value) on single-family houses in cities having a population of 100,000 or more. Data from the Census of Governments[7] show that rates exceeded 4 percent in five northeastern cities but were less than 1 percent in a number of cities, mostly those in the South. The median rate of all 144 cities was about 2 percent. In terms of dollars, a home worth $50,000 would be subject to a levy of $2,000 in a city with a 4 percent rate compared with $500 in a city with a 1 percent rate. Remember, however, that these are citywide averages. Differences at the extremes may be even greater, and similar spreads are sometimes found within states and metropolitan areas. Rates are particularly high in northern cities. In large cities, annual property taxes often absorb 20 percent of gross rentals on apartment buildings. We can expect that property taxes of this magnitude have a significant effect on both the allocation of resources and the distribution of real income.

ECONOMIC EFFECTS

Benefits to property owners are not always closely related to tax liabilities. Consequently, we expect the property tax to alter the allocation of resources as well as the distribution of income and wealth. When the tax is imposed on the use of consumer goods, such as owner-occupied housing and personal property, households can respond by altering the consumption of these items. When applied to business property, it can affect supply price and input mix and, ultimately, the relative prices and quantities of final output.

We begin with a partial equilibrium analysis of the effects of the property tax on prices and resource use in a single community. The conclusions we reach are not sufficient to enable us to evaluate the overall consequences of the property tax for the economy. They do give us insights that are useful to policy makers and voters at the community level, however.

[7]Ibid., pp. 25–27.

Taxes on Housing

The tax on dwelling units may be likened to an excise tax on housing. The rates vary widely, but they are estimated to average more than 15 percent of total consumer outlays on housing, a figure below some excise rates but well above rates under the retail sales tax. Owner-occupiers may try to shift a part of the burden to others by investing less in housing as tax rates rise. Such attempts are partly self-defeating if a large number of homeowners respond in like manner. A tax-induced reduction in the base will necessitate a higher tax rate unless the need for public services drops correspondingly. Redistribution of the tax burden among homeowners will accompany rate changes, however, if some households are more responsive than others to changes in the cost of housing.

Taxes on rental units may be shifted to renters if the supply is responsive to changes in tax rates. If the anticipated return from rental property exceeds the cost (including property taxes) of providing new units, landlords will respond by increasing the stock of rental units. Higher tax rates reduce net returns and, therefore, discourage construction of additional units. The effect of an increase in the property tax accompanied by an increase in the demand for rental units is illustrated in Figure 11–1. The

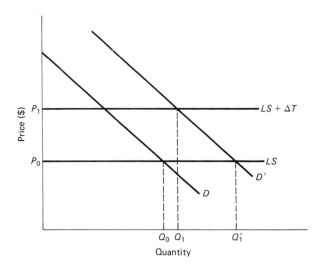

FIGURE 11–1   Effect of tax on residential property in a community with a growing demand for rental housing. An increase in the property tax of ΔT per unit will shift the long-run supply curve upward from LS to $LS + \Delta T$. If community growth shifts demand from D to D', the quantity of housing units will increase from Q_0 to Q_1. Given a perfectly elastic supply curve, rental price will rise by the full amount of the tax increase, or from P_0 to P_1. With no tax increase, the number of housing units would increase to Q_1' with no change in rental price.

tax raises the cost of supplying rental units by ΔT, causing the long-run supply curve to shift upward from LS to $LS + \Delta T$. At the same time, demand shifts from D to D'. In the example, the supply of rental units is assumed to be perfectly elastic in the long run. The rental price rises from P_0 to P_1, and the full amount of the tax increase is absorbed by renters. The quantity of units supplied increases from Q_0 to Q_1. Note that, if property taxes had not increased, the quantity supplied would have increased to Q'_1, and price would have remained at P_0. This example illustrates how the tax can be shifted fully forward in a growing community with a rising demand for housing.

Figure 11–2 illustrates the effect of a tax increase in a community with static demand. In the short run, the stock of housing is fixed, as indicated by the short-run supply curve SS. With no change in demand and a fixed stock of rental housing, price remains unchanged at P_0. No forward shifting occurs, so the full burden falls on landlords. In the long run, the supply curve shifts upward to $LS + \Delta T$. The quantity of rental units supplied will fall to Q_1, and the price will rise to P_1. Because of the durability of housing, adjustment to excess supply takes much longer than does adjustment to excess demand. For this reason, renters are more likely to bear

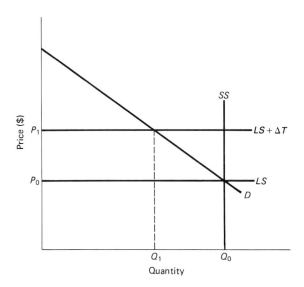

FIGURE 11–2   Effect of tax on residential property in a community with stable demand for rental housing. In the short run, the supply of housing is fixed, as indicated by the short-run supply curve *SS*. Price is demand determined and remains at P_0 after the tax increase of ΔT, so that landlords bear the full burden. In the long run, the supply curve shifts from *LS* to *LS* + ΔT, supply of units drops from Q_0 to Q_1, and rental price rises from P_0 to P_1 as the tax is shifted forward fully.

part or all of the burden of property taxes in communities that are growing than in those that are stagnant or declining. Excess supply of a transitory nature occurs occasionally in growing communities when landlords miscalculate and add too many rental units in too short a time. In either case, competition among landlords will hold rents below long-run equilibrium levels and make forward shifting of tax increases difficult.

The examples shown in Figures 11–1 and 11–2 are for the case where supply is perfectly elastic in the long run. If the long-run supply curve is positively sloped, part of the burden will fall on suppliers in the long run. This is shown in Figure 11–3, where a tax increase shifts the supply curve upward from LS to $LS + \Delta T$. Equilibrium output falls from Q_1 to Q_0, and price rises from P_0 to P_1. The higher tax reduces consumer surplus by an amount represented by the area A (the price increase times Q_0 units) plus B (the excess burden or deadweight loss on the units no longer supplied). Producer surplus is reduced by the area C (loss in net revenue on Q_0 units) plus E (excess burden). The loss in producer surplus is likely to fall on landowners, because the property tax causes land to be used less intensively.

The preceding discussion is based on the assumption that the stock of

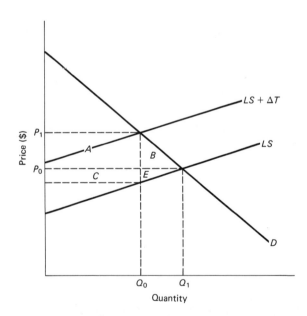

FIGURE 11–3 Effect of tax on residential property with rising supply price and stable demand. In the long run, an increase in the property tax of ΔT will shift the supply curve upward from LS to $LS + \Delta T$. Quantity will decline from Q_1 to Q_0. The price increases from P_0 to P_1, or less than the tax increase. Renters' share of the money burden is shown by area A; producers' share is shown by area C. Excess burden is shown by area $B + E$.

rental units is homogeneous. In most communities, units vary considerably in age, condition, size, location, and so on. It is therefore possible that some types of rental property may be in excess supply with consequent lack of forward shifting, whereas other types are in excess demand. Analysis may be complicated further by interdependence in the demand for different types of units.

Taxes on Business Realty

Real estate taxes on business structures increase costs and encourage firms to try to reduce their use of taxed property by substituting other inputs or reducing the scale of operations. Businesses may try to shift part of the burden to customers or suppliers, but their ability to do so is limited by demand and supply elasticities. Firms selling in the local market might find it easier to shift at least a part of the burden forward than would firms selling in regional, national, and export markets. This is because in most cases the former's major competitors are also local and are subject to the same tax rates. The reasoning behind this conclusion is discussed in greater detail in Chapter 7.

Taxes on Utilities

Privately owned public utilities represent a special case. Their rates are regulated to yield a specified net return on investment. Therefore, higher property taxes generally mean higher utility rates. Most utilities provide service in a number of communities within a state, but ordinarily rates do not vary among communities in accordance with differences in taxes and other costs. As a result, rates in a given community are more likely to reflect the average tax rate in the state than the rate within the community itself. The effect of regulation is that utility customers in low-tax communities within a state subsidize customers in high-tax communities. This sort of disguised equalization is accentuated by the common practice of valuing utility property, most of which is state assessed, at a higher percentage of actual value than other property.

Tax Capitalization

Many writers on property taxation insist that it is important to distinguish between the effects of a tax on land and a tax on buildings and other improvements. The supply of land is fixed.[8] Owners cannot vary the supply in response to changes in tax rates; so a tax on land cannot be shifted forward. Shifting between successive owners can take place, however, if changes in tax rates are *capitalized*.

---

[8]The statement refers to sites. This is not to say that land cannot be made useful by, for example, regrading or draining and filling a swamp.

To illustrate how shifting can take place through capitalization, let us assume that a piece of land is expected to yield an annual rent of $100 per year *in perpetuity*. Given a discount rate of 5 percent, its market value is $100 ÷ 0.05, or $2,000. If an annual property tax of 1 percent of market value is now added, and if it is expected to continue in effect *in perpetuity*, the value of the property will fall to $100 ÷ (0.05 + 0.01), or $1,666.67. If the property is put up for sale after the unanticipated tax is announced, the owner will have to settle for the lower price. The buyer will pay $16.67 a year in property tax and receive a *net* return of $83.33 per year, which is 5 percent of the purchase price of $1,666.67. Therefore, the burden of the tax falls on the person who owns the land at the time of its inception, not on a subsequent buyer who actually pays it. A rate increase that is thought to be permanent will lead to capital losses for current owners; an unexpected rate decrease will lead to capital gains.

Attempts to estimate the extent to which tax capitalization occurs have produced inconclusive results. This is due to the difficulty of specifying a model that accounts for all major factors that influence property values. The actual process is more complicated than the simple numerical example just given would indicate.

First, our example is based on the implicit assumption that public expenditures financed by the property tax have no effect on the income-earning potential of the site. If higher taxes and expenditures make the site more (or less) attractive to potential users, the effect of higher taxes on land values will be dampened (or amplified).[9] Most of the services financed by property taxes (such as police and fire protection, streets, sewers, and parks) increase the attractiveness of land for residential users. Some of these services, especially education, may be of less value to business users.

We also need a more precise explanation of what we mean when we say that the supply of land is fixed. The original productive powers of land in agricultural use are obviously not fabricated. Neither is their supply fixed. Productivity can be maintained only through proper land-use practices. Productivity affects market value. Since property taxes are usually related to market value, landowners can reduce their tax burden by allowing their land to deteriorate.

The characteristic of land that cannot be altered is its location. An acre of land in midtown Manhattan cannot be enlarged, shrunk, or moved to New Jersey. Note that, when we refer to a fixed supply in this sense, we are referring to the supply of sites, not to improvements such as gradings, excavations, or landfills. If an acre of land in a given location cannot be moved, there is no way that its owners can vary quantity supplied in

---

[9]Using the terminology of incidence theory introduced in Chapter 7, an empirical study of the effects of property taxes on land values should be made within the context of balanced-budget incidence.

response to changes in the tax levy placed upon it. The tax does reduce the net income of the owner, however. As a consequence, the market value of the land will be inversely related to the expected future tax levy imposed upon it.

Some sites are more desirable than others because of their location. Locational advantages are reflected in higher return to investment in improvements. Just as more productive farmland will be cultivated more intensively than will marginal land, so will the more advantageously located urban land be developed more intensively. The return to land attributable to its locational advantages is called "location rent," and the capitalized value of location rent is called "site value." Because the supply of sites is fixed, capitalization of taxes has a greater effect on site value than on the value of improvements.

Under certain conditions taxes can also have a significant effect on the market value of improvements. The most likely case is where returns to improvements are high enough to prevent their destruction but too low to justify additions to the existing supply. This was true in the example given of rental units in a city with a stable or declining population. The supply of such property is relatively fixed for the foreseeable future, and rents are demand determined. This is a familiar case in economic theory where returns to a fixed input are less than opportunity cost but greater than zero. The property tax reduces net quasi-rent and therefore reduces the market value of the property.

In those cases where tax capitalization is likely to be significant, policy makers should be aware of the wealth effects of unforeseen changes in tax rates. The windfall gains or losses fall on those who own the property at the time the change takes place. The magnitude of changes in property values can be much greater than the change in annual tax yields. This is true even if the market is much less precise in adjusting for tax changes than our oversimplified example implies.

Taxes on Personal Property and Intangibles

The personal property tax on household and producer goods is similar to an excise tax on the use of the taxed items. Like an excise tax, the tax on personal property provides an incentive to reduce the use of taxed items in favor of untaxed alternatives. The tax on intangibles may cause wealthholders to shift to untaxed assets, sometimes just on assessment day! Some large wealthholders have been known to shift temporarily into marketable, tax-free U.S. Treasury issues, for example. The tax on intangibles is now so insignificant that it has a negligible effect on capital markets. Any state that seriously tries to tax intangibles risks setting off an outmigration of its wealthiest citizens.

Locational Effects

Our discussion of the property tax centers on its economic consequences within a single community. Differences among communities in tax rates and public expenditures also affect the spatial distribution of families and business activities. In metropolitan areas with a number of governmental jurisdictions, firms and households will seek out those communities that offer the most attractive mix of tax rates, public services, and other amenities. This phenomenon is discussed in more detail in Chapter 15.

Over time, there is a tendency for capital to be allocated so as to equate the after-tax rate of return in different uses and locations. If local property tax rates and the public services they finance were identical throughout the economy, property taxes would have no effect on the geographical distribution of capital. Assuming a given level of public services, capital will be attracted to low-tax communities and away from those with high taxes. The influx of capital will tend to increase land rents and wages in low-tax areas, whereas the outflow of capital will reduce land rents and wages in high-tax areas. Because land is immobile, land values will rise in low-tax areas and fall in high-tax areas. Wage differentials will persist unless labor is fully mobile.

Prices of products produced at diverse locations and sold in national or international markets will not be affected by tax differentials because of interregional competition. Goods and services produced and consumed locally, such as rental housing, will tend to become more expensive in high-tax regions because prices must be high enough to offset the higher tax on capital. In this way differences in property tax rates can affect factor incomes, consumer prices, and the wealth of landowners in different regions or communities.

Property Taxes in a General Equilibrium Context

Looked at in a general equilibrium context, the property tax takes the form of a tax on physical capital. Since most privately owned property is subject to the property tax, it can be expected to have an effect on the *overall* return to capital as well as on allocation of capital among alternative uses. The extent to which a property tax would reduce the return to capital depends on the responsiveness of the supply of capital to changes in the average rate of return. As we saw in Chapter 8, empirical evidence is skimpy on the responsiveness of the supply of capital to changes in the rate of return. The issue is not yet settled. It is probably fair to say that most economists regard the supply of capital to be quite inelastic. This view has been strongly challenged by Michael J. Boskin, whose empirical results indicate that the supply of capital is responsive to tax-induced reductions in rate of return.[10] If capital supply is highly inelastic, labor productivity and per capita output would be hardly affected. At least part of the burden of the property tax would fall on wealthholders in general through lower returns on their investments. If capital supply is reduced significantly as a result of the property tax, the smaller capital stock would lead to reduced labor productivity and lower per capita output. Under these circumstances a part of the burden would be shifted to labor in the form of lower real wages.

This line of reasoning is couched in general equilibrium terms. It is meaningful only within the context of differential or balanced-budget incidence. Applying the differential incidence concept, and holding expenditures constant, the distributional consequences of substituting another tax for the property tax must be determined. If the property tax is compared with an income tax, the property tax would fall more heavily on returns to capital than would an equal-yield income tax. Applying the balanced-budget incidence concept, it becomes necessary to relate the effect of expenditures financed by the property tax to the income stream generated by the property.

The Brookings incidence study summarized in Chapter 7 represents an attempt to apply the concept of differential incidence to major taxes in the United States.[11] The authors compare the distribution of existing tax burdens to those of a proportional income tax of equal yield. Supplies of capital and labor are assumed to be fixed. The two variants shown in Table 7–1 reveal quite different incidence patterns for the property tax. The first variant reveals a pattern that is roughly proportional across low and middle incomes and notably progressive among higher-income groups. Estimated rates are 2.5 percent of income in the lowest-income group ($0 to $3,000) compared with 10.1 percent in the top group (over $1 million). This is in contrast to a 3 percent rate for an equal-yield proportional income tax. These estimates are derived by allocating all property taxes on the basis of property income. The presumption here is that the combination of a fixed supply of capital and competitive markets causes property owners to bear the full burden of the property tax.

The second variant is likewise based on the presumption of fixed factor supply. However, the assumption is made that the property tax on improvements—commercial, industrial, and residential—is shifted forward to

[10]For a summary of the literature on the effect of rate of return on saving and investment, see George F. Break, "The Incidence and Economic Effects of Taxation," in Alan S. Blinder et al., *The Economics of Public Finance* (Washington, D.C.: The Brookings Institution, 1974), pp. 150–52. Boskins's results appear in "Taxation, Saving, and the Rate of Interest," *Journal of Political Economy*, 86 (April 1978), S3–S27.

[11]Joseph A. Pechman and Benjamin A. Okner, *Who Bears the Tax Burden?* (Washington, D.C.: The Brookings Institution, 1974).

consumers while the property tax on land is borne by landowners. Forward shifting is brought about by a combination of market power and tax-induced reallocation of capital. The result is an incidence pattern that is unequivocally regressive, with effective tax rates falling from 6.5 percent of income for the lowest group to 0.8 percent for the highest. The average rate is 3.4 percent.

The first variant treats the property tax as a tax on property income. The second treats it as a form of excise tax with forward shifting brought about by a combination of market power and tax-induced reallocation of capital to untaxed uses. The first variant is in line with the general equilibrium analysis cited previously; the second variant is more representative of the orthodox view, which holds that the property tax is regressive or at best proportional. Both variants treat the property tax in a general equilibrium context, since the purpose of the Brookings study is to esimate the incidence of the property tax on an economywide basis. Neither accounts for the factor income or price effects brought about by the reallocation of capital from high-tax to low-tax regions. The latter effects are hidden within the economywide averages.

For policy makers, the general equilibrium estimates are relevant if the goal of a policy change is to reduce (or raise) property taxes nationwide, for example, through an increase (or cut) in the level of federal assistance to local governments. For policy makers at the local level, the Brookings results are not applicable. Changes in a single community would not have an appreciable effect on the nationwide averages. The local property tax rate will have an effect on capital investment within the community, as described in the partial equilibrium models presented earlier. Thus, the general and partial equilibrium models are not inconsistent with each other; they apply to different situations.[12]

SUGGESTIONS FOR IMPROVEMENT

The first step in improving the property tax is to improve valuation. Comparisons of assessed and market values (the assessment ratio) show that substantial variation in the ratios is typical of most assessment jurisdictions. Census of Government tabulations show that for single-family dwell-

[12]The classic reference on the difference between partial equilibrium excise and general equilibrium return-to-capital effects is Peter Mieszkowski, "The Property Tax: An Excise or a Profits Tax?" *Journal of Public Economics*, 1 (April 1972), 73–96. See also Henry J. Aaron, *Who Pays the Property Tax?* (Washington, D.C.: The Brookings Institution, 1975), pp. 18–55. Implications for policy makers at federal and local levels are discussed in Charles E. McLure, Jr., "The 'New View' of the Property Tax: A Caveat," *National Tax Journal*, 30 (March 1977), 69–75.

ings the average deviation of the assessment ratio exceeded 20 percent of its median value in nearly four-fifths of the states.[13] Since tax rates are applied to assessed values, this means that in many communities, on the average, the tax levy on homes of equal value can be expected to differ by 20 percent or more. The tax bill on a home usually amounts to hundreds of dollars, so that the inequities are of considerable importance. What is worse, these figures are for single-family dwellings, which are relatively easy to value.

Differences in assessment ratios are due in part to errors and to the inherent imperfections in the valuation process. They may also reflect market imperfections. Most of the checks on assessors' valuations come from sales data. As we have seen, these data are reliable only in communities where there are a number of sales of relatively homogeneous parcels of property.

Evidence indicates that some assessors systematically value different types of property at different percentages of market value. Systematic differences are often found in ratios for commercial property, large apartments, two- to four-family dwellings, and single-family houses. These differences sometimes result from the deliberate attempts of assessors to vary the tax burden on different classes of property. In a number of communities, assessment ratios on houses differ systematically according to market value. Usually, the ratios are higher on less expensive units, placing more of a burden on less affluent families. In some states, different assessment ratios, usually favoring farm and residential property, are specified by law.

Critics of property tax administration argue that the horizontal inequities attributable to the assessment process—deliberate and otherwise—can be reduced to acceptable levels only by relying on professionally trained personnel appointed to civil-service-type positions. Assessors who are elected or appointed politically are subject to political pressures and usually lack the requisite training. In addition, local assessors should be supervised by a state agency responsible for review and equalization. Differences in assessment ratios for different classes of property should be eliminated unless authorized specifically by law. Differences among assessors' jurisdictions should be removed whenever they affect equity among taxpayers. Inequities can occur when jurisdictions of different assessors overlap a single taxing jurisdiction. The use of assessed values in grant-in-aid formulas is another potential source of inequity.

Progress is being made in the professionalization of assessors. In addition, major changes in the property tax base, notably the gradual elimination of the tax on intangibles and household personal property, are due in part to the desire to avoid the difficult administrative problems that tax-

[13]U.S. Bureau of the Census, "Taxable Property Values and Assessment/Sales Price Ratios," p. 92.

ation of these items entails. In recent years, the job of assessors has been complicated by the high rate of increase in real estate values. Without reassessment every year or two, wide gaps in assessment ratios between old and new structures can appear.[14] If all properties are reassessed periodically, say, once every five years, the tax base will increase in sudden jumps. If taxing bodies do not cut tax rates to compensate for the increase in the base, property taxes will suddenly jump to much higher levels.

Henry J. Aaron's proposal of annual reassessment, made feasible by computerization of records, may be the best way in which to deal with the problem.[15] Elimination of abrupt jumps in taxes should help to hold down taxpayer resistance. In regions where the rate of increase in real estate values exceeds the rate of inflation, however, a cut in tax rates may be necessary as well if strong taxpayer resistance is to be avoided. Failure to deal adequately with this phenomenon has touched off a "taxpayers' revolt" in a number of states.

For years, state laws have put constraints on the property tax levies that can be imposed by local governments. In many cases, the constraints are in the form of ceilings on tax rates, but, as we have seen, inflation in real estate values reduces their effectiveness. The most dramatic reaction occurred in California in 1978. In a referendum, voters approved by a 2 to 1 margin Proposition 13, a constitutional amendment that brought about an immediate 57 percent reduction in property tax revenue, from \$12 billion to \$7 billion. The amendment sets the maximum rate at 1 percent of "full cash value of property." In addition, it constrains to 2 percent a year the growth rate in assessed value of property not sold. New construction and property that is sold are valued at market cost. Given recent inflation rates, the latter provision is expected to lead to a widening discrepancy in tax rates in favor of property under original ownership. Within a year, five other states adopted amendments comparable to Proposition 13, and five more adopted limits on spending.[16]

A likely consequence of constitutional or statutory limits to the property tax is a shift toward greater reliance on grants from higher levels of government. For example, in California a part of the loss in property tax revenue was offset at first by more state aid.[17] Thus, the reduction in local

---

[14]For evidence on the effect of frequency of reassessment on within-jurisdiction variation in assessment ratios, see Karl E. Case, *Property Taxation: The Need for Reform* (Cambridge, Mass.: Ballinger Publishing Company, 1978), pp. 62–69.

[15]Aaron, *Who Pays the Property Tax?*, p. 69.

[16]For a summary of events related to tax limitation in California and elsewhere, see papers by Marion S. Beaumont, William Craig Stubblebine, William A. Niskanen, and Will Myers in *National Tax Association-Tax Institute of America Proceedings*, 1978, pp. 153–75.

[17]Proposition 13 also imposes constraints on the ability of local governments to increase alternative revenue sources and requires two-thirds approval of the California legislature of any increases in state taxes. These provisions limit prospects for tax substitution and are designed to reduce the size of the public sector in California.

expenditures, while substantial, is much less than the cut in property tax revenue. The increase in state aid is likely to be accompanied by a further erosion in local autonomy. The implications of increased reliance on intergovernmental grants are discussed in Chapter 15.

Site-Value Taxation

A more drastic proposal for reforming the property tax comes from those who advocate site-value taxation. They argue that the real estate tax should apply only to the site with complete exemption of all improvements. Rates on land would be raised enough to maintain yields. The effect would be to reduce location rents, perhaps to zero in some cases, thereby reducing site values. Landowners could not avoid their tax liability by withholding land from use. They would still have an incentive to make their sites available to the user able to pay the highest price, because the tax is in the form of a lump sum payable regardless of actual rent receipts. In fact, proponents say, site-value taxation would lead to more efficient use of land because the cost of withholding it for speculative purposes would be greatly increased. Furthermore, by eliminating the tax on improvements, investors would have an incentive to build bigger and better structures and to improve those already in existence. Some of the more optimistic proponents look upon site-value taxation as the cure-all for our problems of slums and urban blight.[18]

Experience with site-value taxation is limited, especially in the United States, and more prudent observers are skeptical of its potential as a panacea.[19] Critics contend that the tax is not workable because of the obvious problem of separating site value from the value of improvements for most pieces of developed realty. They add that, even if this can be done, the redistribution of wealth would be highly inequitable. Higher land taxes would cause owners of land to suffer large capital losses, whereas owners of improvements would stand to gain.

Defenders of the proposal counter with the argument that site values are no more difficult to estimate than are values of other types of realty, especially of a commercial or industrial nature. Given the sorry record of tax assessors, they may be right. As for the wealth effect, they argue that site values are created by the growth of economic activity, not by any effort on the part of the landowner. Wages are the reward for effort; profits

---

[18]The classic case for site-value taxation appears in Henry George's *Progress and Poverty*, first published in 1879. George, an American social reformer, was troubled by the presence of poverty amidst plenty during the early years of American industrialization. He attributed the phenomenon to the rising share of income going to passive landowners in a society undergoing urbanization. George and his followers reasoned that confiscation of land rents through taxation would yield enough revenue to finance all government activities, thereby earning them the title "single-taxers."

[19]Netzer, *Economics of the Property Tax*, pp. 202–4.

and interest are a reward for risk taking and abstention from consumption; but land rents are created by society and should be returned to society through taxation. This argument might be convincing if we were starting from scratch or if all land were owned by its original owners or their heirs. Many owners of land have acquired it by purchase, often with funds acquired through labor or investment in capital. Hence, the argument that they do not deserve location rents (or their capitalized wealth value) is not completely convincing.

Less radical measures designed to encourage investment in buildings and attract new industries have been tried by some communities. The most common is temporary exclusion of part or all of the value of improvements from the tax base for a specified number of years. This practice is often employed on an ad hoc basis following informal negotiation between potential investors and local officials. In some cases, the preferential treatment may be permanent. The net effect is to shift more of the property tax burden to landowners. A part of the burden is also shifted to owners of other types of property, especially homeowners and others not in a position to negotiate for special treatment.

To conclude, the claims of proponents of site-value taxation should not be dismissed without further study and experimentation. A shift of the burden from structures to sites might stimulate additional investment in new construction and improvements. This is especially true in some of our large cities where property tax rates have risen as high as 5 percent of market value. Perhaps a gradual or partial shift in tax base would reduce the wealth effects to acceptable levels. The increased demand for sites that would result from tax relief on buildings might also help to mitigate the depressing effect on site values. It should be added, however, that a shift to a tax on site value removes the property tax even farther from its initial conception as a tax on wealth. The case for site-value taxation is defended more often on allocational than on distributional grounds.

Circuit Breakers

The burden of the property tax on housing is regarded as an onerous burden on low-income families. In an effort to ease this burden, about half the states have introduced some type of property tax "circuit breaker." Circuit breakers generally take one of two forms, the *threshold* type or the *sliding-scale* type. The threshold type provides a rebate when the property tax on an owner-occupied dwelling exceeds a specified percentage of a taxpayer's income. The basic formula for the threshold-type rebate is of the form

$$R = s(T - pY)$$

where

R = rebate (in dollars)
T = property tax on dwelling unit
Y = income
s = proportion of tax above threshold that is rebated
p = threshold as a proportion of income

Only if $T - pY$ is greater than zero (only if the tax exceeds the threshold) is a rebate paid. To illustrate, if $p = 0.05$ and $s = 1$, the state will pick up the entire amount by which the property tax exceeds 5 percent of the tax-payer's income. If $p = 0.05$ and $s = 0.6$, the state will pick up 60 percent of the amount by which the tax exceeds 5 percent of income. For these values of s and p, a taxpayer with a property tax of $600 and an income of $8,000 would receive the following rebates.

$$s = 1; \ p = 0.05$$
$$R = 600 - (0.05)8000 = \$200$$

$$s = 0.6; \ p = 0.05$$
$$R = 0.6[600 - (0.05)800] = \$120$$

The cost of the program is constrained further by upper limits on the amount of rebate payable to a recipient.

The sliding-scale type circuit breaker makes the rebate a percentage of tax paid, with the percentage a declining function of income. The general formula is of the form

$$R = Tp(Y)$$

where

R = rebate
T = property tax on dwelling unit
p(Y) = percentage of tax rebated as a function of income

The rebate formula for elderly homeowners in Iowa is of this form. It provides a percentage rebate that declines in steps from 100 percent for taxpayers with income below $1,000 to 25 percent for taxpayers with income of $7,000 to $8,000. Taxpayers with incomes above $8,000 receive no rebate.[20]

[20]For a description of the Iowa circuit breaker and a comparison of the threshold and sliding-scale approaches, see Steven D. Gold, "A Note on the Design of Property Tax Circuit Breakers," *National Tax Journal*, 29 (December 1976), 477–81.

The threshold formula is most beneficial to families in high-tax communities. It is criticized for providing a bonus of sorts to recipients who live in expensive homes and for subsidizing families with temporarily low incomes. The sliding-scale formula is less selective. It provides some benefits to all homeowners with incomes below the cutoff level.

Some states with circuit breakers provide benefits to renters. In this case, payments are based on rental payments rather than on property taxes. The presumption is that renters pay the tax indirectly in the form of higher rents. We have seen that this may not be the case where the supply of rental housing exceeds the long-run equilibrium quantity. The circuit breaker was introduced as a form of tax relief for the elderly, but five states have extended coverage to all low-income households. Extension to all households increases the cost enormously. According to one estimate, a program restricted to persons age 65 and older costs less than 10 percent as much as an unrestricted program.[21]

Viewed in terms of horizontal equity, a case can be made for extending coverage to all households. By making the rebate a function of income, property tax relief is concentrated on those who need it most. Unfortunately, it adds yet another layer to the host of federal and state welfare programs that are conditioned on income. Circuit breakers add to the work disincentive of other welfare programs, further discouraging persons with low earning potential from labor force participation. This feature is of limited concern when rebates are confined to the elderly, who are not likely to work anyway.

THE PROPERTY TAX:
AN EVALUATION

The property tax has been subjected to harsh criticism for nearly a century. Yet it remains as the leading source of revenue for local governments. The principle of horizontal equity is violated by the substantial intercommunity rate differentials that result from differences in the per capita tax base. Within communities, faulty assessment practices and questionable exemptions lead to wide variation in effective rates. Using income as a basis of comparison, the tax discriminates against households within income categories that have strong preferences for housing and other taxed items. It falls on gross wealth (no allowance is made for claims against property) rather than on net worth, a better measure of taxpaying capacity. Many critics cling to the orthodox view that the property tax is regressive

---

[21]Larry D. Schroeder and David L. Sjoquist, "Alternative Circuit-Breaker Programs: An Analysis of the Size and Distribution of Benefits," *Public Finance Quarterly,* 6 (October 1978), 408.

or at best proportional. Those who view it as a tax on capital argue that it is progressive.[22]

Equity considerations aside, the property tax does have some favorable features. It can be administered locally without undue interference in local affairs. Rates are much more flexible than they are for other major taxes. Specific local outlays are tied to a specific levy, allowing local taxpayers to estimate the cost to the proposed local expenditures—a procedure that aids rational decision making. In addition, elimination of the property tax would lead to a significant but haphazard redistribution of wealth through capitalization, especially in the case of site values. Finally, those who call for its replacement by other revenue sources should not overlook the fact that administration of other major taxes is, as we have seen, far from perfect.

[22]Aaron, *Who Pays the Property Tax?* p. 93.

12

Death and Gift Taxes

We have seen that the two most commonly accepted measures of taxpaying capacity are income and wealth. In the United States, we have made no serious attempt to tax wealth, or net worth, on a year-to-year basis. Wealth is subject to taxation, however, when it is transferred from one individual to another. This usually occurs at the time of death.

BASIC FORMS OF DEATH TAX

Transfers of wealth can be taxed in several different ways. The most common forms are estate, gift, inheritance, and accession taxes.

Estate and Gift Taxes

The estate tax is applied to the net taxable estate left by a decedent. It is sometimes described as a tax on the privilege of transferring property at death. Tax liability varies with the size of the estate and (except for a spouse) is usually unaffected by the number and economic status of the heirs or by their relation to the deceased.

The gift tax applies to a transfer of property between living persons, referred to in legal terms as an *inter vivos* transfer. Tax liability is on the giver, and its main purpose is to prevent wealthholders from avoiding the estate tax by giving away property while they are still alive. The gift tax is intended to apply to large transfers of wealth, not to modest transfers like most Christmas, wedding, or birthday gifts.

Inheritance Tax

The inheritance tax is applied to a bequest or receipt of property from a decedent. Liability falls on the recipient. Thus, the inheritance tax is a tax on the privilege of receiving property from the dead. Rates typically vary directly with the size of the bequest and inversely with closeness of the relationship between heir and deceased.

Accessions Tax

The accessions tax is applied cumulatively to an individual's receipt of property by bequest or gift over a lifetime. Each time an individual receives a transfer of property, its value is added to his or her tax base. Under a progressive rate structure, successive inheritances are taxed at incrementally higher rates. An accessions tax is thought to be superior to an inheritance tax in terms of ability to pay. This is because rate graduation is based on the total amount of wealth inherited during one's lifetime, not on the amount inherited in a single bequest. An accessions tax can also be superior in terms of horizontal equity. Given graduated rates, a person receiving ten bequests of $50,000 each will pay less inheritance tax than will a person receiving $500,000 in a single bequest. Under the lifetime cumulative provision of the accessions tax, each would pay the same amount, assuming that all other provisions of the two taxes treat them equally.

Death and Gift Taxes in the United States

The U.S. government experimented intermittently with death taxes during the nineteenth century. The present federal tax was introduced in 1916. Prior to 1977, the federal government levied separate taxes on estates and gifts. Beginning in that year, the two were merged into a unified estate and gift tax that applies in a cumulative manner to the transfers of property that an individual makes before and after death.

The federal tax is designed to tax only the larger estates. Owing to a sizable exemption, only 1.3 percent of the people who died in 1950 left taxable estates. By the 1970s this percentage had risen to about 7 percent, a result of the combined effects of economic growth and inflation. The Tax Reform Act of 1976, which made major revisions in the estate tax, replaced the exemption with a credit. Its intent was to reduce the number of taxable estates while increasing the tax liability on the largest estates. By 1981, when these amendments were fully implemented, 2.8 percent of estates were subject to the tax. Estate tax provisions in the Economic Recovery Tax Act of 1981 phase in a greatly increased credit and cut the maximum rate. The intent of these revisions is a reduction in taxable estates to less than 0.5 percent of the total and a decline in the effective tax rate on estates that are taxed.

The federal estate tax is a matter of concern to those who plan estate transfers for the wealthy, but it is a relatively insignificant source of federal revenue in spite of marginal rates of 50 percent or more. During the period since World War II it consistently accounted for between 1 and 2 percent of federal tax receipts. In fiscal 1981, the last full year before the 1981 revision began to take effect, the yield was $6.8 billion. Yields are expected to drop during the 1980s. By 1986 it is estimated that the 1981 amendments will cost the U.S. Treasury over $5 billion a year in lost revenue.[1]

State governments began taxing transfers of wealth early in this century, and all states have some type of death tax. Thirty-six states have an inheritance tax. Rates are graduated and are lower for close relatives than for others. They range from 1 to 16 percent on bequests to spouse, child, or parent and from 3 to 30 percent on bequests to nonrelatives. Rates on bequests to brothers and sisters fall in between. The remaining states tax estates, but at rates far below the federal rates. As at the federal level, death taxes are only a minor source of revenue. They currently account for about 2 percent of state tax receipts.

The accessions tax is often recommended by advocates of tax reform, but it has never been adopted or seriously considered at any level of government in the United States. This tax is in effect in two Canadian provinces.

JUSTIFICATION FOR DEATH TAXES

Arguments in favor of death and gift taxes tend more toward the philosophic than toward the economic. One of the most common is derived from the concept of equality of opportunity. In its extreme form, it holds that everyone should start with an equal endowment of property. One way in which to accomplish this is to prohibit any transfer of wealth from one generation to the next, either through a confiscatory tax on estates and gifts or through elimination of all previously held wealth.

The entitlement thesis of John Locke represents the opposite view— a person has a right to dispose of property as he or she wishes as long as it was acquired in a legitimate manner.[2] Included is the right to dispose of one's property by transferring it to others as gifts or bequests. Locke's influence is apparent in the institutions governing property rights in the United States, but it has been tempered by the egalitarianism implicit in

[1]U.S. Congress, Joint Committee on Taxation, *Summary of H.R. 4242, The Economic Recovery Tax Act of 1981* (Washington, D.C.: Government Printing Office, August 5, 1981), p. 61.

[2]For a summary of the arguments in defense of private property, see Gottfried Dietze, *In Defense of Property* (Chicago: Henry Regnery Company, 1963).

the equal opportunity concept. Concern about the effect of concentration of wealth on equality of opportunity is undoubtedly the basis for much of the support for taxes on wealth transfers.

A similar concern, again egalitarian in nature, is the relationship between large concentrations of wealth and political power. Not only are the very rich able to command more economic resources than the rest of us; they are also able to exert a disproportionate influence on our political, social, and cultural institutions. Wealth can be used to buy political influence. It gives wealthy candidates the resources and free time needed to run for political office. For some, it makes it easier to accept the financial sacrifices that may accompany public officeholding. Large-scale philanthropy is alleged to give wealthy contributors undue influence over nonprofit institutions that benefit from their largess.

Whether the power of wealth is exercised for good or for evil is an unsettled question. Perhaps politicians who are independenty wealthy are more trustworthy than the others. Perhaps the allocation of resources to education, culture, religion, and social welfare that derives from philanthropy of the rich is better than we would get if it were all left up to government. Critics of the wealthy are not so sure, and they look to a stiff combination of death and gift taxes as a way of preventing wealthy families from amassing fortunes over successive generations. To be effective, such a tax would have to be levied at close to confiscatory rates on large transfers, and ways would have to be found to prevent tax avoidance.

Another line of argument centers on the importance of wealth as a source of ability to pay taxes. We saw in Chapters 6 and 8 that income is usually regarded as the best single index of ability to pay, but many supporters of the ability-to-pay doctrine would add wealth as a second dimension. One way in which to reach this source of taxpaying capacity would be to level a periodic tax on the net worth of each individual or family. Net worth is often difficult to measure, especially where assets are illiquid. Estimating the value of a family business or an art collection can be a costly undertaking. Because of the high cost of administration and compliance, it may not be feasible to levy such a tax on an annual basis. Some proponents have suggested a levy every five or ten years.

Another alternative is to tax wealth once each generation. Death taxes are the obvious device for accomplishing this, since the property must be inventoried for the legal transfer of ownership anyway.[3] Admittedly, death taxes are not a perfect substitute for a more frequent wealth levy. In particular, they will fail to reach a person who accumulates a large fortune early in life and then dissipates it before death. If the goal of one levy per generation is to be achieved, generation skipping by making bequests or gifts to grandchildren rather than to children must be controlled.

---

[3]For an elaboration on this and related topics, see Carl S. Shoup, *Federal Estate and Gift Taxes* (Washington, D.C.: The Brookings Institution, 1966), pp. 100–17.

Turning to a more strictly economic argument, some economists argue that we should rely more heavily on death taxes and less on other revenue sources, because death taxes have less effect on the allocation of resources. As we have seen in our discussion of other taxes, they can influence decisions on saving, consumption, work versus leisure, use of factors of production, and choices among different consumer goods. The prospect that one's bequests or gifts will be taxed at some future date may influence one's behavior now. Since such taxes are in the future, usually after death, they are thought to have less influence than taxes that must be paid now. If this is true, and if minimization of excess burden—the effect of taxes on resource allocation—is considered desirable, death taxes may be superior to other revenue sources. The effect of death taxes on economic behavior is considered in more detail later in this chapter.

Finally, a word is in order about the treatment of wealth transfers under the income tax. Recall from Chapters 6 and 8 that the accretion concept of income is defined to include the sum of consumption expenditures plus changes in net worth during a given time period. A bequest clearly qualifies as income under this definition. If, as in the United States, bequests are excluded from the income tax base, a death tax can be regarded as a way of closing that loophole.

THE FEDERAL ESTATE AND GIFT TAX

The Tax Reform Act of 1976 merged the previously separate estate and gift taxes into a tax that is applied to the cumulative total of gifts made during one's lifetime plus the estate left at death. In this way, one's tax liability is dependent on the total amount of wealth that one transfers to others both before and after death.

The Tax Base

The basic form of the estate is summarized by the following formula:

Gross estate
Less: Deductions
Equals: Adjusted gross estate
Less: Marital deduction (if any)
Equals: Taxable estate

Note that there is no general exemption under the estate tax. An exemption of $60,000 in effect prior to 1977 was replaced by a credit.

Gross Estate

The gross estate includes the dollar value of all property owned by the decedent at death plus the dollar value of all taxable gifts made during life. Also included is the value of any life insurance owned by the decedent and the dollar value of any trusts over which the decedent retained an option to modify or revoke.

Deductions

Among the allowable deductions are debts, funeral expenses, costs of settling the estate, and bequests to eligible nonprofit institutions. If the decedent transfers property to a surviving spouse, an unlimited marital deduction is allowed. An unlimited deduction is also allowed under the gift tax for transfers of property between living spouses.

Preferential treatment of wealth transferred to a spouse may be defended on several grounds. The recipient of the transfer, most often the wife, may have made a substantial contribution to the partner's earning capacity. Unlike other heirs, receipt of the property is not likely to provide a windfall increase in a spouse's standard of living. Indeed, the transfer is usually needed to prevent just the opposite. Finally, if a once-a-generation tax on wealth is the goal of the estate tax, it can be achieved without taxing transfers between spouses.

The Rate Structure

The tax liability before credits is determined by applying a graduated rate structure to the taxable estate. Prior to passage of the Economic Recovery Tax Act of 1981, the rate schedule contained eighteen brackets with rates ranging from 18 percent on the first $10,000 to 70 percent on taxable estates in excess of $5,000,000. The 1981 revision phases in a top bracket rate of 50 percent. Its effect is to reduce rates in the top six brackets, which apply to estates in excess of $2,500,000. The phase-in will be completed in 1986. At that time, the top six brackets will be combined into a single bracket with a 50 percent rate. The U.S. Treasury estimates that this provision will reduce the tax on large estates by $890 million in 1986.[4]

Tax Credits

The Tax Reform Act of 1976 initiated the phasing in of a unified credit against the gross tax liability. The credit was increased annually from $30,000 for estates of persons dying in 1977 to a permanent level of $47,000 effective beginning in 1981. The $47,000 credit eliminated any tax liability for estates up to $175,625. The Economic Recovery Tax Act of 1981 con-

[4]Joint Committee on Taxation, *Summary of H.R. 4242,* p. 60.

tinued the liberalization of the credit during the period 1982 to 1987. By 1987 the credit will reach $192,800. Its effect is to eliminate any federal estate tax liability on estates of up to $600,000. It is the credit increase that is most responsible for large revenue loss attributed to the 1981 amendment. According to U.S. Treasury estimates, this provision will result in revenue loss of more than $3.8 billion in 1986.[5]

A credit is also allowed for state death taxes. The allowable credit increases with the size of the estate but has a relatively low upper limit. Since the tax must be paid to the federal government if states fail to collect it, all states have enacted death taxes at least high enough to pick up the full credit. Indeed, the credit was introduced in 1926 to discourage states from competing for wealthy retirees by eliminating death taxes completely.

Unification of Estate and Gift Taxes

As indicated, a major feature of the 1976 revision was the unification of federal gift and estate taxes beginning in 1977. Prior to the revision, the gift tax was levied separately on *inter vivos* transfers. Gifts were taxed at lower rates and were not added to property held at death for inclusion in the gross estate.

Under the pre-1977 arrangement, wealthy individuals could achieve substantial tax savings by judicious timing of transfers. By giving away part of their holdings before death, they could take advantage of the lower gift tax rates. In addition, by splitting their holdings between transfers *inter vivos* and at death, they could hold down the value of each, an important consideration under graduated rate structures. The new law goes a long way toward eliminating the advantages of splitting transfers between gifts and estate, but some advantages remain.

Tax Treatment of Gifts

Each individual is allowed an exemption of up to $10,000 per recipient per year ($20,000 for couples giving away jointly held property). Any gift to an individual recipient in excess of the exemption level is taxable under the unified estate and gift tax. The dollar value of taxable gifts is summed over the giver's lifetime. Each year in which taxable gifts are made, the tax liability on the cumulative lifetime total is calculated by applying the rate structure described earlier. A credit is then allowed for gift tax paid in previous years. Thus, in each year the taxpayer pays a tax only on the incremental value of gifts made during that year. The law includes a phase-in provision for gifts made before 1977.

[5]Ibid.

The lifetime unified credit is allowed against gift tax liability. Any portion of the credit not used against the gift tax may be carried forward and applied to the estate. Recall that the value of *inter vivos* transfers in excess of the exemption level is added to the value of property at death in determining the value of the gross estate. To prevent double taxation, a credit for all gift taxes paid prior to death is allowed against taxes due on the estate. Hence, the estate tax in effect applies only to property transferred after death.

By taxing transfers as they accumulate both before and after death, the total tax liability becomes a function of total wealth transfers regardless of timing. In principle, this arrangement eliminates the incentive existing under the previous law to give away part of one's wealth before death. In practice, two provisions of the current law allow tax savings for *inter vivos* transfers. The first is the exemption of gifts up to $10,000 per recipient per year. These exemptions are never recaptured. The second provision excludes taxes paid on gifts made before death from the cumulative estate and gift tax base. Under a graduated rate structure, exclusion of gift taxes from the tax base can result in tax savings on large estates.

An example may help to illustrate how *inter vivos* transfer of part of one's wealth will result in a tax saving. First, take the case of a taxable estate of $2,000,000 transferred in its entirety after death. Under the credit and rate schedule in effect after 1986, the following tax liability applies:

Tax before credit	$780,800
Less: Unified credit	192,800
Net tax due	$588,000

Compare this alternative with the case in which the same property worth $2,000,000 is transferred to a single recipient in two stages. Assume that the wealthholder transfers $1,000,000 to the recipient before death with the remainder transferred after death. These transfers take place as follows:

1. An amount of $1,000,000 transferred to a recipient before transferor's death:

Value of gift	$1,000,000
Less: Exemption	10,000
Taxable gift	$ 990,000
Gift tax due before credit	$ 341,900
Less: Unified credit	192,800
Tax paid in year of gift	$ 149,100

2. Determination of taxable (gross adjusted) estate:

Initial wealthholding	$2,000,000
Less: Initial gift $1,000,000	
Gift tax paid $149,100	1,149,100
Property transferred at death	$ 850,900
Plus: Taxable gift	990,000
Taxable estate	$1,840,900

3. Tax due at death:

Tax gross of credit on taxable estate	$ 516,405
Less: Credit for gift tax paid	149,100
Unified credit	192,800
Tax due at death	$ 367,305

4. Total tax paid on gift and estate transfers:

Gift tax	$ 367,305
Estate tax	149,100
Total	$ 516,405

In this example, the tax liability was reduced from $588,000 to $516,405, for a saving of $71,595.

Evidence indicates that the tax advantage available to wealthy people who transfer a part of their holdings as gifts has only a limited effect on their behavior. Even under the pre-1977 law, when tax savings from *inter vivos* transfers were greater, the wealthy held on to the bulk of their assets until death.[6] Several explanations are offered for their behavior. They include uncertainty over time of death, which encourages delays, loss of control over business enterprises, and unwillingness to give up the power—including influence over the actions of potential heirs—that goes with property. Another consideration is the opportunity cost of money used to pay the gift tax. Payment is due the year after a gift is made, and the opportunity to earn interest on the tax paid is forgone. In the example, interest on the $149,100 compounded annually at 10 percent will exceed the tax saving of $71,595 in less than five years.[7]

ESTATE TAX AVOIDANCE

If ways can be found to transfer wealth across one or more generations without paying a gift or estate tax, the effectiveness of the tax can be undermined. Various schemes for "generation skipping" have been devised

[6]U.S. Treasury data show that, for persons who died in 1959 and who transferred wealth in excess of $1,000,000 only 10 percent was transferred before death. The percentage increased with wealth and was 17 percent for those transferring $10,000,000 or more, indicating that those with the most to gain by making gifts were more likely to do so. See Joseph A. Pechman, *Federal Tax Policy*, 3rd ed. (Washington, D.C.: The Brookings Institution, 1977), p. 232.

[7]Another factor discouraging gifts is the capital gains provision of the federal income tax. The recipient of property transferred by gift takes the basis of the giver, whereas the recipient of a bequest takes as a basis the value of the property at death. Unrealized capital gains at death escape income taxation completely, as described in Chapter 8. An econometric analysis by James D. Adams shows that, when allowance is made for differential treatment of unrealized gains, the effective tax rate on gifts and estates tends toward equality. Large wealthholders are not behaving in an economically irrational manner by transferring most of their wealth as bequests. See James D. Adams, "Equalization of True Gift and Estate Tax Rates," *Journal of Public Economics*, 9 (February 1978), 59–71.

and are often used by wealthy families. The family-controlled nonprofit foundation is another device for avoiding estate taxes. Ownership of assets is transferred to the foundation, but the family retains a degree of control over foundation activities. Legislation has placed restrictions on both these forms of tax avoidance.

Generation Skipping

The most obvious means of skipping a generation is to transfer property from grandparent to grandchild. The generation in the middle is skipped, and the property passed on in this manner is subjected to the estate tax one less time. There is no penalty on this type of transfer under the federal estate and gift tax, but such transfers are often subject to a higher state inheritance tax. Generation skipping may become more common as a result of restrictions on tax avoidance via trusts introduced in the Tax Reform Act of 1976.

A trust is a legal institution with the authority to administer property for the benefit of another individual or institution. Title to the property is turned over to the trust to be managed in accordance with instructions in the trust agreement. It is managed by a trustee, who is usually an attorney, banker, or acquaintance of the person creating the trust.

Under the trust arrangement, a wealthy person can turn property over to a trust before death (and pay a gift tax) or after death (and pay an estate tax). The trust can take a variety of forms, but for purposes of illustration, assume that a wealthy father places part of his property in trust and designates his wife and son as successive life tenants. During her lifetime, the wife receives the income generated by the trust. Upon her death the son becomes life tenant and draws the trust income. Upon his death the trust is dissolved, and the property is distributed to his son (the grandson of its originator) or remainderman. Prior to the 1976 tax revision, this transfer escaped the estate tax completely, thus skipping one generation. The 1976 revision placed an upper limit of $250,000 per recipient (i.e., per grandchild) on the amount of trust property that can be passed on to remaindermen tax free. The rest of the property in trust is added to the taxable estate of the life tenant (the son in our example).

Foundations

Federal law allows unlimited deductions for bequests to nonprofit institutions, including private nonprofit foundations. Some wealthy families have transferred sizable blocks of assets to foundations, and those established by the Ford and Rockefeller families are particularly well known for their support of scientific and educational activities. By controlling the boards of directors, families have in some cases been able to exercise considerable influence over the foundations they have established. In this way, they have continued to exercise power derived from a foundation's assets even though title to the assets has been relinquished.

During the 1960s, Congress became increasingly aware of perversion of the public purposes of some tax-free foundations. A number of corrective measures were written into the 1969 Tax Reform Act, including prohibition of loans to contributors, directors, and officers of the foundation; limits to control by a single family; and a requirement that all income be used for charitable, educational, or scientific purposes. The act also introduced a 4 percent tax on the investment income of foundations.

Family Businesses

If a decedent's assets are held in liquid form, the cash needed to pay the estate tax should be readily available. When the bulk of the estate is in the form of a family business, however, payment may not be so easy. Conceivably, the family may be forced to sell the business, perhaps on unfavorable terms, to raise the needed money. To forestall this necessity, the portion of the tax due on a closely held family business may be paid in installments over a fifteen-year period. Interest is charged on the balance due, with a special rate of only 4 percent on the first $1,000,000 of property.

An additional break is provided for family farms. Farmland may be valued for estate tax purposes according to its use value as farmland. The usual procedure is to capitalize the gross cash rental (net of property taxes) for comparable farmland. The new capitalization rate is the mortgage rate currently charged on new Federal Land Bank farm mortgages. The resulting valuation is likely to be well below the going market value, not only for land on the urban fringe, but for land in rural areas as well. This provision includes restrictions designed to limit its application to family farms operated by the owners. A recapture of some or all of the tax savings takes place if the farm is sold or converted to nonfarm use within 10 years. The purpose of the tax break is to make it easier for farm families to retain control of their enterprises as they pass from one generation to the next. The tax savings can be substantial owing to the rapid increase in farmland values during the past couple of decades.

ECONOMIC EFFECTS

There is no doubt that death and gift taxes affect the timing and the manner in which large wealth holdings are transferred. They may also affect the type of assets that investors hold. In particular, prudent estate planning may call for a switch to more liquid assets in anticipation of the need to pay estate taxes. In this way, death taxes have at least a marginal impact on the allocation of resources.

More uncertainty prevails over the extent to which death and gift taxes affect the aggregate level of saving and consumption. We have seen that, within the context of balanced-budget incidence, any tax can be expected to reduce private expenditures as it releases resources for public use. A more meaningful question is to ask how death and gift taxes affect the consumption-savings mix when compared with an equal-yield tax on income. The usual answer is that a death tax will reduce savings more than an income tax, because the death tax falls more heavily on accumulation (savings) than the income tax. A potential saver has an incentive to accumulate a smaller amount of wealth in order to hold down death and gift tax liability. Individuals with a strong desire to leave an estate of a given size to their heirs would be an exception. They would have to save and accumlate more to pass on an estate of a given size net of tax, but this type of behavior is not considered typical.

The effect of death and gift taxes on recipients is also somewhat unpredictable. Looked at as income, gifts and bequests are transitory in nature, and budget studies indicate that the marginal propensity to save is higher for transitory than for normal income. Thus, to the extent that death and gift taxes lower wealth transfers, they would appear to lower savings more than an income tax of equal yield. An offsetting effect may occur among households that expect to receive sizable wealth transfers in the future. They will have higher expected lifetime income and wealth holdings, and these prospects may cause them to consume more now than they otherwise would.

The consensus view is that death and gift taxes have a greater impact on saving, relative to consumption, than does an equal-yield income tax. Assuming that aggregate demand is maintained at a full-employment level independently of the savings-consumption mix, this would reduce investment and over time would lead to a smaller capital stock.

The federal estate tax allows an unlimited deduction for charitable bequests. Evidence cited in Chapter 8 indicates that the charitable deduction provision of the income tax is an effective device for encouraging high-bracket taxpayers to make contributions. A recent study by Michael J. Boskin indicates that the deduction provision of federal and state taxes on estates and inheritances has a similar effect on charitable bequests.[8]

The effect of the estate tax on charitable bequests can be separated into two components, the wealth effect and the price effect. The wealth effect is expected to have a negative impact on charitable bequests, since

[8]Michael J. Boskin, "Estate Taxation and Charitable Bequests," *Journal of Public Economics,* 5 (January–February 1975), 27–56.

the tax reduces the total amount of wealth available to be split between heirs and charity. The price effect increases charitable bequests, because the deduction provision reduces the cost of a marginal dollar bequeathed to charity by the amount $(1 - t)$, where t is the marginal estate tax rate.

Boskin's results are from an econometric analysis of a sample of federal estate tax returns for 1957 to 1959 and 1969. Results for both time periods show that the deductibility of contributions stimulated bequests to charity that were at least as great as the revenue losses to the Treasury. Among estates subject to the estate tax, the gain to charitable institutions exceeds revenue loss except for estates subject to the highest marginal rates. Boskin's results also confirm the expected negative wealth effect and positive price effect of the tax.[9]

Boskin finds another interesting parallel between the effect of the charitable deduction under the income and estate taxes. In both cases, contributions to educational, scientific, and welfare organizations are much more responsive to tax breaks than are contributions to religious organizations.[10]

If Boskin's estimates are accurate, educational, health, and scientific organizations and nonreligious charities would lose more in bequests than the government would gain in revenue if the charitable deduction were eliminated. Thus, the charitable deduction is an efficient instrument for encouraging the very wealthy to channel wealth into the nonprofit sector. As indicated, whether this is good social policy depends on whether one feels that the money can be allocated more efficiently by the wealthholders themselves or by government operating through the political process.

DEATH AND GIFT TAXES: AN EVALUATION

Death and gift taxes are justified primarily on equity grounds. They promote equality of opportunity, a form of horizontal equity, by limiting the amount of property that an individual can receive as a gift or bequest. By limiting large concentrations of wealth, they are presumed to contribute over time to a more equal distribution of income. Limits on concentrations of wealth can also serve to limit the concentration of political power that accompanies wealth. Finally, taxes on wealth transfers tap a source of tax-paying capacity that is not reached directly by the income tax.

We have no satisfactory measure of the degree to which estate, gift, and inheritance taxes contribute to a more equal distribution of economic welfare or political power in the United States. In light of the modest

[9]Ibid., pp. 40–49.
[10]Ibid., p. 52.

amount of revenue they yield, it is tempting to conclude that the effect is not very great. Prior to passage of the Economic Recovery Tax Act of 1981, the federal estate and gift tax yielded about 1 percent of federal tax revenue. As the provisions of the 1981 legislation become fully effective, even this modest share will decline. Total collections at the state level are less than $2 billion and account for 1.5 percent of state tax receipts. Because death taxes are applied to family wealth holdings no more than once a generation, they do not touch accumulations amassed by persons still living. Only a more frequent wealth or net worth levy would achieve that objective.

Voters and politicians in the United States have been reluctant to resort to heavy taxes on wealth transfers as a means of promoting equality. During the 1972 presidential campaign, a proposal by losing candidate George McGovern for a substantial increase in the tax on estates met with little enthusiasm, even among voters of modest means. Candidate Ronald Reagan, the winner in 1980, advocated elimination of the federal estate and gift tax. In spite of the urgings of egalitarians, Americans still generally hold sacred the right to own property and to transfer it to others through gift or bequest.

No evaluation of the role of gift and estate taxes should overlook allocational effects. Taxes paid after death might have less effect on behavior during life than other types of taxes, but they are likely to have some effect on the amount and uses of savings. In particular, they are more likely to reduce saving than most other taxes of equal yield. This is an important consideration in a country concerned about a sluggish rate of investment and growth. Another feature not to be overlooked is the extent to which the deduction for contributions encourages bequests to nonprofit organizations. The latter consideration is particularly important to people associated with universities, nonprofit cultural and scientific organizations, and health care institutions.

13

Social Insurance and Welfare

Over the past five decades, government has become increasingly involved in providing financial support for persons in need. Benefits are paid to households experiencing loss of income as a result of retirement, unemployment, or loss of breadwinner through death, disability, or desertion. More recently, federal programs have been added to cover much of the cost of medical care for the elderly, disabled, and poor. Many low-income families benefit from food stamps, federally subsidized housing, and energy emergency assistance.

These programs account for roughly one-third of all government expenditures. Annual outlays are well in excess of $300 billion. One program, social security, accounts for about half the total. The rapid growth in social spending that occurred during the 1960s and 1970s spawned mounting criticism.

Some taxpayers and politicians complain about the high cost of welfare and castigate undeserving welfare loafers and chiselers. Social critics are disturbed by the demeaning features of public assistance, the failure of rehabilitation programs, and the inadequacy of income maintenance payments to the poor. The call for ''welfare reform'' is heard from many quarters, but because of disagreement over what direction reform should take, little has been done to change the basic system.

In spite of concerns expressed by critics, the evidence indicates that over the past quarter of a century transfer programs have contributed significantly to the reduction of poverty in the United States. The data in Table 13–1 show the changes in poverty rates between 1959 and 1977. During this period of greatest expansion in government transfers, the percentage of families with cash incomes below the federally designated poverty level declined from 22.4 percent to 11.6 percent. If in-kind transfers such as food

TABLE 13–1   **Number and Percentage of U.S. Families with Money Incomes Below Poverty, 1959 and 1977**

	POVERTY COUNT (MILLIONS)			POVERTY RATE (PERCENTAGE)		
	ALL PERSONS	IN FAMILIES	INDIVIDUALS	ALL PERSONS	IN FAMILIES	INDIVIDUALS
1959						
All	39.5	34.6	4.9	22.4%	20.8%	46.1%
Head 65 and over	5.5	3.2	2.3	35.2	26.9	61.9
1977						
All	24.7	19.5	5.2	11.6	10.2	22.6
Head 65 and over	3.2	1.2	2.0	14.1	7.8	27.3

Source: U.S. Bureau of the Census, *Current Population Reports* (Washington, D.C.: Government Printing Office, March 1979), pp. 13–19.

stamps and medical care are taken into account, the 1977 percentage would be even lower (perhaps as low as 5 or 6 percent). Some of the reduction was due to economic growth, but most was due to expansion of government transfers.

Another striking contrast is the fall in poverty rates among the elderly. In 1959, more than a third of all families with a head aged 65 or over had a below-poverty income; by 1977, this percentage had dropped to 14.1 percent. The massive increases in social security benefits during that time period are a major cause. Indeed, the poverty rate for older persons living in family units is lower than that for the population as a whole. The rate remains relatively high for elderly individuals living alone, particularly among women. Since 1977, the reduction in poverty rates has ceased. The state of the economy coupled with a slowdown in the growth of welfare spending are the major causes.

In this chapter, we focus on the major categories of income maintenance. Noncash transfers, such as subsidized housing and food stamps, programs designed to help the poor become self-supporting through education and vocational training, and programs for veterans are considered briefly. Before examining the major programs in detail, we first consider the rationale for public transfers within the context of the public goods, public choice framework developed in Chapters 2 and 3.

THE THEORY OF INCOME TRANSFERS

Large sums of money are taxed away from those who earn it and are transferred to eligible recipients. No doubt many taxpayers part with their share grudgingly, but it does not follow that everyone required to finance income transfers does so unwillingly. Persons with higher incomes may get utility from the assurance that those unable to support themselves are guaranteed a minimal standard of living. In other words, support of transfers by those who pay may be voluntary and motivated by altruism.

If this is the case, why do we not leave income maintenance in the hands of private charity? One reason is that receipt of transfers by a needy family may be a source of satisfaction to many; there is an element of publicness involved. As we have seen, when publicness or jointness is involved, reliance on private market transactions will generally lead to an undersupply, as exemplified by education. If one donor gives to the poor voluntarily, the effect on relief of hardship is minute. If there are many persons who can be taxed to provide transfers to the poor, the overall effect may be substantial. Consequently, it may be preferable for affluent voters to support public transfers for the poor. Within limits both the taxpayers and recipients can be made better off.

Even if those with higher incomes have no compassion for the poor, they may still favor a government program of income maintenance as a form of insurance. Economic disaster can befall anyone, as many aerospace engineers found out in the 1970s. Hence, anyone who is potentially vulnerable may favor income maintenance as a form of insurance. Obviously, some of us feel more vulnerable than others, and this will be reflected in our political response.

Finally, persons with higher incomes may look upon transfers to the poor as a means of maintaining public safety and social stability. Lack of means to support their families may force some individuals to turn to crime in desperation. In such cases, an adequate income maintenance program serves as a deterrent to crime. Likewise, extreme inequality in the distribution of income and wealth is regarded as a likely stimulant to revolutionary activity. In both instances, the more privileged members of society may conclude that it is in their own selfish interest to support public assistance programs for the poor. If their motives are strictly selfish, however, the well-to-do will support transfers only if they are thought to be a more efficient means of protecting life and property than repression and punishment.[1]

The political process may be used to extend transfers beyond the level that those who pay would accept willingly. In fact the propertied class once opposed universal suffrage out of fear that the low-income majority would vote to divest the wealthy of their property. Some of the constitutional checks built into our system are a reflection of this concern.

---

[1]For a discussion of the insurance and protection motives for redistribution, see Geoffrey Brennan, "Pareto Desirable Redistribution: The Non-Altruistic Dimension," *Public Choice*, 14 (Spring 1973), 43–68. Analyses of the effect of welfare programs on crime and sedition remain speculative. According to a more cynical view, public transfers can provide disaffected individuals with the leisure time needed to plan crime or revolution.

There is no way to determine what proportion of public transfers are forced upon those who pay, but the vocal objections of some indicate a degree of dissatisfaction. Yet the existing disparity in well-being between rich and poor causes us to ask why the more numerous low- and middle-income voters have not used their political leverage to extract more from the rich. We offer no convincing answer. One explanation is that some in the lower-income groups aspire to wealth and are reluctant to obliterate their dream—a reverse twist on the income insurance concept. To many of the poor, however, the prospect of "making it" is likely to be too bleak to support such aspirations. Another explanation, developed by Anthony Downs in his pathbreaking work on an economic theory of democracy,[2] relates political influence to wealth. Because voters are only imperfectly informed on issues, programs, and parties, they are receptive to techniques of persuasion. Political persuasion requires use of the communications media, making political campaigning very expensive. Therefore, persons with wealth exert an influence on political candidates far out of proportion to their numbers. In this way, they discourage further redistribution from rich to poor.

Unfortunately, our existing models of social behavior are too incomplete to give us a thorough understanding of either the initial distribution of income or the redistribution that takes place through the public sector. The distribution of income before taxes and transfers depends on the distribution of ownership of factors of production (i.e., of property and marketable labor skills) and the functioning of markets for factor services. Redistribution depends on a complicated interaction of social institutions, political behavior, and the value judgments of citizens.

We turn now to a discussion of the major instruments of redistribution currently in use in the United States. They include social insurance, public assistance, veterans' benefits, and various forms of aid in kind.

SOCIAL INSURANCE

Extensive programs of social insurance are in effect in all advanced Western nations. Eligible persons receive protection against loss of income, and in a number of countries tax-financed medical services or government health insurance are available. The right to benefits may be earned by prior payment into a special fund, as exemplified by the U.S. social security system. Alternatively, benefits may be financed out of general tax revenue and made available to everyone regardless of economic status. The British national health service is an example of the latter. Tying of benefits to pre-

[2]Anthony Downs, *An Economic Theory of Democracy* (New York: Harper & Row, Publishers, 1957), pp. 236, 257–58.

vious contributions rather than to need or making them available to everyone removes the social stigma associated with public welfare. Thus, social insurance programs are generally looked upon with more favor by taxpayers, politicians, and recipients alike.

Social Security

The social security system is the dominant form of social insurance in the United States. It was created by the Social Security Act of 1935. Initially, the program covered wage earners in industry and trade, about 60 percent of the labor force. It now covers more than 90 percent of all workers, including most self-employed. Many of the remainder are covered by similar federal programs for federal civil service employees and railroad workers. Social security benefits are currently being paid to more than 35 million recipients.

The original program was limited to retirement benefits and unemployment insurance. Subsequent amendments have added benefits for survivors of deceased workers and for workers who are totally disabled. Health insurance under Medicare was added in 1965. Social security is collected via a payroll tax levied on both the employer and employee. Medicare receives supplemental funds from insurance premiums and general tax revenues.

OASDHI.   The system of old age, survivors, disability, and health insurance (OASDHI) is the cornerstone of the American system of social insurance. Benefit payments began in 1940; in 1950, they still totaled less than $1 billion. By 1965 (the year before Medicare payments began), outlays were $19 billion. Since then, growth has been phenomenal. Outlays exceeded $160 billion by 1983 and are expected to approach $200 billion by 1986.

Congress has been forced to raise the tax rate and extend the tax base repeatedly to maintain the solvency of the special trust funds out of which benefits are paid. The original act called for a payroll tax on employee and employer of 1 percent of the first $3,000 of earnings (for a maximum annual payment of $60 split equally between them). The tax rate and base remained at the original level until 1950, when the first of a series of periodic increases went into effect. By 1971, the tax rate on employer and employee had reached 5.2 percent and applied to the first $7,800 of annual earnings (for a maximum annual payment of $811.20). The ceiling on taxable earnings has risen every year since 1971. Under the 1977 social security amendments, the ceiling rose from $17,700 in 1978 to $29,700 in 1981. Since 1981, annual adjustments in the taxable ceiling have been tied to the rate of increase in taxable earnings. The ceiling is expected to exceed $42,000 by 1985. Total tax on employees with earnings at or above the taxable ceiling will then exceed $6,000, more than one hundred times the 1950 maximum. Rates have also continued to rise, and future increases are scheduled. The 1977 amendments set the combined rate on employer and employee at 13.4 percent for the years 1982 to 1984. It is scheduled to jump to 14.3 percent in 1986 and 15.3 percent after 1990. Self-employed persons are subject to the same taxable ceiling but are taxed at a rate equal to about 70 percent of the combined employer-employee rate.

At the time of enactment in 1977, it was thought that the rates and base ceilings set by the 1977 amendments would guarantee the solvency of the social security trust funds at least until the end of the century. Subsequent experience demonstrated that this expectation was overly optimistic, owing to the effect of high rates of unemployment and inflation on receipts and outlays of the funds.[3]

Social security was looked upon originally as a form of retirement insurance. Both employer and employee would pay into a worker's account in a special trust fund. The accumulated payments would be invested in U.S. government securities. Payments into a worker's account would determine the monthly benefits that the worker would receive after retirement.

At its inception, social security could have been established as an actuarially sound form of retirement insurance. Under such a system, the payments into a worker's account plus the accumulated interest on the account would equal the estimated benefits to be paid after retirement. Benefit estimates would be based on anticipated mortality rates. Even as originally enacted, social security was never so pure a form of insurance. The benefit formula has always contained a redistributive component. Benefits are related to a recipient's earnings history in covered employment, but the formula is tilted to provide a higher return on contributions to those with low than with high earnings. Subsequent legislation, beginning as early as 1939, has led to further departures from the insurance concept.

At present, social security is best described as a pay-as-you-go tax-transfer mechanism that taxes those who work and transfers approximately an equal amount to beneficiaries. Thus, if current taxes were to cease while benefits continue at present rates, the entire trust fund would be depleted in a few months. Participants in the program have no contractual right to receive payments, in contrast to annuities issued by private insurance companies. Political support for the program remains strong, however, precluding any abrupt termination of benefits.

As the expenditure trend just cited indicates, Congress has repeatedly raised benefits and extended coverage to new occupations. The impact of inflation on recipients of retirement incomes is a source of continual con-

---

[3]For a discussion of the short-run and long-run financing problems facing social security, see Dwight K. Bartlett, III, "Current Developments in Social Security Financing," *Social Security Bulletin,* 43 (September 1980), 10–20.

cern, but evidence indicates that increases in social security benefits since 1969 have outstripped inflation. Since 1975, recipients have received automatic increases in benefits to offset increases in the cost of living. In addition, Medicare helps to shield the elderly from the effects of rapidly rising medical costs.

Repeated liberalization of benefits and extension of coverage have continually weakened the link between benefits and prior contributions. The erosion of this link may mislead the public, but among critics of social security, it is a matter of concern chiefly to those who believe that individuals should have the right to opt out of social security and buy private insurance instead. Because of the redistributional effects built into the program, individuals with higher wage and salary income might be tempted to invest their employee and employer contributions in a private retirement program. Benefits to lower-income workers would be reduced, however, exposing them to the threat of more extreme poverty in their old age unless welfare payments from other sources were raised.

There is little opposition to forcing people to participate in some type of retirement program, private or public. If people are allowed to opt out of any contribution to a retirement program, some will do so and end up on the public dole without having contributed when they were working.

Reform proposals.   In the past, much of the criticism of social security centered on the payroll tax as a means of finance. The tax applies to wage and salary income below the taxable limit and allows no exemptions or deductions. It is therefore more of a burden on low-income and middle-income workers than on persons with high incomes. This feature has been attenuated in recent years with the rapid increase in the limit on taxable earnings. The payroll tax is also alleged to discriminate against two-earner families, since the earnings of both are taxed.

Although tax liability is split equally between employees and employers, the incidence depends on the supply and demand elasticities in the labor market. The employers' share adds to labor costs and is presumed to reduce aggregate demand for labor. Since aggregate labor supply is thought to be highly inelastic, it is usually agreed that most of the burden falls on workers in the form of lower wages.[4]

Some critics favor elimination of the payroll tax and the separate social security trust funds. They would be replaced by a social insurance program financed out of general revenue. In this way benefits could be financed by the income tax, which could be raised substantially in exchange for elimination of the payroll tax. Although a switch to general fund financing may make sense in terms of taxpayer equity, an attempt to make

[4]The view that labor bears the full burden of the payroll tax is defended in John A. Brittain, *The Payroll Tax for Social Security* (Washington, D.C.: The Brookings Institution, 1972). His analysis is questioned in Martin S. Feldstein, "The Incidence of the Social Security Payroll Tax: Comment," *American Economic Review*, 62 (September 1972), 735–38.

the shift might weaken public support for the program. The program was originally sold to the public as a form of social insurance in which beneficiaries earn the "right" to benefits on the basis of their prior contributions. Because of the strong public acceptance of the contribution principle, it is not likely that the payroll tax or trust funds will disappear.

It is possible, however, that some future Congress will choose to provide payroll tax relief by supplementing the trust funds with a transfer from general revenues. Several options have been suggested. The most modest calls for temporary general fund supplements when the unemployment rate exceeds a certain limit, say, 7 percent. This would relieve the squeeze that sometimes occurs during recessions. A second option would shift the health insurance program (about 20 percent of outlays) or the disability insurance program (about 10 percent of outlays) to general fund financing. A more ambitious change calls for an equal sharing with one-third of the funding coming from general revenues, employees, and employers.

The present method of financing social security does have one feature that makes it attractive to fiscal conservatives. The channeling of payroll tax revenue through special trust funds on a pay-as-you-go basis precludes Congress from financing benefit increases with budget deficits. Once the principle of general fund financing is accepted, this source of fiscal discipline would be undermined.

Another controversial feature of social security is the retirement test. This provision is designed to restrict benefit payments to potential beneficiaries who continue to work after age 65. Under provisions contained in a 1978 amendment, potential recipients aged 65 to 69 are allowed to draw full retirement benefits if they earn less than the earnings exemption. Benefits are reduced by 50 cents for each dollar of earnings above the exemption. (The exemption, set at $6,000 in 1982, is to be adjusted upward annually by a wage index after 1982.)[5] The earnings test is consistent with the original philosophy of social security. The program was intended to provide a partial source of earnings replacement when earnings cease because of death, disability, or retirement of a worker. If an individual continues to work beyond normal retirement age, there are no lost earnings to replace. Nevertheless, the earnings test is looked upon by many older workers as an undue constraint on their right to work. Receptive members of Congress have already relaxed the test. The major deterrent to its elimination has been the cost to the hard-pressed retirement trust fund, estimated at about $7 billion annually.

The continued rise in labor force participation by women has spawned new concerns about the original intent of the social security system. The creators of the system had in mind the needs of the traditional

---

[5]The retirement test formula causes benefits to drop to zero when earnings reach or exceed the exemption plus twice the annual benefit. For the average worker reaching age 65 in 1983, this figure is about $15,000. The retirement test is more strict for workers who exercise the option to retire on reduced benefits between ages 62 and 64.

family with a working husband, a nonworking wife, and dependent children. Thus, it provides for survivors' benefits in case of death of the worker. Retirement benefits include an allowance for an elderly dependent spouse or widow (or widower) of a covered worker.

If a wife works long enough to qualify for benefits on her own account (a maximum of forty quarters of covered employment), she may either draw benefits on her own account or draw dependent's benefits on her husband's accounts. Obviously, she will draw whichever benefit amount is larger. If the wife works during most or all of her adult life and has earnings roughly comparable to her husband's, she will draw more on her own account than as her husband's dependent. In this case, each spouse will draw from separate accounts (and neither will get dependent's benefits). If the wife worked only intermittently or if her earnings are far below her husband's, she will draw on his account and get no benefit from taxes paid into her account. Treatment of the spouses is reversed in cases where the husband works less or has much lower earnings than the wife.

Some proponents of women's rights have expressed concern over the treatment of women who are full-time housewives. They are eligible for spouse's benefits but never accumulate rights on their own account. The provision granting spouse's benefits to divorced persons who have been married to a covered worker for more than ten years represents one attempt to compensate housewives for the value of their services.

Various options exist for dealing with these perceived inequities. One alternative is to combine the accounts of husband and wife into a single account with benefits split equally. Another is to allow recipients to draw benefits from more than one account. As in the case of elimination of the earnings test, a major obstacle to the latter alternative is the additional cost that would be imposed on the system.[6]

Prospects for the future.   Most past and present social security beneficiaries have received a very favorable return on their payments into the system. During its early years, the number of workers paying into the system was large relative to the number receiving benefits. Until recently, Congress encountered little resistance to the tax increases needed to finance extension and liberalization of benefits. Now the situation is changing as the system reaches maturity. The payroll tax is the second most important source of federal revenue, with a yield more than twice that of the corporation income tax and two-thirds that of the individual income tax. Many families with low and middle incomes pay more in payroll tax than in any other tax, even if one counts only the employee share.

In spite of provision for continued rapid expansion in tax yield, there is growing concern that revenues will fall short of projected benefits unless

---

[6]For a discussion of the issues, see Marilyn R. Flowers, *Women and Social Security: An Institutional Dilemma* (Washington, D.C.: American Enterprise Institute, 1977).

additional revenue sources are found or benefits are scaled down. The squeeze is expected to become most severe after the year 2010 when the cohort born during the post–World War II baby boom begins reaching retirement age. If present demographic trends continue, the ratio of workers to beneficiaries will fall from the present 3 to 1 to about 2 to 1. These ratios are far below those of the 1950s and 1960s and are an inevitable result of the maturing of the system. One consequence is that for future retirees the return on previous payments into the system will be much lower (perhaps even negative) than for those who retired prior to 1980.

Long-range projections by Social Security Administration actuaries indicate that by the year 2030 social security, excluding Medicare, will absorb more than 16 percent of taxable earnings, compared with about 11 percent now. If Medicare (which now absorbs about 2.6 percent) is added, it is possible that social security will absorb as much as one-fifth of earnings. We cannot be certain that future generations of workers will be willing to allow themselves to be taxed at such levels.

Current and future funding problems reflect a change in the role of the program. The original intent was to create a system of retirement insurance that would provide retired workers and their dependents with an income floor. Additional support would come from private pensions, savings, interfamily transfers, and, where necessary, public welfare programs. The massive increases in benefit levels, particularly those enacted during the 1970s, have converted the program into the major source of retirement income for most beneficiaries. The 1977 amendments to the Social Security Act adopted a method of benefit calculation that will perpetuate the change in emphasis. Congress chose to tie benefit levels to increases in money wages by means of wage indexing. The effect of this procedure is to cause benefit payments to new retirees to increase at the same rate as earnings of workers. Assuming that labor productivity continues to grow, the real income of new retirees will increase over time at the same rate as the real income (before taxes) of those still working.

The present arrangement is a source of concern for several reasons. Most obvious is the tax burden that it will impose on future generations, particularly after the year 2010. As an alternative to reduction in scheduled benefits, there is growing support for a scheme to postpone the retirement age. Workers can now retire with full benefits at age 65 or with reduced benefits after age 62. Many workers opt for early retirement, even though monthly benefits are reduced (by up to 20 percent for those retiring when they reach age 62). The proposal receiving the most attention calls for raising the age for full benefits to 68 and the minimum age for reduced benefits to 65. If postponement of retirement is adopted, it would probably be phased in gradually and would not be set at 68 until the year 2000 or later.

Another concern is over the effect of social security on private saving and private pension plans. Private savings and pension funds are channeled into the capital markets where they contribute to capital formation and economic growth. Social security is a transfer system that finances the consumption of beneficiaries out of tax revenues. It seems reasonable to conclude that greater reliance on social security will reduce the level of private saving and investment, although this hypothesis has not been confirmed by the empirical evidence.[7] In addition, a government program lacks the flexibility that can be built into private pension plans. Social security is a product of the political system. It is intended to meet the needs of the majority and cannot be adapted easily to the needs of individuals in atypical situations or occupations.

Future Congresses and administrations will face the responsibility of reassessing the program, but they will not have the easy options available to their predecessors. Current members of the work force have accumulated obligations for future benefits. As we have seen, these obligations are not of a contractual nature, but politically they would be difficult to reduce.[8]

If high rates of inflation persist, any attempt to shift from social security to greater reliance on private pensions and savings will be undermined. Social security benefits are indexed against inflation. Government can provide this protection, because it finances benefits out of tax revenues that rise with prices and wages. It is not possible for the private sector to provide so secure an inflation hedge. Those who retired on fixed private pensions ten years ago have seen the purchasing power of this income source decline by more than half. Only if they are also drawing indexed benefits from social security or a similar government program are they likely to have avoided a substantial drop in their standard of living. If we as a society cannot bring inflation under control, we will be forced to rely on government transfers as the major source of retirement income.

Unemployment Insurance

Income maintenance during periods of temporary unemployment is provided for wage earners in covered industries through unemployment insurance (UI). The program is administered jointly by federal and state governments and is financed by a payroll tax on employers. The federal UI tax is levied at a rate of 3.4 percent on the first $6,000 of annual earnings (yielding a maximum of $204). Firms are allowed a credit for payment of

---

[7]Martin Feldstein attracted much attention with his startling estimate that social security depressed personal saving by 30 to 50 percent, but his results were shown to be the result of a computational error. See Martin Feldstein, "Social Security, Induced Retirement, and Aggregate Capital Accumulation," *Journal of Political Economy,* 82 (September 1974), 905–26. The error was exposed by Dean R. Leimer and Selig D. Lesnoy, "Social Security and Private Saving," a paper presented at the 93rd Annual Meeting of the American Economic Association, Denver, Colorado, September 1980.

[8]The political problems are described in Martha Derthick, "How Easy Votes on Social Security Came to an End," *The Public Interest,* 54 (Winter 1979), 94–105.

state UI tax of up to 2.7 percent of the tax paid on the first $6,000 of earnings (a maximum credit of $162). All states take full advantage of the credit, and nearly all have found it necessary to levy taxes in excess of the credit amount. Benefits to unemployed workers are paid out of earmarked state trust funds.

Firms with below-average rates of unemployment are granted tax reductions. The reductions serve to place more of the tax burden on firms that create more unemployment. In a sense, unemployment is treated as an externality and the UI payroll tax as a corrective. This arrangement is called *experience rating.* It assigns some of the social cost of unemployment to firms and industries with the highest incidence of unemployment and gives firms with poor ratings an incentive to seek ways to reduce layoffs.[9]

The UI program is characterized by considerable interstate differences in weekly benefits. Payments are a function of previous wages. The reduction in income is supposed to be large enough to encourage recipients to look for new jobs. Because unemployment benefits are exempt from most income and all social security taxes, however, the reduction in income is overstated if unemployment benefits are compared with gross wages. In some cases, work disincentive is a cause for concern.[10] Those who remain unemployed may draw benefits for a minimum of twenty-six weeks. Some states extend the period beyond the minimum or provide automatic extension to thirty-six weeks when unemployment of covered workers exceeds specified levels.

INCOME-CONDITIONED TRANSFERS

Social insurance programs are designed to serve the general population. Eligibility for benefits is derived from previous labor force participation and is dependent on such eligibility criteria as age, disability, or temporary unemployment. Welfare programs, in contrast, are designed to assist those who lack the earning capacity and wealth needed to provide themselves with socially acceptable minimal living standards.

The task of providing income supplements to families with inadequate

[9]Evidence indicates that even in states that make the greatest use of experience ratings, the practice does not assign the full cost of UI to firms with high unemployment rates. For a discussion of the issues, see Joseph M. Becker, *Unemployment Insurance Financing* (Washington, D.C.: American Enterprise Institute, 1981), pp. 63–87.

[10]See Martin Feldstein, "Unemployment Compensation: Adverse Incentives and Distributional Anomalies," *National Tax Journal,* 27 (June 1974), 231–44. Since this article was written, unemployment compensation has become subject to the federal income tax for certain higher-income workers, as described in Chapter 8.

resources seems simple enough. It would appear to call for a properly designed system of transfers that would boost the incomes of all households up to some target level. To do so, however, requires transfers that are income conditioned. In other words, welfare benefits paid to each family must be dependent on income that the family receives from other sources. The difficulty with this arrangement is that the family can increase welfare benefits by reducing its income from other sources. Earnings, or income from work, are generally considered most vulnerable to the disincentive effects of income-conditioned transfers.

Work-disincentive effects provide a serious challenge to designers of transfer programs. If welfare benefits discourage people from working, the program may fail to achieve the goal of improving economic well-being. Much or all of the gain in income from the transfer will be offset by a fall in earnings. Recipients will become more dependent on government and will lose any benefits gained from work force attachment.

Two options are available to policy makers for countering the work disincentive effects of welfare transfers. One is to force able-bodied adult recipients to work in order to qualify for benefits. Payments are made contingent on acceptance of a job. If no job is available, the recipient is required to accept a public service job. The other option is to design a welfare benefit structure that tempers the work-disincentive effect. The latter option is exemplified best by the negative income tax.

A full-fledged negative income tax, or NIT, has never been adopted, but some of its basic features have been incorporated into existing programs. For this reason, and because of the way in which it treats work disincentives, a discussion of the NIT serves as a useful prelude to an examination of existing welfare programs.

Negative Income Tax

Among the various proposals for welfare reform, the negative income tax has attracted the most attention. A properly designed and administered NIT would concentrate payments where they are most needed in a way that does not discriminate among different classes of poor. By basing benefits on a standard formula, it would free recipients from the capricious demands of the welfare bureaucracy and eliminate the large geographical spread in benefit levels. In fact, according to Milton Friedman, who is usually credited with popularizing the idea, the NIT could replace the "grab bag" of existing programs and enable us to dismantle the entire welfare bureaucracy.[11]

[11]The literature on the negative income tax is now voluminous. Major seminal works include Milton Friedman, *Capitalism and Freedom* (Chicago: University of Chicago Press, 1962), pp. 190–95; and Christopher Green, *Negative Taxes and the Poverty Problem* (Washington, D.C.: The Brookings Institution, 1967).

Conceptually, the NIT is simple. Each family unit is entitled to a basic allowance that varies with family size. If the family receives no income from other sources, it keeps the entire allowance, which becomes a guaranteed minimum income. For each dollar of other income that the family receives, its basic allowance is reduced by a fraction of a dollar as determined by the NIT rate schedule. Thus, a family with other income will have more total income than will a family of identical composition that has no other income.

These relationships can be shown by a simple formula if it is assumed that the marginal tax rate, that is, the reduction in allowance that results from a $1 increase in income, is a constant.

Let

B = basic allowance
Y = earnings
t = tax rate (applied to earnings up to break-even level)
P = net payments

Then,

$$P = B - tY$$

If $Y = 0$, then $P = B$, the full basic allowance. Setting $P = 0$, we can solve for Y_b, the break-even income or minimum income at which NIT payments cease:

$$Y_b = \frac{B}{t}$$

To illustrate, suppose that $B = \$5,000$ and $t = 0.5$. We get the following combinations of allowance income, other income, and total income:

Y	P	Y+P
$ 0	$ 5,000	$ 5,000
2,500	3,750	6,250
5,000	2,500	7,500
7,500	1,250	8,750
10,000[a]	0	10,000

[a]Break-even income.

The relationships among program parameters are shown in Figure 13–1. The basic allowance is shown by OB on the income axis. Net payments are represented by the vertical distance between line segment BC and line OL. They fall to zero at the break-even level of earnings, Y_b. The NIT tax rate is measured by the ratio CD/BD.

Our simple example hides some serious practical difficulties that must

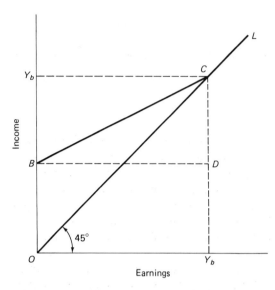

FIGURE 13–1   **Negative income tax (NIT).** If the earnings are the only source of income, the earnings-income locus is represented by the 45° line *OL*. The maximum NIT benefit for an individual with zero earnings is represented by *OB* on the income axis. With a constant NIT tax rate, benefits decline to zero at the break-even income Y_b. Total income, equal to earnings plus benefits, is represented by the line *BCL*.

be faced if a national NIT is to be implemented. For example, we assumed that all income counts against the basic allowance. Contrast this to the many exclusions and deductions allowed in determining taxable income under the individual income tax. Doubtless, we would want a broader definition of income for NIT purposes than for ordinary income taxation, but it is not clear how broad. Social policy objectives and administrative feasibility must be considered.

Of greater import is the conflict among income, incentive, and cost goals. The disincentive effect is of particular concern. As with the income tax, the marginal tax rate reduces net wages and lowers the price of leisure, encouraging the worker to substitute leisure for work. Unlike the income tax, the income effect of the transfer also discourages work. Several government-financed experiments were undertaken in the 1970s to test the magnitude of the work-disincentive effects of a variety of NIT formulas. The results indicate modest reductions in work effort for men and more substantial reductions for married women.[12] The same disincentive effect is present in any income-conditioned program.

[12]Albert Rees and Harold Watts, "An Overview of the Labor Supply Results," in J. A. Pechman and P. M. Timpane, eds., *Work Incentives and Income Guarantees* (Washington, D.C.: The Brookings Institution, 1975), pp. 60–87.

If the NIT is to eliminate poverty, the basic allowance must be at least as high as the poverty line. If work disincentives are to be tempered, the marginal rate must not be too high; but a low t and a high B can lead to a high break-even income. Returning to our example, if $B = \$5,000$ (below the federal poverty line for all but single-person families) and $t = 0.5$, break-even income, Y_b, is $10,000. Fifty percent is a high marginal tax rate that might have serious disincentive effects. Lowering t to $33\frac{1}{3}$ percent will raise Y_b to $15,000 and entitle many more families to benefits. If the marginal tax rate is to be kept at t, it would be necessary to relieve eligible families from all other taxes based on income, including federal and state income taxes and the social security payroll tax. The net result would be a substantial increase in the cost of the welfare program coupled with a reduction in the number of households paying taxes.

The definition of the family unit and the timing of income are among the other troublesome features of the NIT. We have discussed these problems in connection with the personal income tax, and they are similar in nature under the NIT. The timing problem could be more crucial for families with limited resources, however, if there is a long lag between a drop in income and receipt of transfer payments.

The practical problems of implementing some form of NIT would be most serious if the plan were to encompass all families whose income is temporarily or permanently below the poverty level. An all-inclusive program would simplify our welfare system and narrow the scope of administrative discretion, but the benefits of uniformity may not be worth the cost. For persons who cannot work, the various devices for overcoming the disincentive effects are unnecessarily cumbersome. If we retain unemployment compensation, the timing probelm becomes less urgent. Perhaps the NIT approach would be most useful if it were limited to families with employable heads. It could provide an income supplement to the working poor—the group most often denied cash benefits under existing welfare programs—without overlapping social insurance and public assistance programs directed at persons who are unable to work.

Wage Supplement

The wage supplement proposal represents an attempt to attain the goals of the NIT without as strong a work disincentive. It calls for a government subsidy to the hourly wages of low-wage workers. The subsidy would be highest for workers with the lowest wage rates. As rates increase, the subsidy would be reduced by a fraction of the increase up to a cutoff level. Because the subsidy would increase the hourly earnings of eligible workers, it would have the same effect on work effort as an increase in market wages. The income effect would discourage work, but the substitution effect, by making leisure more expensive, would encourage work. The net effect cannot be predicted *a priori*.

The wage supplement is superior to the NIT with respect to work incentives, but it has other features that make it less attractive. Unlike the NIT, payments are determined by a worker's wage rate, not family income. Some payments are likely to go to families not in need of income maintenance. Examples include families with more than one earner, especially if teenagers living with parents are eligible. The supplement would be difficult to calculate for self-employed or for persons working in family businesses. There is some fear that employers would respond by paying lower wages, although their ability to do so would be constrained by labor market conditions. Finally, the program provides benefits only to those with jobs. Other programs would be needed for those unable to work or to find employment.

PUBLIC ASSISTANCE PROGRAMS

The general category of public assistance encompasses a variety of programs that provide needy families with income support and social services. Recipients must apply for assistance and demonstrate through a "means test" that they lack the financial resources needed to maintain a socially acceptable living standard.

Public assistance or "welfare" began in this country as a responsibility of local governments, and much of the responsibility remains at that level today. The American system is modeled after an English system that evolved out of the Elizabethan poor laws. Bruno Stein identifies the goals of the Anglo-American system as combining financial support and social services for the deserving poor with pressure for maximum labor force participation and for holding down welfare costs.[13]

In most states, public assistance is administered by county or municipal welfare agencies under the supervision of state agencies. In the others, the program is administered by the state through local offices. Federal participation began with passage of the Social Security Act of 1935, which introduced federal matching funds for aid to select categories of welfare clients. The cost is thus generally shared by the three levels of government. Cash transfers are supplemented by a variety of benefit-in-kind programs, including subsidized medical care, food, housing, and energy assistance.

Categorical Assistance

The federally subsidized categorical programs included old age assistance (OAA) and aid to the needy blind (AB), the permanently and totally

[13]Bruno Stein, *On Relief* (New York: Basic Books, Inc., 1971), pp. 43–48.

disabled (APTD), and families with dependent children (AFDC). The so-called "adult categories"—OAA, AB, and APTD—were federalized in 1974 and combined into the Supplemental Security Income (SSI) program. New minimum benefit levels exceeding those set by most states were put into effect with full federal funding. A number of states, however, still continue to supplement federal SSI payments. The SSI program provides basic income support for the needy aged and disabled not covered by social security. Social security recipients whose benefits are deemed inadequate are eligible for supplemental payments. Like social security, SSI benefits are indexed to protect recipients against inflation.

The AFDC program is the largest of the categorical cash grant programs. It was envisioned originally as a source of support for widows with dependent children, but a majority of recipient families are headed by women who are separated, divorced, or were never married. The cost of AFDC is shared by the federal and state-local governments. The federal share ranges from 50 to 65 percent, depending on the income level of the state. The state-local split is subject to considerable interstate variation.

Federal regulations allow extension of benefits to families headed by able-bodied unemployed males, but only about half the states have added this option. In the remaining states, an unemployed father is forced to desert his family if its members are to become eligible for AFDC. For this reason, AFDC is blamed for bringing about family disintegration and worsening the economic condition of families it is supposed to help.

Americans traditionally emphasize self-reliance and the work ethic, an attitude that accounts in part for the social stigma associated with welfare. A strong work disincentive is built into AFDC benefit schedules, however, in seeming contradiction to our basic attitudes. This is a result of changes introduced in the Budget Reconciliation Act of 1981. Prior to passage of this legislation, states were required to disregard a portion of household earnings in calculating monthly benefits. The earnings "disregards," as they were called, were prescribed in the "30 and ⅓" rule. AFDC families could earn up to $30 per month without a loss of benefits; they could also keep one-third of all earnings in excess of $30. In effect, this meant that benefits could decline only two-thirds of a dollar for each additional dollar earned. (Note the similarity to a negative income tax with $t = 0.67$.)

Since 1981, families have been allowed these disregards only for the first four months in which they have earnings. After that, benefits are cut by a dollar for each dollar of earnings. As long as earnings are below the benefit cutoff, the effective tax rate is 100 percent (or the equivalent of $t = 1$ under a negative income tax)[14]

Federal law allows AFDC families to deduct some work-related ex-

---

[14]AFDC families are not likely to be faced with income tax liabilities. Without the earned income tax credit, described in Chapter 8, the social security payroll tax would push the marginal rate above 100 percent for many working families on AFDC rolls.

penses and child-care costs from earnings before benefits are calculated. The 1981 Budget Reconciliation Act imposed stricter limits on these deductions, however, adding to work disincentives. These changes represent a clear break with policies in effect since the 1960s. AFDC no longer resembles the negative income tax, nor can it be regarded as a form of income supplement for the working poor.

The intent of these changes is to cut welfare costs by limiting benefits to recipients who cannot work. The attempt is likely to fail, however, because the dollar-for-dollar cut in benefits destroys the incentive to work. Only if welfare agencies are able to force employable members of welfare families to work will the new approach succeed.

In an effort to overcome the disincentive effects of AFDC, the work-incentive (WIN) program is in effect in most areas. It requires beneficiaries over age 16 to register for work training or employment programs to be eligible for benefits. Recipients who are full-time students, are disabled, or are needed at home to care for children under age 6 or for incapacitated family members are exempt. A major obstacle to success of the WIN program is the lack of suitable jobs for participants. A few localities have experimented with "workfare," under which AFDC recipients "earn" benefits by working in various public sector service jobs. In spite of evidence that workfare has not been very successful, it remains a popular concept among some advocates of welfare reform. Workfare is likely to receive more emphasis as a result of the recent changes in federal law.

Academicians are often critical of the way in which local welfare agencies administer the welfare program. Each family declared eligible for assistance is assigned to a caseworker who is supposed to visit the family periodically. The caseworker is to assess family needs, provide counseling on family problems, and make sure that the family is not violating any of the eligibility rules. The practice of combining the roles of counselor and enforcer of regulations is alleged to undermine the family's confidence in the caseworker. The social work philosophy, which favors much latitude to allow the caseworker to tend to each family's specific needs, may also lead to undue agency interference in the life style of the family. The effectiveness of caseworkers is eroded further by heavy case loads and inadequate training and experience. Only a minority of caseworkers have had training in social work, and low pay and other features of the job lead to high turnover.

Perhaps the most damaging weakness of all is the lack of uniformity among states in eligibility and benefit levels. Aside from falling into one of the eligible categories, applicants must demonstrate through a "means test" that their income and net worth are low enough to qualify for assistance. Once the family becomes eligible, benefit levels range from about $100 to more than $500 per month for a family of four—differences far in excess of differentials in cost of living.

General Assistance

Needy families and individuals who do not fit into the four federally subsidized categories are forced to apply for general assistance (GA). The GA programs are financed fully by state and local governments and are administered by their welfare agencies. In some states, GA provides income supplements for the working poor; in others, it is limited to emergency relief available only to those in dire need. For those who qualify, benefit levels are roughly comparable to those paid under AFDC with interstate differences of comparable magnitude.

BENEFITS IN KIND

Cash transfers are only one way in which the living standards of the poor can be improved. An alternative is aid in kind, guaranteeing a minimal provision of basic necessities such as food, shelter, and medical care. These necessities can be provided free of charge, or their cost to low-income families can be reduced through subsidies. Defenders of aid in kind argue that society in general benefits when everyone is guaranteed an adequate diet, decent housing, and adequate medical care. In technical terms, they are arguing that there is a public good component associated with private consumption of acceptable levels of life's basic necessities and that, without a public subsidy, some households would not attain these levels.

Government subsidies may be used as devices to increase the supply of certain goods to low-income families. Examples include low-income housing, hospitals, and clinics. Public funds may also help families of modest means to meet the burden of extraordinary outlays such as major medical bills or the cost of post high school education for their children.

The principle of granting benefits in kind, however, is not without critics. If the public sector gives a family aid in kind instead of an equivalent amount in dollars, it is accused of interfering with the family's right to consumer choice. The family would rather have $100 in cash than in food stamps, because with cash it could still buy $100 worth of food; but it could spend a part or all of the $100 on other things if that is its preference. The weakness in this argument is that it fails to account for the public good aspect of consumption of necessities. If voters are more willing to vote to have themselves taxed to provide needy persons with necessities than with cash, the alternative for the needy family may be $100 in food stamps or $50 in cash. Given this choice, it is not at all clear that the family would prefer the cash.

A shortcoming of some forms of aid in kind is the failure of the public to provide services to everyone who meets the income test. This is often true in the case of subsidized housing for the poor. Authorities must then resort to some form of rationing, and inequities in the treatment of the poor are an inevitable result.

Finally, it must be remembered that income-related aid in kind can have disincentive effects. A reduction in aid that is tied to marginal increases in income discourages work effort in the same way as does a reduction in cash transfers. A point that should not be overlooked by policy makers is that, while the disincentive effects of any one program may not be great, the combined effect of several may be substantial. A study by Henry Aaron indicates that this problem is already serious and that it could get worse if more income-conditioned subsidies are adopted.[15] A related difficulty occurs when eligibility for benefits ceases once income reaches some upper limit. The purpose of the upper limit is to deny benefits to those who presumably need no assistance, but for families within a few dollars of the limit, it can mean that a few more dollars of income may cost them many dollars worth of aid in kind. This is the equivalent of a marginal income tax of over 100 percent. Aside from the disincentive effect, it creates an incentive to families so affected to try to hide a portion of their income.

Turning to specific programs of aid in kind, the most important are for food, housing, and medical care. The food stamp program extends the broadest coverage. Eligibility standards are uniform throughout the country. The stamp allotment varies inversely with family income and size. A notable feature of the program is the large number of working poor eligible for benefits.

Federally subsidized housing for low-income families dates back to the Public Housing Act of 1937, which established the public housing program. The goal of this and subsequent legislation is to hold housing costs for the poor to a maximum of 25 percent of family income. In many communities, especially in urban areas, it is not possible to provide decent housing to low-income families within this guideline. Heavy federal subsidies allow local public housing authorities to provide publicly owned dwelling units to low-income families, including many welfare families, at rents that they can afford. Since only the poor are eligible to live in public housing, the inhabitants are plagued by many of the problems characteristic of low-income neighborhoods in general. As a result, the quality of life in public housing projects is sometimes notably unpleasant, and critics have begun to question the feasibility of this solution to the housing problem.

In recent years, the federal government has begun experimenting with new ways of providing housing for the disadvantaged. These include subsidized mortgages for private landlords who rent to low-income families at below market rates and rent supplements, under which the government

---

[15]Henry J. Aaron, *Why Is Welfare So Hard to Reform?* (Washington, D.C.: The Brookings Institution, 1973).

picks up a part of the rental fee. The rent supplement is potentially the most revolutionary approach, because it allows low-income families to move into middle-class neighborhoods with better schools and amenities and better proximity to job opportunities. Rent supplements were introduced as part of the Johnson administration's "War on Poverty," but limited funding and other constraints have prevented them from having much impact on the housing problems of the poor.

The federal government has been subsidizing middle-income homeowners for years through FHA and VA mortgage insurance that insures lenders against default, thereby reducing mortgage costs to the homeowner. More recently, the government introduced an interest subsidy that reduces the cost of home ownership for eligible low-income families. Eligibility standards are strict, but present levels of funding make it possible to satisfy the demand of only a fraction of the families who qualify.

For years, the medical needs of the poor were financed out of state and local welfare budgets or through the charity of hospitals and physicians. The federal contribution was included in federal matching grants to state and local welfare agencies. The Medicaid program was introduced in 1965, along with Medicare, to provide separate funding of medical care for the poor. Medicaid is the most costly of all welfare programs. It is financed jointly by federal and state governments and is administered by the welfare agencies. Persons receiving SSI and AFDC are automatically eligible for Medicaid benefits, and some states have extended coverage to other low-income families. As with public assistance, the individual states are allowed to set benefit and eligibility standards. As one would expect, interstate differences are substantial.

Education and Vocational Training

The tax-transfer and aid-in-kind programs discussed thus far provide immediate income support and other assistance to recipients. Other government programs are directed toward longer-term solutions to the poverty problem. A detailed discussion of these programs is beyond the scope of this book, but a brief account may help to present a more complete picture of social policy in the United States.

One way in which to deal with poverty is to invest in education and vocational training that increase the value of marketable labor skills. Economists call this "investment in human capital." The underlying philosophy—helping people to help themselves—is politically appealing, and the major thrust of Lyndon Johnson's "War on Poverty" was in this direction. Among the policy instruments that have been used are federal aid to school districts with large enrollments of pupils from low-income families, the Head Start program of remedial education for preschoolers from disadvantaged homes, and programs such as the Job Corps that provided vocational training for teenagers. Programs also exist for adults in need of vocational training and upgrading.

VETERANS' BENEFITS

Virtually all federal programs for veterans or their dependents and survivors are administered by the Veterans Administration (VA). Some of the benefits are unrelated to the income or financial status of the recipient. These include pensions to retired career and reserve personnel, payments to war orphans, and monthly payments for service-connected disabilities. In some cases, the disability undoubtedly reduces earning capacity, but the payments are made even if earning capacity is obviously not affected. Veterans are eligible for free medical treatment for ailments contracted while in service, but a means test is applied to admission to VA hospitals for treatment of other illnesses.

Aged veterans without adequate income from other sources may qualify for special pensions. Coverage may be extended to dependents and survivors. Thus, veterans' benefits are a form of delayed compensation for persons who served in the armed forces. Only to a limited degree can they be regarded as a form of welfare, but one study shows that about half the cash benefits go to families with pretransfer income below the poverty level.[16]

Effectiveness of Existing Programs

The American system of welfare is said to be degrading to recipients, inimical to work effort and self-reliance, badly administered, and too expensive. Differences in benefit levels and eligibility requirements result in substantial horizontal inequities in treatment of the needy, and many of the poor receive no benefits whatsoever.

In spite of its weaknesses, the social insurance and public assistance system does redistribute a sizable amount of income (roughly 15 percent of GNP). As the data in Table 13–1 indicate, the United States has experienced a substantial reduction in the poverty rate since 1959. Government programs do lift many families out of the poverty category, and they provide more than half the income of the posttransfer poor. Within the low-income population, however, the distribution of benefits is notably uneven. Among the least likely to receive aid are the working poor.

Not all recipients of government transfers are poor. The percentage of dollars going to the poor is highest for the means-tested cash public assis-

[16]Benjamin Bridges, Jr., "Redistributive Effects of Transfer Payments Among Age and Economic Status Groups," Staff Paper No. 10 (Washington, D.C.: Social Security Administration, Office of Research and Statistics, 1971), p. 15.

SSI = Cash
AFDC = Law

tance programs (SSI, AFDC, GA). One study estimates that 87 percent of benefits go to the poor. As expected, the percentages are much lower for social insurance programs such as OASDI (58 percent) and Medicare (48 percent).[17] Given the different nature of the various programs, such results are to be expected.

SUMMARY

Social insurance and public assistance are the major components of the American system of income maintenance. The social security system is the dominant form of social insurance. It provides retirement, disability, and survivors' benefits for workers in covered employment. Eligibility is established through labor force participation. Benefits are financed through a payroll tax. Since 1966, social security has provided hospital and subsidized medical insurance for persons over 65.

Public assistance is financed and administered jointly by federal, state, and local governments. The federal government provides basic cash transfers for the needy aged, blind, and disabled under the Supplemental Security Income program. The federally subsidized AFDC program provides cash transfers to needy families with dependent children. Pensions are provided for indigent veterans. Needy persons outside these categories generally are not eligible for federally assisted cash transfers, but they may qualify for general assistance programs funded wholly by state or local governments.

Low-income families may qualify for aid in kind in the form of food stamps, medical care, housing subsidies, and various training and educational grants. Aid in kind can be used to guarantee minimum consumption of necessities for all families regardless of income, but with the possible exception of food stamps, such universal availability is far from being achieved.

The proliferation of income-conditioned programs of cash and noncash transfers has created a potentially serious disincentive problem for poor persons who can work. Even if no cash transfers are involved, additional earnings may be offset by reduction or total loss of subsidies for food, housing, education, and medical care. In some states, the problem is compounded by loss of property or sales tax relief. Greater coordination of income-conditioned transfers at federal and state levels is clearly desirable.

[17]Robert D. Plotnick and Felicity Skidmore, *Progress Against Poverty* (New York: Academic Press, Inc., 1975), p. 178.

14

Public Debt

During national emergencies such as war, Americans have accepted the inevitability of public indebtedness. Our first century of history demonstrates this. The federal government assumed the various state government debts incurred in waging the revolution against England. During the Civil War, national debt increased from less than $100 million in 1860 to more than $2.6 billion in 1865. More than $200 billion of our current national debt accumulated during World War II. Over the years', there has also been a willingness to use government debt in constructing capital facilities. Typically, these are long-term projects that yield benefits over an extended period of time. Since the beneficiaries include persons living in future, it is sometimes regarded as only fair that they too contribute something toward the cost of capital facilities.

At times, however, the national debt has become a highly charged, emotional issue. Some persons regard a large national debt as a threat to everything from the economic system itself to our moral fibre. Periodic congressional debates over the legal "debt ceiling" are spirited, drawing considerable attention to our national debt and encouraging visions of America enslaving future generations with burdens unjustly imposed. In any event, our large public indebtedness is likely to be with us for a long time to come.

PUBLIC INDEBTEDNESS OF
THE FEDERAL GOVERNMENT

Generally, the term "national debt" refers to the indebtedness of the federal government. There are many reasons for distinguishing carefully between federal and state-local debt. One reason is that state-local debt is incurred mainly to finance specific public investment projects. There are notable exceptions. For example, both the Louisiana Purchase and the Panama Canal were financed with the receipts from bonds issued for those particular ventures.

The reasons for federal government indebtedness are generally quite different from explicitly financing particular capital undertakings. Usually, federal debt is issued simply because higher taxes are not acceptable, or it is issued (or retired) because of stabilization reasons. During World War II, for example, the government relied upon a civilian labor force for the high rate of production required. Personal income tax rates were increased and the base broadened. Taxes were not raised sufficiently to finance the war fully, however. Raising taxes to that level might have reduced the work effort of the civilian labor force. In other words, the supply of labor might have decreased. This effect of higher taxes would have conflicted with the national intent to increase the supply of labor by inducing women to enter the labor force and encouraging overtime work. The decision, therefore, was to cover federal expenditures only in part with tax revenues and to make up the difference with the proceeds from issuing bonds.[1]

Federal debt is also incurred because of fluctuations in economic activity. The debt may be planned or unplanned. The Employment Act of 1946 declared that the federal government would use "all practicable means" to promote "maximum employment, production, and purchasing power." Among the practicable means is debt. A budgetary deficit, with the difference between expenditures and tax revenues financed with debt, may be planned to stimulate the economy. At times, however, budgetary revenues may fall short of budgetary expenditures because of an unexpected downturn in economic activity. Under such circumstances, there would be an unplanned increase in debt.

Our national debt consists of securities issued by the U.S. Treasury. The amount of national debt has grown tremendously since 1900. Periods of social disturbances, particularly the Great Depression and World War II, were periods of rapidly increasing national indebtedness. During the 1930s, debt more than doubled, rising from $16 billion in 1930 to $43 billion in 1940. It rose to $269 billion by 1946, when World War II ended. In the 1980s, after three decades of hot and cold wars and a hot- and cold-running economy, the nation's debt went over the $1 trillion mark.

The relative significance of the national debt can be expressed in a number of ways, but none truly provides an adequate measure. National debt per capita, for example, invites an analogy with individual private debt. By the early 1980s, the federal government owed more than $5,000

---

[1]A major consequence of this decision was that consumer demand exceeded supplies of consumer goods available at government controlled prices. Nonprice rationing had to be used to allocate resources and to distribute output. Such rationing had disincentive effects on work effort, but not as great as raising taxes even further would have had.

for every man, woman, and child in the United States. The analogy ignores earning capacity as a measure of ability to carry indebtedness, however. National debt as a percentage of GNP, on the other hand, at least gives us some sense of the capacity to carry debt. In other words, it gives some perspective of the burdensomeness of servicing and amortizing the national debt. The ratio of national debt to GNP was well above unity by the end of World War II but declined from 1946 until it flattened out at about one-third in the 1970s.

Another way of getting some sense of the ability or capacity to carry debt is to focus on the interest costs only and to relate these charges to GNP. Interest charges on the federal government's debt have increased tremendously, particularly in the 1970s, when the amount rose from $20 billion in 1970 to $65 billion in 1979. However, the annual interest charge is only about 3 percent of GNP. Basically, the interest charges are paid with revenues raised from taxation of incomes. If GNP is taken as an indication of incomes and the ability to carry debt, then the relative burdensomeness of servicing the debt has not increased significantly since World War II. It rose from about 2 percent in 1950 to about 3 percent in the early 1980s. It rose because interest-bearing debt grew faster than the economy.

The Types of Interest-Bearing Treasury Notes

The public debt of the federal government is the sum of federal securities issued by the U.S. Treasury. Almost all the public debt is interest bearing. Basically, there are two kinds of issues, special and public. The special issues are securities issued to public enterprises and trust funds. The social security trust fund, the federal employees' retirement fund, and the unemployment insurance trust fund all have invested in special issues.[2] Public issues are marketable and nonmarketable securities held by U.S. government agencies and trust funds, Federal Reserve banks, and private investors such as commercial banks, mutual savings banks, insurance companies, nonfinancial corporations, savings and loan associations, state and local governments, and individuals.

Marketable securities include bills, notes, and bonds. "Marketable" means that an owner can convert these securities into cash by selling them in an established secondary market. The federal government itself does not redeem such securities before maturity, and it does not guarantee bond prices. Therefore, marketable securities are risky. If an investor chooses to convert a bond into cash prior to its maturity date, a capital loss might be suffered if rising interest rates have depressed bond prices below face value.

---

[2]U.S. government agencies and trust funds also hold public issues.

The main difference between bills, notes, and bonds is maturity. Treasury bills have a maturity of one year or less. Usually, they are issued with maturities of twelve months, but the maturities are as short as three months. Treasury bills are sold at weekly auctions in $10,000 denominations. They are sold at a discount and pay no interest. The investor's return is the appreciation in value to maturity. Treasury notes have a maturity of one to ten years, and bonds more than ten years. In contrast to bills, both notes and bonds have a coupon rate of interest. The Treasury does not sell either notes or bonds at auction. The Treasury announces the price, coupon rate, and length to maturity of notes and bonds, and then invites the public to subscribe on or before the date of issue. Interested buyers generally subscribe through a commercial bank or a brokerage house. If the Treasury misjudges the market for an issue, then the issue will be oversubscribed or undersubscribed. If the issue is oversubscribed, purchasers receive prorated shares. If the issue is undersubscribed, the Federal Reserve System will maintain an orderly market by purchasing the remainder.

Nonmarketable issues can be held only by the initial buyer. Mainly, these securities are special issues for government agencies and are held by various trust funds of the federal government. They are also held by state and local governments and by foreign governments. The familiar Series E savings bond is a nonmarketable issue. Savings bonds are sold to individuals. The U.S. government guarantees an interest return on these bonds if held to (or beyond) maturity. If a savings bond is converted into cash prior to maturity, the only loss is a portion of the interest return. The holder is fully protected against capital losses.[3] Also, in the 1960s when the United States incurred deficits in its balance of payments, the deficits were settled with nonmarketable, interest-bearing depository series bonds rather than with gold. Some foreign governments had what they regarded as an excess accumulation of dollars and wanted to settle in gold rather than in dollars. They were officially requested and persuaded to purchase U.S. government securities instead. Some of these securities were denominated (i.e., payable) in dollars and some in foreign currency to protect the buyer from capital losses in the event that the dollar was devalued.[4] Currently, there are several nonmarketable securities that are foreign series, foreign currency series, or foreign government series.

---

[3]During World War I, the U.S. government sold "liberty bonds" as marketable securities. Liberty bonds were sold to individuals, many of whom were more patriotic than knowledgeable about financial markets. In the postwar period, interest rates rose and the market value of unmatured securities fell. People felt cheated and victimized. During World War II, nonmarketable "victory bonds" were issued to individuals in order to protect them against capital loss.

[4]The foreign currency series were called "Roosa bonds" after Undersecretary of the Treasury Robert Roosa who was credited with the idea.

Ownership of U.S. Treasury Securities

Who owns the securities that make up the indebtedness of the U.S. government? Approximately one-third of the national debt is held by U.S. government accounts (such as trust funds and public enterprises) and Federal Reserve banks. When the revenues of federal trust funds and public enterprise accounts exceed expenditures, the surplus is invested in U.S. government securities. Most important is the OASDHI (social security) trust fund, which holds special issues. The Federal Reserve System's holdings are marketable securities acquired in open-market purchases to execute monetary policy. Open-market operations consist of purchases and sales of Treasury securities by the Federal Open Market Committee. These transactions have significant effects on the supply of money, the availability of credit, and cost of credit.

The remainder of the national debt is held by state and local governments, individuals, commercial banks, nonbank thrift institutions, financial intermediaries, corporations, and miscellaneous other investors. For these classes of investors, U.S. Treasury securities serve the highly important function of providing assets that offer a high degree of safety, stability, and liquidity. Such securities are held partly because they are regarded as riskless. The federal government can be counted on to pay principal and interest on schedule. No one believes that the federal government will default. If the holder of a marketable government security wants to convert into cash before maturity, however, selling on the over-the-counter secondary market may result in a capital loss if prices have declined. In this sense, marketable Treasury securities are risky. Such securities are also held because of the income. Corporations, financial institutions, and state and local governments often have large cash balances, which earn no interest income, and they can hold interest-earning government securities instead. Finally, since specialized dealers make markets in these securities, particularly bills, the securities are highly liquid.

Servicing and Managing the Public Debt

As a debtor, the federal government must meet certain responsibilities. These responsibilities can be separated into servicing and managing the federal debt. Debt service refers to paying interest on outstanding securities and paying the principal of any debt that is being retired. Debt management refers to refunding operations that involve payments of principal from the sale proceeds of new issues, that is, replacing mature debt with new issues of securities.

If the federal government's budget is in deficit and new debt is accumulating, then the type and maturity of the securities to be issued must be determined. If debt is decumulating, the securities to be retired must be determined. Even if the federal government's debt is stable and unchanging in amount, some securities are maturing, and these issues must be refunded or "rolled over." The type and maturity of the securities issued for refunding must be determined. Decisions about the type of security issued, the maturity of securities, and other related questions are central to debt management. Basically, there are two objectives of debt management. Put most simply, decisions regarding the type and length to maturity of debt are made with the objectives of (1) minimizing interest expense and (2) contributing to stabilization goals through the impact that funding and refunding have on the economy's liquidity.

Since the end of World War II, short-term interest rates were usually, but not always, lower than long-term rates.[5] The average length to maturity of marketable, interest-bearing public debt was shortened. It declined from more than nine years in 1946 to less than four years in the 1970s and early 1980s. A major part of this trend was to take advantage of lower short-term interest rates.[6] Also, inflationary trends encourage relatively short maturity structures. Short-term debt enables the Treasury to avoid commitments to high-interest costs over a long period.

Another objective of debt management is to contribute to stabilization goals such as full employment and stable prices. Among the factors that influence the economy as a whole is liquidity. Short-term securities are simply more liquid (i.e., convertible more easily and more quickly into cash) than are long-term securities. Cash can be used for transactions purposes; securities cannot. Conversion of securities into cash contributes to spending; conversion of cash into securities deters spending. Thus, increased liquidity generally supports a higher level of aggregate spending and thereby has an expansionary effect on the economy as a whole. On the other hand, decreased liquidity generally sustains a lower level of aggregate spending and thereby has a depressing effect on the economy as a whole.[7]

[5]The reasons for this tendency involve risk, liquidity, and expectations. The holder of any security, regardless of its length to maturity, bears the risk of capital loss in the event that it is sold for cash before maturity. Changes in interest rates cause prices of long-term securities to fluctuate more than short-term securities, however. This factor alone can influence rates so that they are higher on long-term securities. If inflationary expectations are rising, then nominal interest rates may be expected to rise in the long run, and present long-term rates may be higher. If inflationary expectations are waning, on the other hand, then nominal interest rates may be expected to fall in the long run, and present long-term rates may be lower. Finally, rates may differ due to investor preferences. Banks and corporations prefer more liquidity than do insurance companies, and this relative preference for short-term or long-term securities may influence rates. At any given time, all these factors and others have impact on interest rate differentials.

[6]Why issue any long-term securities at all? There are many reasons. Current long-term rates may be lower. Also, frequent refunding required by short-term debt means relatively high administrative costs. Finally, the interest minimization objective may conflict with stabilization goals.

[7]These generalizations apply to changes in the average length of marketable interest-bearing public debt *held by private investors*.

If debt management is used as a means of promoting stabilization goals such as full employment and stable prices, the maturity of the debt can be manipulated to influence liquidity. In a period of recession, the maturity of the public debt can be shortened, which increases the liquidity of the economy. In a period of inflation, the maturity of the public debt can be lengthened, which "mops up" liquidity. The potential for impact on the economy should be kept in perspective, however. Whatever the relation between the stock of liquid assets and consumer or investor spending, shortening and lengthening the maturity of public debt alone has a very small effect on this stock at any given time. Debt management can make a contribution to the overall fiscal policies of the federal government, but it plays a supporting role to the main actors, including changes in taxation, government expenditure, and the supply of money.

Disguised Money Creation

If the federal government does not collect enough taxes to pay for its expenditures, then it must print currency or issue bonds to finance the deficit. Real borrowing is the case in which persons or groups exchange some of their current purchasing power for a government obligation to provide an income return in the future. When currency is created, there is no person or institution giving up purchasing power in exchange for governmental obligations. A problem arises because some bond or debt issue may actually be disguised money creation rather than borrowing.

Money creation can be disguised when the federal government finances its deficits by "borrowing" from the Federal Reserve System (the Fed) and, supported by the Fed, from commercial banks. No person or institution gives up any purchasing power. In fact, purchasing power is created for the federal government in exchange for its debt. Interest is paid on the debt instruments held by the Fed and commercial banks, but the interest income is paid for creating money and purchasing power for the federal government rather than for sacrificing purchasing power as is the case of real borrowing.

The effects of real borrowing and disguised money creation are different. Real borrowing transfers purchasing power from the private sector to the public sector with no additional purchasing power created in the process. Disguised money creation involves creation of government purchasing power without any corresponding reduction in private purchasing power. Thus, there is additional purchasing power created. In an economy with excess demand for goods and services, money creation causes still more excess demand and the price level to rise. The effect of financing government expenditures with disguised money creation under conditions of excess demand is like a tax on money balances. The burden of the "tax" falls on those who hold money balances. Real borrowing, on the other hand, does not necessarily cause still more excess demand, because it is basically a transfer of purchasing power. There may be small effects on aggregate spending in the economy if persons or groups who sacrifice purchasing power have relatively low marginal propensities to consume.

Outstanding debt and debt issue contain both real borrowing and disguised money creation. The failure to distinguish between the two is unfortunate because "debt" and "borrowing" lose meaning in ordinary usage of the words. Also, two quite different operations are confounded although they can have quite different effects on the economy. For example, in an environment of inflation, confusing money creation for real borrowing can give public debt a bad name.

The Burden Controversy

Many people fear that we have "mortgaged our future." In other words, many people believe that, when we use deficit financing to pay for goods and services provided today, we are shifting the burden of payment onto future taxpayers who must service and amortize the debt. For a time, economists made light of the popular view that the burden of public debt is shifted to future generations.

Basically, what economists had in mind was the *real* cost or *real* burden. Suppose that the government sells bonds to the public and uses the proceeds to finance typewriters, computers, and aircraft carriers. To manufacture these goods, resources such as labor, materials, plant and equipment, and energy are used in production. Inputs of these resources have alternative uses in the private sector, and output of goods and services for private consumption is reduced. The reduction in production of these goods is the real cost to society of the goods financed with debt. According to this view, the cost of World War I rested with citizens who, during the war itself, sacrificed production of consumer and capital goods. The manufacture of armaments required steel, copper, and coal; drill presses, metal lathes, and dies; carpenters, machinists, and welders; and countless other materials, capital, and labor. The real cost of those armaments was the sacrifice of goods that could have been but were not produced with the same inputs of these resources. Whether financed with taxes, debt, currency creation, or conscription, the *real* cost or burden of armaments was borne by the 1914–1919 generation that sacrificed command over resources.[8]

What happens when the debt is repaid, that is, when it is amortized and serviced at some time in the future? Is there a burden imposed at that time? According to this view, the answer is no. Suppose that the govern-

---

[8]Economists holding this point of view would concede that later generations were affected because wars diminish private capital formation. If later generations "inherit" a diminished stock of capital, their real incomes are presumably lower than otherwise.

ment raises taxes at some time in the future to retire the debt. The government collects tax revenue from taypayers and uses the revenues to make payments to bondholders. Retirement of the debt is merely a *transfer* among people living at the time. There is no *net* burden. Nor does the debt repayment divert any productive resources from the private sector to the public sector. Consequently, there is no reduction of private production at the time of repayment.

In 1958, a well-known economist, James M. Buchanan, came to the defense of the popular view and argued that the burden of debt was shifted to future generations.[9] Buchanan did not question that production of private goods is reduced when debt is created. He argued that the reduction is not a burden. The resources used to manufacture typewriters, computers, or armaments that government purchases are diverted from the private sector. However, Buchanan argued, the people who give up command over these resources when they purchase bonds do so *voluntarily*. In return for reduced current output and consumption of private goods, those who purchase bonds receive government's promise of interest and principal to be paid at some time in the future. Consumption is reduced now in order to enjoy greater consumption later. No one, according to Buchanan, bears a burden at the time that government borrows to purchase typewriters, computers, or armaments. In this sense, bondholders agree to reduced consumption in exchange for securities, and they also are among the beneficiaries of the goods purchased by government.

What happens in the future when the debt is retired? The earlier view of economists was that there is no net burden, only a transfer among taxpayers and bondholders. Buchanan argued that there is a net burden after all. Bondholders do not gain; they merely exchange one asset for another, bonds for money. And taxpayers lose; they pay the higher taxes to retire the debt. Since bondholders do not gain and taxpayers lose, there is a net burden.[10]

The controversy over the burden of the public debt—whether the burden can or cannot be shifted from one generation to a future one—is not likely to be resolved here. Both sides agree that present, not future, resources are used up as government spends the proceeds of a bond issue. If taxation had been imposed, we could have traced the impact and incidence of the taxes to identify and estimate where the final burden of *financing* the expenditure rests among income and even occupational groups.

[9]James M. Buchanan, *Public Principles of Public Debt* (Homewood, Ill.: Richard D. Irwin, Inc., 1958).

[10]This simplification of the controversy can be complicated by introducing distinctions between the case in which all debt is held domestically by citizens and the case in which some debt is held by foreigners or by relying on various assumptions that affect to some degree the conclusions of the basic argument. These seem unnecessary to the purpose here, which is to elucidate the fundamental dispute.

With debt, we can do essentially the same thing, and it seems clear that the incidence of public debt rests on those who eventually must pay the taxes to service and amortize the debt. In the sense of incidence, "burden" examines how the burden of taxation or debt is distributed among income groups or occupational groups, whether any such groups are members of present or future generations.

LOCAL AND STATE
GOVERNMENT DEBT

Generally, local and state governments borrow to finance capital projects. They sell bonds to finance construction of schools, streets, waste treatment and disposal systems, and other capital facilities. Taxes collected to pay for these capital facilities can be spread over their useful lives. In large part, this is an equity consideration. People move from one state to another, or from one city to another within a state. Borrowing and then repaying with taxes spread over the useful lives of capital facilities is a way of distributing cost among those who utilize them over time rather than, say, concentrating cost on those who live in a state or city at the time a capital facility is built. Sometimes this is called a "pay-as-you-go" system. Even paying for capital facilities as they are built may not impose undue cost on residents who subsequently move. Some or all of the cost may be recovered through higher prices for property. People consider present and expected levels of taxation in their decisions to acquire property. They may pay higher prices for property in a community that has no outstanding indebtedness because it does not require a higher level of taxes in future years to retire debt. Potential buyers may not be well informed, however, and the property market may not efficiently discount or capitalize or reflect anticipated levels of taxation.

Local and state governments also borrow in anticipation of tax receipts. At the local level, for example, property taxes are often paid annually. Toward the end of the twelve-month period prior to collection, a local government might have to borrow to meet current payrolls and other obligations. A loan may be negotiated with a local commercial bank rather than floating a security issue. Such borrowing in anticipation of tax receipts is short-term borrowing. At both local and state levels, outstanding debt is mostly long-term debt.

Since local and state governments borrow to finance capital projects, the major objective of debt management is to minimize the interest expense. Consequently, the reasons for debt differ between the federal and state-local levels, and the objective of debt management at the state-local level is not complicated with the goals of stabilization policy. The mode of authorization also differs. Many local and state governments are prohibited by law from incurring debt without authorization from the qualified voters in a referendum on the project and the bond issue. Often, a qualified, rather than a simple, majority is required for approval. In some jurisdictions, a qualified majority of *eligible* voters is necessary.

Serial Issues

Bond financing must cover the interest payment and principal repayment. Once, the common method of meeting these obligations to service and amortize the debt was the "sinking fund." The idea was to collect enough tax revenues for this purpose each year to pay the annual interest charges and also to add to funds "sunk" into a fund to repay the principal when the bonds mature. The sinking fund would accumulate through tax revenues and through earnings from investment of the fund. Management of sinking funds is technically demanding and proved to be beyond the competence of many local government officials. Consequently, "serial bonds" have replaced, for the most part, the sinking fund.

With a serial issue, a fraction of the total issue of bonds is scheduled for redemption each year until the issue is retired. In other words, a capital facility is financed by bonds that have different maturity dates, usually with the maturities spread over the life of the facility. A sinking fund is not required. Outstanding indebtedness diminishes over time. Serial issues avoid many of the problems of managing a sinking fund. However, management skill is still required. Usually, new issues are sold to underwriting syndicates on the basis of bids. The interest rate on new issues is critical in many cases. Bids may be rejected because money market conditions may drive interest rates up beyond statutory limits where such limits apply. Also, high interest rates may make some capital projects so expensive that feasible tax revenues or user charges may be inadequate. In such cases, capital projects may be postponed or canceled.

General Obligation and Revenue Bonds

In conventional bond financing, the obligation to pay interest and repay principal is secured by the general tax power of government itself. This just means that payment is guaranteed by the "full faith and credit" of the government borrowing the money. The general taxing powers of government are committed to meet interest payments or principal repayments. Revenue bonds, on the other hand, do not commit the full faith and credit of the issuing government. These bonds are secured by a claim on fees, charges, or rents paid by users of a capital facility. Revenue bonds were relatively insignificant in amount as recently as 1950 and still secondary in importance through 1960. Since the late 1970s, however, the dollar amount of new issues of revenue bonds has exceeded that of general obligation bonds.

Historically, there have been limitations and even prohibitions on the amount of general obligation indebtedness that states and local governments may undertake. State and local governments have no real control over money market conditions under which they borrow. They borrow funds as favorably as they can, but the cost of borrowing differs substantially from one government to another depending on *credit ratings*. Both states and local governments can and have defaulted on their debt obligations. For example, both New York City and Cleveland have defaulted. When a major city defaults, the credit ratings of other governmental units also tend to worsen. In large part, debt limits have been imposed because market forces often are not sufficient to restrain local borrowing. Debt limits discourage overextension and the external harmful impact that default can have even on responsible governments. For whatever reason, debt limits are common. At the local level, debt limits are tied to the valuation of taxable property. In these cases, outstanding general obligation indebtedness cannot exceed a certain percentage of the value of real property in the local jurisdiction. There are many ways for local governments to circumvent the limitation. One is to turn to revenue bond financing that is exempted from debt limits.

Revenue bonds are commonly used to finance waterworks, electric plants, and other utilities for which users are billed for service. Roads and bridges are sometimes financed with revenue bonds. Tolls collected are used to service and amortize the debt. Interest rates on revenue bonds are higher than on general obligation bonds because the full faith and credit guarantee is regarded as more certain than a claim on revenues collected from use of a particular facility.

In some cases, governments and quasi-governmental agencies or corporations have issued revenue bonds as part of a plan to influence industrial location. Sometimes, these are called "industrial development bonds." The idea is to issue revenue bonds to finance the construction of facilities that are leased to privately owned businesses. The interest rate on these bonds may be lower than what a firm would be charged if it were borrowing to finance the same facility. One reason for the lower rate is that interest earned from ownership of these revenue bonds is exempted from federal income taxation.[11] Consequently, the terms offered to business firms may be attractive enough to induce them to locate their industry in a community or state.

[11]There are limits on the size of projects for which industrial development bond financing can qualify for federal tax exemption. In 1969, Congress provided that the tax-exemption privilege be limited to issues not exceeding $5 million.

Federal Income Tax Exemption
of State-Local Bond Interest

Exemption of interest earned from state and local bonds from federal income taxation is a substantial subsidy to capital projects undertaken by these governments. The exemption originated in the *immunities doctrine* that it is unconstitutional for one government to tax an "instrumentality" (i.e., bonds and salaries) of another government. This was the finding of the U.S. Supreme Court in *McCulloch* v. *Maryland,* a case that arose when the State of Maryland endeavored to tax banking operations conducted by the federal government. This historic decision in 1819 stated that "the power to tax is the power to destroy." Bond interest and the salaries of government employees were exempted from taxation by another government. In 1918, however, the Supreme Court held that the immunities doctrine did not prohibit taxation of salaries by another government as long as the taxation does not single out these salaries for taxation. This finding enabled the federal government to tax salaries of state-local government employees. The findings also enabled the taxation of interest paid on state and local bonds, but as a matter of *policy,* such interest is still exempted from federal taxation. In other words, the federal government *can* tax interest on state and local bonds without violating the immunities doctrine, but the federal government *chooses* not to.

The exemption subsidizes capital projects by permitting state and local governments to borrow at lower costs than would be the case if interest on bonds were taxable. This tax-exempt feature is very attractive to investors with high incomes. If these investors are in a 50 percent marginal tax bracket, then the rate of return on state or local bonds is, in effect, double the yield on other investment alternatives. State and local governments have formed an effective ally in high-income investors, and together they are motivated by self-interest to resist any attempts to remove the tax exemption. Yet the exemption is an inefficient means of helping state and local governments. The cost savings that these governments enjoy from exemption is *less* than the loss of tax revenues to the U.S. Treasury. The difference in what it costs the Treasury and what it benefits these governments is the gain to high-income owners of state-local bonds. If interest on the securities were taxed, the U.S. Treasury could give the same dollar amount of aid to state and local governments that they currently enjoy and save money. State and local governments would be no worse off, the Treasury would be better off, but high-income investors would be worse off. These governments, along with high-income investors, still resist loss of exemption. State and local governments fear that any alternative would leave them more vulnerable to federal interference and less secure in general.

CONCLUSION

The question of how to finance government expenditures is central to public finance. Several revenue sources are feasible and available, and judgment among them is comparative. Debt finance must be compared with other revenue sources, usually tax finance. More so than taxation, debt finance tends to shift costs beyond the period when expenditure is undertaken. Its burden may be relatively difficult to perceive. Such observations do not close out debt finance from preference over taxation when, for example, financing a long-lived project built with high initial costs. They do point up the opportunity to choose debt finance for the principal reason that debt is more politically convenient and expedient than taxation. While not for this reason alone, it certainly is numbered among the reasons cited by economists, politicians, and others who favor a constitutional amendment that would require an annually balanced budget.

15

Fiscal Federalism

From the beginning, governmental functions in the United States have been divided among federal, state, and local jurisdictions. To a degree, governmental division of labor is prescribed in the Constitution. Among the activities assigned to the federal government are control over the money supply, regulation of foreign and interstate commerce, the issue of patents and copyrights, and conduct of international relations. The remaining functions of government may be assumed by the states. Local governments are creatures of the individual states, and there are considerable interstate differences in the powers and functions delegated to them.

Both the scope and distribution of governmental functions have evolved over time. The forces affecting this evolution are only partly economic. Nevertheless, the economic factors underlying what is often called "fiscal federalism" are sufficiently important to warrant a detailed examination.

ECONOMICS OF FISCAL DECENTRALIZATION

Those who are concerned about the trend toward centralization of governmental power often advocate reversing the trend and bringing government "closer to the people." Even though the meaning of this catch phrase is not always clear, an application of the concepts of public goods and public choice may help to give it content.

Gains from Decentralization

By decentralizing government, tax and expenditure decisions are placed at the community level. In this way, voters of each community choose public services that reflect their own preferences. To illustrate, take the simple case of two communities, Lynden and Blaine. The 100 citizens of Lynden have identical demands for a public good. Each wants to spend $50 per person, or $5,000 in total, to provide the good to their community. The 200 citizens of Blaine also have identical demands for the same public good. Each favors expenditure of $100 per person or $20,000 in total. Take for granted that each community is unaffected by expenditures in the other. If Lynden and Blaine are fiscally independent, their citizens will vote to tax and spend $5,000 and $20,000, respectively, for the public good. Each community is supplied with just the amount demanded.

Now suppose that Lynden and Blaine are placed under a single government that requires an equal per capita expenditure on the good in both communities. The citizens of Blaine can outvote the citizens of Lynden by a margin of 2 to 1. Thus, the 300 citizens of Lynden and Blaine will consume the good at the level of $100 per capita or $30,000 in total. The citizens of Blaine still get the quantity they want, but the citizens of Lynden are forced to consume too much. If Lynden and Blaine had different preferences but the same number of voters, some sort of compromise would be necessary. For example, they might agree to spend $75 per capita. In this case, Lynden gets too much, but Blaine gets too little.

This simple example illustrates the most obvious argument for fiscal decentralization. When the costs and benefits of a public good are confined to a community, local autonomy allows choice according to community preferences. In a society in which individuals can move easily from one community to another, differences in community preferences can be expected to increase over time. The reason is that households will be attracted to communities offering a package of public services closest to their preferences. This tendency is known as the *Tiebout effect* after the late Charles Tiebout, who first analyzed the phenomenon in a formal model.[1]

A decentralized system of local government is most likely to contribute to an efficient allocation of resources if local expenditures are financed

[1]Charles M. Tiebout, "A Pure Theory of Local Expenditures," *Journal of Political Economy*, 64 (October 1956), 416–24. Empirical support for the Tiebout theory remains inconclusive. A recent study of towns in Pennsylvania shows substantial dispersion in the demand for public goods within communities. The authors speculate that other considerations, such as job proximity and transportation costs, may be of at least equal importance in choosing where to live. See Howard Pack and Janet Rothenberg Pack, "Metropolitan Fragmentation and Local Public Expenditures," *National Tax Journal*, 31 (December 1978), 349–62.

by local taxes. By tying benefits to costs, local residents have an incentive to avoid overspending. This conclusion is based on the presumption that there is no *spillover* of either costs or benefits to residents of other communities. Such fiscal isolation is not likely, however, especially if local jurisdictions are small enough to achieve substantial homogeneity of preferences.

Limits to Decentralization

The argument just cited is clearly of importance in deciding how to allocate governmental activities among units of government. It is also subject to several qualifications. First, as indicated, it may not be true that all costs and benefits of locally financed public goods are confined to the local community. Second, there may be economies or diseconomies of scale in the production of public goods. Third, the optimal area for provision may differ significantly among public services. Finally, there may be great differences in wealth and income and thus the fiscal capacity of governmental units. Among the more striking examples are the "rich" and "poor" enclaves observed in and around some of our large cities.

Spillovers. The geographic distribution of beneficiaries differs considerably for various types of public good. The deterrent power of national defense provides protection for the entire country and, to varying degrees, for our allies. On the other hand, the benefits from the services of a municipal fire department are concentrated largely on the residents of a single community. Thus, defense is provided by the national government, while fire protection is a local affair.

In principle, the boundary of the governmental unit providing a public good should coincide with the spatial distribution of those who benefit. If the governmental unit extends beyond those who benefit, gains from decentralization are lost. If the boundary does not enclose all beneficiaries of a public service, some of the benefits "spill out" to residents of other jurisdictions who presumably do not pay for it. From an allocational point of view, this type of spillover becomes a matter of concern if it contributes to underprovision of the good in question.

To illustrate, suppose that a public good is provided by Lynden. In Figure 15–1, the line D_r shows the demand by residents of Lynden. Suppose that benefits spill over into neighboring jurisdictions and that D_n shows the demand of nonresidents. Total demand, D_t, is obtained by summing D_r and D_n *vertically*. S is the supply curve for the good. The actual quantity provided by Lynden will depend on its public choice mechanism and tax instruments, but presume that the quantity chosen is OQ_r. The socially optimal output is OQ_t, which takes into account the demands of residents and nonresidents. Underprovision is likely, because taxpayers and

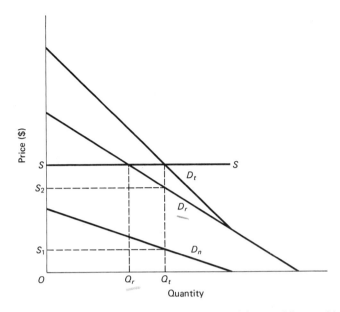

FIGURE 15-1   Benefit spillover. The demand for a public good by residents of the government unit providing it is represented by D_r; demand of nonresidents is represented by D_n; and total demand is represented by D_t. If only demand by local residents is considered, supply will be suboptimal at Q_r. A subsidy of S_1, added to the residents' price of S_2, equates supply and demand at the optimal output Q_t.

politicians in Lynden have no incentive to consider the demand of nonresidents and nonresidents have no way of influencing choice.

Underprovision might be avoided by extending the boundaries of Lynden to include all who benefit, but this procedure may add new problems. As we indicated, when it is necessary to resort to the voting mechanism, it is desirable to group voters in such a way that their preferences are as homogeneous as possible. As the size of a jurisdiction is increased, however, differences in voter preferences are likely to become more pronounced. Therefore, in considering the size of a governmental unit, the gains from including all who benefit from a collectively financed good must be weighed against the losses arising from greater diversity of preferences.

Another practical difficulty occurs in trying to identify beneficiaries. Most who benefit from police protection in New York City are residents, but some benefits spill over to nonresidents who work in or visit the city and even to those who have commercial connections with New York firms. People from all over the world are among the beneficiaries, but it seems farfetched to argue that the New York Police Department should be placed under the control of a world government or even the national government in Washington. Extending the boundary to an area that wide would encompass too many nonbeneficiaries.

In practice, therefore, benefit spillovers are inevitable. In those cases where the consequences are considered serious, potential gains from more efficient provision of public services provide affected parties with an incentive to seek means of improving the situation. When the number of governmental units involved is small, units benefiting from spillover might negotiate directly with the provider. Units receiving benefits can encourage providers by compensating them directly for expanded output. Bargaining costs and uncertainties over the value of benefit spillovers are likely roadblocks to such agreements. The past half-century has been marked by accelerated growth in more formal means of dealing with spillovers. These have taken the form of intergovernmental grants and regional compacts.

Intergovernmental grants typically flow from higher to lower levels of government. They take a variety of forms but are generally directed at a specific governmental activity. Grants are discussed in detail later in this chapter. The United States has also experienced a growing interest in the use of federal inducements to encourage such activities as areawide urban planning and regional control of air and water quality.

In recent years, most attention has focused on benefit spillovers. Misallocation can result from cost spillovers as well. If a governmental unit can shift some of its tax burden to nonresidents, residents do not have to pay the full cost of public services. Residents of the tax-exporting jurisdiction will then have an incentive to vote to expand output beyond the optimal level. Shifting to nonresidents may be achieved by taxing businesses that are owned by or sell to outsiders. States with valuable mineral or energy resources sometimes shift tax burdens to nonresidents by levying a severance tax on the output of mines, oil and gas fields, or forests. For example, severance taxes account for more than 20 percent of state tax revenue in Alaska, Louisiana, Oklahoma, and Wyoming. States like Florida with attractive recreational resources find ways to tax tourists. The federal government deliberately relieves residents of all states from bearing the full burden of financing public services by allowing an income tax deduction for most states and local taxes. Cost spillovers through exporting of tax burdens thus help to offset the tendency toward undersupply attributable to benefit spillovers. They do so only in the global sense, however. All expenditures are affected, not just those with significant benefit spillovers.

Cost of production.   Benefits and spillovers are demand phenomena. The cost of production is also relevant in choosing the proper configuration of governmental units. Economies of scale are likely to be present in the production of governmental services, at least when output levels are relatively low. If governmental units are too small to achieve minimum unit cost, taxpayers must absorb the cost of the attendant inefficiencies. If units are too large, diseconomies may be present.

We know surprisingly little about the shape of cost curves for individual governmental services. Attempts at estimation, using observed data from a cross section of different sized units, have met with only limited success. One reason is the difficulty of specifying comparable units of output. The output of a plant that produces a single homogeneous physical product like three-penny nails is easy to measure. Defining a unit of output for a police department, court of law, or high school is much more difficult. It is also difficult to adjust for such factors as differences in labor costs, geographical area covered, and scope and quality of service.[2]

Complementarities and interactions among different activities add a further complication. For example, cities may cut costs by locating several departments in a single building, which allows them to share space, supply inventories, switchboards, and computer facilities. Interactions occur among the activities of police and fire departments, building inspectors, and public health personnel.

Our ignorance of the determinants of production costs weakens their proper impact on decisions about the size and configuration of governmental units. The importance of cost considerations is weakened further when governments can contract for services with outside suppliers. If a jurisdiction is too small to gain the full benefit of economies of scale in the production of a particular service, it might choose to buy the service from a larger adjacent area. For example, a small suburb might buy water and sewage treatment services from an adjacent city. By doing so, however, the suburb can lose budgetary flexibility. The city could provide a higher level of sewage treatment than that preferred by voters in the suburb. This puts the suburb in the position of choosing between a high-cost local treatment plant or a purchase of "too much" treatment from the city. In this case, the suburb loses out on one of the benefits of decentralization.

Voter control. After weighing the benefits of decentralization, the extent of spillovers, and costs of production, the boundaries of the units providing each public good or service must be set. It is conceivable that a different-sized unit may be optimal for each separate governmental activity. The result would be an incredible tangle of overlapping taxing and spending jurisdictions, each with its own electorate and governing body. Voters would be overwhelmed with issues and candidates, and many

[2]For a discussion of conceptual issues and examples of empirical estimates of cost functions for local governmental services, see Werner Z. Hirsch, *The Economics of State and Local Government* (New York: McGraw-Hill Book Company, 1970), pp. 167–84.

would give up in despair. In such an environment, voter control would break down. Tax and expenditure decisions would no longer reflect the preferences of citizens.

One way in which to avoid chaos while taking advantage of some of the complementarities and interactions just noted is to consolidate a number of functions under a single governing body. Of course, this is what has happened. Citizens vote for federal, state, city, and county officials. In some cases, they may vote separately for court officials or members of boards responsible for schools, parks, or other special-purpose functions. In this way, the demands on the voter are made more manageable, but at a price. The consolidation of governmental functions places an additional constraint on the determination of governmental boundaries, adding to the potential for spillovers and inefficient production.[3]

Fiscal equity.   Substantial differences in fiscal capacity—the ability to finance government—appear to be common among governments at all levels. The vast disparity in wealth among nations is common knowledge. In the United States, per capita income in the richest states is about double that in the poorest. Disparities within states are often greater.

The existence of substantial differences in fiscal capacity of governmental units within a federal system is a cause for much concern. It means that the variety and quality of public services will be lower and/or average tax rates will be higher in the poorer jurisdictions. This condition violates the principle of horizontal equity. Comparing two taxpayers with equal ability to pay, one who lives in a rich state is likely to have to pay lower taxes and/or enjoy a higher level of public services than is his or her "equal" in a poor state. In addition, fiscal inequities can contribute to an uneconomic allocation of resources. Residents of a rich state get more public services per dollar of taxes than do residents of poor states. This encourages location or relocation of residences and businesses in rich states. To the extent that the location or relocation decision is due to the presence of rich neighbors rather than to real economic advantages, too many people and resources will concentrate in the richer state.[4]

Our example refers to states. The same forces are at work at the local level. Especially in metropolitan areas, there is a tendency for taxpayers to cluster in communities according to economic status. Zoning regulations and other restrictions often preclude entry of low-income families into high-income suburbs. Poor people simply cannot afford to buy or rent housing in a wealthy community. In this way the Tiebout effect, which can

---

[3]For a more formal analysis, see Gordon Tullock, "Federalism: Problems of Scale," *Public Choice*, 6 (Spring 1969), 19–29.

[4]See James M. Buchanan, "Federal and Fiscal Equity," *American Economic Review*, 40 (September 1950), 583–99. Reprinted in Buchanan, *Fiscal Theory and Politcal Economy* (Chapel Hill: University of North Carolina Press, 1960), pp. 170–89.

promote a more efficient use of resources by local governments, can also serve as a source of substantial inequality in fiscal capacity and quality of life.

The tendency for households to locate in richer jurisdictions may be tempered by differentials in the prices of public services. The cost of providing services may be lower in low-income regions, in part because wages of public employees are lower. This offsetting effect is likely to be of greater significance between regions, for example, Snowbelt versus Sunbelt, than within a given metropolitan area.

FISCAL COORDINATION

It should be clear that there is no way in which to achieve total fiscal independence for the governmental units that make up our federal system. Ways have been devised, however, to mitigate some of the undesirable consequences of fiscal interaction. These include means for coordinating the taxing functions of federal, state, and local governments and for transferring funds between governments, usually in the form of grants from higher to lower units.

Allocation of Revenue Sources

Governments at the federal and state levels have considerable freedom in choosing a tax structure. Local governments, as creatures of the individual states, are subject to many more legal constraints. The degree of local autonomy varies from state to state.

Aside from legal constraints, the autonomy of state and local governments is constrained further by economic considerations and administrative capabilities. Tax differentials encourage movement of persons and capital investment across jurisdictional lines. States and communities are consequently reluctant to get "too far out of line" in their choice of tax bases and rates. Interstate and intercommunity competition undoubtedly holds down taxes on businesses. This is particularly true of taxes on manufacturers who are not tied to a particular location by the need to be close to customers or sources of raw materials. Tax concessions designed to attract industry are common. State industrial development commissions often advertise their "favorable tax climate."[5] State-local tax structures are generally less progressive (or more regressive) than are federal taxes. This is due in part to the fear of driving out high-income residents.

[5]Some state and local governments try to attract industry by constructing facilities and leasing them to private businesses. The facilities are financed by industrial development bonds. The federal income tax exempts interest on state-local securities, keeping interest rates on industrial development bonds below the rates paid by private firms. This source of indirect subsidy for private firms is described in Chapter 14.

For administrative reasons, larger governmental units have more options in choosing among alternative revenue sources. The federal government can administer personal and corporate income taxes more efficiently than can states because of its ability to gather information from divergent sources. The Internal Revenue Service (IRS) gathers information on wages subject to withholding and on interest and dividend income earned within the territorial limits of the United States. In addition, the federal government has a greater capability than does any other entity to monitor the flow of income from foreign sources. No state could possibly rival the capacity of the IRS to collect and process information needed for enforcement, nor could an individual state match its nationwide network of tax auditors and investigators. Only because they are allowed access to federal tax files are state and local governments able to rely on income taxes as a reasonably reliable and equitable revenue source. For similar reasons, the federal government administers excise taxes more efficiently than do the states. If it chose to do so, it would enjoy comparable advantages in administering a retail sales tax.

Administrative inadequacies and competition from surrounding communities discouraged all but the largest local governments from independently levying major general taxes other than the property tax. Even in the case of property taxes, poor quality of administration in many localities has forced state governments to take steps to improve assessment procedures, as described in Chapter 11.

The increasing professionalization of municipal employees coupled with improvements in data processing may make it easier for local governments to tap new sources of local revenue. Their ability to do so, however, is often constrained by state laws. A common example is a law requiring voter approval by referendum before a new local tax can be levied.

Fiscal Accommodation

Because of fiscal interdependence and constraints on revenue-raising capacity, the different levels of government have experimented with a variety of ways of accommodating each other's needs. A common response involves partial or total transfer of a function to a higher level of government. Such transfers may be motivated by a desire to improve program administration, account for spillovers, or take advantage of the superior revenue-raising capacity of the higher level of government.[6]

Allowing different levels of government to tax separate bases is another remedy that is often advocated. To a degree, this practice has been

---

[6]Some functions may be transferred to a higher level of government if groups favoring their expansion enjoy stronger political representation at higher levels. See Kenneth V. Greene, "Some Institutional Considerations in Federal-State Fiscal Relations," *Public Choice*, 9 (Fall 1970), 1–18.

followed in the United States. Income taxes are most important at the federal level, retail sales taxes at the state level, and property taxes at the local level. It is questionable as to whether this division has been dictated by deliberate design or by the demands of tax administration. In recent decades, the trend has been toward diversification and overlap as states and localities sought to expand their revenue capacity. The overlapping of tax sources has encouraged governments to seek out ways of tax accommodation. Among the most important arrangements are tax supplements, tax sharing, deductibility, and credits.

Tax supplement. Under this arrangement, a subordinate governmental unit is allowed the option of imposing its own rate on a tax base already used by a higher unit. An optional local levy added to a state sales tax is the most common example. The state collects the whole tax and returns the local portion to the subordinate unit. The local unit may or may not have complete autonomy in choosing the supplemental rate, but it does not have the option of forgoing the tax. Supplements preserve a degree of local autonomy, but the subordinate unit must accept the base described by the collecting unit. Administration is improved, and taxpayer compliance is simplified. This scheme does not eliminate tax competition or fiscal inequality among jurisdictions.

Tax sharing. Under tax sharing, the collecting jurisdiction returns a portion of the tax revenue to the subunit in which it is collected. The portion is typically a fixed percentage of the total collection. The subordinate unit has no control over the base or rate. Elimination of local option avoids the distorting effect of tax differentials on location decisions. Proportional sharing does not compensate for unequal fiscal capacity. It may create inefficiencies by constraining local decision making.

Tax deduction. The federal government allows taxpayers who itemize to deduct state and local income, sales, and property taxes from taxable income. State and local business taxes can be deducted as business expenses. Consequently, the net cost of paying deductible state and local taxes is reduced for those taxpayers claiming the deduction. The deduction is thus a form of subsidy for state and local governments. It has the effect of increasing state-local tax revenues at the expense of federal revenue. It also moderates interarea differences in tax burden. On the other hand, deductibility reduces overall tax progressivity, because the tax saving is greater in higher rate brackets. Deductibility may reduce taxpayer resistance to higher state and local taxes, but the gain in state-local revenue is generally thought to be considerably less than is the loss in federal revenue. Finally, deductibility is not an effective instrument for reducing the unequal fiscal capacity among states and localities.

Tax credit.   A tax credit permits a taxpayer to subtract from tax owed to a higher level of government some or all of tax paid to a subordinate unit. For example, the federal government allows a credit against the federal estate tax for death duties paid to state governments. The amount of the credit is limited, however, and death taxes levied by the states generally exceed the credit. All states levy duties at least up to the maximum allowed by the credit. If they did not, they would lose the revenue to the federal government. The original intent of the federal credit was to encourage all states to levy some type of death duty.

Credits can be used to encourage greater uniformity among subordinate jurisdictions with respect to tax instruments and tax rates. Unlike income tax deductions, credits need not concentrate most of their tax-saving benefits on well-to-do taxpayers. In fact, upper limits on credits may have the reverse effect. In practice, credits are similar to tax sharing. Unlike sharing, credits do not eliminate duplication of administration at two levels of government.

Tax credits can be used to promote horizontal accommodation among taxing bodies. For example, U.S. corporations that pay income tax on income earned abroad are generally allowed a credit against their U.S. corporation income tax liability for taxes paid to foreign governments. The purpose is to avoid double taxation by two sovereign nations. Similar provisions apply to individuals earning income abroad. Within the United States, states commonly grant income tax credits for taxes paid by their residents on income earned in other states.

Tax treaties and compacts.   Treaties are sometimes used between taxing jurisdictions to prevent double taxation of each other's residents. Neighboring states may sign an agreement under which persons residing in one state and working in the other will pay income tax only in the state of residence. These agreements are most likely to come about in cases where the flow of income between states is roughly equal.

Tax compacts among a number of states deal with some of the enforcement and equity problems created by state taxation of interstate business. Among the more important are compacts dealing with corporation income taxes and with user taxes imposed on interstate truckers. These compacts have reduced some of the problems attributable to taxation of interstate commerce, but inequities and inefficiencies still abound.

Grants-in-Aid

The most important development in fiscal federalism during the past half-century has been the enormous growth in grants-in-aid from higher to lower levels of government. Most of the grants are earmarked for specific uses. They have been accompanied by increased centralization of control over the activities of recipient governments. The trend toward centralized control, particularly at the federal level, has aroused growing opposition. Recipient governments are generally eager to accept the money, but they seek more autonomy over the way in which it is spent. Determination of the proper role of intergovernmental grants is the key issue facing our federal system in the 1980s. Before we turn to specific policy issues, however, it will be useful to describe the major forms and purposes of grants-in-aid.

Taxonomy of grants.   Grant instruments take a variety of forms. This is to be expected, since grants are intended to serve a number of different purposes. Some grant programs are in the form of an *entitlement.* Benefits are paid in accordance with a prescribed formula to all eligible governmental units. Federal revenue sharing and most state grants to local school districts are examples. Other programs award grants on a competitive basis to governments that apply. Federal project grants for community development and urban park facilities are examples.

Grants can be classified according to their essential characteristics.

I. *Unconditional (or general) grant:* a transfer of funds from the donor government to the recipient government with no strings attached. In its pure form, the recipient government can use the money as it pleases. Unconditional grants are much like tax sharing, except that the amount returned to recipient governments need not equal the revenue collected within their borders. Because unconditional grants permit redistribution of tax revenue within a federal system, they are often touted as a device for reducing inequality in fiscal capacity.

II. *Conditional (or specific) grant:* a transfer that must be used by recipient governments for restricted purposes, usually spelled out in detail in the grant agreement. Major types and subtypes include the following.

    A. *Matching grant,* which requires the recipient government to put up a specified amount of its own money for each dollar it receives from the donor government.

        1. *Proportional match,* under which the recipient and donor governments share the cost of each unit of a service provided by the recipient. The grant thus becomes a subsidy. The proportion assumed by the donor government may be constant or may vary according to such factors as level of output of the subsidized service and the fiscal capacity of the recipient government. Matching grants may be "open ended" or "closed ended." The open-ended grant puts no upper limit on the number of dollars payable by the donor government, although the donor's share of incremental costs may decline as program levels rise. Under a closed-end proportional grant, the donor places an upper limit on the number of dollars payable to a recipient. In this way, the donor retains control over its maximum liability.

        2. *Incremental match,* under which recipient governments must bear

the full cost of a program up to a prescribed minimum level before matching funds are made available. By forcing recipient government to finance a minimum effort on their own as a condition of eligibility for grant money, the donor government hopes to expand provision of the favored activity at less cost to itself.

B.   *Specific block (or nonmatching) grants,* which require the recipient government to spend the money for a prescribed purpose. The amount of the grant does not vary directly with the expenditure of the recipient government on the specified activity. Specific block grants increase the ability of recipient governments to finance specified services. They do not provide the per unit reduction in price that occurs with a matching grant. Thus, nonmatching grants have an income effect. There is no substitution effect, because they do not affect the per unit cost of the specified service to the recipient government. The following are the two basic varieties of specific block grants:

1.   *Nonincremental block grant,* which provides the recipient government with a lump-sum payment regardless of the amount of its own funds that it spends on the specified service.

2.   *Incremental block grant,* which requires the recipient government to spend a minimum amount on the specified service to qualify for a lump-sum payment.

Economics of grants.   Grants-in-aid can be used to help equalize fiscal capacity or to improve the allocation of resources within a federal system. The purpose of the grant must be specified before its form is selected. As noted, residents of a rich community can expect more government services per tax dollar than can their horizontal equals in a poor community because of the greater taxpaying capacity of their neighbors. If the goal of a grant program is to reduce this type of fiscal inequity, an unconditional grant that transfers tax revenue from richer to poorer jurisdictions is most suitable.

Some measure of fiscal capacity is required if grants are to be used to promote fiscal equality among units of a federal system. One of the simplest measures is per capita personal income. A variant of this is the excess of personal income over poverty-level income on a per capita basis. These data are reasonably reliable for large units such as states, but they are of dubious reliability for most local jurisdictions. Moreover, tax and benefit spillovers undermine the reliability of personal income as a measure of fiscal capacity. In particular, per capita personal income may substantially understate the taxpaying capacity of states that can gain large amounts of revenue by taxing tourists or exports of oil or minerals.

A measure proposed by the Advisory Commission on Intergovernmental Relations (ACIR) has attracted a great deal of attention. ACIR recognizes that state and local governments rely on a variety of revenue sources and that there are substantial interstate differences in revenue structures. ACIR initially proposed that taxpaying capacity of each state be defined as the per capita revenue that would be obtained by applying the national average rate to each source of state and local tax revenue.[7] More recently, nontax sources such as user charges have been added to give a more inclusive measure of revenue capacity.

The ACIR measure of per capita revenue capacity in the state with highest capacity (Alaska) exceeded the capacity of the lowest state (Mississippi) by a ratio of 3 to 1. In other words, applying average national rates to state and local sources would yield three times as much revenue per resident in Alaska as in Mississippi. By contrast, if per capita personal income is used as a capacity measure, the ratio of highest to lowest capacity is only 1.8 to 1.[8]

Owing to data limitations, the ACIR revenue capacity would be even more difficult to measure than personal income for many small local jurisdictions. Yet differences in fiscal capacity are thought to be far greater among local units of government than among states. If grants-in-aid are to be used to reduce these differences, then some measure of capacity, however imperfect, must serve as a basis for grant allocation.

Finally, revenue capacity applies to only one side of the budget. On the expenditure side, some communities are presumed to have greater need than others for public services. Communities with a large number of low-income families have greater need for welfare and similar programs. Large numbers of children increase the need for school expenditures. Once the expenditure side of the budget is introduced, however, the distinction between general fiscal capacity and financing of specific programs begins to break down. It becomes unclear whether the allegedly greater "need" for certain outlays should be accommodated by unconditional grants or by conditional grants limited to specific uses. The inability to separate need from fiscal capacity is undoubtedly responsible for the common practice of incorporating a redistributional element into many conditional grant programs. This feature is dealt with in more detail in a subsequent discussion.

Up to this point, the discussion has centered on the overall revenue-raising capacity of a governmental unit in a federal system. Ultimately, the chief concern is with the way in which horizontal equals—persons with equal taxpaying capacity, as discussed in Chapter 6—are treated in a fiscal system. In terms of the ethical standard of horizontal equity, or equal treatment of equals, each taxpayer should receive the same benefits and pay the same amount of taxes as fiscal equals in other jurisdictions. In most cases, an unconditional grant-in-aid program based on some measure of fiscal capacity of recipient governments would not be capable of achiev-

[7]Advisory Commission on Intergovernmental Relations, *Measuring the Fiscal Capacity and Effort of State and Local Areas* (Washington, D.C.: Government Printing Office, 1971).

[8]*Intergovernmental Perspective*, 7 (Summer 1981), 31.

ing horizontal equity among individuals. Local autonomy in matters of taxation is likely to lead to interstate and intercommunity differences in the progressivity (or regressivity) of the tax structure. Differences in the cost of public services and in the need of citizens add an additional complication. Therefore, a grant program designed to equalize the fiscal capacity of recipient governments cannot also be expected to achieve horizontal equity among individuals.

Where spillovers of benefits of public expenditures occur, efficient allocation requires a system of intergovernmental transfers that will equate costs and benefits at the margin. Otherwise, as pointed out, beneficiaries of spillovers will become "free riders," and there will be a tendency toward underprovision.

Referring back to Figure 15–1, if D_r is the demand for a public service by residents and D_n is the demand for nonresidents, there will be a tendency for OQ_r units to be produced in the absence of a transfer. A grant of OS_1 per unit added to the residents' price of OS_2 per unit would encourage expansion of output to the socially optimal level of OQ_r. In other words, efficient allocation requires a conditional matching grant at a ratio of spillover to total benefits, or OS_1, to OS in Figure 15–1.

All this presumes that benefits can be measured, but as we saw in Chapter 2, it is not generally possible to determine the demands of individuals when publicness is involved. To the extent that the political process approximates demand, however, the presumption remains that benefit spillovers will lead to underprovision in the absence of intervention by higher levels of government, particularly in cases involving a number of government units. Hence, conditional matching grants are prescribed in such cases.

FEDERAL GRANTS

Federal grants to state and local governments are not new. As far back as the early 1800s, the federal government transferred title to federal land to the states. The states converted these land grants into cash through sale to settlers. After the Civil War, land grants to all the states were earmarked for the support of agricultural colleges, marking the inception of today's system of land-grant universities. Federal grants grew slowly but steadily until the New Deal era of the 1930s. That decade saw the introduction of joint state-federal categorical welfare programs, as described in Chapter 13. State and local governments also benefited from federally financed public works projects, a part of depression-era efforts to create jobs and revive the dormant construction industry.

The most profound changes occurred during the two decades from

1960 to 1980. During that period, federal grants to state and local governments grew from $7 billion to $83 billion. The number of individual grant programs increased from 150 to 498. Nearly all were earmarked for specific purposes, primarily in the areas of health, welfare, education, and transportation. Using grants as a policy instrument, the federal government assumed greater responsibility for dealing with a variety of social problems. Meanwhile, recipient governments became more dependent on federal money. By the end of the 1970s, federal grants financed 24 percent of state-local expenditures, compared with 15 percent in 1960. Large cities became particularly dependent on federal largesse. By the end of the last decade, the nation's forty-seven largest cities received half as much in federal aid as they raised from their own revenue sources; in 1957, the figure was 2.6 percent.

Major changes in our federal system occurred with the inception of President Lyndon Johnson's Great Society in the mid-1960s. The goal of Great Society programs was to cure social ills such as poverty, hard-core unemployment, poor schooling, inadequate housing and medical care, and urban decay. Specifically targeted federal grants were the means. Many grant programs bypassed the states and were directed at local governments, school districts, and locally controlled independent agencies.

The categorical grant programs of the Great Society clearly failed to produce the quick solutions envisioned by their originators. Hard-core unemployment and urban decay remain. The reduction in poverty and privation that has occurred during the past two decades is attributable more to the cash and in-kind transfer programs described in Chapter 13 than to investments in human and social capital that Great Society grants were designed to promote. Defenders of the Great Society argue that underfunding is at least partly to blame for its failures. Monies needed to finance the grant programs were siphoned off to finance the war in Vietnam. Anticipated budget surpluses turned into deficits as Congress and the Johnson administration tried to fight wars against poverty at home and on the battlefield in Asia without raising taxes.

President Richard Nixon, who took office in 1969, expressed a desire to recast the system of federal grants that he had inherited. He acknowledged the need for federal participation in the effort to deal with the nation's domestic problems. He hoped to do so, however, by allowing recipient governments to exercise more control over the expenditure of grant monies. This would be accomplished in two ways. First, a number of specifically targeted grant programs would be consolidated into less restrictive categorical block grants. Second, a portion of federal grant money would be channeled into a program of general revenue sharing. The latter program was to be the cornerstone of President Nixon's "New Federalism." His original proposal called for a permanent allotment of a percentage of federal income tax revenue to the states. The money was to be allocated among states on a per capita basis. Each state in turn would be free to allocate the money in accordance with its own priorities.[9]

Efforts of the Nixon administration to consolidate numbers of specifically targeted grants into a few less restrictive block grants met with little success. Congress jealously guarded its ability to attach strings to federal grant money. It did eventually accept the idea of general revenue sharing, but in more restrictive form. Details of the program are described in the paragraphs that follow.

The basic thrust of federal grant programs did not change markedly during the administrations of Gerald Ford or Jimmy Carter. One trend, begun in the 1960s, did accelerate during the next decade. This is the practice of exercising federal control over grant recipients in areas well beyond the specific grant categories. Some of the controls are designed to ensure that federal money is spent efficiently and for the intended purpose. Grant recipients must satisfy federal planning and administrative regulations and submit to federal audits. Other controls are intended to promote national social priorities that may bear little or no relation to the objectives of particular grant projects.

Examples of the latter are the various *cross-cutting* requirements, many of which are imposed across the board on federal grants. Some relate to civil rights. They include regulations prohibiting discrimination and providing for the protection of disadvantaged groups, including the elderly and handicapped. Others deal with such diverse matters as environmental impact, historic preservation, animal welfare, and relocation assistance for persons displaced by public works projects. Another type of control is the *crossover sanction,* under which grants in one area are used to influence state or local policy in another. Well-known examples include loss of highway funds to states that fail to adopt the 55 m.p.h. speed limit or that fail to regulate billboards on interstates.[10]

The proliferation of programs imposes great inconvenience on recipient governments. This is particularly true of grants earmarked for specific projects, many of which are awarded on a competitive basis. Major recipients, such as states, large cities, and even some state universities have es-

---

[9]The idea of revenue sharing did not originate with the Nixon administration. Henry Simons in 1938 outlined an income-tax-sharing arrangement and defended it with arguments very much like those used by Nixon. See Henry C. Simons, *Personal Income Taxation* (Chicago: University of Chicago Press, 1938), pp. 214–18. In the 1960s, the idea was resurrected by Walter Heller and Joseph Pechman.

[10]See David R. Beam, "Washington's Regulation of States and Localities: Origins and Issues," *Intergovernmental Perspectives,* 7 (Summer 1981), 8–18. Beam identifies fifty-nine cross-cutting requirements. Two-thirds have been added since 1969.

tablished offices in Washington, D.C., or have hired grant consultants to ensure that grants for which they may be eligible are not overlooked.[11]

Federal Grant Formulas

The various grants were enacted at different times under the aegis of different congressional committees and executive agencies to meet a wide variety of perceived needs. Thus, there is considerable variation in grant design. In the previous section, two purposes of grants were cited, promotion of fiscal equality among jurisdictions and correction for spillovers. Redress of fiscal inequality requires unconditional grants inversely related to fiscal capacity, while correction for spillovers requires matching grants. The formulas actually used in federal entitlement grant programs often mix these two functions, one redistributive and the other allocational. Some federal grants also incorporate a "need" component that crudely reflects the demand for the particular service being subsidized.

Conditional grants. Federal grant formulas contain an allotment component that determines the allocation of appropriated funds among states. Matching grants contain a second component that determines the state and federal share.

In its simplest form, the allotment component allocates funds among states on the basis of each state's share of the target population. Algebraically, the formula is of the form

$$A_i = S \frac{P_i}{P_t}$$

where

A_i = allotment to ith state
S = appropriation in dollars
P_i = target population in ith state
P_t = total target population

As an example, the federal grant for support of agricultural education allots to the ith state a share of the total appropriation that is equal to the ith state's share of the total U.S. farm population. The intent is to allocate grant money on the basis of need as measured by each state's share of the identified population of beneficiaries.

[11]For an excellent historical account of the evolution of federal grants, see George F. Break, "Fiscal Federalism in the United States: The First 200 Years, Evolution and Outlook," in Advisory Commission on Intergovernmental Affairs, *The Future of Federalism in the 1980s* (Washington, D.C.: Government Printing Office, July 1981), pp. 39–65.

For a number of grants, the allotment formula is modified to allow for differences among states in fiscal capacity. As mentioned, fiscal capacity is not easy to define or measure. Federal grant formulas use per capita income as a capacity measure, perhaps because it is simple and because estimates are readily available, at least at the state level. One commonly used formula is the following:

$$A_i = S \frac{P_i\,(1 - 0.5\ Y_i/Y)}{\sum\limits_{j=1}^{51} P_j\,(1 - 0.5\ Y_j/Y)}$$

where

P_i, P_j = population in ith or jth state
$j = 1, \ldots, 51$ (50 states plus District of Columbia)
Y_i, Y_j = per capita income in the ith or jth state
Y = per capita income nationwide
A_i and S are as defined previously.

The effect of the inclusion of per capita income in the manner shown is to weight the formula so that it increases the allotments of states with low per capita incomes at the expense of states with high per capita incomes. The allotments to states with incomes at or near the national average are about the same with or without weighting based on income.

Allotment formulas similar to those shown are used to allocate conditional block grants to states. They set the maximum amounts for which individual states are eligible under closed-end matching grants. To receive its full matching allotment, a state must match the federal contribution by putting up a specified percentage of its own funds. Many of the programs have a uniform federal matching percentage so that the federal government picks up the same percentage of program cost in all states that participate in the program. The federal share differs among programs, however, ranging from 33⅓ percent to 90 percent. Other programs have a variable federal matching percentage. The federal share varies inversely with the fiscal capacity of the state. The federal match is determined by a formula such as the following:

$$F_i = 1 - 0.5\frac{Y_i}{Y}$$

where

F_i = the percentage of program cost assumed by the federal government in the ith state
Y_i = per capita income in the ith state
Y = per capita income nationwide

Thus, a state with average per capita income would get a federal matching grant of 50 percent; a state with per capita income 25 percent above the national average would get a federal match of 37.5 percent $[1 - 0.5(0.75)]$.

The effect of inclusion of per capita income in the matching formula is to increase the federal subsidy in the poorer states and reduce it in the richer states. Unless it can be demonstrated that benefit spillovers are greater from poor than from rich states, this procedure cannot be justified on allocational grounds. If the goal is to promote fiscal equity, it can be satisfied more directly by unconditional block grants. Block grants augment the fiscal capacity of poor states without distorting expenditures patterns, whereas matching grants encourage states to switch outlays from unsubsidized to subsidized activities.

To summarize, conditional matching grants can be categorized according to allotment component and the matching percentage. These two components can be fitted together in four ways, as shown. All the combinations shown are used in federal grant programs.

Allotment	Matching Percentage	
	No capacity adjustment	Capacity adjustment
No capacity adjustment	1	3
Capacity adjustment	2	4

Revenue sharing.   The closest approximation to an unconditional grant yet adopted by the federal government is the so-called revenue-sharing program introduced with the passage of the State and Local Fiscal Assistance Act of 1972. Revenue-sharing grants are not without restrictions, but recipient governments are allowed much greater latitude than they are under conditional grants earmarked for special programs. The 1972 legislation called for an annual appropriation of about $7 billion. One-third was allocated to states, with the remaining two-thirds going to general-purpose local governments such as cities, counties, or townships.

The original program was in effect for five years. In 1976 it was amended slightly and extended through 1982. Appropriations remained at about $7 billion with no attempt to adjust for inflation. The share going to the states has been deleted since fiscal year 1981, with funding dropping to about $4.6 billion. This occurred at a time when federal deficits were large and when many states enjoyed budgetary surpluses. The future of general revenue sharing remains clouded.

Each state's revenue-sharing allotment is determined by a three-factor formula reflecting population, tax effort, and per capita income. Allotments vary directly with population and tax effort, inversely with per capita income. States may substitute a five-factor formula that also factors in urban population and income tax collections. The five-factor formula allows states with large urban population a somewhat higher share of the revenue-sharing appropriation in recognition of the financial crises faced by many large cities. Within each state, funds are allocated to local government on the basis of population, tax effort, and the inverse of per capita income.

The revenue-sharing program was promoted by the Nixon administration as a device for decentralizing governmental power. To the extent that recipient governments use revenue-sharing funds to cut taxes without cutting expenditures, it results in a substitution of federal for state-local revenue sources. Those who regard federal taxes as more equitable would find this result unobjectionable. The inclusion of a tax effort component in the allotment formula tends to discourage tax substitution and encourage recipient governments to increase expenditures instead.

The Future of Federal Grant Programs

The most frequently heard criticism of federal grant-in-aid programs may be stated very simply: too much power is centralized in Washington, D.C. Most federal grants are accompanied by rigid control over the use of funds. Federal bureaucrats who administer the programs are deemed to be too remote to exercise control intelligently. They are bombarded with reports prepared at great expense and containing more information than they can reasonably digest. Neither Congress nor federal agencies can possibly design programs with enough flexibility to accommodate the diverse local conditions.

If the system is so bad, why does it not change? One reason is that recipient governments have become so dependent on federal money. Total withdrawal of federal monies would lead to serious budgetary dislocations. On the other hand, recipient governments are eager to gain more control over the way in which grant money is spent. This paves the way for a possible compromise—a cut in the amount of federal grant money in exchange for a loosening of federal control over the way in which it is spent. One way of achieving this goal would be to consolidate a number of separate grant programs into largely unrestricted categorical block grants.

Another means of simplifying the system would be to channel federal grant money only to the states. It would then be up to governors and state legislatures to decide how to allocate grant money to local governments. Instead of dealing with thousands of governmental entities, the federal bureaucracy would deal with only fifty. Proponents of this form of fiscal decentralization point out that states are now much more able to handle such responsibilities than they were in 1960. During the 1960s, a U.S. Supreme Court decision forced state legislatures to redistrict on a one-person, one-vote basis. This helped to free many state legislatures from minority control and made them more representative of the needs of all citizens, especially those in urban areas.

The administration of President Ronald Reagan has proposed these and other more radical changes. Among the latter is a proposal to phase out selected federal grant programs over the remainder of the decade. During the interim, the targeted programs would be financed out of a special fund financed by earmarked excise taxes and an excess profits tax on oil. At the end of the phase-out period, federal support would cease, along with the earmarked taxes.

The phase-out would last long enough to enable recipient governments to accommodate to the transfer of responsibility. Some programs would be dropped. Others would be financed from state and local taxes. Cuts in federal income tax rates and elimination of some federal excises would, it is argued, make it easier for state and local governments to raise taxes if more revenue is needed.

The outcome of this effort and its effect on the U.S. federal system are not easy to predict. Previous administrations, particularly those of Richard Nixon and Gerald Ford, were largely unsuccessful in attempts to carry out much less radical reforms. Many members of Congress continue to resist efforts to weaken federal control. They are supported by spokespersons for groups benefiting from existing programs. Among the most vocal critics of change are officials of the hard-pressed larger cities and representatives of low-income and minority groups. Both groups express the fear that they will receive less favorable treatment from governors and legislatures than from the U.S. Congress.

STATE GRANTS TO LOCAL GOVERNMENTS

Prior to the depression of the 1930s, local governments were largely autonomous financially. The property tax was the prime source of general revenue for both state and local governments. During the 1930s, many property owners were unable to pay property taxes. States were forced to switch to sales and income taxes. Since that time, states have increased their grants-in-aid to local governments substantially. They now exceed $75 billion per year (not counting passthrough of federal aid) and account for over one-third of local expenditures.

Most state grants are categorical in nature, with the bulk of the funds going to education, roads, and welfare. Local funding of primary and secondary education has aroused the greatest concern. This is because of the great variation in the per pupil tax base among school districts within a state. In the landmark case of *Serrano* v. *Priest* (1971), the California Supreme Court ruled that extreme inequality in expenditure per pupil deprived students in poor school districts of an equal opportunity to receive an adequate education. The court declared the local property tax unconstitutional as a revenue source for schools. Similar rulings have been handed down in other states.[12] Objections of the type cited in *Serrano* v. *Priest* could be met by a statewide property tax levy for schools, but the most probable reaction is to rely more on other sources of state revenue for school finance.

State aid to school districts varies substantially among states, both in amount and in form. Special grant categories for school construction, transportation, and education of the handicapped are common. The most pervasive form of general grant is the school foundation plan. Foundation grants are designed to equalize expenditures per pupil among all districts, regardless of the size of the district tax base.

The basic foundation formula is the form:

$$F_i = EP_i - rV_i$$

where

F_i = the state foundation grant to the ith district
E = state-authorized expenditure per pupil
P_i = enrollment in the ith district
r = mandatory state property tax for schools
V_i = property tax base of ith district

In its pure form, r is set so that the district with the highest assessed value per pupil will raise enough revenue from the property tax to meet the authorized expenditure per pupil. That district receives no state aid. Every other district receives enough state aid to enable it to spend E dollars per pupil. Algebraically, this amounts to $EP - rV$ for each district, with the district raising rV from the local property tax. Obviously, if the plan is to be equitable, assessors must be required to equalize all assessments in the state at the same percentage of market value.

In practice, the foundation formula contains a variety of modifications to the pure form. Adjustments in authorized expenditure per pupil are made for differences in grade composition. State appropriations may cover only a fraction of the amount needed for full funding, requiring poor districts to raise property tax rates above the prescribed rate, r. Often, the

[12]Ferdinand P. Schoettle, "Judicial Requirements for School Finance and Property Tax Redesign: The Rapidly Evolving Case Law," *National Tax Journal*, 25 (September 1972), 455–72.

expenditure per pupil, *E,* is set at an unreasonably low level, requiring districts to levy supplemental taxes to reach acceptable levels. Nevertheless, the foundation plan does represent a step in the direction of equal expenditure per pupil and thus serves to meet some of the objections to local finance cited by the court in *Serrano* v. *Priest.*

SUMMARY

An economic case can be made for decentralization of many governmental functions. By placing tax and expenditure decisions at the local level, the residents of each community are able to provide themselves with the level and variety of collectively financed goods and services that meet local preferences. If all communities were economically self-contained entities, a strong case could be made for substantial decentralization. Unfortunately, communities are not self-contained. Benefits of some public expenditures spill out to nonresidents who do not pay for them. This phenomenon can lead to an underallocation of resources to some government services when viewed from the perspective of society at large. Spillouts of costs via tax exporting can have the reverse effect.

Other limits to decentralization include economies of scale in the production of public goods, problems of voter control that are eased by consolidation of a variety of governmental activities under a single unit, and the great differences in fiscal capacity of geographical subunits that make up our federal system. Fiscal inequities lead to differences in tax burdens for persons of equal taxpaying capacity living in rich and poor communities, violating standards of horizontal equity. Communities with limited fiscal capacity may be unable to meet what society at large regards as minimum standards in education or public assistance programs without some form of outside assistance.

Intergovernmental matching grants can be devised to overcome the effects of spillovers of benefits. Specific block grants can assure that every governmental unit meets minimal national standards in selected program areas. Unconditional block grants related inversely to fiscal capacity can be used to ease the fiscal burdens of poor communities and states.

Several hundred federal grant programs provide assistance to state and local governments, and states operate a variety of grant programs for schools and other local activities. The grant programs do not fall neatly into the categories indicated by purely economic conditions. For example, they often combine allocational and capacity elements through such devices as variable matching grants. In addition, recipient governments are usually required to accept a number of other conditions to qualify for federal or state funds.

Finally, different levels of government have worked out a variety of techniques for harmonizing revenue sources. Since the 1930s, the move has been away from separation of sources, although the retail sales tax is left mostly to the states and the property tax is now almost exclusively used by local governments. When different levels of government rely on the same tax base, they may resort to tax sharing or supplements, deductions, and credits as a means of accommodating to each other's needs.

Name Index

Subject Index

Expenditure
$$C = Y - \Delta NW$$